The International Handbook on Computer Crime

The International Handbook on Computer Crime

Computer-related Economic Crime and the Infringements of Privacy

Ulrich Sieber

Institute of Criminology and Economic Criminal Law, University of Freiburg, Federal Republic of Germany

JOHN WILEY & SONS

Chichester · New York · Brisbane · Toronto · Singapore

Library of Congress Cataloging-in-Publication Data:

Sieber, Ulrich, Dr.
  The international handbook on computer crime.

  Bibliography: p.
  Includes index.
  1. Computer crimes. 2. Computers—Access control.
  I. Title.
  HV6773.S54 1986   364.1′68   86-15670
  ISBN 0 471 91224 7

British Library Cataloguing Data:

Sieber, Ulrich
  The international handbook on computer crime
  1. Computer crimes
  I. Title
  364.1′62   HV6773

  ISBN 0 471 91224 7

Typeset by Inforum Ltd, Portsmouth
Printed and bound in Great Britain

Contents

For my academic mentor,
Professor Dr iur. Dr iur. h.c. Klaus Tiedemann,
from whom I learned the value
of comparative legal research

Preface and Acknowledgements

Computer crime has become a subject of international concern in recent years due to worldwide advances in computers, close international co-operation in data processing, and an increasing transnational data flow via international communications networks. Consequently, fighting computer crime cannot be continued at a national level but must be extended by close international co-operation, especially in the fields of criminological research, clarification and reform of prevailing legal provisions, development of security measures, and prosecution of computer crime.

This book is intended to initiate this international effort. The author's German books, *Computerkriminalität und Strafrecht* (2nd edn, 1980) and *Informationstechnologie und Strafrechtsreform* (1985), provide a detailed criminological analysis of computer-related economic crime and respective West German law. In contrast, this book is extended to an international overview of all kinds of computer crime, a comparative analysis of the legal situation in major Western countries, a presentation of the most important security measures discussed at an international level, as well as an analysis of problems arising in the field of prosecution.

The work presented in this book is based on a continuing study of the field of computer-related crime and information law which the author has been carrying out at the Institute of Criminology and Economic Criminal Law at the University of Freiburg in close co-operation with research institutes in other countries since 1974. The book is also founded on the author's work as an attorney in the field of information law and as a lecturer in computer crime and computer security. The international legal aspects of the study originate from his work as a consultant for the Organization for Economic Co-operation and Development (OECD) in Paris, for which he prepared a comparative legal study which became the basis of section IV.A. Analysis of the international aspects has also been supported by his activities as a member of the Legal Observatory for the Community Information Market of the Commission of the European Communities and as a scientific member of the Select Committee of Experts on Computer-related Crime of the Council of Europe, for which he prepared a draft study which became the basis of subsection IV.A.2c and Section IV.B.

As the issue of computer crime is a most topical one and subject to very rapid changes, work in this field can only be carried out in close co-operation with researchers in several countries. Consequently this study is based not only on the author's work but is also the result of many contributions by friends and colleagues. It is not possible to mention all who have contributed to this research. However, the author would especially like to thank for their help Mr Jay Bloombecker (Los Angeles), Professor Dr Pierre-Henri Bolle (Neuchâtel), Ms Martine Briat (Paris), Professor Dr Jean Cosson (Paris), Mr Kevin J. Fitzgerald (East Malvern/Australia), Ms Michèle Franke (Montreal), Mr Hans-Peter Gassmann (Paris), Professor Dr Nico Keijzer (Amsterdam), Mr Paul Kenneth (Paris), Mr Manfred Kindermann (Böblingen), Mr Lauri Lehtimaja (Helsinki), Mr John F. Ley (Barton/Australia), Professor Dr Jaime Malamud-Goti (Buenos Aires), Mr Finn Meilby (Copenhagen), Dr Manfred Möhrenschlager (Bonn), Professor Dr Fermin Morales Prats (Barcelona), Mr. C.G.B. Nicholson (Edinburgh), Professor Dr Noriyuki Nishida (Tokyo), Mr Donn B. Parker (Menlo Park), Ms Betina Pasquali (Buenos Aires), Mr Alexander Patijn (Amsterdam), Dr Lorenzo Picotti (Bologna), Mr Donald K. Piragoff (Ottawa), Ms Charlotte M. Pitrat (Paris), Dr Carlo Sarzana (Rome), Mr Stein Schjolberg (Oslo), Dr Gabriele Schmölzer (Innsbruck), Professor Dr Bart de Schutter (Brussels), Mr Artur Solarz (Stockholm), Professor Dr Dionysios Spinellis (Athens), Mr Erik Tersmeden (Stockholm), Professor Dr Guy P.V. Vandenberghe (Amsterdam), Dr Ken Wong (Manchester), and Dr Erwin Zimmerli (Zurich). Above all, the author is most grateful to his academic mentor, Professor Dr Dr Klaus Tiedemann (Freiburg i. Br.), for his constant support.

An international analysis of a new and quickly changing phenomenon will hardly be without omissions. All deficiencies of the present study fall uniquely within the author's responsibility. The author would like to apologize to all researchers whose works might have been overlooked. He would appreciate being informed of their research and thus having them participate in the international co-operation which is intended by the present publication.

Ulrich Sieber
Freiburg i.Br., March 1986

I.

Introduction: The Emergence of a New Threat

Western societies are currently encountering a second Industrial Revolution. This 'revolution of informatics', which is replacing the work of human minds by machines, will be more transformative than the mechanical Industrial Revolution of the nineteenth century, which replaced physical work by machines. The worldwide advances of business and personal computers, the increasing extent of storage and processing capabilities, the miniaturization of computer chips installed in industrial products, the fusing of information-processing and new information communication technologies, as well as research in the field of artificial intelligence, all illustrate the present development, often described as the turn to the 'information age'.[1]

This triumphant march of computer applications not only has an advantageous side but also leads to the crucial importance of the operation and security of computer systems for business, administration, and society. In the business community, for example, the majority of monetary transactions is administered by computers in the form of deposit money. Balance sheets are prepared with computer support. A company's entire production is frequently dependent on the functional ability of its data-processing (DP) system. Furthermore, many businesses store their most important company secrets in a computer. Modern administration relies on computer technology and databanks in a similar way. Sea, air, and space-control systems, medical supervision as well as Western defence also depend to a great extent on modern computer technology.[2]

Because of this dependency, the increasing level of criminal offences involving DP systems registered over the last decade in the United States, Western Europe, Australia, Japan, and now even in the socialist States represents a threat to individual companies as well as to a country's economy and society as a whole. This danger has been increasingly recognized in recent years and has led to national and international concern about the new threat which is called 'computer crime'.

According to a definition worked out by a group of experts invited by the

1

OECD to Paris in May 1983,[3] the term *computer crime* (or 'computer-related crime') is defined as any illegal, unethical, or unauthorized behaviour involving automatic data-processing and/or transmission of data. The breadth of this definition is advantageous, as it permits the use of the same working hypothesis for all kinds of criminological, criminalistic, economic, preventive, or legal studies. Obviously, this does not prevent each of these studies from dealing only with the phenomena of computer crime, which cause computer-specific problems in its own discipline.[4]

Using the broad definition of the OECD as a working hypothesis,[5] this book will provide an international survey of the main problems surrounding the new phenomena. In the proceeding chapter the various forms of computer crime are described. The third chapter covers the extent, impact, and future development of computer offences. In the three chapters following this phenomenological analysis, the manner in which the legislature, business community, and law-enforcement agencies have so far dealt with these problems are discussed, as well as those measures which ought to be taken in the future. Finally, a summary stresses the need for further action and international co-operation.

II.

The Phenomena of Computer Crime

Up to the present three main groups of computer crime (falling within the OECD definition) have been revealed: computer-related *economic crimes* such as computer fraud, computer espionage, and computer sabotage; computer-related *offences against personal rights*, especially against the citizens' right to privacy; and computer-related *offences against superindividual interests* such as offences against national security, control of transborder data flow, integrity of computer-based procedures and data-communication networks, or democratic legitimation of computer-based parliamentary decisions.

The following analysis of these phenomena is arranged according to the actual frequency and importance of the respective acts. It first describes the various computer-related *economic crimes* (*infra*, A). Then it investigates the group of computer-related *infringements of privacy* (*infra*, B). Finally the remaining *other phenomena* and definitional questions are discussed (*infra*, C).

A. COMPUTER-RELATED ECONOMIC CRIMES

Computer-related economic crimes constitute the main field of computer crime today. Excluding accidental and negligent damage to computer systems, six main categories of computer-related economic crimes have been developed. These are
(1) Fraud by computer manipulations against DP systems;
(2) Computer espionage and software theft;
(3) Computer sabotage;
(4) Theft of services;
(5) Unauthorized access to DP systems; and
(6) Traditional business offences assisted by DP.[1]

3

1. Fraud by Computer Manipulation

Fraud against DP systems by computer manipulation involves the changing of data or information for purposes of financial gain. The following analysis describes the objects, the methods used, and the perpetrators of this new type of fraud.

a. OBJECTS OF COMPUTER-RELATED FRAUD

The objects of computer-related fraud are *data representing assets* in DP systems. In the majority of computer fraud cases the assets represented by computer data are *intangible objects* such as deposit money, claims, working time, credit ratings, and results of calculations of balances. Cases known at present are primarily manipulations concerning salaries, invoices, pensions, and social security payments as well as manipulations of the account balances of bank computers. Because of the increasing replacement of cash money by deposit money, this field of computer crime will also be the main area of computer fraud in the future. In Europe the trend towards a cashless society is especially illustrated by the widespread system of money transfer orders and giro services, which became the main payment systems in both the private and the business sectors. In the United States the replacement of cash money and paper-based payment systems with 'electronic blips' is especially shown by point-of-sale (POS) and other electronic funds transfer systems (EFTS), in which payments are made by inserting a plastic card into a terminal connected to a computer. All over the world, EFTS are common in the banking area. The four major funds transfer systems in the United States—Fedwire, Bankwire, CHIPS, and SWIFT, for example—transmit about $300 billion per day domestically and $600 billion per day internationally.[2]

> It is obvious that these developments in the economic and technical areas attract criminals for special reasons. Because the sums transferred or processed by computer systems are very high and because electronic money can be 'created' by the perpetrator, the amounts of losses in these cases are generally very high. The widely reported case of Mark Rifkin is an example. In 1978 he fraudulently managed to get $10.2 million transferred from the Security Pacific National Bank in Los Angeles to a New York bank account by means of a telephone call.[3]

In some cases the data being the object of computer fraud represent *tangible and corporeal objects* which are taken away by the perpetrator after the manipulation of the computer system. This concerns especially cash money, materials, merchandise, or goods. Manipulations concerning these classic objects of crime generally result in smaller losses than manipulations of intangibles, since the losses here are limited by the actual amount of goods available.

Two West German cases which were reported to the police in 1984 and 1985 can be singled out as examples of fraud concerning such classic objects of inventory. In the 1984 case a programmer and a stock clerk had altered the program and the databases of a spare-parts store's computer so that spare parts taken away by them were invoiced at very low prices. The losses in this case amounted to DM 31 000.[4] In a similar case in 1985, which also concerned the manipulation of spare parts, the perpetrators embezzled merchandise valued at about DM 300 000.[5]

A *specific group* of computer crime cases primarily concerning tangible cash money, goods, and services registered by computer systems has now been made possible by the increasing number of *cash dispensers* installed by banks and by *electronic high-efficiency vending machines* equipped with electronic sensors.

In Japan the installation of *cash dispensers* (CD machines) and automatic teller machines (ATMs) is the most advanced in the Western world. By 1981 23 627 CD machines had been installed and 66 450 CD cards were in use. As a result the manipulation of cash dispensers represents one of the main problems of computer crime. In 1981, 288 cases of CD crime were known to the police, 83.3% of which involved the use of stolen cards, 9.7% the use of forged cards, 4.9% cards received by fraud or blackmail, and 2.1% lost-and-found cards. The number of cases reported to the police increased to 472 in 1982 and to 642 in 1983.[6] In the United States the US Bureau of Statistics estimated that in 1983 banks suffered losses of about $70–100 million by the illegal use of CD cards. (For the manipulation techniques used in these cases, see *infra*, b, pp. 9 *et seq*.)

A similar development is now taking place in the field of *electronic high-efficiency vending machines*. Here, too, in Japan the technical development of these machines is the most advanced in Western countries. At the end of 1982 in Japan there were about 4 900 000 automatic vending machines, 200 000 of which were high-efficiency machines which could read and identify banknotes. The first manipulation of these systems was reported to the police on 30 July 1982 at Osaka. From this date until December 1982, 328 cases in 37 prefectures were reported, of which 181 concerned vending machines; 98, money-changing machines; 43, amusement machines; four, pin-ball machines; and two, automatic ticket machines. At the end of 1982, 39 of these cases were cleared and 58 people were arrested, of whom 23 were members of organized crime groups.[7]

An analysis of the *differences between traditional fraud and computer fraud* in the field of the objects of the crime shows that the assets now represented and manipulated in DP systems were the target of traditional fraud long before the computer existed. This is also true in the field of intangible assets, because the change from tangible to representative or symbolic assets in countries' economies started centuries ago. However, what is new about the object of computer manipulations is the fact that the information representing these assets is no longer stored on paper, in a visible, easily readable form but in an invisible and machine-readable concentrated form in electronic storage devices. This *change from paper-represented assets to paperless-represented assets* is, as will be shown later, the reason for problems both in the scope and the detection of crime and in the application of existing legislation. Concerning the object of the crime, computer-related and traditional property crimes differ not only in this qualitative aspect but also quantitatively. This *quantitative difference*, which is caused by the *high values handled in DP systems*, will be dealt with later in connection with amounts of losses in computer crime.[8]

b. MODI OPERANDI: THE METHODS OF MANIPULATION

As the information stored in DP systems is no longer handled by humans but by computers, the offender now has to proceed differently in order to achieve his aim of changing information. It is therefore the *mode of perpetration* which forms the *main difference between traditional fraud and computer fraud*.

For a better understanding of the various *methods of manipulating DP results* the computer has to be regarded as a DP system, i.e. as a system into which the data to be processed and the required type of processing are fed (via the program and additional console inputs) and which automatically outputs the result of this processing. The offender can either feed the computer incorrect data from the beginning (input manipulations), interfere with the correct processing of the computer (program, console, and hardware manipulations), or subsequently falsify the initially correct result given by the computer (output manipulations). In computer systems using data communication, especially remote DP, additional manipulations in the field of data transfer are possible. Special methods of manipulation also exist in the field of cash dispensers. All these manipulation techniques have been successfully applied in practice.

Input manipulations make up the majority of computer manipulations discovered up to now. These can be carried out mainly by the adding, omitting, changing, exchanging, or incorrect posting of input. Such 'data-diddling' is primarily committed by clerks, data typists, transaction participants, and operators responsible for the collection, checking, transmission, and input of data to be processed.

> As an example of an input manipulation committed by a clerk, the case of a savings bank in South Germany can be cited. The female perpetrator, who was working as a teller in a local branch of the bank, in February 1983 transferred DM 1.3 million to her friend's account early in the morning by simply inputting the respective credit into her terminal. The bank's well-developed control and safety system would have detected this manipulation no later than noon. However, the online transmission of the credit by remote DP and the speed of a modern computer system made it possible for the teller's friend to withdraw three cheques totalling DM 1.28 million some minutes later at another branch of the bank.[9]
>
> Another example of a typical input manipulation is the case of a DP employee in Zurich who succeeded in manipulating the automatic foreign payments transac-

tions of one of the biggest Swiss banks. The employee, who was working as an operator and data-checker for the bank, intercepted various transfer orders from his accomplices in the encoding department of the bank and then, instead of feeding the computer the correct transfer amounts, fed a thousand times the amount each time. He cleverly avoided the security measures set up by the bank in order to prevent such manipulations. Thus, when DM 98 were, for example, deposited in Frankfurt, his accomplices, drawing the money in Lugano and Davos, did not receive 100 Swiss francs but 100 000 Swiss francs. Similarly, for their $97 deposited in New York, they did not receive 251 but 251 000 Swiss francs. The perpetrators made a profit of about 700 000 Swiss francs through these manipulations. They were sentenced to prison and put on probation in 1976.[19]

Compared with input manipulations, which in many cases can be carried out without any knowledge of DP, the *modus operandi* of *program manipulations* is more computer-specific and, above all, much more difficult to discover. These manipulations are committed either by *changing the company's existing programs* (especially by adding 'Trojan-horse' routines or using special versions of the 'virus-programs', described below) or by *applying additional programs*, written by the perpetrators. These additional programs can either be self-written or standard utility programs which are powerful tools for emergency situations and able to bypass most security measures (for example the widespread 'superzap' utility).[11] The following examples show that the offender can use such program manipulations to bypass security checks and tuned circuits set up for the prevention of computer offences and that he can disguise his crime almost perfectly.

The offender was employed as a programmer at a large West German corporation. Using a program especially written for the purpose, he entered the information on the salaries of fictitious people into the data memories containing company salary information and inputted his own account as the account to which the fictitious salaries should be transferred. This salary manipulation, which was successfully carried out even in this simple form at several West German companies,[12] would have been discovered in the company concerned as the computer prepared wage-slips, checklists, account summaries, and balance sheets which were carefully checked and evaluated by the company. In order to prevent discovery by these control printouts the offender first made changes in the salary payments program to ensure that no pay-slips were printed for payments to the fictitious employees and that the payments did not appear in the checklists produced by the computer. By further manipulation of the program which produced the company's accounting summaries and balance sheets the perpetrator finally succeeded in having the embezzled amounts deducted from the income tax to be paid to the tax office. Thus the sums did not appear as deficient amounts in the company's accounting summaries and balance sheet. The offender fraudulently made DM 193 000 before the manipulation was discovered by chance. In 1978 he was sentenced to two years' imprisonment for fraud and breach of trust.[13]

In another case the head of the DP department of a cable-drum factory in South Germany created special 'correctional programs' which put the debit items of an accomplice's firm at zero. The implementation of further programs provided that during his vacations and absence no debit lists indicating debits for the accomplice's firm could be printed and that the unpaid sales to the accomplice's firm did not appear in the databases creating the factory's balance sheets and statistics. Thus from 1977 to 1982 the perpetrators were able to receive equipment worth DM 4 153 000 without paying for it. In 1983 both perpetrators were sentenced to prison for five and a half years.[14]

As indicated above, correct processing of the computer can be subject to crime not only by program manipulations but also by the abuse of mechanical control elements or integrated circuits of the DP system. The most spectacular case of these *console or hardware manipulations* occurred in West Germany in the mid-1970s and involved concealment of speculative foreign exchange dealings at the Herstatt Bank.

The entire accounting operations involved in the foreign exchange and currency transactions of the Herstatt Bank were recorded via the console of a small computer and subsequently transferred to the bank's central computer. The bank's employees succeeded in covering up a number of speculative foreign-exchange deals by pressing an 'interrupt' key on the console of a small computer so that the data for these foreign-exchange transactions were not transferred to the bank's central computer. In this way it was possible to make the small computer produce a perfectly correct confirmation of the transaction for the contractor without an accounting record being made in the bank's central computer. This method of operation made it possible to cover up the losses and keep down the apparent overall level of future business. In addition, the employees were able to declare the losses as the bank's business and succeed in private deals for their own accounts later.

A particularly interesting aspect of this case was the way in which the offenders bypassed a security measure written into the program. In order to avoid improper use, the small computer's program was designed to print out the word 'interrupt' on the accounting form produced by the computer as soon as the 'interrupt' key was pressed. The perpetrators prevented this error message, which would have necessarily led to discovery of the manipulation, by removing the accounting form from the system after it was completed but before the 'interrupt' key was pressed. The word 'interrupt' was therefore not printed on the form but on the empty drum.

It was estimated that amounts totalling several billion US dollars had not been recorded in the accounts or had been falsified. Finally, the speculations led to the bankruptcy of the Herstatt Bank in 1974 and to losses of the bank's customers of about $1.2 billion. The 70-year-old director of the bank could not be prosecuted for a long time but finally in 1984 received a prison sentence of four and a half years for bankruptcy and breach of trust. As an appeal by the director was partially successful in October 1985, the decision is not yet final. Some of the senior executive officers received long-term prison sentences in 1983.[15]

Remote DP systems, used with increasing frequency in recent years, provide a particularly interesting variation of the manipulation techniques described here and will be of great significance in the future. If the computer is connected to remote DP via the public telephone network or other methods of data-communication the offender can carry out manipulation from his own home, using his own DP terminal and without personally entering the offices of the company affected by the crime. International telecommunications systems are even offering the possibility of 'transnational computer crime', committed in one country and taking effect in another.

One of the first manipulations via remote DP took place in the early 1970s when an American student succeeded in linking a private terminal in his apartment via the public telephone network to the Pacific Telephone Corporation's central computer. He thereby authorized the delivery, free of charge, of goods worth about $1 million.[16]

This student was a forerunner of the many computer enthusiasts described below who are now causing problems by manipulation, destruction, and sabotage of computers via remote DP. Because the methods of manipulation in telecommunications systems are used more often for espionage purposes and depend to a great extent on the security measures of the respective DP system, they will be described more thoroughly in the following chapters, which deal with computer espionage and the circumvention of security measures.

Special methods of manipulation also exist in the field of *cash dispensers*. The above-mentioned Japanese statistics demonstrate that these methods present a variety of phenomena, and range from simple trickery to highly sophisticated forgeries of magnetic cards.

The range of simple methods to manipulate cash dispensers was illustrated in a Japanese case of 1983. The perpetrator drew about 11.47 million yen in cash by using 32 cash cards which he had stolen from the clothes of people in tennis club dressing rooms and from elsewhere. In 17 cases the perpetrator discovered the secret identification numbers of his victims by making correct guesses from the date of birth given on the victims' driving licenses. In 14 cases he elicited the number from the victims by posing as a bank employee. In one case he found a memorandum of the registration number when he was stealing the cash cards.[17]

The following method, which has been successfully applied hundreds of times in the United States and Japan, shows how simple such manipulations can be in cases of insufficient technical safety measures. The perpetrators, disguised as CD machine repairmen, waited until a customer had activated the machine by inserting his plastic card and giving his secret personal identification number. At this point they intervened and informed the customer that the machine was not working properly and recommended that another machine be used. After the customer had left, the perpetrators went to the first machine, which was still activated, and withdrew the maximum amount possible.[18]

More sophisticated techniques of *modus operandi* make use of the fact that magnetic entries in most CD cards can be copied and changed (the new West

German CD cards contain a special MM-mark which—up to the present—prevents copying of the cards). The knowledge necessary for the manipulation of the magnetic entries can be obtained to a great extent from the public international norms concerning CD cards (see, for example, ISO-norm 4909). The necessary equipment does not cost more than a few thousand dollars. In 1976 a French engineer managed to change the magnetic entries of the French 'cartes bleues'. Since then, similar acts have occurred in many countries. In Italy, for example, three perpetrators produced 3000 copies of an Italian student's bank card and managed to draw about 300 million lire from the cash dispenser's offline system of the Banca Populare di Milano in various cities of north Italy during the weekend of 18 November 1984. Two of the perpetrators were arrested and charged with aggravated fraud. However, it is unclear if this statute or the statutes of theft or private forgery can be applied.[19]

A highly sophisticated technique was practiced in Japan in 1982. An employee of the Telecommunication and Telephone Corporation intercepted a bank's online communication, deciphered the information using the information from his own cash card, and obtained 1.33 million yen by using a forged test card. He was arrested on 16 February 1982.[20]

In West Germany a wave of intelligent cash-dispenser manipulations started in 1985/6. In September 1985 two television journalists from Hamburg managed to manipulate their CD cards and create overdrafts by using a magnetic card reader, a personal computer, and a self-written program. They recorded the act and on 27 October 1985 showed the film on West German television. This inspired two unemployed 'computer freaks' from Cologne to develop the following technique. They inserted a blank copy of a CD card into a cash dispenser and then fitted the card reader with a special auxiliary device. After a customer had inserted his card into the auxiliary device the blank card was pushed into the bank's card-reader. Since the customer's personal code number did not match that of the specifically prepared blank card, the cash dispenser seized the blank card and indicated the permanent withdrawal of the card to the customer, who then left. The perpetrators took the customer's card out of the auxiliary device and investigated the code by analysing the buttons of the keyboard, which they had previously sensitized with small drops of oil. The correct sequence of the four code numbers discovered was ascertained by testing the 24 possible combinations: The security routine, which should have seized the card after three false inputs, was circumvented by copying the card and changing the automat after two incorrect inputs or by manipulating the card's security counter for wrong inputs. The perpetrators embezzled about DM 80 000. As a result of constant observation through hidden video cameras they were caught on 16 January 1986. However, other perpetrators who use a similar technique have not yet been discovered.[21]

According to the latest information originating from the 'hacker scene', several computer freaks are currently deciphering the (DNS-) algorithm of the pool code with which the code numbers can be analysed on the basis of the information stored in the cards. They are also developing techniques which capture and analyse the radiation of the cash dispensers as well as special transparent foils which can be put onto the keyboards in order to electronically register the code. The author expects that these techniques will soon be successfully developed. In the field of credit card systems, some professional groups seem to be preparing a plan for copying a large number of cards by using special card-readers installed in ordinary retail stores. Having gathered a great deal of card information, they then intend to make a large number of falsified cards.[20]

In the future, prevention of these acts will only be possible by improved security measures, such as the replacement of magnetic cards by 'intelligent' chip cards, described below (pp. 128 *et seq*).

Specific methods of manipulation are also used in the above-mentioned *manipulations of high-efficiency vending machines*, which are equipped with sensors able to read and identify banknotes.

> In the Japanese case of July 1982 described above (p. 5) the perpetrator introduced into the machine a piece of paper similar in size to a 1000-yen note with a magnetic tape attached to it. This made it possible to make use of blind points on the magnetic detection sensors and to obtain money from a money-changing machine at an amusement centre in Osaka. Most of the other Japanese cases of manipulation were conducted in a similar way.[22]

The manipulation techniques described above are often combined with each other by the perpetrator, resulting in *complex manipulation techniques*.[23] In most cases, manipulations are carried out not just once but many times. This *permanence* and—in some cases—*automatic working of the criminal effect* is one of the most striking characteristics distinguishing computer fraud from traditional fraud.[24] The possibility of frequently repeating the act which forms the basis of this phenomenon is due in the first place to the fact that, as a rule, the workflow in the DP area is strictly organized. Once a loophole has been discovered, the offender can exploit it as often as he wishes. In the case of program manipulations and changes in master data frequent repetition of the act becomes an automatic working of the act, as the computer automatically repeats the manipulation each time the program is used or an item of master data (e.g. a gross salary) is called without the offender having to do anything. For example, in a case in south Germany the offender caused a total of 111 illegal transfers by means of two incorrect inputs.[25] Perpetrators have further developed this characteristic into the so-called 'salami technique' by taking many 'thin slices' of financial transactions (which no-one misses) and transferring these amounts to a favoured account.[26]

c. PERPETRATORS

As far as the perpetrators are concerned, empirical studies in West Germany indicate that more than 90% of the manipulations detected were committed by *employees* of the victimized companies. About 60% of the perpetrators detected (especially in the field of input manipulations) did not have *skills* in the field of DP and the number of cases involving specialists taking advantage of their superior skills in systems analysis and programming was relatively small.[27] However, the question as to whether this is due to the fact that systems analysts and programmers commit fewer crimes than generally assumed or to the fact that the manipulations of these people are especially difficult to detect cannot be answered with certainty. The West German results are supported by recently published studies which concentrate on the field of embezzlement.[28] Older studies, which do not differentiate between the various forms of computer crime, indicate a higher percentage of programmers among the perpetrators. This is supposedly due to the numerous cases of software theft committed by programmers. In most cases revealed so far, at least in Europe, the criminal *motive* was financial gain.

However, in the *future* these findings are expected to change. Due to remote DP and the increasing use of cash-dispenser installations, the number of manipulations committed by *non-company personnel* will rise. As a result of improved safety measures, which will prevent simple manipulation schemes, the percentage of manipulations of DP specialists and the *collusion* of several employees will increase. The challenge to overcome other companies' safety measures by remote DP as well as the desire to extend one's technical expertise will gain more importance as a *motive*, especially for young computer enthusiasts, in the fields of manipulation and espionage.[29]

2. Computer Espionage and Software Piracy

a. OBJECTS OF ESPIONAGE

Like computer manipulations, computer espionage represents one of the most frequently used forms of computer crime. It is particularly lucrative for the perpetrator and dangerous for the company affected because of the valuable information stored in the computer centres of most companies:

In all businesses the primary targets of computer espionage are the *computer programs*. The value of these new objects of crime is illustrated by the fact that the worldwide market for sold computer programs (not including self-produced software) was estimated in 1985 at approximately $55 billion. Computer espionage in the commercial sector also concerns computer-stored *cost accounts, balance sheets, and customer addresses*. The centre of attraction in the technical sector is *development, research, and production data*, and *computer-chip designs*. The value of chip designs, for example, is demonstrated by the market for integrated circuits which amounted to approximately $17 billion in 1983 and increased by about 100% in 1984.[30]

Whereas computer programs and chip designs constitute a new object of espionage, the above-mentioned data were the targets of industrial and commercial espionage even before the invention of the computer. However, the high concentration of data in electronic memories, especially tapes, discs, and chips, and the possibility of using a computer to copy data quickly and unobtrusively are leading to new dimensions of industrial and commercial espionage in this sector.

The new possibilities of DP espionage can be illustrated by a case of computer espionage in which the author conducted a check of recordings on a computer and analysed them. At first they seemed to show that only harmless programs had been used on a particular day. However, in reality a number of programs disguised by common names were concealing special programs, written by the offender, which could be used to compress and copy large volumes of data in a short time. Analysis of the various check programs then revealed that within twelve hours the offender had copied all the programs and files comprising the company's essential business data and had taken them away on a single magnetic disc.[31]

b. MODI OPERANDI

As far as the *modi operandi* of computer espionage and theft of software are concerned, the most frequently used method to obtain data is the *copying of data files*. In the field of mass-marketed programs the copying of programs is a rapid standard technique, which, however, can be made more difficult by specific program routines against copying (see subsection V.C.3.g). In the field of non-mass-marketed programs and other data (especially 'tailored software') copying is mainly done by utility programs (in protected companies especially by 'superzap'), by self-written programs (sometimes passed off as regular application programs), or by 'Trojan-horse' routines which are built into privileged application programs.

Further computer espionage ranges from traditional to specific, highly sophisticated computer techniques. Traditional *'personal' techniques* used for computer espionage are, for example, the corruption or extortion of employees, the infiltration of employees from other companies, especially for a short working period (often referred to as the method of 'hello–goodbye'), or the interviewing of employees responding to dummy advertisements for new jobs and describing their present work.

Traditional 'technical' approaches to obtain computer-stored information have also been based on *embezzlement of data files*, secret *cable connection* to computers, or the installation of *transmitter units* in computer systems. The traditional technical method of *exploitation of outdated data* can range from 'scavenging' printouts or carbon paper of multiple-part forms in waste bins; tapes and discs which were used for data-carrier interchange but not completely erased; or data stored in the buffer storage area of a computer after job-execution.

The *radiation and 'electronic fields'* generated by computer terminals and electronic typewriters can be intercepted, analysed, and recorded from distances of up to 3000 feet using standard television and recording equipment which can be obtained reasonably cheaply and easily stored in a car parked near the computer centre. It is said that this picking up of radiation is a standard technique of the Eastern bloc's Secret Service.

In the field of *telecommunications systems* special techniques to penetrate data centres in order to obtain unauthorized access to information have been applied. Many users here think they are well protected by passwords, but in many cases this safety measure can be easily circumvented if standard passwords are used (they are often not changed by the users). Hoax telephone calls and other techniques are often used to outwit legal users. Technical interception and wiretapping are also resorted to and will be the main *modus operandi* in future international data networks. The techniques of *wiretapping* in order to obtain passwords and other secret information from telecommunication and teleprocessing systems may range from a coil on a drop-wire to the picking up of stray microwaves from satellites or terrestrial stations or penetrations of data-switching computers. Because of the computer's great working speed and its abilities to sort, match, disseminate, and copy information, wiretapping of a computer communication can be much more efficiently organized and is much more dangerous than the traditional wiretapping of an oral communication.[32]

> In the press, abuses of telecommunication systems have been discussed mainly in connection with cases of young computer enthusiasts 'joyriding' computer networks and data centres. An example for such abuse is the well-known case of some 15- to 25-year-old computer enthusiasts who belonged to the '414 Gang' of Milwaukee (USA) and other groups of so-called 'hackers'. In 1983 they obtained access to the data banks of the Los Alamos National Laboratory, the Security Pacific Bank in Los Angeles, the New York Sloan–Kettering Cancer Center, the Massachusetts Institute of Technology, the McClellan Air Force Base in Sacramento, the Norwegian Telephone Administration, and other institutions.[33]
>
> These acts were investigated by the FBI and a committee of Congress in the United States and received great publicity in the press. It must be stressed, however, that it is not these teenagers or 'whizzkids' but the professional or politically motivated perpetrators who create the main danger in the field of computer espionage via public telephone and telecommunication lines. There is no doubt that, in the long run, the professional criminals will learn the technology used by the hackers or will persuade the hackers to work for them.

c. PERPETRATORS

Apart from these acts committed by hackers and from the well-known copying of mass-marketed programs practised by computer-users and software-dealers, the theft of software and data is committed primarily by disloyal *employees* of the victimized company (especially shortly before leaving a job) and by *licensees* in breach of contract. Most of these people are acting in favour of *competing national firms*.

The attempted espionage attack on IBM by more than 20 individuals working for Hitachi, which the FBI discovered in its famous 'sting operation' in 1982,[34] showed that espionage for the benefit of *foreign firms* is becoming increasingly important. Computer espionage and unlawful export of computers infringing Western embargo laws are practised especially by the *Eastern bloc's Secret Service* in Western countries. A long-term plan for DP espionage drawn up in 1964 by the East German Secret Service was already revealed in West German court proceedings in 1976. In the Soviet Union theft of high technology is organized by the State Security Committee (KGB) and by the Chief Intelligence Directorate of the Soviet General Staff (GRU). These organizations are supported by Western companies which have specialized in the illegal export of computers and other high technology to Eastern-bloc countries. In 1983, 11 containers with computer systems (including a Digital VAX 11/782) were confiscated in Hamburg and Haelsingborg, Sweden, on a ship bound for the Soviet Union. The work of the Eastern bloc is also made easier by the negligence of many Western companies, which, in search of new markets, often close their eyes to the need for security.[35]

3. Computer Sabotage

a. OBJECTS OF SABOTAGE

The high concentration of data stored in the electronic devices mentioned above, along with the dependence of many companies and administrative authorities on DP, make computer sabotage another particular danger for business and administration. The objects of computer sabotage are the tangible computer facilities as well as the intangible data containing computer programs and other valuable information.

b. MODI OPERANDI

The field of the *modi operandi* can be differentiated between methods of causing physical damage and those of causing logical damage. The most frequently practised *methods of causing physical damage* are *igniting or bombing a building*. These techniques are especially applied by outsiders.

> As an example, the bombing attack against the West German MAN computer centre in 1983 can be cited. The act was committed by terrorists in order to protest against the participation of the MAN Company in the production of Pershing and Cruise missiles. Since the safety copies of the data in the computer centre were not affected the losses were limited to about DM 2 million.[36]

For insiders, mainly in cases of labour and other social conflicts within the company, the following additional *techniques of physical destruction* are recommended by left-wing European underground magazines: gluing emery paper onto the electronically readable parts of cards in order to destroy badge- and card-readers; inserting iron cuttings, paper clips, or small pieces of aluminium foil into computer devices in order to cause electrical short-circuiting for some time afterwards; pouring coffee, saline solution, and caustic cleaning agents into the operator console and other equipment; blowing smoke, hair-spray, and other gases into devices; putting a container of hydrochloric acid in front of the air-conditioning's induction pipe or suction fan; causing extreme temperatures by sabotaging the air-conditioning or by heating computer parts with lit cigarettes; interfering with the electric power station, switching office, or communication lines; and cutting cables or putting mice under a raised floor where they could gnaw through the insulation of electrical wiring and even the wires themselves.[37]

The most popular method of causing *logical damage* is through the use of *crash programs* which can erase large volumes of data within a short period. These programs can be utility, self-written, or 'Trojan-horse' routines built into application programs or into the operating system.

> An example of computer sabotage by using computer programs to erase data is the following case involving a south German engineer. He erased the comments of a valuable computer program on the disc before leaving the company so that it could not be modified easily by other programmers and the company almost lost a contract worth about DM 1 million. The accused programmer declared that he had copied the comments on to another disc in order to save space on the original one, and that the second disc must have been lost after his leaving. Although he was acquitted of the charge in the first instance, his declaration was disproved in the second, and he was found guilty of breach of trust.[38]

Crash programs can be executed at a later stage, after the perpetrator has left the firm. A special variation of sabotage techniques using such *'time-bombs'* is the implementation of a so-called *'cancer'-routine* in an application program. This consists of a few time-consuming program instructions and a set of commands which cause the self-reproduction of the 'cancer'-program in another, arbitrarily chosen, part of the application program during each run. When the application program slows down due to the increasing number of 'cancer-routines', these routines may be detected and taken out of the program by the user. However, if only one routine is overlooked, the 'cancer' will continue to reproduce and spread.

A most dangerous modification of the 'cancer-routines' are *'virus-programs'*, which have been tested successfully in the United States since 1983. Since 1985 these have been described in European underground newsletters and hacker information sheets.[39] Virus programs are self-reproducing programs which copy and implement themselves in other programs and data files to which they have access and which are not yet infiltrated, thus spreading through all shared resources. If such programs are implemented in privileged programs, in utility programs (which are often used by privileged programs and therefore can work as formidable 'Trojan horses'), in the compiler or in other parts of the operating system, or even in free programs offered to system operators on a system's bulletin-board, the virus-program can infiltrate the whole DP system and even complete networks. This is extremely dangerous, because virus-programs in a 'damage command' can not only carry destruction routines (such as loops or erasure commands) but can be combined with 'time-bombs' which are activated at preset times or later when the whole system or network (including the safety copies of the programs!) is already infected by the 'virus'. Special 'evolution viruses' can carry additional self-modifying 'hiding commands' which are able to counteract later automatic detection and elimination of virus-programs by the victim's special search programs. The virus-programs can be written in a few hours by ordinary programmers without any special skills. A case in Berlin, in which on 31 January 1986 (shortly after a strike by the university tutors) the university's computer system began to work increasingly slowly, is possibly the result of a virus-program containing time-consuming routines. However, this case has not yet been cleared.[40]

In *teleprocessing systems* it is possible to carry out sabotage programs via telecommunication lines from some distance away. Cases involving computer sabotage by remote DP are reported from the United States in particular. In 1980, for example, a group of 8th-grade students of the New York Dalton School were able to use their school's training computer to penetrate the databanks of various Canadian companies and the federal government and, in some cases, to destroy their data.[41]

Further techniques to cause *logical damage* which have been revealed are: erasing data by magnets or degaussers; operating a power-off switch during a production run; putting a plug, chip, or printed-circuit motherboard into an incorrect socket; or changing labels, tape numbers, and other data.[42]

This detailed description of sabotage techniques could be criticized on the grounds of the danger of their criminal use. However, it is given here because many victims of computer sabotage are unfamiliar with these sophisticated techniques and have suffered additional loss due to their inability to identify the effects of such techniques as deliberate acts of sabotage. Instead, they searched for system defects for a long time, thus giving the perpetrator more time to continue his criminal activities. In addition, it must be taken into account that, especially in terrorist circles and among hackers, these techniques are already well known.[43]

c. PERPETRATORS

The majority of acts of sabotage recorded in Western countries up to the present have been committed by angry *employees seeking revenge*, protesting against rationalization of their company, or just wishing to retire early.

> In one case in West Germany a similar but more unusual motive was found. This was the operator's wish to enjoy an amorous rendezvous with the wife of the repairman in charge of the computer. By putting a plug into an incorrect socket the operator ensured at least two hours of free time for himself and two hours of guaranteed work for his rival on several occasions.[44]

A second, more serious, group of perpetrators consists of *ideologically motivated terrorists*, who often regard the computer as a symbol of State control and suppression and as an essential component of the armaments industry.

These politically motivated attacks against computer centres began with acts of sabotage against armaments factories in the United States by opponents of the Vietnam War, the explosions caused by the East-Asian Anti-Japan Armed Front, and the numerous bomb attacks by the Red Brigades in Italy. They spread to France with the spectacular attacks against computer manufacturers committed in Toulouse during the Easter weekend of 1980 by the 'Committee for the Liquidation and Subversion of Computers (CLODO)'. Initiated by proclamations and instructions in some left wing magazines they have spread to West Germany as well, especially with the above-mentioned bombing of the MAN company's computer centre in September 1983 and a variety of other bombing attacks in 1984 and 1985. Some of these bombings, such as those against the SCS and the MBP companies committed in 1985, were claimed by 'revolutionary cells' to be protests against increasing rationalization and the job-destruction of computers.[45]

Another group of perpetrators could emerge from the *business community*. Th aim of computer sabotage committed by companies can be to gain an advantage over their competitors or to facilitate the take-over of a company.[46]

In a West German case in 1984 an employee combined such computer sabotage with a software theft. While he was selling good copies of the stolen programs, the original programs of his former employer were handicapped by time-consuming routines, some of which occasionally showed pictures of jumping-jacks and clowns on the users' screens.[47]

A particularly threatening financial motive in computer sabotage underlies the cases of 'bitnapping', in which computer programs or other data are stolen in order to be used as a means of extortion.

4. Theft of Services

The unauthorized use of DP systems, often referred to as theft of services or 'time-theft', is very widespread in the DP sector. The objects of this activity are the processing, storage, and transmission services of computer hardware and very often also programs and other data, which are used by DP employees for their own purposes. In some cases time-theft, especially if committed by employees, does not cause considerable damage to the company concerned, and represents less of a danger than the offences described thus far. However, the company's interest can be severely affected by abuse of remote DP systems (by using the company's account numbers or rented computers for which the actual time of utilization has to be paid), or when the company loses its services or customers by blockade system or by 'blacking' of the labour of its employees.[48]

Such a case is the subject of a charge brought before a court in South Germany. The Public Prosecutor has accused four university professors of having used the university computer for several mathematical problems on behalf of private corporations without having entered this work properly into the university's accounts. Instead they had formed a private association named 'Institutsgemeinschaft der Universität eV' and had entered their activities into this association's accounts. There appears to have been receipts of more than DM 350 000 in the accounts of this association, part of which does not appear to have at least been spent according to the university's budgetary rules (e.g. for overtime payments, increases in salary, travelling expenses, etc.). The Public Prosecutor has charged the professors with breach of trust.[49]

5. Unauthorized Access to DP Systems and 'Hacking'

Unauthorized access to DP systems via remote DP which is not committed for manipulation, fraud, espionage, or sabotage purposes but simply for non-financially motivated 'joyriding' of another company's computer (*'hackito ergo sum'*), can be categorized as a special form of 'theft of services'. The new videotex systems, which often lack adequate safety measures, have considerably increased the possibilities for such acts.

'Pure' unauthorized access to DP systems is primarily committed by juvenile hackers, who have a variety of motives. They may intend to improve data- and consumer-protection; they may want to overcome the challenge of a company's security system; they may enjoy infiltrating important databanks; or they may want to boast among friends or to the press. As an analogy to Sutherland's sociological term 'white-collar crime' one could call these acts 'short-pants crime'.

When some cases become public these acts of hacking can be useful for the detection of loopholes in computer systems. However, in general they are dangerous, because data may be destroyed by negligence, system blockades may be caused, and security deficiencies found by acts committed as a challenge may be subsequently used for financial fraud.[50]

Numerous examples of such 'hacker stories' can be found in the press, and the case of the Hamburg 'Computer-Chaos Club' may be singled out. A representative of the *German Post* had dismissed the reports of the club on loopholes in the West German videotex system as being 'nonsense'. Two members of the club therefore continuously called an information page, which the club offered in the videotex system of the *German Post*, by using the name and password of a Hamburg savings institute. Because each request for the page was charged DM 9.97 to the account of the savings institute and as the club members continued the page's request for one night by use of a special computer program, they collected DM 134 000 on the club's account before they made the action public at a press conference held in the office of the Hamburg Commissioner for Privacy Protection on 19 November 1984.[51]

6. The Computer as a Tool for Traditional Business Offences

In the preceding cases companies were damaged through manipulations of their own computers, primarily by their own employees. However, in recent years the possibilities of computer misuse have been increasingly utilized by the management of fraudulently operating companies to commit general business offences at the expense of business partners, consumers, investors, or governmental agencies. The majority of cases discovered up to now involve the manipulation of computer-administered revenues, accounts, balance sheets, stock-taking lists, and tax declarations. The erasing of stock-keeping lists and balance sheets to disguise business offences and to render penal procedures more difficult is also a frequently practised method. In a West German bankruptcy case in 1980, for example, the offender attempted to attribute a manipulation to an accidental mistake in computer-handling. The application of computers to simulate and organize crimes has been revealed particularly in the field of check-kite simulation and drug dealing.[52] The best-known example of a computer-assisted general business offence is the American Equity Funding case, which led to some of the most extensive losses caused by computer manipulations in the United States.

The swindle practised by the Equity Funding Corporation, an insurance company, consisted of the sale of fictitious life-insurance contracts to a reinsurer. This case of assignment of bogus claims was greatly facilitated by the corporation's DP system. Without the use of DP the offenders would have been forced to fill out and falsify an insurance contract with a large number of social security and medical entries concerning the insured person for each of the fictitious contracts sold. The DP system, with the individual insurance contracts stored in the master file, eased this work. As the reinsurer was willing to accept the DP printout from the Equity Funding Corporation as evidence of the existence of the insurance contracts taken on, the offenders simply had to add the data of the fictitious insurance contracts to the data on the master file. The corporation did not undertake the laborious task of feeding individual fictitious contract data, together with correct data, via the routine intended for this purpose, but instead used magnetic tapes containing the data of old contracts already issued. A specially written program was used to change the old insurance numbers and multiply both the premiums and insurance sums to be paid by a factor of 1.8. Further computer programs ensured that the fictitious data were entered into the company's balance sheet, thus driving up the share rates of the corporation. By automating the production of bogus policies in this way, a total of 56 000 fictitious insurance contracts with a sale value of more than $30 million were fraudulently produced by special computer programs and sold to another company between 1970 and 1972. It probably would not have been possible to achieve this amount by manual falsification of insurance contracts. The manipulation was discovered because a member of the staff with knowledge of the crime betrayed the plan after an argument with his boss. The head of the company was sentenced to 8 years' imprisonment and 21 other members of the staff, including three from the DP department, also received long prison sentences.[53]

B. COMPUTER-RELATED INFRINGEMENTS OF PRIVACY

The discussion surrounding the second main group of computer abuses, that of computer-related infringements of privacy, is considerably older than that concerning computer-related economic crimes. However, because of the small number of severe criminal cases[54] and the dependency of the evaluation of most privacy infringements on a difficult balancing of interests, these cases have been discussed more in terms of public, civil, and labour law problems than as a matter of criminal law.

Even today, in many cases an evaluation of privacy infringements as 'abusive', 'illegal', or 'criminal' is still difficult because often a balancing between the rights of an individual to his privacy and the rights of society to information is necessary. This balancing of interests not only causes different evaluations of the legality of the respective acts in various countries but also different concepts of the role which criminal law should play in this field. Because of these legal uncertainties and differences it is important to stress that this chapter only analyses potential threats and abuses, and that the classification of these acts as illegal or criminal can only be done by a legal evaluation given in Chapter IV.

Criminological research and systematic phenomenology of potential computer-related infringements of privacy which are (*de lege lata*) or should be (*de lege ferenda*) criminal has not until now been well developed. As a clear definition and classification of the sphere of privacy for the purpose of criminological systematization does not seem to be available the following survey analyses the respective cases by differentiating the various modi operandi of privacy infringements. Using this criminological approach one can differentiate between:

(1) The production and use of incorrect data (the classical field of infamation offences);
(2) The illegal disclosure or misuse of data (partly covered by traditional offences protecting professional secrets);
(3) The illegal collecting and storing of data; and
(4) Infringements of formalities and information rights of privacy laws.

1. Use of Incorrect Data

Privacy infringements committed by the use of incorrect data can be divided into two phenomenological types of abuses: (a) the manipulation and erasure of data by unauthorized persons; and (b) the collection, storage, processing, or disclosure of incorrect data by their legitimate holder.

a. MANIPULATION AND ERASURE OF PERSONAL DATA BY UNAUTHO-RIZED PERSONS

As far as incorrect personal data originate from computer manipulations committed by unauthorized persons, both the illegal and the criminal character of the act are easy to determine. The same is true when the contents of databanks are changed by the erasure of data. These cases, which often not only infringe upon the privacy rights of the individuals concerned but also upon the economic interests of the holder of that information, have been discussed above.[55]

b. COLLECTION, PROCESSING, AND DISSEMINATION OF INCORRECT DATA BY THEIR LEGITIMATE HOLDER

It is obvious that the collection, processing, or dissemination of incorrect data by its holder is also illegal. When these acts are committed knowingly the evaluation of the criminal character of the act does not raise major problems either. However, in most cases in the DP area, especially in the field of credit-reporting systems, the use of incorrect data in general is only caused by negligence. In such cases, most legal systems provide civil and administrative remedies for the abuses, which are not generally considered to be criminal.

> As an example, the American case of *Thompson* v. *San Antonio Retail Merchants Association* may be cited. This concerned the credit agency SARMA, which utilized a computerized 'automatic capturing' feature. Each subscriber to the credit-reporting service used its own terminal to feed identifying information about a particular consumer to SARMA's computer. This then displayed the credit-history file that most nearly matched the information fed in by the subscriber, who was free to decide whether or not he would accept the displayed file as that of the consumer for whom the request had been made. When the subscriber did accept the file, SARMA's computer automatically captured into the file any non-pre-existing information from the subscriber's terminal.
>
> This system caused great problems for the plaintiff by producing a mixture of his file and of that of a man who ultimately became delinquent and was discharged as a bad debt. As a result, the plaintiff's applications for credit cards were denied. Numerous efforts to discover and remedy the problem failed. Only after the plaintiff's lawsuit had been filed was the mistake corrected.
>
> The trial court found that the credit denials had been caused by SARMA's failure to follow reasonable procedures to ensure the maximum possible accuracy of its files, and awarded the plaintiff $10 000 damages plus $4 485 attorney's fees. The appellate court upheld the trial court's judgment and stressed that even if there were no out-of-pocket expenses caused by the negligence, the consumer would have been entitled to recover under the Fair Credit Reporting Act for humiliation and mental distress. It agreed with the trial court that in this case the humiliation and mental distress had been substantial enough to warrant the $10 000 award.[56]

2. Illegal Collection and Storage of Correct Data

Privacy and personal rights can not only be affected by the use of false data but also by the collection and storage of correct data. An 'abusive' character of such acts can either consist of (a) the methods by which the data were gathered or (b) the content of the data.

a. ILLEGAL TECHNIQUES OF OBTAINING DATA

On the techniques to obtain data a variety of acts can be listed which are clearly detrimental infringements of privacy. Examples of such clear 'abuses' are wiretapping, bugging, illegal access to another person's data files by infringement of security measures, etc. In future the growing use of personal computers, data networks, and mailboxes will lead to an increase in these infringements. As an example of these intrusive techniques a West German hacker case can be cited which illustrates the whole range of infringements in private-user data networks:

> The 16-year-old perpetrator, among others, programmed 'data traps' which collected the personal identification data of other videotex systems-users. Furthermore he manipulated and destroyed the data files of some users, changed the valid passwords of others (who could therefore no longer work with their system), and sent libellous letters by using false sender-identifications.[57]

However, in many other areas the question whether a certain act is legal or illegal remains open. Computerized video-surveillance and recognition of people undertaken by police agenices, for example, will raise considerable problems in the future.

b. ILLEGAL CONTENTS OF STORED DATA

The second aspect which can render the storage of information illegal is that the content of the information is not supposed to be stored. Without legal limitations the expanded possibilities to collect, process, and transmit large amounts of information could be used to create excessive profiles of individuals, households, or groups of people. However, the question of who is supposed to store what kinds of information is one of the most difficult in privacy-protection. It is especially important for credit-reporting systems, police, intelligence and other administrative agencies, personal information systems in the field of labour registration, and registration of private consumption of new media services.

> In the field of labour registration the legality of data storage is being discussed, especially in Italy, where unions are focusing on this question. In a case in northern Italy, for example, a multinational computer company installed two control systems called 'Service Level Reporter' and 'Resource Access Control Facility'. A trade union denounced the managers of the company to the Magistrate of

Milan, arguing that the control systems were a violation of section 4 of the Workers' Statute (Law No. 300 of 5 May 1970; for the public sector see section 23 of Law No. 93 of 29 May 1983). This provision forbids control at a distance of the activities of workers in that 'by the use of instruments which allow personal access, connected to the fulfilment of duties, it becomes possible for the employer to control quantitatively the activity of the employee'. According to section 38 of the Workers' Statute, violations against section 4 are punishable by a fine of between 100 000 and 1 million lire or by imprisonment of between 15 days and 1 year. The company argued that the system was used only for the protection of company assets and for correct planning and management of the automation system. The Magistrate of Milan cited the managers of the company for violation of section 4 above. The proceedings are still in progress.[58]

3. Illegal Disclosure and Misuse of Data

A third group of privacy infringements is constituted by the illegal disclosure and misuse of data. With respect to the legal evaluation of these acts a distinction can be made between acts concerning secret personal data and those concerning non-secret personal data.

a. PERSONAL DATA COVERED BY TRADITIONAL SECRECY PROTECTION

The illegal character of the disclosure of personal data in general is clear when these data are covered by traditional statutes protecting special secrets. This is especially the case in the fields of medicine, banking, etc. To a certain extent this is also true for acts in which data are misused, i.e. when information is legally collected and stored but used for a purpose other than that for which the data were obtained.

> The threat to personal data in the banking sector was illustrated by a case concerning the Swiss Bankgesellschaft in 1983. In this the French customs investigation and exchange control services had somehow obtained three tapes containing bank-account information on French citizens. As the French customs administration, who were looking for illegal currency exports and tax-evaders, could not decipher the tapes they offered 500 000 French francs to two employees of the Swiss Bankgesellschaft for this service. In 1983 these employees brought six of the bank's tapes containing its operating programs to a guarded French data centre in Rennes, where French officials and the two perpetrators tried to make operable a Univac System 1100, which was identical to the Swiss bank's system. The act was detected when a third employee of the bank, who was later asked for additional information in Switzerland, realized that a printout of the bank's system had been produced on paper not available in the bank's computer centre. In the proceedings the courts assumed that the attempt by the French customs to read the personal tapes was not successful. Nevertheless, the two perpetrators received prison sentences of 2 years and 3 months and of 4 years.[59]
>
> The threat to privacy in the field of police information systems was illustrated by an Austrian case in which a police officer of the Federal Police of Vienna had, from

1961 to 1978, given to a private detective data from the register of criminal records, the register of persons, the file of police searches, and Interpol files. The police officer was sentenced on account of 'breach of secrecy by a public servant'.[60]

b. NON-SECRET PERSONAL DATA

In other areas it is difficult to decide whether the disclosure and use of personal data is detrimental to society and should be called abusive, illegal, or criminal. This is especially true in the case of information-exchanges between various government agencies or between credit-reporting agencies and their clients.

> The issue of whether computer matching by government agencies violates the constitutional right of privacy was addressed in the case of *Jaffess* v. *Secretary of Health, Education, and Welfare.* In this a list of persons receiving veteran's disability benefits was matched against a list of social-security recipients. This comparison was made because the amount of a veteran's payment is dependent upon annual income from other sources, including social security benefits. When a computer cross-check revealed that the plaintiff had not reported his social security income as required by law, his veteran's benefits were accordingly reduced. The court rejected the plaintiff's claim of a constitutional guarantee of privacy, finding that the right of privacy does not prevent intra-agency disclosure of information obtained in the course of conducting regular agency functions. The disclosure of Jaffess's benefits to the Veterans Administration under the matching program was clearly warranted because the Veterans' Administration is statutorily obliged to take such payments into consideration. A violation of the right of privacy would only occur if the government possessed 'highly personal and confidential information which has been given under compulsion of law and with an expectation of privacy and where the dislosure of such information is unnecessary for the advancement or inconsistent with the fundamental purpose for which the data was obtained'.[61]

4. Infringements of Formalities of Privacy Laws

The difficult balancing of interests necessary to differentiate between legal and illegal collection, processing, and disclosure of personal data in many States has led not only to the criminalization of substantive infringements of privacy but also to the creation of formal duties of registration or of licensing the processing or transmission of personal data. In many States the violation of these formal duties as well as other duties to inform or support supervisory agencies or individuals concerned are sanctioned by penal provisions, creating new criminal offences. Prosecutions based on these new provisions are, however, only rarely carried out.

> The case of the French company SKF can be cited as an example. SKF had stored information concerning the private life, political opinions, and union membership of job-applicants in a manual storage device without reporting it to the French National Commission on Information and Liberties. This constituted

an infraction of section 42 of the French Law on Data Processing, Data Files, and Individual Liberties of 6 January 1978 (providing a maximum penalty of 5 years' imprisonment). The French Commission for Information and Liberties handed the case to the State Prosecutor, who is demanding a fine amounting to one year of the company's turnover.[62]

C. FURTHER ABUSES AND QUESTIONS OF DEFINITION

Because of the increasing expansion of computer techniques in all areas of social life, computer-abuse will not be confined to economic and privacy offences but will also extend to most other classic crimes.

1. Offences Against State and Political Interests

This extension of computer crime can be illustrated in the field of *political, State, administrative, and judicial interests.*

> In 1976 a committee of inquiry of the West German state of Baden-Württemberg investigated the question of whether a Secretary of State had manipulated a computer analysis in order to situate a dumping-ground for toxic waste in the electoral district of a political opponent.[63]
>
> Further abuses of computer technology in the political domain concern shifts of power between government and parliament caused by different access to databanks. Political abuses could also happen, for example, through manipulation of political elections by computer-based alterations of electoral districts.[64] The possibility of direct manipulations of election results was illustrated in the 1986 election in the Philippines, when computer personnel refused to continue to work because of alleged orders to manipulate the results.
>
> Administrative and judicial interests were affected in a West German case when a programmer was manipulating the result of his blood alcohol test.[65] In another West German case a group of people was accused of attempted erasure of certain names from the police's file on wanted persons.[66]

2. The Extension to Offences Against Personal Integrity

The possible extension of computer crime to offences against human lives has already been correctly analysed by the Japanese *White Book on Police* in 1983.[67] This describes the incident of 18 January 1979 when an aircraft, landing at JFK Airport in New York with the Russian Ambassador on board, was endangered by computer manipulation by an air-traffic controller. The misrouted flight of a Korean jumbo jet in 1984, which was assumed to have been caused by a programming error in its navigational computer and which ended with its being shot down by a Russian fighter, also illustrates the theoretical possibility of such grave consequences due to computer-error or manipulation. The vulnerability of air- and traffic-control systems has also been shown by the terrorist attacks in 1985 on the computer and communications systems of Tokyo Airport and the Japanese railways. Threats to the *lives of people* caused by computer manipulation are also possible in the fields of computerized hospital supervision systems, control systems for nuclear power plants, and of air, sea, and road transport systems. The malfunctioning of the North American NORAD defence system, 'detecting' an attack by Soviet weapons which in reality had not taken place,[68] shows that manipulation and sabotage in the field of highly computerized defence systems could have even graver consequences. The American SDI system will considerably increase the dependency of Western defence systems on computers, since it will require large numbers of computers, sensors, and software.

3. Resulting Questions of Definition

This extension of computer abuses and computer crimes leads to the question as to whether the above accepted *definition and concept* of computer abuse or computer crime has become too broad to have any scientific or practical value. It is true that for an approach which is only based on substantive penal law, the last-mentioned offences neither pose any specific legal problems nor have anything in common with computer-assisted economic or privacy offences. However, considering also the criminological aspects of *modus operandi* and circumvention of safety measures, the development of security measures for computer-users, or the detection, prosecution, and proving of computer crime, all the cases discussed above pose similar problems. Therefore it is recommended to keep the broad OECD's definition for criminological and general-purpose studies and restrict specific studies concerning legal problems, security measures, and prosecution to the specific areas which are creating problems in these fields.

III.

Extent, Impact, and Future Development of Computer Crime

1. Extent of Computer Crime

The question of the scope of computer crime is one of great controversy. Whereas in the 1970s the significance of computer crime was denied by some authors, today estimations can be found indicating that one in forty computer centers is affected by computer crime, that only 1% of all computer offences are detected, and that only one in 22 000 perpetrators is sentenced to prison.[1] However, as far as these figures are concerned it must be stressed that scientifically sound methods do not allow any reliable statements to be made about the actual scope of computer offences. Only estimates based on substantiated experience are possible. Thereby two aspects must be considered: the *number of known cases* and the *problem of undetected offences* (the 'dark figure').

a. THE NUMBER OF KNOWN CASES—A SURVEY OF INTERNATIONAL EMPIRICAL COMPUTER CRIME STUDIES

Cases of computer crime have been described in many publications in recent years. However, most of these have no scientific value because they are unverified newspaper reports, secondary literature, or popular books in which the writers often quote each other without critically examining the sources of their information. Worldwide, only a few empirical research studies provide reliable information. An exact comparison between these is not possible because of the different underlying definitions of the phenomena investigated as well as the different research methods of selection and verification. Nevertheless it can be stated that the number of perfectly verifiable computer crimes in all reliable empirical studies is not very large.

The earliest statistical research in the field of computer crime was undertaken in the **United States** by *SRI International* (Stanford Research Institute

International) in Menlo Park, California, in 1971, which up to March 1985 had collected about 1600 cases of computer-abuse that had taken place since 1958. However, this number includes all kinds of computer-abuse (including civil suits and other non-criminal matters) and both verified and unverified cases, some of which are based only on newspaper reports. A more reliable but also not necessarily representative result was obtained by the SRI in 1979, when a questionnaire was sent to 72 district attorneys who participated in the Economic Crime Project of the Law Enforcement Assistance Administration. Forty district-attorney offices reported a total of 244 cases of respondent-defined, computer-related crimes brought to their attention, 191 of which were prosecuted and 167 resulting in a conviction.[2]

In the United States in 1976 a second study was conducted by the *General Accounting Office* (GAO), when ten federal investigative agencies searched their files for cases of 'computer crime', resulting in 74 cases, 69 of which were recognized by the GAO.[3]

In 1980 the *National Center for Computer Crime Data* (NCCCD) initiated a third study which initially was based on a 1980 copy of the databases of the SRI. In 1985 the Center published the preliminary results of its new 'Computer Crime Census' project, which is intended to become part of the Center's annual statistical report. In the course of this study, the NCCCD surveyed over 130 prosecutors' offices to determine the significance of the new computer crime laws passed since 1976. This investigation resulted in 52 cases of computer crime being prosecuted pursuant to State computer crime laws. Two of these cases had gone to trial and 13 were still pending.[4]

Additional empirical studies in the United States have been conducted by the American Institute of Certified Public Accountants and by the American Bar Association. The EDP Fraud Review Task Force of the *American Institute of Certified Public Accountants* (AICPA), which was founded in 1978, sent questionnaires to banks and insurance companies and published a report on this survey in 1984. This shows that 9405 banks were surveyed, of which 5127 responded: 105 of these respondents reported they had experienced at least one case of what was believed to be EDP-related fraud. After reviewing the details of these cases, the AICPA determined that 85 conformed to the study's definition. Another questionnaire was sent to 1232 insurance companies: 854 responded and identified 40 cases that they believed to be EDP-related fraud. Of these cases submitted, 34 conformed to the study's definition. The survey participation was voluntary and the Task Force was aware of some significant cases that were not reported and therefore not included in the study.[5]

A Task Force on Computer Crime of the *American Bar Association* in February 1984 distributed a lengthy survey to approximately 1000 private organizations and public institutions. It received 275 respondents, 27% of which stated to have sustained 'known and verifiable losses due to computer crime during the last twelve months'.[6]

In the **Federal Republic of Germany** the first empirical computer crime study applying approved criminological research methods was conducted by the author in a research project started in 1974 at the *Institute for Criminology and Economic Criminal Law of the University of Freiburg*. In order to avoid methodological doubts concerning the verification and method of selecting cases arising in the first Stanford Research Institute study and in a case collection of the private West German security consultant Von Zur Muehlen published in 1973 (and revealing 54 unverified cases of computer crime[7]), statistical statements were restricted to perfectly verifiable cases of computer-related economic crimes (i.e. cases for which the original court records could be obtained). Thirty-one of these were described and analysed in detail in the first publication of this study in 1977. For the second edition of the research project published in 1980 about a dozen more verified court records were included. In a publication of the continued study prepared for the legal committee of the West German Bundestag in 1984/5 the general statistical work was not continued because hundreds of cases of software theft brought before the courts in 1984 and 1985 showed that general statistics on computer crime were becoming of little value and had to be replaced by specialized studies concentrating on specific phenomena such as computer-related fraud, espionage, sabotage, privacy infringements, and other selected areas.[8]

In the Federal Republic of Germany in 1983 cases of computer crime were also determined by a special study carried out by the *Max-Planck Institute for Foreign and International Penal Law* at Freiburg in the context of 'Countrywide Registration of Economic Crimes'. This study revealed 38 investigations by the public prosecuters in the period 1975 to 1983.[9]

The increase in computer crime cases caused by software-thefts (especially by juvenile perpetrators) indicated early in the University of Freiburg's research was then confirmed by an inquiry of the West German *Federal State Investigation Agency* (Bundeskriminalamt), which had asked police agencies to report on known cases of computer crime. The inquiry revealed nine cases in 1980; eight in 1981, nine in 1982, and 11 cases in 1983. In 1984 the following numbers of cases were reported: 212 (involving 553 suspected persons) of computer espionage and software-theft (95% of these cases involved illegal copying of programs and only six concerned highly valuable software), six cases of computer fraud (all reported by the state of Nordrhein-Westfalen!), two of computer sabotage, and two of unauthorized use. An estimated 300–500 additional software thefts reported by one state *in toto* are not included in these figures.[10]

In 1984 the first empirical study on computer-related privacy infringements was published. The study, which had been conducted at the *University of Tübingen*, used the statistics of the Federal State Investigation Bureau (Bundeskriminalamt) and investigated all infringements against the Federal Data Protection Act and against the State Data Protection Acts which had been prosecuted from 1977 to 1982. This resulted in 159 cases for which police records could be obtained. The majority of these cases were only minor ones: 142 were stayed, eight resulted in a demand for an order of summary punishment, and nine were brought to trial.[11]

In **Australia** a comprehensive collection of computer-abuse cases was started in 1975 by the *Computer Abuse Research Bureau at the Caulfield Institute for Technology*. This study revealed a total of 96 reported cases of computer-abuse during the period 1975 to 1982 and a total of 150 cases until 1985.[12]

In the **United Kingdom** the *Local Government Audit Inspectorate* in 1981 invited the business community to report on cases of computer fraud. The agency received 319 replies which resulted in 67 cases of computer crime and a number (79%) of companies which had not been affected by computer fraud. For its 1985 Computer Fraud Survey the Audit Commission for Local Authorities in England and Wales received 943 replies from local and state authorities and commercial organizations. The 943 replies, which constituted a 55% response rate, resulted in 77 cases of computer fraud.[13] Another UK study published in 1984 by the private security consultant *Wong*, of BIS Applied Systems, Manchester, found 95 cases of computer crime.[14]

An international study of the **Commission of the European Communities** in 1983 collected cases of computer risks (including accidental risks) from Belgium, France, West Germany, Italy, and the United Kingdom since 1979. The study examined more than 260 cases of accidents or abuses concerning information technology, 115 of which could be presented in detail in a case study. Of these, 66 involved deliberate actions (40 cases of theft or embezzlement, 21 of sabotage or direct attack, and four of strikes), 41 cases involved accidental risks (especially damage by floods, fire, and lightning), and seven were considered as 'miscellaneous'.[15]

In **Finland** an empirical survey on data security was conducted in 1983 and 1984 by the *Centre for the Development of Data Technology* and the Data Processing Society. The questioning of 650 Finnish organizations showed that many more cases of computer-abuse were detected than reported to the authorities. Most of them had been petty and had therefore been settled out of court. Until the end of 1984, 21 computer-related crimes had been reported to the *Finnish police*, most of them involving software piracy.[16]

In **Sweden** in 1985 *Artur Solarz* published his detailed criminological research. He analysed all the verified serious embezzlement offences in Sweden from 1981 to 1983. These 351 cases included 38 computer-related embezzlements. In addition, Solarz investigated 10 computer-related embezzlements in 1979 and 1980.[17] The *Swedish police* until 1984 reported about 20 cases of computer-related crime.[18] On 16 January 1986 the Swedish government decided to set up a consultative group for studies on vulnerability problems.

In **Austria** in 1984 a study on computer crime was conducted at the *University of Graz*. The research, which was published in 1985, did not consist of a systematic collection of computer crime cases but described several verified Austrian computer-crime cases.[19] The Austrian *Ministry of the Interior*, to whom all security agencies have to report cases of computer crime, registered 30 relevant cases until the end of 1985.[20]

In **Belgium** the *International Criminal Law Centre* and the *Economic Law Centre of the University of Brussels* sent a questionnaire to 650 computer-users in order to investigate the impact of computer crime. The results of the study had not been received at the time of writing.[21]

The relatively small number of computer-crime cases revealed in those research projects was confirmed by **additional police statistics** published in several countries in recent years. In **Japan** a study of the *Central Police Bureau of Tokyo* for 1971–83 showed 36 cases of 'classic' computer crimes and the following number of manipulations of cash dispensers: in 1975, eight cases; in 1976, 23; in 1977, 64; in 1978, 131; in 1979, 187; in 1980, 212; in 1981, 288; in 1982, 472; and in 1983, 642.[22] In **Switzerland** the police department of the *Canton of Zurich* in November 1985 reported a total of 15 cases of computer crime.[23]

b. THE PROBLEM OF THE 'DARK FIGURE'

The relatively small number of verifiable computer crimes does not permit any conclusion concerning the number of actual cases, as the number of undiscovered offences in computer crime is suspected to be considerably high.

This assumption is due first, to the low proportion of computer offences which become known due to the specific difficulties of detection and proof in the DP sector. Second, many of the offences that are discovered are subjected to the internal disciplinary procedures of the companies concerned rather than being reported, due mainly to a fear of damage to the company's reputation and of loss of confidence by investors, shareholders, and customers or in order to facilitate the compensation for the damage done. Third, cases reported to the law-enforcement agencies are not always systematically prosecuted since effective treatment requires special knowledge as well as high expenditure in terms of time and money. Finally, it is a matter of chance whether reported cases of computer crime are discovered among other cases of fraud and breach of trust, because the criminological term 'computer crime' does not appear in official legal administration statistics.[24]

> The relevance of these factors was clearly illustrated in a survey conducted by the Ontario Provincial Police between 1980 and 1981: of 321 responses received from 648 companies questioned, only 13 companies reported experience of a loss through computer crime; only five of these 13 incidents were reported to the police at that time, and it seems that only three prosecutions were undertaken.[25]
>
> Additional problems which arise from special police statistics, even when the research has strong administrative support, are illustrated in the above-mentioned inquiry of the West German Federal State Investigation Agency. In this all police agencies were asked to report on known cases of computer crime. However, according to the information currently available, many verifiable cases were not included in the police reports. It seems that many police agencies had difficulties in applying the technical definitions used in the inquiry. In addition, not all police agents were properly informed of the existence of the reporting system. Furthermore, the 300–500 cases of software-theft reported *in toto* by one State seem not to be included.[26]

As the above-mentioned four factors for determining the level of undiscovered offences must be multiplied many times, the scope of computer crime should be estimated as being considerable. However, due to the reasons discussed, precise figures cannot be given.

2. Extent of Losses

Various international inquiries into computer crime show different amounts of losses in computer crime which are likely to be the result of the different disclosure techniques in the respective States and research areas. However, all the studies demonstrate that losses in computer crime are much more severe than those in traditional crime.

Whereas the losses in the majority of traditional fraud cases in the **Federal Republic of Germany** are less than DM 10 000, in most cases of computer manipulation discovered in the Federal Republic the statistical investigation carried out by the author in 1977 indicated that the losses ranged from DM 200 000 to DM 300 000. The losses in the majority of computer manipulations discovered in the Federal Republic between 1977 and 1982 ranged between DM 500 000 and DM 1 500 000. Subsequently, a general statistic was not formulated because of the growing disparities between the various groups of phenomena. Whereas the losses in fraud by computer manipulation continued to increase (two cases in 1983 showed amounts of about DM 4 million and DM 5 million), the large number of software-thefts committed by minors as well as the cases committed by hackers led to only small amounts.[27]

In the **United States** a study by the Stanford Research Institute International in 1975 indicated an average loss of $450 000 and in 1979 an average amount of $1 685 000. However, this figure is based on the verified and unverified cases described above.[28] In the previously mentioned study by the US General Accounting Office, a monetary loss could be determined in 49 of the 69 cases. The total loss was $2 161 413 and the average was $44 110.[29] The study by the National Center for Computer Crime Data revealed the following figures: 18 cases of 'theft of money' with an average loss of $5 254, two cases of 'theft of programs or data' with an average loss of $81 000, and five cases of 'damage to programs or data' with an average loss of $93 600.[30]

In **Australia** the national survey carried out by the Computer Abuse Research Bureau at the Caulfield Institute of Technology between 1975 and 1982 revealed losses ranging from nil to $900 000 and average losses of about $32 000 per case. According to the Institute's 1985 statistics the average amount is $77 565.[31]

In the **United Kingdom** the study by Wong, the private security consultant, based upon 95 cases, found average losses of around £31 000 in the field of computer fraud and £1.2 million in computer-related arson and bombing.[32]

In **Japan** 15 of the 19 input manipulations registered by the Central Police Bureau of Tokyo in 1982 showed losses of more than 10 million Yen.[33]

In **Sweden** Artur Solarz's study revealed that the average amounts embezzled were 137 000 Swedish crowns for ordinary embezzlement and 196 000 crowns for computer-related embezzlement.[34]

In the above-mentioned study by the **European Commission** the amounts of misappropriations could be analysed in 23 cases: 15 misappropriations related to sums of over 150 000 ecus each, of which two major banking cases suffered losses in excess of 10 million ecus each. The 13 other cases caused an average loss of 1 million ecus. The average for the eight 'small' misappropriations run at more than 40 000 ecus (1 ecu at that time equalling 54 US cents).[35]

The *reason for the high losses* in computer-related property crimes is primarily the high value of DP-stored data. In the field of *fraud* this was illustrated by the high sums administered in electronic funds transfer systems or stored in computer-based accounts. The perpetrator can even exceed the existing accounts by creating fictitious values, because fraud of deposit money stored in DP systems, in contrast to traditional embezzlement, is not limited by the actual amount of money at hand in a cash register. The previously described[36] permanent and automatic working of the acts, including the 'salami technique', also help to create considerable amounts of losses in the field of computer fraud. In the area of computer *espionage*, the high value of DP-stored data has been mentioned.[37] In the field of *sabotage* it is especially the dependence of firms, administrative units, governments, and economies on DP systems which make computer crime a serious threat. It has already been illustrated that the destruction of a computer centre and its computer-stored data can easily lead to the risk of bankruptcy for a firm which does not possess adequate back-up facilities. It is also clear that a political plan for computer sabotage, comparable with the above-mentioned[38] East German plan for DP espionage, could lead to severe harm for Western defence and economy. Therefore, it is primarily the potential harm to society, not the actual losses revealed in cases up to the present, which make computer crime a serious threat for Western industrialized nations.

3. Future Developments

The problems caused by computer crime are bound to intensify in the future.[39] Increasing computerization, particularly in the administering of deposit money, in the balancing of accounts and stock-keeping, in the field of electronic funds transfer systems, and in the private sector, as well as new computer applications such as electronic home banking, electronic mail systems, and other interactive videotex systems will lead to increases in the *number of offences and losses*. In cases of fraud, espionage, and sabotage this prediction is supported by the previously discussed[40] number of manipulations of cash dispensers in Japan, which was twelve times that of all other 'classic' computer offences. In addition, the cheap modems and terminals which have been brought on the market during the last two years and have opened up the possibilities of computer crime by means of telecommunication to a large group of non-company individuals, as well as the interactive videotex systems currently being installed in Europe, will permit this development to continue.

The examples of cash dispensers, remote DP, and interactive videotex systems show that the new applications of DP systems will not only lead to an increasing number of crimes but also to *new phenomena and abuses* not yet known. Further changes in the field of *modus operandi* will be caused by new safety measures which will eliminate most of the simple manipulation techniques which currently prevail. However, it will also provoke new techniques of circumvention, as can be seen by the increasing number of cases of collusion among several perpetrators—a reaction to improved control techniques. The main techniques of security-measure circumvention will therefore be discussed in Chapter V.

International computer networks will lead to *transnational computer crimes* committed in one country via remote DP with results in others. If the prevention of computer crime is not harmonized, this development will include the emergence of '*computer crime havens*'.

As far as the *perpetrators* are concerned it must be expected that governments, terrorists, and criminal organizations will also utilize the possibility of computer crime. This was illustrated in the 1960s, when the East German Secret Service's plan for long-term DP espionage strategy was discovered. It is also demonstrated by the suspected involvement of the Mafia in a number of American cases of computer crime.

Changes will also result in the field of the *victims*. Whereas today in most cases the victims are the companies who own the computer, in the future the number of consumers being hit by computer crime will increase. This will especially be the case in the field of cash-dispenser cards, interactive videotex systems, and other consumer networks, as well as in the area of fraud against personal computer-users. There is therefore no doubt that the question of preventing computer crime and of concentrating efforts to overcome the specific difficulties of detection in the DP sector will be of great significance in the future.

4. The Need for Further International Criminological Research

Precise knowledge of the rapid changes regarding the phenomena and characteristics of computer crime is a necessary prerequisite for the development of preventive safety measures, for law reform, and for an effective prosecution of crime. Continued criminological research in this field is therefore an absolute necessity.

This criminological research should be carried out with close international co-operation. Not only does computer crime exist in all countries, but it also tends to be an international or transnational problem, and some countries can profit by the experience of others. This international co-operation should be based on a uniform categorization and differentiation of computer-crime cases and a common method of data-gathering in order to allow differentiated evaluations of the various types of computer crime as well as an international comparison. The application of computers in most areas of life and the international data networks have condemned non-differentiating global and national research work to the archives of the past.

IV.

The Legal Problems of Computer Crime

The legal comprehension of computer-abuses by *substantive law* is creating problems in two areas: computer-related *economic crimes* and computer-related *infringements of privacy*. Other computer-abuses mentioned above, such as homicide committed by computer manipulation, have not caused major legal problems, since the laws protecting respective traditional interests are formulated primarily in terms of results and not in terms of *modi operandi*. However, especially in Anglo-American law, the use of computers is causing *procedural problems* in all areas of crime, particularly as far as the admissibility of computer-generated evidence and the jurisdiction in transnational computer crime cases are concerned. Consequently, this chapter will discuss three main legal issues:

(A) The legal comprehension of computer-related economic crime;
(B) The legal comprehension of computer-related infringements of privacy; and
(C) The procedural problems of computer crime.

The additional question of prescription of legal requirements for computer security is mentioned in subsection V. B.2.c.

A. COMPUTER-RELATED ECONOMIC CRIMES[1]

In the field of computer-related economic crime the main question in all Western countries is to what extent the existing provisions of *substantive penal* law cover the new forms of offences. In most countries the problems are caused by the fact that the respective penal provisions, some of which date back to the last century, primarily protect physical, tangible, and visible objects against traditional acts. In contrast, computer crime affects not only

37

these traditional objects represented by new media (such as deposits stored in computer records) but also involves new objects in some areas (such as computer programs or the use of DP facilities) and, in most cases, new methods of commission (such as manipulating a computer instead of cheating a person).[2]

In certain areas, especially insofar as protecting computer programs is concerned, the new values and objects in the DP area are creating similar problems for *substantive civil law*. These problems are closely related to those of penal law: penal law often supports and refers to civil law by protecting civil rights (e.g. in the field of copyright) and the violation of penal provisions also generally entails liability for losses. Furthermore, as various legal systems of social control are, to a certain degree, interchangeable, penal provisions in one country sometimes correspond to civil provisions in another (as in the field of trade secrets and copyright protection).[3] The following international comparative survey on the legal response to the new phenomena therefore deals with both the penal and civil law coverage of computer crime.[4]

The following analysis will differentiate between:
(1) Fraud by computer manipulation;
(2) Computer espionage, software piracy, and high-technology theft;
(3) Computer sabotage;
(4) Theft of services;
(5) Unauthorized access, as well as
(6) Computer-related tax fraud.
Individual treatment of these phenomena is not only carried out for clarity and systematization but forms a prerequisite for an analysis of most legislative systems, which—in contrast to some American legislative tendencies—strictly differentiate between these groups of phenomena.

1. Fraud by Computer Manipulation

a. PROBLEMS OF TRADITIONAL LAW

In the field of fraud by computer manipulations many criminal law systems *de lege lata* face considerable difficulties in applying traditional legal remedies.

Theft, Larceny, and Embezzlement
The statutory definitions of *theft, larceny, and embezzlement* in many legal systems require that the offender take an 'item of another person's property' (see, for example, section 127, Austrian Penal Code; sections 461 and 463, Belgian Penal Code; section 379, French Penal Code; sections 242 and 246, West German Penal Code; section 624, Italian Penal Code; section 235, Japanese Penal Code; section 461, Luxembourgian Penal Code; and for the United Kingdom section 4 (a), English Theft Act 1968). Their applicability, therefore, depends on the circumstances of the particular case, especially on

the object and *modus operandi* of the crime.

The provisions can be applied directly if the perpetrator, using the computer, misappropriates *tangible property*, such as cash, cheques, or inventory. However, when money is taken from *cash dispensers* the provisions concerning theft already create problems for some legal systems since it is questionable whether the money was 'taken' against the owner's will. As far as unauthorized users abusing other people's cards, Austrian, Belgian, French, West German, Japanese, and Swiss courts as well as leading opinions in Italy and Portugal apply the provisions of theft. When a legitimate holder of a bank cash-dispenser card exceeds his credit, in some countries such as Belgium there is a tendency to adopt the same approach. However, the French Supreme Court (Cour de Cassation), in a decision of 24 November 1983, judged this conduct to be only a breach of a contractual obligation which does not fall under the provision of theft (section 379, Penal Code) or any other penal provision.[5]

As was shown above, in the majority of computer fraud cases the object of crime was computer-stored data representing *deposit money*. Countries which include such money in the statutory definitions of theft and embezzlement—e.g. Canada, the Netherlands, Switzerland, the United Kingdom, and most of the American States—cover at least some of these cases of fraudulent 'appropriation' of intangible objects (see, for example, section 282 and the definition of 'property' in section 2 of the Canadian Criminal Code; sections 310, 311, 321, and 322, Dutch Penal Code; sections 137, 140, and 141, Swiss Penal Code; and, for the UK, sections 1 and 4(1) of the Theft Act 1968). However, many countries, such as Belgium, West Germany, Greece, Luxembourg, and Japan, cannot treat these cases as theft or embezzlement, because deposit money is not considered to be a tangible item but a claim.[6]

Fraud

The statutory definitions of *fraud* in most legal systems—e.g. in Austria, Denmark, Finland, West Germany, Greece, Italy, Japan, Luxembourg, Norway, Sweden, and Switzerland—require that a *person be deceived* (see, for example, section 146, Austrian Penal Code; section 279, Danish Penal Code; section 263, West German Penal Code; section 386, Greek Penal Code; section 640, Italian Penal Code; section 246, Japanese Penal Code; section 496, Luxembourgian Penal Code; chapter 9, section 1, Swedish Penal Code; or section 148, Swiss Penal Code). As the 'deception' of a computer is inappropriate in this case, the applicability of the fraud provisions in these countries always depends on whether or not the offender has also deceived a person checking the data.

In a few countries, however, the provisions of fraud are interpreted *more broadly*, e.g. as illustrated by the 'manoeuvres frauduleuses' in the Belgian and French statutory definition of fraud ('escroquerie'), the new court decisions in the Netherlands, the respective Canadian fraud provisions, the American statutes of mail, wire, and bank fraud, and the American laws concerning conspiracy to defraud (see, for example, section 496, Belgian Penal Code; sections, 338, 387, and 388, Canadian Criminal Code; section 405, French Penal Code; and section 326 of the Penal Code of the Netherlands). In Canada, for example, this is illustrated in the case *R. v. Marine Resource Analysts Ltd*, in which the accused were convicted of attempted fraud concerning the monetary worth of the computer service as they had used another person's account number in order to gain access to the computer system. Similarly, in *R. v. Kirkwood*, the accused, who sold and rented videotapes which had been unlawfully duplicated, was convicted of defrauding the holder of the respective rights despite the absence of deceit, falsehood, or relationship between the accused and the victim. The dishonest acts (knowingly in breach of copyright) caused both an actual and a risk of prejudice to the economic interests of the owner of the distribution rights and copyright. This 'dishonest deprivation' constituted fraud.

In England the question of whether a machine can be 'deceived' has not yet been clearly answered (see section 15, Theft Act 1968 on 'obtaining property by deception' and section 2 (1) (b) Theft Act 1978). In a fiscal decision (*R. v. Moritz* (1981)) concerning VAT returns the judge held that 'deception' required a human mind which could be deceived. Contrary to English law, the Scots law of fraud does not pose any problems, since it is based not on the concept of 'deception' but on that of 'false pretences'.[7]

Credit-card Fraud
In some countries there exist special provisions on *credit-card fraud*. However, only in a few (and in exceptional cases) is it possible to apply these provisions to cases of cash-dispenser manipulations. This may be so, for example, with the traditional section 301.1 of the Canadian Criminal Code, describing as an offence to (a) steal, forge, or falsify a credit card, (b) possess, use, or deal in any other way with an unlawfully obtained credit card, or (c) use a credit card that one knows has been revoked or cancelled. Yet it has been considered difficult to apply this provision to all types of automated teller machines and bank or service access cards (for the reform of the provision in 1985, see below p. 47). In any case, since credit-card fraud statutes can only be used in specific cases of cash-dispenser manipulation they are not an instrument generally capable of dealing with computer manipulations.[8]

Breach of Trust
The statutory definitions of breach of trust, or 'abus de confiance' in some countries such as in Austria and West Germany, only apply to *offenders in high positions* and not to punchers, operators, and programmers. In addition in some legal systems—such as those of Belgium, France, or Luxembourg— there are restrictions concerning the *protected objects* (see, for example, section 153, Austrian Penal Code; section 491, Belgian Penal Code; section 408, French Penal Code; section 266, West German Penal Code; section 247, Japanese Penal Code; and section 491, Luxembourgian Penal Code;

similar problems are also posed by section 159 of the Swiss Penal Code on 'Ungetreue Geschäftsführung').[9]

Forgery and Related Offences
The provisions of *forgery* in most countries—e.g. Austria, Belgium, France, Finland, West Germany, Italy, Luxembourg, and Switzerland—require *visual readability* of the statement embodied in the document and therefore do not cover electronically stored data (see, for example, section 223, Austrian Penal Code; section 193, Belgian Penal Code; section 145, French Penal Code; section 267, West German Penal Code; sections 485 and 476, Italian Penal Code; sections 193–214 Luxembourgian Penal Code; and sections 110, No. 5, 251–7, and 317, Swiss Penal Code). As far as visible computer printouts are concerned there are additional problems regarding the questions whether or not the printout constitutes an *'original' instrument* and a *(human) declaration*. Furthermore, the question is whether the printout is a *false document* or just a genuine one containing incorrect statements of facts, as only the provisions of forgery of certain public documents (see, for example, section 271, West German Penal Code) punish incorrect statements (for the ordinary provisions of forgery, see especially Chapter 14, section 1 of the Swedish Penal Code, requiring that the act be committed 'by writing the name of another person' or 'obtaining another's signature'). However, the wide definitions of forgery in the Australian Penal Codes of New South Wales or Victoria and the punishment of illegal entries into the magnetic part of cash-dispenser cards as forgery by Japanese jurisdiction and Dutch and French literature exemplifies a different understanding of classic forgery provisions (see section 83 (1), Australian Penal Code of Victoria, section 225 of the Penal Code of the Netherlands, and section 150 French Penal Code).

In addition to the classic statute of forgery, in West Germany a special new provision on *'falsification of technical recordings'* exists (section 268, Penal Code); however, this provision in the DP area can only be used in very few cases. In Belgium, section 211 of the Penal Code can be applied to falsifications by public employees in the field of telecommunication services. In Austria in certain cases special provisions on falsification and suppression of proof used in judicial proceedings can be applied (sections 293 and 295, Austrian Penal Code).[10]

The provisions on *'false accounting'* can only be used in specific cases if documents for accounting purposes are concerned (see, for example, sections 283b, West German Penal Code, or section 17 of the English Theft Act 1968. The provisions of *counterfeiting* in all legal systems require the making of false money. The duplication of 'electronic blips' obviously cannot be said to be counterfeiting.[11]

Summary and Conclusion
In most countries, computer manipulations that have been prosecuted up to the present could be punished according to existing provisions, but there is *no*

guarantee of a general punishability. In some countries such as West Germany and Greece this is a consequence of the respective constitutions which require precise wording and a narrow interpretation of the provisions in order to prevent arbitrary abuses (see, for example, article 103 (2) of the West German 'Grundgesetz' or article 7 of the Greek Constitution). Problems of interpretation are less pronounced in those Western legal systems with more liberal rules of interpretation or broader provisions. Consequently, most Western legal systems are facing difficulties and are looking for solutions *de lege lata* in order to avoid stretching the wording of existing provisions or taking refuge in analogy. The need for new penal provisions to cover computer manipulation was and is being discussed, particularly in Austria, Australia, Belgium, Canada, Finland, France, West Germany, Greece, Japan, the Netherlands, Norway, Sweden, Switzerland, the United Kingdom (England and Scotland), and the United States.[12]

b. NEW LAWS ENACTED

In a number of countries statutory law has already been rewritten in order to cover computer fraud.

The Swedish Data Act of 1973
The *Swedish* Data Act of 4 April 1973 was the first legislation with a provision against computer-related property crimes. The law deals mainly with personal data but also contains a general section (section 21) stating that 'any person who unlawfully gains access to a recording for automatic data processing or unlawfully alters or obliterates or enters such a recording in a file, shall be sentenced for data trespass'. Since this provision primarily concerns unauthorized access, it is to be addressed later.[13]

United States Legislation from 1976 to 1985
The second country to adopt special legislation against computer-related property and economic crimes is the *United States*. There, new legislation, though being first elaborated on a federal level, was first enacted on a *State level*. The Federal Computer Systems Protection Act, proposed by Senator Ribicoff in 1977 and not yet passed, became a model for many of the 45 States which have already enacted computer-crime legislation. Most of the new State laws are not restricted to the field of computer fraud but also include provisions on theft of software and services, destruction of data, attacks on computer equipment, and unauthorized access to computer systems. Generally speaking, it can be said that the great majority of these laws define 'property' as anything of value, including intangible property and computer data. Most of the laws penalize unauthorized access to or use of a computer system for the purpose of wilfully and knowingly (1) devising or executing any scheme or artifice to defraud (or extort) or (2) obtaining money, property, or services by means of embezzlement, false or fraudulent

pretences, representations, or promises (such acts, which are often called 'fraud' or 'fraud in the first degree' are usually punished more harshly than other computer crimes), as well as intentional access, alteration, or destruction of computer hardware, software, or data (such acts, which in some States are called 'fraud in the second degree' or 'misuse', are usually punished less severely.) Examples of this 'creating an act' technique can be found, among others, in the legislation of Arizona, California, Colorado, Delaware, Florida (of special interest because it differentiates and systematizes offences), Georgia, Hawai, Illinois, Kentucky, Louisiana, Michigan, Missouri, Montana, New Mexico, Rhode Island, South Carolina, Tennessee, Utah, and Wisconsin. The suggested State Legislation of the National Association for State Information Systems of 1981 goes even further by imposing a misdemeanour penalty for being criminally negligent in failing to provide adequate computer security.

However, especially in recent legislation in some States, there is also a tendency to incorporate computer-related crime into the general provisions of the penal codes. The Virginia legislature, for example, simply defines computer time and services to be property that may be the object of larceny, embezzlement, or false pretences (for more details, see below); according to the legislature of Massachusetts the term 'property' includes electronically processed or stored data. The new criminal code of Alaska provides that in a prosecution for an offence that requires 'deception' as an element 'it is not a defence that the defendant deceived or attempted to deceive a machine' (including a vending machine, computer, or automated teller machine); and the legislature of Ohio expanded the definitions of 'property', 'services', and 'writing' in the Criminal Code to make them applicable to computer-related crime.

On the *federal level* the *Federal Computer Systems Protection Act* proposed by Senator Ribicoff in 1977 (amended in 1979 and revised in 1980) was reintroduced in Congress on 31 January 1983 by Senator Nelson. While this bill was stalled in a subcommittee, the '*Counterfeit Access Device and Computer Fraud and Abuse Act of 1984*', sponsored by Mr Hughes, was approved by the US House of Representatives in July 1984, a year after its introduction. The 'Counterfeit Access Device and Computer Fraud and Abuse Act of 1984' aimed at both credit-card and computer fraud by including within chapter 47, title 18, of the US Code a provision on 'fraud and related activity in connection with access devices' (section 1029) and a provision on 'fraud and related activity in connection with computers' (section 1030). In the federal domain of jurisdiction, the latter proposes punishment for whoever '(1) knowingly accesses a computer without authorization or, having accessed a computer with authorization, uses the opportunity such access provides for purposes to which such authorization does not extend, with the intent to execute a scheme to defraud . . . or (2) knowingly accesses a computer without authorization . . . and by means of one or more instances of such conduct knowingly uses, modifies, or discloses information in, or prevents authorized use of, such computer'.

Whereas the provisions against credit-card fraud and counterfeit access devices were passed in the *Credit Card Fraud Act of 1984* (Publ.L. 98–473, §1029), the provisions on 'fraud and related activity in connection with access devices' were criticized by the US Department of Justice at a hearing held on 9 August 1984 by the House Judiciary Committee's Subcommittee. As a counterproposal, the *Department of Justice* suggested the '*Federal Computer Systems Protection Act of 1984*', which in the federal domain of jurisdiction would penalize 'whoever having devised or is intending to devise any scheme or artifice to defraud, or for obtaining money or property by false or fraudulent pretenses, representations, or premises, or to embezzle, steal, or convert to his use or the use of another, property not his own, for the purpose of executing such scheme or artifice or embezzlement, theft or conversion or attempting to do so, knowingly accesses or attempts to access a computer'. According to the definition given in the bill, 'property' includes, but is not limited to, 'financial instruments, information, including electronically processed or produced data, and computer program and computer software in either machine or human readable form, computer services and any other tangible or intangible item of value'. Like its predecessors, the bill also provides penalties for sabotage and mere unauthorized access to computers. It also contains a special forfeiture provision which is particularly interesting: upon conviction, the court shall authorize the Attorney-General to seize all property or other interest declared forfeited under the act. If a property right or other interest is not exercisable or transferable for value by the United States, it shall expire, and shall not revert to the convicted violator. The United States shall dispose of all such property as soon as commercially feasible making due provision for the rights of innocent persons.

The Department of Justice's criticism of the *Counterfeit Access Device and Computer Fraud and Abuse Act* and the presentation of its own bill on 5 October 1984 in the frantic last days of the 98th Congress effected a compromise which led to only a very restricted version of the former Act being passed. The passed Counterfeit Access Device and Computer Fraud and Abuse Act is limited to unauthorized access to computers used by or on behalf of the Federal Government, customer and consumer records maintained by federally regulated financial institutions, and credit-reporting agencies. It does not cover private or business records other than those enumerated. The Act applies to anyone who 'knowingly accesses a computer without authorization, or having accessed a computer with authorization, uses the opportunity such access provides for purposes to which such authorization does not extend', and thereby either (1) obtains certain classified national information, (2) obtains customer or consumer information maintained in certain financial institutions or credit-reporting agencies, or (3) knowingly uses, modifies, destroys, or discloses information in, or prevents authorized use of, such computer, if such computer is operated for or on behalf of the Government of the United States and such conduct affects such operation. Coverage of fraud in the field of federal jurisdiction was excluded from the legislation.

According to congressional sources it is expected that committees will hold hearings in order to expand the law to cover all computers used in interstate commerce. These hearings will be based on, among others, the above-mentioned Federal Computer Systems Protection Act 1984 (Senators Hughes and Nelson, see HR 930), a bill sponsored by Senator Wyden (HR 995), a bill sponsored by Senator Hughes (HR 1001), the above-mentioned Department of Justice bill, and a more general bill dealing with data-transmission protection (sponsored by Senators Leahy and Mathias).[14]

Law Reform in the United Kingdom, especially the Forgery and Counterfeiting Act of 1981

The third country which has adapted its legislation to computer-related economic crimes is the *United Kingdom*, where the Forgery and Counterfeiting Act of 1981 came into force on 28 October 1981. Replacing the numerous forgery offences in statute and common law, the Act in part 1, sections 1–4 describes the offences of forgery, copying a false instrument, using a false instrument, and using a copy of a false instrument. Part I, section 8(1) (d), of the Act includes a special section defining the false 'instrument' as a.o., 'any disc, tape, sound track or other device on or in which information is recorded or stored by mechanical, electronic or other means'. Moreover, in section 10(3) the Act defines that 'in this part of this Act references to inducing somebody to accept a false instrument as genuine, or a copy of a false instrument as a copy of a genuine one, include references to inducing a machine to respond to the instrument or copy as if it were a genuine instrument or, as the case may be, a copy of a genuine one'. Sections 1 and 3 of the Act have recently been invoked in England in the prosecution of persons who are alleged to have obtained access to a computer system by the use of false identification. However, the cases are not yet closed. The question as to whether or not an additional reform of English law is necessary is being considered by the Law Commission as part of its program of codifications of the criminal law.

Part 1 of the Forgery and Counterfeiting Act does not apply to Scotland. As far as Scottish law is concerned, in 1986 the Scottish Law Commission, which had been dealing with the problems of computer crime since 1984, published a detailed analysis of Scots law which was sent out for comments. The Commission assumed that there was no computer-specific need for reform of the provisions of fraud and uttering, suggested the criminalization of unauthorized access to DP systems, and drew attention to several uncertainties which are of much wider application than just in relation to computer crime.[15]

Australian Legislation from 1983 to 1985

In Australia the legal situation varies from territory to territory. The Commonwealth of Australia has plenary legislative powers in the field of criminal justice in the Australian Capital Territory (ACT) and in other Commonwealth Territories. In the other jurisdictions, the Commonwealth's responsibility for criminal law is limited to matters which relate to its powers under the Constitution. Furthermore, the legal situation is inhomogenous since in some States the law is codified, whereas in others it rests largely upon the common law.

Two Australian jurisdictions have already passed specific provisions relating to computer crime. In 1983 a new section 276 of the *Northern Territory* Criminal Code was enacted. Section 276, subsection 1, punishes with imprisonment of up to 3 years 'any person who unlawfully alters, falsifies, erases or destroys any data processing material with any fraudulent intention'. Subsection 2 provides for punishment of up to 7 years, if the act is committed 'with the intent that an incorrect data processing response will be produced and with the intent that it may in any way be used or acted upon as being correct . . . to the prejudice of any person, or with intent that any person may in the belief that it is correct, be induced to do or refrain from doing any act'. In addition, section 1 of the Criminal Code contains definitions stating that (1) 'alters' includes 'adds to'; (2) 'data processing material' means all information and programs used in or with a DP system; and (3) 'data processing response' covers any printout, response, or result obtained from the operation of a DP system.

In 1985 in the *Australian Capital Territory* the 'New South Wales Crimes Act 1900 in its application to the Australian Capital Territory' was amended by a new section 115 on 'Dishonest Use of Computers'. Section 115, subsection 1, provides for that 'a person who, by any means, dishonestly uses or causes to be used, a computer or other machine, or part of a computer or other machine, with intent to obtain by that use a gain for himself or herself or another person, or to cause by that use a loss to another person, is guilty of an offence punishable, on conviction, by imprisonment for 10 years'. Subsection 2 defines a 'machine' as 'a machine designed to be operated by means of a coin, banknote, token, disc, tape or any identifying card or article'. In addition to these provisions, new draft proposals to amend the Crimes Act with respect to forgery are currently under consideration (the wording of the proposed sections 137C–137D of the Act is given in Appendix 2).

In 1983 the National Companies and Securities Commission had already prepared a draft working paper on the substantive law aspect of computer crime. The Commission made its submissions in the form of a proposal for a *New South Wales* Crimes (Computer Abuse) Act. In the field of computer manipulations the Commission applied a broad 'property approach'. It suggested expanding the common-law concept of larceny by broadening the definition of 'property' (section 4 of the Crimes Act) to 'computer-related property' (including intangible software) and by replacing the intention of larceny with the intention to 'temporarily or permanently' deprive the owner of the property. The Commission also proposed the introduction of the offence of unauthorized use of computer time, or 'accessing', into the law of larceny. Further provisions deal with the breaking and entering of computer installations, criminal damage to computers and computer-related property, falsification of computer data and software, and use of computer-related property for fraudulent purposes.

The State of *Victoria* lacks specific legislation governing computer crime. However, it adopted several Theft Act Provisions of the United Kingdom. The definition of 'property' in section 71 of the Victorian Crimes (Theft) Act 1973 (No. 8425 of 1973), for example, includes 'money and all other property real or personal including things in action and other intangible property'. In order to study the legal problems of computer crime the law department installed a working group. Furthermore, the Victorian Society for Computers and Law published draft provisions for computer-crime legislation. In *Tasmania* a research paper prepared for the Law Reform Commission of Tasmania also proposed to enact several new computer-crime statutes.

Law reform in the various territories of the Commonwealth of Australia is now being discussed by the *Standing Committee of the Attorneys-General*. This Committee comprises the Commonwealth Attorney-General, the Attorney-General of each Australian State, the Attorney-General of the Northern Territory, and the Attorney-General of New Zealand. Its aim is to achieve a common approach to the legal problems of computer-related crime and to develop *model legislation* suitable for all jurisdictions.[16]

The Canadian Criminal Law Amendment Act of 1985

In 1985 Canada adopted comprehensive computer-crime legislation by enacting the Criminal Law Amendment Act 1985 (S.C. 1985, c. 19), which was passed in the House of Commons on 24 April 1985, received the Royal Assent on 20 June 1985, and came into effect on 4 December 1985. As far as computer crime is concerned, the Act is primarily intended to punish unauthorized interception and destruction of computer systems (see *infra*). However, the new Act also affirms that the provision on credit card fraud (section 301.1 of the Criminal Code) extends to all types of automated-teller machine and bank or service access cards. In addition, the definition of 'document' for offences concerning forgery of documents is amended to include any 'material, on which is recorded or marked anything that is capable of being read or understood by a person, computer system or other device'.[17]

The Danish Law on 'Data Kriminalitet' of 1985

Denmark effected the first comprehensive reform in European computer crime by enacting the 'Penal Code Amendment Act of 6 June 1985 om aendring of straffeloven—Datakriminalitet', effective on 1 July 1985). As far as computer manipulations are concerned, the Act introduces a new section 279a of the Penal Code which convicts for computer fraud 'any person who, with the intention of procuring an unlawful gain for himself or for a third party, in an unlawful manner alters, adds or erases data processing programs or by other unlawful means tries to manipulate the result of such data processing'. In addition, the Act includes 'computer fraud' in the provision on receiving stolen goods (section 284, Penal Code). The Act also contains special amendments concerning computer sabotage and unauthorized access, all of which will be discussed below.[18]

The West German 'Second Law for the Prevention of Economic Crime' of 1986

In the *Federal Republic of Germany* the 'Second Law for the Prevention of Economic Crime' (Zweites Gesetz zur Bekämpfung der Wirtschaftskriminalität—2. WiKG) was passed in the Bundestag on 27 February 1986 and in the Bundesrat on 18 April 1986. The law, which had been discussed by law reform commissions since 1976 and in parliament since 1982, was promulgated on 15 May 1986 and will come into force on 1 August 1986. As far as computer manipulations are concerned, the Act contains two main amendments. First, the provision on 'fraud' is supplemented by a provision on 'computer fraud' not requiring that a *person* be deceived (section 263a, Penal Code). The new provision punishes 'any person who with the intention of procuring an unlawful gain for himself or a third party causes loss to another by influencing the result of a data processing by improper programming, by the use of incorrect or incomplete data, by the unauthorized use of data, or by otherwise interfering without authorization with the processing'. Second, the Act amends the provision on forgery by a new provision on 'falsification of data of legal significance'. The wording of the new section 269 does not require the visual perceptibility of the forged instrument. It covers 'any person who for purposes of deception in a legal transaction stores or alters data such that their reproduction would yield an ungenuine or falsified document or who uses data thus stored or altered'. As additional amendments in the field of forgery the Act introduces a modified section 274, Penal Code, on 'suppression of stored data' as well as specific modifications concerning forgery of public documents (sections 271, 273, and 348, Penal Code). The Act also contains amendments concerning unauthorized access, unauthorized use, computer sabotage, and espionage of trade secrets, which will be discussed below.[19]

c. BILLS PLANNED

Amendments in Switzerland, Austria, and Greece

In *Switzerland* the Ministry of Justice published in 1985 the draft proposals of the Committee of Experts for the Revision of the Penal Code, which started its work in the field of property and economic crime in 1978 and submitted its report in 1982. The draft proposals contain several new statutes covering computer manipulations. A new section 147 of the Penal Code on 'fraudulent misuse of data processing systems' covers certain computer manipulations procuring a transfer of value. Section 150 (formerly section 151) on the 'unauthorized use of services' punishes, among others, 'any person who knowing that payment is required uses . . . a service which a data processing system supplies or which an automat arranges'. The revised sections 251 and 317 include in the provisions of forgery the act of producing 'a paper of legal significance which creates the impression that it is the result of an independent data processing record'. An additional amendment concerns section 251 (2) on false book-keeping. The further provisions of the bill concering removal of property, damage to property, and violation of manufacturing or business secrets will be discussed below.[20]

In *Austria* amendments to the Penal Code similar to those in West Germany were suggested in 1985: The Austrian Ministry of Justice proposed a new section 147a on computer fraud and new sections 227a and 229a on forgery and suppression of stored data.[21]

In *Greece* a working group of the Ministry of Justice is preparing a draft of new provisions on computer fraud, forgery of computer data, breach of secrecy, unauthorized copying or use of computer programs, and unauthorized access to DP systems. The results of this draft could also be similar to the West German, Swiss, and Austrian reform projects.

Amendments in the Nordic Countries
The amendments proposed in the Nordic countries also resemble those in West Germany, Switzerland, and Austria. In *Sweden* in November 1985 the Ministry of Justice presented to parliament a bill suggesting the amendment of the section on fraud (chapter 9, section 1, of the Penal Code) by a new subsection. This subsection is especially interesting as it intends to cover not only computer fraud but also any kind of fraudulent handling of slot machines and similar devices. According to the new subsection, 'any person who, by presenting incorrect or incomplete information, by altering a program or a recording or otherwise without permission affects the results of an automatic information processing or a similar automatic process in a way which involves gain for the offender and loss for someone else, shall likewise be sentenced for fraud'.[22]

In *Norway* the standing Committee on Criminal Law Reform presented in 1985 a report on computer-related crime and suggested an amendment to the general fraud provision (section 270, subsection 1, number 1 of the Penal Code) which would punish 'any person who with the intention of procuring an unlawful gain for himself or for a third party . . . by using incorrect or incomplete information, by altering computer programs or by other means in an unlawful manner influences the result of data processing, and thereby causes prejudice of property or the risk of prejudice of property'.[23]

In *Finland* a government draft proposal in 1986 suggested a similar amendment to the general fraud provision (chapter 36, section 1, of the Penal Code). The proposal goes back to the work of the Finnish Penal Code Revision Committee which is undertaking a general revision of the Penal Code and which in June 1984 published its first draft proposals concerning

crimes against property and economic interests. In addition to the amendment of the fraud provision, the government draft proposes a provision on
'fraud involving an instrument of payment' in order to solve the problems
created by the introduction of deposit money and the use of bank, credit, and
other similar records (chapter 37, section 8, of the Penal Code). Furthermore,
the Finnish Committee suggests broadening the offence of forgery by providing that the forged 'document' includes 'any recording produced by a plotter,
a calculator or other similar device, or any magnetic or other data carrier used
in electronic data processing, provided it is admissible as legally relevant
evidence of rights, obligations or factual circumstances' (chapter 33, section 1
of the Penal Code). The additional amendments proposed by the government
draft concerning computer espionage and damage to property as well as the
additional proposals of the Finnish Working Group on Informational Crimes
will be discussed below.[24]

The Solutions in France and Portugal
In *France* the Commission for the Revision of the Penal Code also suggested a
provision covering the fraudulent use of automatic systems with the intention
of depriving another. The Commission proposed to distinguish this provision
from the traditional fraud provision and to insert it in a special chapter of the
Criminal Code dealing with computer crime and also including other computer-related economic crimes as well as the penal provisions of the French
Privacy Law. In February 1986 the French Ministry of Justice presented its
proposals for the new chapter VII of the Penal Code on 'Informational
Crimes'. These proposals include provisions on the fraudulent obtainment of
programs, data, or other elements of an automatic information-processing
system (section 307–1), the illegal use, communication, or reproduction of a
program, data or other elements of an automatic information-processing
system (section 307–2), the destruction, alteration, or hindering of an automatic information-processing system (section 307–3), as well as the illegal
profit gained by fraudulent use of an automatic information system (section
307–4; for the details of these provisions see *infra*). The proposals also
contain detailed provisions on special sanction for persons and companies.[25]
   In *Portugal* computer-related offences are defined in an even closer context
with the respective privacy legislation. In 1984 the Ministry of Justice proposed a Data Protection Bill that deals primarily with personal data but also
contains general provisions against computer crime. Section 43 of the bill
punishes the illegal modification or erasure of computer data or computer
programs. According to section 44, punishment for qualified theft is attached
to certain cases of manipulation which affect a transfer of value.[26]

d. COMPARATIVE ANALYSIS OF REFORM PROJECTS
If one compares the different reform proposals concerning computer fraud
and takes into account the various legal systems in which they are to be

implemented it can be said that the *content* of all the reform proposals aims at penalizing the *same activities* to a high degree, with the exception of unauthorized access to DP systems, a question which will be discussed in more detail below.

The problem of which *types of provisions* should cover fraud by computer manipulation reveals a *difference* between the various legal systems. Whereas most Continental legal systems cover or aim to cover computer manipulations by provisions on *fraud, forgery*, or provisions similar to those mentioned above, Anglo-American and a few other systems also tend to incorporate the object of computer fraud, especially deposit money, into the provisions on *theft, embezzlement*, and *larceny*.

Differences between the present reform projects also exist in the area of *legislative technique*, where two opposing approaches and a compromise between the two can be found. Most American proposals and the above-mentioned Swedish Data Act of 1973 provide one *general provision against computer-related crime*, including different forms of attack, such as manipulation, destruction, theft, and unauthorized use of or access to DP systems. Contrary to the 'global' approach, the English Forgery and Counterfeiting Act 1981, the new Canadian and Danish legislation of 1985, the American State statues of Alaska, Massachusetts, Ohio, and Virginia as well as the new Austrian, Finnish, West German, Norwegian, Swedish, and Swiss reform proposals use a more 'evolutionary' approach. This introduces the new objects and methods of computer-related crime into the traditional criminal legal system by *modifying the existing offences*, extending the definitions of existing offences (such as theft, embezzlement, fraud, or forgery), or supplementing the present provisions with new specific provisions according to the needs of DP media. A *compromise* between the 'global' and the 'evolutionary' approach is taken by the Portuguese Data Protection Bill, which consolidates various distinct provisions on computer crime, as well as by the French Commission for the Revision of the Penal Code, which proposes to consolidate the various provisions on computer crime in a special chapter of the Penal Code.

e. SUGGESTIONS FOR LEGAL POLICY

In order to arrive at an international consensus on computer crime it is recommended that all legal systems first ascertain that the manipulation of data with the intent to cause an illegal transfer of funds is covered by the traditional provisions on fraud or by a similar provision on '*computer fraud*', neither of which presupposes that a person is being deceived. The 'intent to cause an illegal transfer of funds' means an 'intent to deprive another in order to gain illegal profit', as is required by several Continental law fraud statutes. However, this is only meant to be a minimum recommendation, since in Canada, England, and the United States, among others, an intent to deprive the victim is usually sufficient, even if the perpetrator does not wish to benefit himself or others.

Because of the dependency on electronically stored data, a provision should govern the alteration of certain data stored in DP systems (especially data used for recognizing rights or obligations and those used for legal purposes) by unauthorized persons with the intent of influencing (human or computerized) decisions. Visual perceptibility of the embodied statement should not be required by this kind of *'forgery of DP-stored data'*. A more extensive criminalization of data-alteration by persons acting within their ordinary function could be reached by provisions (to be discussed below) which protect the integrity of DP systems (especially mischief and unauthorized access) but not by a concept of 'forgery', because many legal systems espouse the concept of a 'false' (unauthentic) document and do not include a genuine document containing incorrect statements of facts. An exact definition of the acts covered could be left to national laws by describing the crime as the 'alteration of programs and data stored in DP systems with the intent to commit forgery'.

A more comprehensive incrimination of computer fraud by the provisions of theft, larceny, embezzlement, or credit-card fraud should be left to the discretion of individual countries, because adequate provisions on fraud and forgery are sufficient to counteract fraud by computer manipulations. In addition, incorporating intangible property into the provisions on theft and embezzlement would, in many European countries, conflict with the wording and principles of these laws. According to all present legislation, the perpetrator must act *knowingly* and dishonestly in order to be guilty under the new provisions.

At least for Continental countries, the above-described *evolutionary legal technique* is preferable, especially for reasons of systematization and acceptance of law. To this end, the *general provisions* of penal legislation should be implemented as far as possible.[27] A definite proposal for a specific legal technique, however, cannot be given, as each country must consider the leading principles of its own constitution and its individual legal system.

Because penal statutes depend on the respective legal systems general suggestions for the *wording* of reform proposals also cannot be made. However, as computer technology is rapidly improving, the dangers of linking the definitions to present technology must be stressed. The necessary definitions of 'computer fraud' and 'forgery of DP-stored data' should be expressed, as far as possible, in *terms of function rather than technology*.[28]

2. Computer Espionage, Program Piracy, and Copying of Chips

Penal and civil coverage of computer espionage and program piracy are among the most topical and economically significant legal questions in the field of computer crime today. A systematic legal approach has to distinguish (1) the general protection of all computer-stored data (including databases and computer programs), (2) the additional special protection of computer programs, and (3) the special protection of computer chips.

a. PROTECTION OF GENERAL DATA IN COMPUTER SYSTEMS

aa. Traditional Property Law

When information is acquired by *taking away another person's tangible information-carriers* (such as paper-listings, tapes, or discs) the classic penal provisions of theft, larceny, or embezzlement in all Western legal systems do not create any special problems. Yet the ability of DP and communication systems to copy data quickly, inconspicuously, and often via telecommunications facilities has replaced most of these traditional 'information-carrier thefts' with acts of copying information onto data devices. Therefore the question arises as to what extent *pure acquisition of intangible information* can or should be covered by these provisions.

In most *Continental law countries*, such as *Belgium, West Germany, Italy*, or *Luxembourg* one is reluctant to apply the traditional provisions on theft and embezzlement to the unauthorized abstraction of information, since these laws generally require the taking of tangible property with the intention of permanently depriving the victim (see, for example, section 461, Belgian Penal Code; sections 242 and 246, West German Penal Code; and section 624, Italian Penal Code).[29] However, in some Continental law countries the application of the traditional provisions on theft and embezzlement seems possible at least in cases in which a tangible data-carrier is, for a certain time, possessed by the perpetrator. This is true, for example, of *France*, where the Chambre Criminelle de la Cour de Cassation, in a decision of 8 January 1979, judged the photocopying of a document as theft according to section 379 of the Penal Code. French legal literature, however, argues against extending this decision to a general concept of theft of information.[30] Similar considerations can be found in *Austria* (concerning section 127 of the Penal Code).[31] In the *Netherlands*, the Arnhem Court of Appeals, in a decision of 27 October 1983, went even further when it assumed that data represented a 'good' in the sense of section 321 of the Dutch Penal Code. It convicted an employee of embezzlement for having copied computer data and programs for the purpose of setting up his own business.[32] Arguments for similar results might arise in countries in which the law of theft has been applied to electricity, such as in *Greece*, where energy is considered to be a 'thing' in the sense of section 372, subsection 2, of the Penal Code, or in *Finland*, where the Supreme court in 1950 ruled *ex analogia* that electric energy may constitute 'goods or money' in the sense of the provision on theft. In *Belgium* and *Italy* energy is also considered to be an item in the sense of theft (section 461, Belgian Penal Code; and section 624, Italian Penal code).[33] However, the idea that it is possible to apply the same principles to both 'intangibles' is questionable. First, it is not possible to equate energy and information. Second, in the case of the theft of energy the energy is taken away, whereas in the case of unauthorized acquisition of information, the information remains with the holder.

In the *United Kingdom*, which has long applied the law of theft to electricity (see, for England, the Larceny Act 1916 and also the Victorian Theft Act), the English Theft Act 1968 defines 'property' to include 'money and all other property, real or personal, including things in action and other intangible property'. *English* law, however, demonstrates that a simple extension of the objects of traditional theft provisions is not sufficient to include theft of intellectual property, since the particular section requiring the intention of 'permanently depriving the other of it' still seems to be addressed to tangible objects. It is true that there are some English court decisions in which an intention to deprive temporarily is considered to be sufficient for theft in cases of temporary removal of articles. However, in *Oxford* v. *Moss* The English Court of Appeal in 1979 held that confidential information (i.e. university examination questions surreptitiously obtained by a student) did not fall under the meaning of intangible property of section 4 of the Theft Act 1968. In a commentary on that case it was suggested that the prosecutor might have fared better had he used section 6, subsection 1, of the 1968 Act which deals expressly with 'borrowing'. That view may, however, be questioned, since in the recent decision *R.* v. *Lloyd and Others* the English Court of Appeal held that the temporary borrowing of films for the purpose of copying them did not fall under section 6 of the Theft Act 1968. As far as *Scotland* is concerned, the Scottish Law Commission also concluded that Scots criminal law does not penalize the taking of information; this does not apply to the taking of that on or in which the information is stored or recorded.[34]

In the majority of the territories in *Australia* the situation is similar to that of the English law. This is especially the case for the State of Victoria, which adopted several Theft Act Provisions of the United Kingdom. Compared with section 4 (1) of the English Theft Act 1968, the definition of 'property' in section 71 of the Victorian Crimes (Theft) Act 1973 (No. 8425 of 1973) also includes 'money and all other property real or personal including things in action and other intangible property'. The basic definition of theft in section 72 (1) also requires that the perpetrator 'dishonestly appropriates property belonging to another with the intention of permanently depriving the other of it'. In contrast to this limitation of the traditional property law, the above-discussed reform proposals of the National Companies and Securities Commission for a New South Wales Crimes (Computer Abuse) Act advocate a broader 'property approach' and a provision on 'larceny of computer-related property' (including computer software and information) with the intention to 'temporarily or permanently' deprive the owner of the property.[35]

A strong tendency towards a 'property theory' of intellectual values can be found in the legislation of some States of the *United States* which have been imposing criminal penalties for theft of trade secrets since 1964. In some American States, courts regard computer data as property in the sense of traditional larceny provisions. However, extending the provisions on theft to cover information is raising problems. In contrast to *Hancock* v. *State of California*, where 'theft' of programs were affirmed, it was held in *Ward* v. *The Superior Court of California* that theft of a program contained in a computer's memory could not be regarded as 'theft' of an 'article' within the scope of the definition of crime contained in the relevant statute. In *People* v. *Home Insurance Company* a Colorado court also refused to regard electronic impulses (concerning confidential hospital records) as tangible property within the meaning of the respective statute (which afterwards was amended by a comprehensive definition of property in a general computer crime statute). In *United States* v. *Seidlitz*, in which computer software was copied using a remote terminal, the attempt to apply the crime of interstate transportation of stolen property also was found legally impossible, as no 'transportation' of the property (movement from its source) could be proven to have occurred. Similarly on 28 June 1985 in *Dowling* v. *United States* the Supreme Court of the United States decided in a six to three decision that selling records by infringing on copyright did not fall under the National Stolen Property Act (18 USC § 2314), which should be restricted to stolen tangible items. To avoid such problems in many States the legislature has now defined computer data or trade secrets as 'property' or a 'thing of value', thus making the application of the larceny provisions or new general provisions on computer crime possible. An even broader property approach has been chosen by section 73.2 of the Lousiana Statutes Annotated. According to section 73.2 (A) (2) the intentional 'disclosure, use, copying, taking or accessing, without consent, of intellectual property' is considered an offence against intellectual property. According to section 73.2 (C) the provision shall not apply to the 'disclosure, use, copying, taking, or accessing by proper means as defined in this subpart' (including discovery by independent invention, reverse engineering, discovery under license, or authority of the owner, etc.). Section 4 (d) of the Videotex Association's Model Computer Crime Act of 25 January 1985 goes even further by punishing whoever intentionally and without authorization, among others, 'copies or uses any computer data'. Because of the difficulties arising with such property protection of information a number of American States have recently enacted special provisions concerning the theft or disclosure of trade secrets which exist separately from the general larceny provisions. Florida and Missouri legislation against computer crime exemplifies a computer-specific approach for trade secrets and contains special provisions applying to the disclosure of data forming trade secrets.[36]

Canadian jurisprudence currently seems to be following the American development, but has not yet finally resolved the problem. In *R.* v. *Stewart*, in which a union member attempted to copy a confidential payroll printout containing the addresses of a hotel's employees, the Ontario High Court of Justice dismissed the indictment for mischief, fraud, and theft in the first instance and decided that confidential information was not property in the sense of the law of theft (section 283, Criminal Code of Canada). The Ontario

Court of Appeal, however, overturned the decision and convicted him for counselling theft. Although an absolute discharge was granted, the perpetrator momentarily has appealed his conviction to the Supreme Court of Canada, which is going to decide the question in the coming months. The Canadian Sub-Committee on Computer Crime of the Standing Committee on Justice and Legal Affairs, which considered the problem in the course of reform discussions, has now opted against the property approach and stated that Parliament would be ill advised to try to protect information by granting a proprietary interest in it.[37]

Because of differences in the nature of tangible property and intellectual values (property implies exclusivity while information is more of a public good which cannot be entirely 'captured' by one person), the difference between traditional property rights and intellectual property rights (for example, concerning the question of ownership and possession), and the difference between traditional theft of tangible things and the theft of information (where the relevant information is only copied and remains with the owner), a *theory of property* should be *denied* for general protection of *intellectual values*. It must also be remembered that civil law does not regard information *per se* as protectable and that, even with the statutory monopolies of copyright, patent, trademark, and industrial designs, the creator, inventor, or designer of the work is only given exclusive ownership rights within certain limits (especially with respect to time and geographic areas). Therefore it seems dangerous and unnecessary to protect by means of penal law values which are not even addressed by civil law. Furthermore, as far as penal law is concerned, it often strains the language to speak of a 'taking' of information or of 'depriving the victim'.

Similar arguments are also made against applying the provisions of possession of property obtained by crime or of receiving stolen goods (see, for example, section 312, Canadian Criminal Code, and section 257, West German Penal Code)[38] At least from the viewpoint of Continental law countries, there is no doubt that a solution independent from the larceny and theft provisions is preferable.[39]

bb. Trade Secrets and Unfair Competition Law

The Present Legal Situation
Because of the problems in applying the general property law to cover trade secrets in *most Continental law countries* the misappropriation of someone else's data or the illegal abstraction of secret information is covered by special provisions against the *betrayal or misappropriation of trade secrets*. These provisions protect trade secrets by prohibiting certain condemnable acts of obtaining information either by provisions of the Penal Code or penal or civil provisions of Acts against Unfair Competition. This concept of Trade Secrets Protection and Fair Competition is in harmony with modern American information theory, which rejects the static 'property theory' and turns to

procedural 'relationship theories' and 'entitlement theories' by looking at the relationship between discloser and disclosee.

As far as computer data and programs are kept secret, the *criminal provisions of trade secrets law* can represent an effective weapon against traitors and users who act in bad faith. In *West Germany* if a trade secret is disclosed or used by an employee during his employment or by any person *contra bonos mores* effective penal and civil protection is available, in particular in sections 17, 18, and 20 of the Act Against Unfair Competition (Gesetz gegen unlauteren Wettbewerb), even if a misappropriated program has been considerably altered. In most Continental law countries the legal situation is similar, as can be illustrated, for example, by section 13 of the *Swiss* Act on Unfair Competition and sections 162 and 273 of the Swiss Penal Code, sections 11, 12, and 19 of the *Austrian* Act Against Unfair Competition, or sections 16 and 17 of the Greek Act on Unfair Competition. However, there are also countries with trade-secret provisions which are only partially sufficient, such as the *French* statutes which are limited to industrial trade secrets (section 418, French Criminal Code), the *Luxembourgian* law (section 309, Penal Code), and the *Belgian*, *Dutch*, and *Italian* provisions, which have loopholes vulnerable to espionage committed by outsiders (see, for example, section 309, Belgian Penal Code; section 623, Italian Penal Code; or section 273, Netherlands Penal Code, which is limited to employees infringing contractual obligations concerning secrets). The penal provisions of the *Finnish* Improper Trade Practices Act 1978 are criticized as inadequate and vague.

In most of these Continental law countries, however, the penal provisions against industrial (and commercial) espionage are backed up by more comprehensive *civil provisions*. Section 1 of the *West German* Act Against Unfair Competition, for example, gives additional civil protection against slavish imitation and parasitic competition. Similar results originate from section 1 of the *Austrian* Act on Unfair Competition, section 54 of the *Belgian* Fair Trade Practices Act of 14 July, 1971, section 2598 of the *Italian* Civil Code, sections 1382 and 1383 of the *French* Civil Code and its related theories of 'unfair competition', 'act of interference', and 'enrichment without reason due to the illegal utilization of somebody else's intellectual work', or the general concept of unfair competition and the law of tort based on section 1401 of the Civil Code in the *Netherlands*.[40]

In the *United States* trade-secret and unfair competition law is generally State law, and for the most part it is not statutory. However, as previously mentioned, some States have enacted penal provisions concerning illegal disclosure or theft of trade secrets, and in many States special provisions against computer crime (including theft of data and programs) have been initiated. Furthermore, the National Conference of Commissioners on Uniform State Laws in 1980 recommended a 'Uniform Trade Secrets Act', which has since been adopted in several States such as Arkansas, Delaware, Idaho, Indiana, Kansas, Louisiana, Minnesota, North Carolina, and Washington.

In contrast to the narrow and cautious view taken by the English judiciary, the American judges have made unfair competition an extremely broad cause of action, which is limited only by the doctrine of federal pre-emption (especially regarding the federal patent and copyright legislation). Considering trade-secret protection of computer programs, US courts have found that widespread distribution of commercial programs to many hundreds of recipients does not forfeit the trade-secret status of the underlying program provided that the licence agreements place restrictions on use and disclosure of the programs on each recipient.[41]

The *Canadian* Criminal Code also does not contain an offence of disclosure of a trade secret; criminal protection can be sought only under the provisions concerning secret commissions and criminal breach of trust. Civil proceedings for an alleged misappropriation of a trade secret must rely upon the law of contract or equity for causes of fiduciary relationship, breach of confidence, and the doctrine of unjust enrichment. This works fairly well when there is a clear confidential relationship between two parties; the protection, however, becomes uncertain when the trade secret is conveyed to third parties.[42]

The *United Kingdom*, as well as the *Commonwealth of Australia,* have no special criminal legislation in the field of trade-secret protection. In England, in certain cases the issue of breach of confidence can only be applied.[43]

In *Japan*, too, no criminal-law provisions or other statutes exist which explicitly cover unauthorized disclosure of, or access to, trade secrets. Civil trade-secret protection is also not well developed and must be sought under general tort provisions or contract law.[44]

Reform Proposals
Reform proposals for penal and civil trade-secret protection have been made in various countries. The above-described *Danish* Penal Code Amendment Act 1985 in Section 263 (breaking open a letter, wiretapping, *et al.*) and section 264 (infringement of domestic peace) added qualifications which apply if the acts are committed 'with the intention to procure or make oneself acquainted with information about trade secrets of a company'. In *West Germany* the above-mentioned 'Second Law for the Prevention of Economic Crime' of 1986 enacted an amendment to the Unfair Competition Act. The new section 17, subsection 2, of the Unfair Competition Act punishes not only the use but also the acquisition of trade secrets by technical means, by copying, or by removal of copies.[45] In *Switzerland* the previously mentioned proposals of the Committee of Experts for the Revision of the Penal Code extended section 162, Penal Code, on the violation of manufacturing or business secrets. The *Swedish* Committee on the Protection of Trade Secrets suggests a new act on trade secrets, expanding the sections on trade secrets in the Unfair Competition Act 1931 (lagen om illojal konkurrens). The proposed new legislation, which is still being discussed, distinguishes between industrial espionage and abuse of commercial secrets in commercial relations

and in employer–employee relationships.[46] The *Finnish* government's draft proposals of 1986 include new provisions on trade espionage (section 3), breach of trade secrets (section 4), and misappropriation of trade secrets (section 5) to be implemented in chapter 30 of the Penal Code. The provisions are of special interst, since they include computer-specific elements such as the 'unauthorized entry into a data processing system or data transmission network, provided it is protected against outsiders' (section 3, no.1) or 'spying with the help of a technical device' (section 3, no.3). The Finnish reform proposals also suggest expanding the use of court injunctions in order to prevent the use of another's trade secret.[47]

In *Canada,* too, a draft trade-secret protection act is being prepared by a joint federal/provincial committee which is studying the problem in the broader context of economically valuable business information in general and not only industrial secrets.[48] In the *United Kingdom* the Law Reform Commission recently recommended a legislative scheme which would involve the creation of a new statutory tort. In the *United States*, in the field of civil trade-secret protection the above-mentioned model of the proposed Uniform Trade Secret Act is advocated. In the field of penal law, however, the reform is founded on the establishment of both trade-secret protection and of general provisions against computer crime which include the illegal acquisition of all computer-stored data (see *supra*).[49]

On the *international level* the Standing Committee of the Consultative Assembly of the Council of Europe adopted a criminal model law on the protection of manufacturing and commercial secrets.[50]

Evaluation and Suggestions for Legal Policy
As far as *future policy-making* is concerned the international trend towards *trade-secret protection* should be *encouraged*. Trade-secret protection is not based merely on natural rights to property but primarily on the conviction that certain ends ought to be promoted and regulated by law: without a certain degree of such protection, research and its costs would be put at risk.

However, in order to avoid the monopolization of information trade-secret protection should be restricted to certain *intolerable acts* of obtaining information, and not be extended to a protection of information *per se*. Consequently, a more comprehensive interpretation of the crime of unauthorized duplication of information is not desirable, and would interfere with the traditional well-balanced copyright system.

Even if copyright law applies to computer programs (see *infra*), the value of trade-secret law is not rendered obsolete by the applicability of copyright law in this field, since trade-secret law is able to *protect ideas, information, and innovations*, and thus covers elements not protected by copyright law. Similarly, copyright law remains valuable because trade-secret law does not apply to the field of non-secret programs distributed in source code as well as to cases in which the secret is disclosed or in which examination of the programs allows a purchaser of the product to discover the secret. Furthermore, trade-secret law generally cannot be used against third parties who may acquire the secret in good faith (for example, buying illegally obtained data from the perpetrator).

In the course of drafting penal statutes in the field of trade-secret law the various *levels of exchange of information* must be differentiated, especially in the area of national and international exchange of information, exchange of information in commercial relationships, and exchange of information in employer–employee relationships. *International information-exchange* shows the political dimensions of trade-secret law; whereas industrialized countries are interested in preventing the misappropriation of certain nationally originated processes by other countries, developing countries, in particular, resist such laws vehemently, as they would impede the free flow of information and technology between the 'have' and 'have-not' countries. As far as the *internal and external enterprise exchange* of information is concerned, special attention must be paid to the balancing of the interests of *employers and employees* with special regard to the mobility of labour. Employees are not permitted to make use of their employers trade secrets for private profit during their employment but should be entitled to at least take their general work experiences with them after termination. Trade-secret protection, therefore, can be qualified by and is dependent on the status of the perpetrator.

In order to achieve an international consensus it is *recommended* that all Western legal systems—either in their Penal Codes or in Unfair Competition legislation—establish *penal trade-secret protection* backed up by adequate *civil provisions concerning unfair competition*. These penal and civil provisions should generally apply to all trade secrets (treated as such by their holders) and not be limited to the computer and DP area. Special regulations for employer–employee relationships are necessary. The trade-secret provisions should not only be applicable when trade secrets are disclosed or used but also in cases of pure acquisition of the information by technical means, such as copying. As information technology has extended not only the dimensions but also the techniques for misappropriation of information, these means could—as the Finnish bill shows—also comprise computer-specific attacks, such as illegal access to DP systems.

cc. Protection of Special Secrets and Relationships

Protection of Special Types of Information
As far as special secrets and *particular types of information* are concerned, a more extensive criminal protection is already in place. Sensitive military, technological, and diplomatic information, for example, is protected in all countries by provisions of *treason* and *illegal exports* of certain technologies. As the provisions of treason in general do not show computer-specific problems, and are applicable only to a small area of computer-stored information, they are not dealt with in detail here. As far as export regulations are concerned, however, it may be mentioned that the US Defense Department

recently demanded stiffer controls of computer exports and the inclusion of software in the list of high technology whose export from the United States has to be reviewed under the Export Administration Act. This question is currently being considered by the Co-ordinating Committee for Multilateral Export Controls (COCOM) in Paris.[51]

Another example of special protection of particular types of information are the provisions on illegal disclosure of *personal data* in the various data-protection acts and bills. These provisions will be dealt with in section B along with the other infringements of privacy, since this section focuses on the protection of economic interests.

Protection of Special Legal Relationships
Specific protection of secrets also applies to special relationships—such as the work of State officials and certain employees—where additional protection is supplied by criminal provisions against disclosure of information by *public officers*, employees of the *postal* and/or *telecommunication services*, or members of *special professions* (see, for example, in Austria, sections 122 and 125, Penal Code, and sections 17 and 44, Postal Act; in Canada, the offences of secret commissions in sections 383, Criminal Code; in France, section 41 of the 'Code des Postes et Télécommunications'; in West Germany, sections 203, 204, 353 b, 354 and 355, Penal Code; in Switzerland, sections 320 and 321, Penal Code; in the UK section 6 of the Post Office Act 1969; and in the United States 18 USC §§1902 to 1980 and 15 USC §552 (b) (1) (1976)). In some countries a protection of information against unauthorized disclosure also originates from the provisions on criminal *breach of trust* or 'abus de confiance' (section 296, Canadian Criminal Code; section 408, French Penal Code; section 266, West German Penal Code; and section 247, Japanese Penal Code). In special cases the provisions on *corruption* may also apply (see, for example, section 12 of the West German Act Against Unfair Competition and sections 331–4, West German Penal Code, or sections 177–9, French Penal Code). Since these provisions do not specifically aim at the DP area, they shall not be analysed here.

A notable *computer-specific* extension of penal provisions protecting *professional secrets* is worth mentioning. This concept has been especially considered but rejected by the *French* Commission for the Revision of the Penal Code. The commission has discussed extending professional secrecy (section 378, Penal Code) to a general *'secret informatique'*. The new provision was considered to be constructed in analogy to the provision protecting the legal requirement concerning confidential medical communication (section 378, Penal Code) and to cover information entrusted to persons working in the field of DP. Similarly, the *Portuguese* Data Protection Bill contains provisions based on the concept of infringement upon professional secrecy in the DP area (sections 38, 39, and 40). A similar approach can be found in section 12 of the *Italian* Law No. 121 of 1 April 1981 on the Regulation of the State Police Administration. Section 12, in connection with sections 7–11 of this law, punishes an officer who illegally communicates or uses data of certain governmental data centres; a wider-reaching punishability now is intended by section 29 of the Italian privacy bill of 5 March 1984. In *Finland* the Working Group on Informational Crimes has reviewed all criminal provisions on professional and other secrecy in order to consolidate the present penal regulations. The working group suggests the creation of a general provision on 'breach of secrecy' and a more specific provision concerning breach of communication secrecy. This provision would cover oral communications, letters, and all kinds of telecommunication (see, especially, number 3 of the provision on breach of communication secrecy).[52]

Such provisions protecting professional secrets should be examined very carefully, particularly in countries with a well-founded tradition of safeguarding professional secrets (see, for example, the general protection of the 'segreto professionale' in section 622, Italian Penal Code). However, one should also consider that confidential information in the DP area is, to a great extent, covered by trade-secret protection, privacy laws, and traditional professional secrets. Furthermore, the definition and delimitation of persons working in the field of DP will be difficult, especially in view of the widespread use of personal computers, and provisions concerning the infringement of professional secrets vary considerably in Western countries. Therefore it is doubtful whether such legislation would be appropriate for all countries. In any case, there is no international consensus on the respective role of criminal, administrative, and civil law in this field.

dd. General Criminal Protection of DP-stored Data
The previous analysis shows that Western legal systems do not recognize a general penal provision which punishes the illegal use, communication, or reproduction of data. Besides criminalizing certain unfair methods of obtaining information they only protect specific kinds of (especially secret) information. The question whether or not the special features of automatic DP can justify or even necessitate special treatment of DP-stored data, i.e. a general protection of DP-stored information against illegal reproduction, has been raised specifically by the new 1986 proposal of the French Ministry of Justice for a new section 307–2 in the Penal Code. This proposed section punishes 'the use, communication or reproduction of a program, of data or of any other element of an automatic information processing system, which infringes upon the right of another'. This provision, which came to the author's attention upon completion of this book and the underlying OECD report, should be carefully examined in order to avoid an overcriminalization.

Since in the future most information will be stored in DP systems, there is the probability that any provision concerning the reproduction of data stored in automatic information-processing systems will turn into a general provision concerning the reproduction of information. Therefore a criminal sanction against the illegal reproduction of all kinds of DP-stored data will probably come into conflict with the freedom of information processing and the well-balanced traditional system of intellectual property rights (for details on copyright, see *infra*). Therefore at least on the international level it does not seem to be appropriate to recommend a provision which punishes the general reproduction, use, or communication of all kinds of DP-stored data.

ee. Protection by the Law of Contract

Finally, the (*non-criminal*) law of contract must be mentioned since it has become one of the *major structures* for the protection of information against the unauthorized acquisition and use of information in DP practice. The weak point of contractual protection is that contracts generally only bind the involved partners and do not cover infringements of rights by third parties. The advantage of contract law, however, is the possibility of adapting the legal situation to the necessity of each individual case. Therefore a proper formulation of contracts does not only engender rights which are important in cases of litigation but will also prevent actions in dubious grey zones and reduce the risk of later lawsuits by providing legal certainty. Furthermore, civil sanctions laid down in contracts can deter perpetrators from committing certain acts leading to civil remedies. Obligations to give information and disputed programs to expert witnesses for comparison can also facilitate the preparation of a lawsuit.

The applicability of contract law protecting computer-stored data ranges from contracts concerning licensing of *general knowhow* to the regulation of the use of *data banks*. Its main scope of application, however, lies in the production and licensing of *computer programs*. There contract law has developed into one of the most important forms of protection. As far as the protection of information against illegal acquisition and use is concerned, contracts with employees, software package contracts, or software development contracts should always consider clauses of non-disclosure of information and non-removal of data-carriers, rights concerning specified uses and licensing of programs, rights to modify sources, moral rights of copyright, and admissibility of security measures built into computer programs.[53]

b. ADDITIONAL PROTECTION OF COMPUTER PROGRAMS

The above-discussed legal structures, especially trade-secret law and contract law, not only apply to all computer-stored data but also act as important means of protection for computer programs.[54] However, since these legal systems are restricted to secret programs, special relationships, and/or specific acts of accessing information they cannot guarantee fair and untroubled trade with computer programs. Considering the previously mentioned discrepancy between the cost of computer programs and that of reproducing them,[55] an adequate protective system for the trade of computer programs must also cover non-secret programs (which is especially important for mass-marketed programs) and apply to third parties.

This additional protection of computer programs is of great importance, because in recent years software has developed into the heart of computer technology, and the software industry has become more and more important in all national economies. For example, in the United States from 1982 to 1983 the software and services industry grew by 22% and generated $32.6 billion in annual revenues, and this is projected to grow to $90 billion by 1988. In West Germany the market for computer software was estimated at DM10.8 billion in 1984 and DM13 billion in 1985.[56]

In all Western countries such additional protection is sought especially in the areas of (1) patent law, (2) copyright law, and (3) special protection structures for computer programs. While these additional legal systems will be discussed, trademarks protecting the names of programs and their reputations[57] will be omitted.

aa. Patent Law

In most *European countries* there is general agreement that, except for the small number of programs which include a technical invention, the protection of computer programs by patent law is not possible. This is based on the general principle that patentable inventions must not only be new and original but also suitable for industrial application, and therefore give a solution to a technical problem. Consequently schemes, rules, and methods performing mental acts are not regarded as patentable inventions. Due to this principle, article 52 (2) and (3) of the European Patent Convention (EPC, Munich, 1973) excludes patentability of computer programs as such. In most European countries this limitation of patentability can be found in the national patent legislations (see, for example, for *Austria*, section 1, para.2, no. 3, Patent Law, amended 8 June 1984; for *France*, sections 6 and 11, Patent Law, no. 68–1 of 2 January 1968, modified by law no. 78–742 of 13 July 1978 and law no. 84–500 of 27 June 1984; for *West Germany*, sections 1, para. 2, no.3 and para. 3, Patent Law of 5 June 1936, amended on 16 December 1980; for *Italy*, section 12, Patent Law, no. 1127 of 29 January 1939, modified by law no. 338 of 22 June 1979; and for the *United Kingdom*, section I (2) (c) of the Patents Act 1977; for a different result see the *Belgian* Patent Law of 21 May, 1854).[58] According to a new set of guidelines from the European Patent Office, the interpretation of the term 'computer programs' as such should be as narrow as possible. However, at present, patent protection of computer programs does not play an important role in Europe.[59]

In the *United States* a patentable invention must come under one of the statutory categories of section 101 of the Patent Act of 19 July 1952 (35 USC §101), these being machines, processes, manufactures, compositions of matter, and improvements to any of the above. Unlike European countries, there is no express exclusion of computer programs from patent protection, though case law excludes from patentable subject-matter the laws of nature, physical phenomena, and abstract ideas. Amongst the excluded ideas are mathematical formulae, algorithms, and purely mental steps. A claim for mathematical formulae or algorithms of computer programs therefore is not successful. Nevertheless, American courts have recognized patent-protection with respect to certain processes incorporated into computer programs and software in 'firmware form' in a more generous way than has been the case in most European countries.[60] The *Canadian* Patent Appeal Board has adopted the same principles, since the Canadian Patent Act resembles its American counterpart more than its British one.[61] The *Australian* patent law on the other hand, is modelled after English common law.[62]

The *Japanese* Patent Office, which published its guidelines for examination of inventions concerning computer programs, also restricts patent protection to creative technical ideas which employ laws of nature. Consequently, Japanese patent protection is not regarded as a major source of software protection. However, the number of patent applications involving computer programs is reported to be close to 10 000 every year.[63]

This more *generous treatment* of computer-related innovations which has been followed in Europe, the United States, and Japan should be *continued*. By excluding computer software from patent protection, patent offices all over the world would become archives for the technology of the past. However, an *amendment of the patent law* enacting general patent-law protection for computer software is *not feasible*. As patent law grants the owner of an invention a monopoly over its use, manufacture, and sale, extending the patent law would result in a monopolization process. In addition, the cost and time needed to examine an apparent invention would be excessive. As patent protection involves publicizing the invention, third parties would also be able to copy and improve the software.

bb. Copyright Law
Because patent law cannot offer much protection to computer programs, in recent years the centre of attention has shifted to copyright protection. Since a growing number of countries are seeking to protect computer programs by copyright law the problems caused by its application both for civil and criminal law are now becoming the focus of discussion.

The Availability of Copyright Law
The applicability of copyright law to computer programs has been discussed in all Western countries during the last twenty years. In order to avoid legal uncertainty, a number of them have explicitly provided copyright protection for computer programs.

The main initiator of such a legislative reform has been the *United States*. The American Constitution grants Congress the power to promote the progress of science and useful acts by securing, for a limited time, for authors and inventors the exclusive rights to their respective writings and discoveries. Based on this power and on the report of the Computer Software Sub-Committee of the Commission on New Technological Uses of Copyright Works (CONTU), Congress passed the Computer Software Copyright Act 1980. Section 101 of this Act declares computer programs to be literary works protected by copyright. It defines a computer program as a set of statements or instructions to be used directly or indirectly in a computer in order to bring about a certain result. In order to obtain copyright protection, American copyright law—in contrast to European and Commonwealth law— requires that a copyright notice be placed on all publicly distributed copies from which the work can be visually perceived, either directly or with the aid of a machine or device (17 USC §401 (a) (1982)). Registration of the work is not required until prior to commencement of infringement litigation, but early registration is desirable because only registered works can benefit from certain strong statutory remedial protection, specifically, the availability of so-called statutory losses (i.e. losses which the copyright-owner need not prove) and attorneys' fees. This requirement of registration is a disadvantage of American copyright protection of computer programs as it can reveal the secrets of the program to a competitor. However, registration of source code in abbreviated or otherwise 'identifying' form is permissible. Based on the new Copyright Act 1980, the United States Court of Appeals in its decision of 30 August 1983 confirmed that programs expressed in object code, programs embedded in a ROM, and computer-operating system programs can be subject to copyright protection. Considering the extensive case law supporting copyright protection of computer software it can be stated that, in the United States, copyright protection applies to programs of any type, in any form, and in any medium of expression.[64]

The legislative option for copyright protection of computer programs in 1984 was also chosen by *Australia*. On 7 June 1984 the Australian Parliament enacted the Copyright Amendment Act 1984 (put into force on 15 June 1984) which includes computer programs in the copyright law as a type of literary work, irrespective of their medium of fixation. Prior to this law reform, the Federal Court of Australia for New South Wales had already affirmed, on 29 May 1984, that computer programs stored in ROMs and EPROMs could be copyrighted.[65]

Other common-law countries are now following this example of deciding the question explicitly through amendments to copyright acts. In the *United Kingdom*, section 1 (1) of the Copyright (Computer Software) Amendment Act 1985, which received the Royal Assent on 16 July 1985, also expressly grants copyright protection of literary works to computer programs. The new law goes back to a report of the Whitford Committee (1977) and a government Green Paper in 1981. Based on the old Copyright Act 1956, copyright protection for computer programs was applied in several cases in 'Anton Piller' orders or at the stage of interlocutory injunction.[66]

In *Canada* the Sub-Committee on Computer Crime of the Standing Committee on Justice and Legal Affairs suggested in 1983 that the Canadian Copyright Act 1924 (based on the English Copyright Act 1911) should be amended to include computer software in order to stop legal uncertainty and to give the victims of computer crime as much support as possible. In October 1985 the House of Commons Sub-Committee on the Revision of Copyright published its report, calling for revision of the Copyright Act 1924. It recommended that computer programs be protected in the Copyright Act as a separate category of work with a term of protection of the life of the author plus fifty years. The Government intends to review the Copyright Act and it will be issuing its response to the Sub-Committee's recommendations in 1986. As far as jurisdiction is concerned, in *International Business Machines Corp.* v. *Ordinateurs Spirales, Inc.* (26 June 1984) the Federal Court decided that computer programs in both source and object form are protected under the present Canadian copyright law. Furthermore, the courts have granted a number of interlocutory injunctions supporting copyright in computer programs under section 4 of the current Copyright Act.[67]

In 1985 *West Germany* was the first Continental law country to explicitly provide copyright protection for computer programs in the Copyright Amendment Act of 24 June 1985 by classifying 'programs for data processing systems' as protected works in the catalogue of section 2, para. 1, no.1, of the West German Copyright Act. Before this legislative reform, a number of civil appeal courts such as the Federal Labour Court and (in its notable 'Inkassoprogramm' decision of 9 May 1985) the Federal Civil Court (Bundesgerichtshof) had affirmed the copyrightability of computer programs. However, according to the Inkassoprogramm decision of the Federal Civil Court (which remains applicable after the Copyright Amendment Act 1985) only highly creative programs are protected by copyright.[68]

A few days after the West German law reform the *French* law no. 85–660 of 3 July 1985 (loi relative aux droits d'auteur et aux droits des artistes-interprètes, etc.) included software in section 3 of the traditional Copyright Law no.57–298 of 11 March 1957 (loi sur la propriété littéraire et artistique). However, software is subject to special conditions defined in part 5 of the law (see *infra*). Under the old Copyright Act 1957 there had been a tendency by the courts to recognize the copyright protection of computer programs, especially in civil decisions (whereas in a decision of the criminal section of the Cour d'Appel de Paris of 4 June 1984 the legality of copyrighting a video-game program was denied).[69]

In *Italy* a divergence between civil and penal jurisdictions has taken place. Civil decisions of the Tribunal of Turin of 17 October 1983 and of the Preture di Pisa of 11 April 1986 recognized that software related to video games is protectable as an expression of 'work of the intellect of a creative character' under sections 1 and 2 of the Italian Copyright Act 1941. In a decision on 1 June 1983 concerning the seizure of illegally copied software, the Pretore di Milano also stated that in the field of civil law it could be possible to consider computer programs as works protected by sections 1 and 2 of the Copyright Act, but that this civil approach is not admissible as far as the penal provisions of sections 171 and 172 of the Copyright Act are concerned, since this would be an impermissible analogy in the field of penal law. In a similar case, the Pretore di Padova followed this view in his decision of 15 December 1983. However, contrary to the Pretore di Milano, the Pretore di Padova applied section 517 of the Italian Penal Code, which make it a crime to sell falsified products ('Vendita di prodotti industriali con segni medaci del commercio'). Yet the Pretore di Bologna seems to be applying copyright protection to computer programs, since he recently ordered an expert witness to identify the disputed programs.[70]

In the *Netherlands* there has been a substantial number of court decisions since 1981 confirming that copyright protection exists for computer software. In order to establish a higher degree of legal certainty an interministerial 'Piracy Working Party' in August 1984 recommended that section 10, no.11, of the Copyright Act (Auteurswet) 1912 (amended by the law of 27 October 1972) be changed to specifically mention 'computer programs in source or object codes' as works susceptible of copyright protection.[71]

Denmark, Finland, and *Sweden* are also planning clarifying amendments to their copyright laws. Furthermore, *Norway* and *Spain* are considering a applicability of the present copyright law. Similarly, in *Belgium* no bill is being concerning computer software is not considered necessary because of the applicability of the present copyright law. Similarly, in *Belgium* no bill is being discussed at present, but the academic literature assumes protection by the present law (sections 1 and 10 of the Copyright Act of 22 March 1886) as well.[73] In Switzerland the legal situation remains open.[74]

In *Japan* the Agency for Cultural Affairs of the Ministry of Education introduced the Copyright Amendment Bill which passed the National Diet on 7 June 1985 and which came into force on 1 January 1986. The new law expressly mentions 'program works' in the list of examples of protected works and defines a program as 'an expression of combined instructions given to a computer so as to make it function and obtain a certain result' (for the former special programs law of the Japanese Ministry for International Trade and Industry, see *infra*. In several cases, Japanese courts have confirmed copyright protection for both source programs and object codes stored in ROMs. On 13 January 1985 the Tokyo District Court, for the first time, found the criminal law applicable to copyright infringement of computer programs.[75]

Copyright protection of computer programs also exists outside OECD member countries. As a forerunner of the legislative changes described above, the *Philippines* were quick to recognize computer programs as subject matter for copyrighting in Presidential Decree no. 49 of 14 November 1972, effective 6 December 1972. As early as 1983, *Hungary* also adopted legislation which places computer programs under copyright law (Decree no.15 of the Minister of Culture of 12 July 1983). Before this decree was issued, two judgments of the Municipal Court of Budapest had affirmed copyright protection of computer programs. Similarly, *India* amended the Copyright Act 1957 by the Copyright Amendment Bill No. XIX of 1984, which enlarges the definition of a literary work to include computer programs. In the Republic of China (Taiwan) the new Copyright Act put into force in July 1985 also introduced computer programs in the catalogue of protected works. Court decisions applying copyright protection of computer programs can also be found in *Argentina* and *South Africa*.[76]

Major *international organizations* have also tended towards copyright protection of computer programs, especially the Commission of the European Communities (which is preparing a Green Book on this question), the World Intellectual Property Organization and UNESCO (which held a joint meeting in 1985 concerning software protection), and finally the OECD (which discussed the problem in the ICCP Committee in the context of the growth of the software industry).[77]

The stated trend towards general applicability and refinement of *copyright protection* for computer programs containing an original work of authorship should be *encouraged*, especially as it is the most practical means of protection now available at the international level. Copyright law provides a balance between the production and the dissemination of information in the field of computer programming. Being based on protecting the expression of an idea, not the idea itself, it only protects the material form of the program and not the underlying algorithms and knowhow.[78] Copyright law, therefore, offers appropriate protection against software piracy and against the acquisition of software by third parties acting in good faith, but does not lead to the monopolization of new ideas and knowhow. Copyright law also provides legal protection which, to a certain extent, is internationally consistent by virtue of the Universal Copyright Convention (UCC) and the Bern Convention for the Protection of Literary and Artistic Works (BCC).[79] This is especially important, as software products are traded and utilized on an international scale.

The Scope of Copyright Protection
The fundamental recognition of the copyrighting of computer programs is only a first step. In order to create an effective copyright system, several problems concerning the scope of copyright protection have to be solved. These are primarily civil law problems. However, as most penal provisions on copyright offences refer to the respective civil provisions, these problems also determine the range of the respective criminal offences. The present analysis will therefore give a short survey of the main questions.

The scope of copyright protection for computer programs depends, in the first instance, on an exact definition of the *object of copyright protection*. The most decisive question concerns the level of originality necessary for copyright protection and the actual contents of the program which warrant protection. Despite the international trend towards copyright protection of computer programs, these questions are answered differently in various countries. In United States' copyright law, for example, originality is of a very modest level, since the work need only originate from an author and in some way be non-conventional. Almost any authored computer program would be likely to qualify. Similarly, in the Netherlands there are no severe demands on the originality of the program. Yet in West Germany, the Federal Civil

Court, in its famous 'Inkassoprogramm' decision, stated that only outstanding programs containing a high level of originality are protected by copyright.[80] Further problems relating to the object of copyright protection concern the protectability of computer-generated results, such as computer music, computer graphics, and computer-generated programs.

Furthermore, the scope of copyright protection for computer programs is dependent on a definition of the *acts covered by copyright*. An important question in this respect is whether the use of a program can be considered as a copyright infringement.[81] It is also problematic whether a legal software user infringes the author's copyright when he rents out the software for a fee. The distinction between inadmissible adaptation and permissible fair use[82] as well as the interpretation of contracts between the authors and users of programs[83] create further problems. The admissibility of back-up copies and private copying are also major issues.[84]

In civil-law countries the *moral rights* raise additional questions. These do not concern common-law countries, who view copyright essentially in property terms. There copyright may be sold and dealt with as any other property. In contrast, civil-law systems conceive copyright as involving a personal right, reflecting the character of the author, who is entitled to certain moral rights, including that of controlling amendments. The application of these rights to the DP area has resulted in considerable difficulties for the program-user.[85]

Having considered these problems, for most countries the question remains whether courts will be able to solve these questions in a satisfying way. If not, legislative changes will be necessary. *Such legislative changes* can be found already in the above-described copyright amendment acts. The *American* Computer Software Copyright Act 1980 (17 USC 117) limits the owner's exclusive rights to a computer program by permitting the copying and adaptation for archival purposes and in the operation of a computer.[86] The *Australian* Copyright Amendment Act 1984 also permits owners of authorized copies of programs to make additional copies, and modifies the definition concerning the translation of a program.[87] The *United Kingdom* Copyright (Computer Software) Amendment Act clarifies that the conversion of a computer program into a different computer language or code is an adaptation, and that the reduction of any work to a material form shall include reference to the storage of the work in a computer (section 1 (2) and 2).[88] The *West German* Copyright Amendment Act 1985 in section 53 (4) prohibits 'private copying' of computer programs.[89] The *French* Law no.85– 660 of 3 July 1985 goes even further, and grants ownership rights to employers for works produced by employees in the execution of their working contract (section 45), limitation of the moral right (section 46), protection against unauthorized use and permission to produce back-up copies (section 47), limitation of protection to 25 years (section 48), and special regulations concerning the 'saisie-contrefaçon' (a kind of 'Anton Piller order', section 50). It also limits the protection of foreign programs to countries giving equal protection to French programs (section 51).[90] The *Japanese* Copyright Amendment Act 1985, among others, limits the moral right concerning the integrity of computer programs by permitting necessary modifications, permits owners of authorized copies of programs to make additional copies or adaptations deemed necessary in order to use the programs in computers, and prohibits the use of infringing copies of programs in computers for business purposes.[91] A similar situation can be found in the field of the presently discussed reform proposals. The report of the *Swedish* Committee on the Revision of the Copyright Law, for example, suggests amendments concerning private copying, adaptation, and rental or lending of computer programs.[92]

Assuming that courts in various countries will decide these questions in unsatisfactory and divergent ways, and considering the differences between the resulting legislative changes, the above-mentioned *International Organizations* such as the European Commission, the European Council, the OECD, and WIPO/UNESCO, should try to find a common solution to these questions before national legislation will make such uniformity much more difficult. This could best be done in the course of the ongoing work of WIPO/UNESCO in this field.

The Necessary Reform of Penal Law
In the field of copyright law the role of penal law was, for a long time, evaluated differently in various countries. Whereas in common-law countries copyright law resorted rarely, if at all, to penal sanctions, civil-law countries punished infringements of copyright by lenient criminal sanctions. The increase in program, music, and video piracy has now removed most of these differences, and is, in most countries, creating effective criminal deterrents against copyright infringements. Although some of the new laws are still confined to phonographic products, most of them are of a general nature.

In *Italy* the new law No. 406 of 29 July 1981 concerning urgent measures against the unlawful copying, reproduction, import, distribution, and sale of unauthorized phonographic products contains penalties of up to 3 years' imprisonment. The new *Swedish* law No. 284 of 19 May 1982, amending the law of 1960 on copyright concerning literary and artistic works, provides for penalties of up to 2 years. In *Finland* the Copyright Act was amended by law No. 442 of 8 June 1984 (An Act Amending the Act Relating to Copyright in Literary and Artistic Works). Copyright violations which formerly had a maximum penalty of 6 months are now punishable by up to 2 years' imprisonment (section 56, Copyright Act; see also section 56a and 62, Copyright Act, as well as sections 18, 18a, and 23 of the new Act on Rights in Photographic Pictures, law No. 443 of 8 June 1984). In *West Germany* the above-mentioned Copyright Amendment Act 1985 inserted the new sections 108a into the Copyright Act, according to which the copyright infringements of sections 106 and 108 (imposing penalties of up to 1 year's imprisonment) can be punished with up to 5 years' imprisonment if committed regularly for purposes of gain. The *French* law no. 85–660 of 3 July 1985 also revises and stiffens the provisions of sections 425, 427, 428, and 429, Penal Code. In *Denmark* a legal amendment from 1985 now provides a maximum penalty of up to 1 year's imprisonment. In the *Netherlands* a new reform proposal of the Ministry of Justice includes penalties of up to 4 years' imprisonment.[93]

In the *United States* the Piracy and Counterfeiting Amendments Act of 24 May 1982 enacted penalties of up to 5 years' imprisonment for copyright infringements (17 USC § 506 (a), 18 USC § 2318). In the *United Kingdom*, the Copyright Act 1956 (Amendment) Act 1982, which received the Royal Assent on 13 June 1982, amended section 21 of the Copyright Act 1956 so as to make it an offence to be in possession of an infringing copy of a sound-recording or cinematograph film by way of trade. The Copyright Amendment Act 1983 included penalties of up to 2 years' imprisonment and contained special regulations for the issuance and execution of search warrants with respect to sound-recordings and cinematograph films. Similarly, section 3 of the above-mentioned Copyright (Computer Software) Amendment Act 1985 made software piracy a criminal offence in a like manner with respect to sound-recordings and cinematograph films. In *Canada* the House of Commons Subcommittee on the Revision of Copyright proposed increasing the maximum fine for criminal copyright infringements to $1 million. The new copyright law of the *Republic of China* (Taiwan) 1985 includes penalties of up to 5 years' imprisonment.[94]

Most of these reform proposals also stipulate that severe copyright infringements should not be prosecuted only after the injured party has filed a complaint but also in general, on the public prosecutor's own initiative (see, for example, section 62 of the new Finnish Copyright Act). In West Germany, where a request by the injured party is generally necessary, the act may be prosecuted in the absence of such a request when the public interest warrants prosecution (section 109 of the Copyright Act).

These efforts towards more effective penal protection are justified, since attacks against intellectual property deserve the same attention by the penal law as the more conventional attacks on tangible property have received.[95] The reluctance to criminalize copyright infringements still prevailing in some common-law countries, especially in Australia, should be counteracted by adequate civil-law provisions permitting private copying and/or limiting criminalization to severe cases causing high economic damage or committed regularly for gain.

cc. Special Protective Structures for Computer Programs
In addition to existing provisions, special protective structures for computer programs are under discussion. The most detailed discussion of such proposals has been by the *World Intellectual Property Organization (WIPO)* which, in 1978, published model provisions for computer programs similar to, but more comprehensive than, copyright protection. It also proposed a treaty dealing with international protection. However, in view of the increasing

trend towards copyright protection at the national level, a committee of experts recommended in June 1983 that a special protection structure and treaties should not be considered for the time being but, if necessary, at some later point in time. In April 1984 a 'Working Group on Technical Questions Relating to the Legal Protection of Computer Software' was re-examining definitions, in particular the definition of the term 'computer software'. During a joint meeting of WIPO/UNESCO, held in Geneva from 25 February to 1 March 1985, a great number of participants regarded computer programs as works deserving protection by copyright; only several delegations and participants voted for an immediate *sui generis* protection.[96]

At the national level, proposals to develop special protective structures for computer programs have been discussed, especially in *Japan*. The Information Industry Committee of the Japanese Ministry of International Trade and Industry (*MITI*) on 9 December 1983 published a 'Proposal with respect to Rearrangement of the Foundations for Software—Aiming towards Establishment of Legal Protection for Computer Software'. It proposes to substitute existing copyright protection with a new program law which is based primarily on industrial property-law concepts and borrowed provisions from Japanese patent law. According to the respective 'MITI-bill', published on 14 December 1983, the producer of software should be granted the right to use and duplicate software if he registers the software with a formal government agency. The bill demanded a compulsory licence for special cases. As a deterrent against software piracy it also provided injunctions, loss claims, and penal provisions. The MITI proposal caused a major trade row with the United States, which accused MITI of assisting Japanese industry in copying foreign-made programs. After the option of the above-mentioned WIPO/UNESCO conference for copyright protection, MITI dropped the bill in March 1985.[97]

In *France*, in June 1984, the Ministry of Industry and Research also suggested a 'droit *sui generis*'. The proposed law was intended to complement copyright law. It required the registration of the program at a state agency and protected non-evident elements of programs which could result from new algorithms and from combinations of known algorithms. The producer of the software should be granted, among other things, the right to copy, translate, and use the program for a period of 20 years. Yet after the above-described enactment of the French Copyright Amendment Act the realization of these legislative plans does not seem very likely.[98]

Sui generis legislation, which in recent years has been discussed by scholars and practitioners in many countries, is supported at present only by the governments of *Brazil, Greece,* and the *Soviet Union*.[99]

In case copyright protection proves insufficient, proposals of *sui generis* protection should be examined. A prerequisite to any further discussion, however, would be the resolution of what subject matter, especially which elements of programming, should be protected. Since trade (and theft!) of computer software has reached international proportions, worldwide protection has become a necessity. Any new legislation therefore should be developed and co-ordinated not only at a national but also at an *international level*. However, for the time being, the development and harmonization of copyright protection seem to be a more promising possibility.

c. ADDITIONAL PROTECTION OF INTEGRATED CIRCUITS[100]

Computer programs are not the only new economic values created by modern computer technology. With regard to the miniaturization of computers and the development of 'fifth-generation' computers, the technology of integrated circuits is becoming increasingly sophisticated. An integrated circuit or chip consists of two or more layers composed of conducting, semiconducting, and insulating material in a predetermined three-dimensional pattern, and is designed to perform electronic circuitry functions. Modern integrated circuits have structures of about 0.5 μm (1/1 000 000 m) in size and can contain more than 1 million transistors on a silicon disc of about 1 cm². In 1983 worldwide sales of computer chips were estimated to total $17 billion and in 1984 this number grew by an estimated 100%.[101]

The development of new and improved integrated circuits can take several man-years of design effort and requires high levels of investment. At the same time, there are methods which allow the chip's design to be analysed and copied within a few weeks at a fraction of the original production cost. A chip development costing about $1 million, for example, can be analysed and copied for about $10 000 (whereas reverse engineering of this chip would amount to about $100 000). If such copying is not prevented, the copied chips can be produced and marketed much more cheaply soon after the release of the original chip.

Since the widespread use of copied chips can significantly reduce the return on investment and consequently affect the motivation and the ability of the developer to invest in new chip designs, this is the classic example of a situation where the efforts of the original designer should be protected, it being in the public interest to encourage further innovation. The subject matter of the desirable legal protection should be the original design or topography of the semiconductor integrated circuit, and not the information stored in the chip or the procedure to produce the chip. Thereby a monopolization of ideas must be prevented in order to reach a balance between protection and competition.

Protection by Traditional Law
In most countries it still remains unclear to what extent chip designs are protected against reproductions by patent law, copyright law, registered designs, trade-secret law, and competition law.

Patent law may be applicable in the field of manufacturing methods or circuit configurations. However, as far as the layout or topography of the chip is concerned, the degree of inventiveness necessary for patent protection in general is not met by most chip designs. The laws on *registered designs* show similar problems; however, they could result in a broader protection in some countries.[102]

The application of *copyright*[103] differs. In some countries, such as the United States, copyright protection for integrated circuits is not available because purely utilitarian works are excluded from copyright protection (section 17, USC §101).[104] Other countries such as Australia, the Netherlands, Sweden and the United Kingdom, include utilitarian works in the protection of copyright. Sections 1 and 10 of the Dutch Copyright Act 1912, for example, include works of applied art, drawings, and industrial designs, and sections 3 and 9 (8) of the Copyright Act 1956 and the Design Copyright Act 1968 of the United Kingdom extend protection to drawings, engravings, and photographs, independent of their aesthetic appeal. However, even in these countries the scope of protection is different. In the Netherlands and in the United Kingdom reproduction implies, *inter alia*, the conversion of a two-dimensional preliminary form into a three-dimensional form and vice versa (see section 14 of the Dutch Copyright Act and section 48 (1) of the United Kingdom Copyright Act). In contrast, section 71 of the Australian Copyright Act 1968 provides that 'the making of an object of any kind that is in three dimensions does not infringe the copyright in an artistic work that is in two dimensions', and vice versa, 'if the object would not appear to persons who are not experts in relation to objects of that kind to be a reproduction of the artistic work'. A similar result holds true for West German copyright law.[105]

In many countries *trade-secret law* and *competition law*, and *law of tort*, though playing an important role, also show limitations, especially concerning the secret character of chip designs (which can be revealed by reverse engineering of marketed chips) and the time of protection by competition law.[106]

New Acts and Bills and their International Co-ordination
In the *United States* special protection for computer chips was given by the Semiconductor Chip Protection Act 1984, passed on 16 May 1984 and signed into law on 8 November 1984.[107] The Act is codified as chapter 9 of title 17 of the US Code and will be administered by the Copyright Office. It creates a new form of intellectual property law, different and independent from any preceding law. The protection consists of an amalgam of patent and copyright principles but also contains new features. The protected works are defined in 17 USC § 901 (a) (2) as 'a series of related images, however fixed or encoded (A) having or representing the predetermined three-dimensional pattern of metallic, insulating, or semiconductor material present or removed from the layers of a semiconductor chip product; and (B) in which series the relation of the images to one another is that each image has the pattern of surface of one form of the semiconductor chip product'. Section 908 (a) of the Act requires registration at the Copyright Office of a claim

requesting protection in a mask work to be made within two years of first commercial use of the work. Under section 905 of the Act, the owner of a protected mask work enjoys, for a period of 10 years, the exclusive right to do and to authorize any of the following: (1) to reproduce the mask work by optical, electronic, or any other means; (2) to import or distribute a semiconductor chip product in which the mask work is embodied; and (3) to induce or knowingly cause another person to do any of the acts described in paragraphs (1) and (2). The law, however, permits analysis of chips by 'reverse engineering' (in practice, it is therefore advisable to document reverse engineering in order to be able to prove it). The law further includes 'innocent infringer' provisions according to which the liability of a *bona fide* purchaser of an illegally produced chip is limited to payment of adequate royalties for chips sold after having knowledge of the infringement. The law does not provide for the use of criminal sanctions which were considered in the parliamentary discussions. Foreign chips are protected only on the basis of reciprocity; however, the Secretary of Commerce may upon a petition extending protection to foreign nationals under certain conditions, especially when the foreign nation is making good-faith efforts and reasonable progress in chip protection. Several countries have already submitted such a request and have received an interim order (e.g. Australia, Canada, Japan, the Netherlands, Sweden, the United Kingdom, and the European Communities).[108] Since the temporary protection of integrated circuits marketed before 1 July 1983 takes effect only if registration was made at the Copyright Office before 1 July 1985, integrated circuits marketed outside the United States can only be protected if the US government gave a positive reply to a request prior to July 1985 or if the foreign firms transferred all their rights concerning their integrated circuits to their American subsidiaries.

In *Japan*, on 31 May 1985, an 'Act Concerning the Circuit Layout of a Semiconductor Integrated Circuit' was promulgated.[109] The Act defines a 'semiconductor integrated circuit' as 'a product having transistors or other circuitry elements which are inseparably formed on a semiconductor material or an insulating material or inside the semiconductor material, and designed to perform an electronic circuitry function' (section 2 subsection 1). A 'circuit layout' is defined as 'a layout of circuitry elements and lead wires connecting such elements in a semiconductor integrated circuit' (section 2 subsection 1). The creator of a circuit layout may obtain registration to establish a 'circuit layout right' at the Ministry of International Trade and Industry (section 3). This 'circuit layout right' grants its holder the exclusive right to use the circuit layout (section 10) for a period of 10 years. 'Using' in the sense of the Act means (1) the manufacture of semiconductor integrated circuits by utilizing the circuit layout and (2) the transfer, lease, exhibition for the purpose of transferring or leasing, or the import of semiconductor integrated circuits manufactured by utilizing the circuit layout' (section 2 subsection 3). However, like the American law, the Japanese law does not cover the manufacture of a semiconductor integrated circuit which is made by 'utilizing the regi-stered circuit layout for the purpose of analyzing or evaluating the semi-conductor integrated circuit'. The Act contains provisions concerning infringement of rights (especially sections 22, 25, and 27), special provisions on persons acting in good faith (section 24), and empowers the court to request documents necessary for the assessment of damage (section 26). Contrary to United States' law, the Act has no reciprocity provision for the protection of foreign chips. It also includes various penal provisions which punish 'any person who infringes a circuit layout right or a sole use right' (section 51), 'any person who has obtained registration for establishment by fraud' (section 52), as well as various acts of officers or staff member of the registration organ (sections 53, 54, and 55).

In *Europe* the Commission and the Council of the European Commuities under Articles 100 and 113 of the Treaty Establishing the European Com-munities are preparing a Council directive on the legal protection of original topographies of semiconductor products. On 31 May 1985 the Commission submitted a proposal for a Council Resolution concerning a Community framework which was accepted by the Council on 19 June 1985. Based on this resolution, the Commission then submitted a proposal for a Council Directive in December 1985 (KOM–85–775).[110] This directive would ensure the desirable and speedy convergence of the legislative measures which are to be taken in the near future in several European states. As it is intended to be limited to basic questions and to leave matters of detail to the Member States, it would allow the realization of the new laws to take place in different forms. In *West Germany*, for example, the Ministry of Justice in November 1985 submitted a first unofficial pre-draft of provisions for the protection of the topographies of semiconductor chip products. This pre-draft contains a criminal provision applying to 'any person who, without the required consent of the bearer of the protective right, in situations other than those permitted by law, reproduces a protected topography or offers or brings into circulation semiconductor chip products or means of production which contain an unlawful reproduction'. Contrary to this approach of creating a specific new law, the *Swedish* government intends to extend copyright protection to integrated circuits.

Furthermore, at the international level the *WIPO* in June 1985 proposed a draft treaty on the protection of intellectual property with respect to inte-grated circuits. In November 1985 the question was considered at a joint meeting of *WIPO/UNESCO* in Geneva.[111]

These international efforts, aimed at a harmonization of the new national legislations, should be strengthened. Since a *criminal sanction* for the infringement of the protected rights is appropriate it might be recommended to criminalize the infringement of the exclusive right of the owner of a protected chip design. In order to avoid overcriminalization, only acts committed with the intent to exploit the chip design commercially should be punished.

3. Computer Sabotage

a. PROBLEMS OF TRADITIONAL LAW

In the field of computer sabotage the intangible nature of assets stored in DP systems also presents legal problems. The provisions on mischief in most countries require that tangible property be damaged. This occurs when computer hardware is physically damaged. Problems appear, however, in the above-mentioned cases of *non-physical (logical) damage*, especially when data are erased or when access to a computer system is denied by purely electronic means.

According to the prevailing opinion in most countries, such as Austria, Canada, Denmark, West Germany, Greece, Italy, the Netherlands, Norway, and the United Kingdom, the deliberate damage or destruction of information on tapes or discs is considered to be *damage to property, vandalism, or malicious mischief* (see section 125, Austrian Penal Code; section 291, Danish Penal Code; section 303, West German Penal Code; section 381, Greek Penal Code; sections 420 and 635, Italian Penal Code; section 350 of the Penal Code of the Netherlands; and section 78 of the Criminal Justice Act 1980 of Scotland or the Criminal Damage Act 1971 of England). This result is supported by the argument that the perpetrator either damages or interferes with the function of the physical tape or disc upon which the information is stored. Such construction can be applied especially in Canada, where the offence of mischief (section 387, Criminal Code) includes both the damage or destruction of tangible property and the obstruction, interruption, or interference with the lawful use of tangible property or with any person in the lawful use or operation of tangible property. In the case of *R. v. Turner* (1984, Ontario High Court of Justice) the accused altered some intangible computer programs that were contained on computer tapes, with the result that the programs would not operate properly. While the alteration or destruction of the intangible data did not constitute the offence of mischief, the resulting interference with the use of the tangible tape containing the altered intangible data was held to constitute mischief. In other criminal codes, however, such as in Belgian, Finnish, New York or Tasmanian State law, the erasure of information without damaging the physical medium does *not* fall under the provisions of damage to property, since electric impulses are not considered to be 'tangible property' and interference with use of the physical medium is not considered to be 'destruction' (see, for example, sections 528 and 559, Belgian Penal Code; and section 273, Tasmanian Criminal Code). In cases of denial of access to authorized users, the legal situation is unclear in many countries.[112]

However, no computer-related problems are generally created by provisions concerning offences against statutory *obligations to keep books*, which can be applied in certain cases of computer sabotage (see, for example, section 283b, West German Penal Code; and sections 166 and 325, Swiss Penal Code).[113]

b. NEW ACTS AND BILLS

In several countries legislation extending the present law of *mischief* to cover new forms of non-tangible values in the DP area has been enacted or proposed.

In the *United States*, in the legislation of most *States* this has been accomplished by including the respective conduct in the above-mentioned *comprehensive computer crime legislation* (see, for example, section 502 (a) and (d) of the Californian Penal Code of 1 January 1985). In some States there exist more specific provisions on the destruction of computer equipment (see, for example, section 53a–251 (f), Connecticut Statutes) and/or on the 'interruption of computer services' (see, for example, section 53a–251 (d), Connecticut Statutes, or section 934, Delaware Code Annotated). However, there are also States which include computer sabotage in comprehensive general provisions of damaging property (see, for example, section 11.46.484 (a) (1), Alaska Statutes). An 'evolutionary' technique of law reform was used by section 9A.48.100 of the Revised Code of Washington, which declares for the purpose of sections 9A.48.070 to 9A.48.090 that 'physical damage', in addition to its ordinary meaning, shall include 'the alteration, damage, or erasure of records, information, data, or computer progams which are electronically recorded for use in computers'. At the *federal level*, the above-mentioned American Federal Computer Systems Protection bill of 1984 proposes to punish in a similar manner 'whoever knowingly and wilfully without authorization damages, destroys or attempts to damage or destroy a computer or knowingly and wilfully without authorization damages or attempts to damage any computer program, or data contained in such computer'. However, the Counterfeit Access Device and Computer Fraud and Abuse Act 1984 does not adopt this comprehensive provision but only includes certain cases of computer sabotage by punishing whoever 'knowingly accesses a computer without authorization . . . , and by means of such conduct knowingly uses, modifies, destroys or discloses information in, or prevents authorized use of such computer, if such computer is operated for or on behalf of the Government of the United States and such conduct affects such operation'.[114] Section 43 of the *Portuguese* Data Protection Bill also captures all kinds of erasure or modification of data or programs in one comprehensive provision.[115]

In contrast to this comprehensive approach prevailing in the United States' and Portuguese legislation, the 'evolutionary' technique of *modifying the traditional statutes* is espoused in a number of states. The above-mentioned *Swiss* bill advocates a reformed section 144 (2), Penal Code, which punishes 'any person who, without authorization, alters or erases electronically stored data or programs'.[116] The *Finnish* Penal Code Revision Committee suggests equating damage to data to damage inflicted on tangible property. In addition, the Finnish reform proposals suggest a specific provision on 'obstruction of communications'.[117] Similarly, the *Canadian* Criminal Law Amendment Act 1985 adds a new subsection 1.1 to section 387 of the Criminal Code designated 'mischief in relation to data'. This amendment is of special interest, as it is not limited to the erasure of data but punishes whoever wilfully and without legal justification, excuse, or colour of right '(a) destroys or alters data; (b) renders data meaningless, useless or ineffective; (c) obstructs, interrupts or interferes with the lawful use of data; or (d) obstructs, interrupts or interferes with any person in the lawful use of data or denies access to data to any person who is entitled to access thereto'.[118] The 'evolutionary' technique of modifying the traditional statutes is also espoused by the *Swiss* Committee of Experts, who advocate a reformed section 144 (2), Penal Code,[119] and by the *Finnish* government's bill, which suggests equating damage to data to damage inflicted on tangible property (chapter 35, section 1 of the proposed Penal Code).[120]

The West German, Austrian, and French reform proposals do not change the existing provisions of 'damage to property' but suggest *specific provisions against computer sabotage* or against damaging and suppression of computer data. The *West German* 'Second Law for the Prevention of Economic Crime' enacted two new provisions which follow the traditional provision on 'damage to property' (section 303, Penal Code). The new section 303a punishes the erasure, suppression, rendering useless, and modification of data with imprisonment of up to 2 years, whereas section 303b includes a *special qualification* for these acts and for the destruction, damaging, rendering useless, removing, and modification of computer systems or of a data carrier, if this interferes with data processing which is of essential importance for another's enterprise or an administrative agency.[121] In *Austria* the Federal Ministry of Justice also suggested amending the traditional provision on 'damage to property' by a new section 126a of the Penal Code. Paragraph 1 of this provision is similar to paragraph 1 of the new West German section 303a, whereas paragraph 2 provides more severe sanctions in cases in which losses exceed 10 000 or 200 000 Austrian Schillings.[122] The *French* provision proposed in 1986 by the Ministry of Justice covers 'the destruction or alteration of an automatic information processing system or a part of it, or any hindering or falsification of its functioning, if the act is committed knowingly and infringes upon the right of another person'. The provision will be part (section 307–3) of the general chapter on information crimes being implemented in the Penal Code.[123]

In addition to the West German law, the new *Danish* law on computer crime of 6 June 1985 has specifically dealt with *severe cases* of computer sabotage by including DP systems in section 193 of the Penal Code. This provision now punishes 'any person who, in an unlawful manner, causes major disturbances in the operation of public means of communication, of the public mail service, of telegraph or telephone systems, radio or television systems, data processing systems, or of installations for the public supply of water, gas, electricity or heating'.[124] A similar new proposal concerning 'national vulnerability' is suggested by the *Norwegian* Standing Committee on Criminal Law Reform of 1985 (section 151b of the Penal Code). This provision holds that 'whoever renders useless, damages, or puts out of operation a collection of information, or a construction for energy supply, broadcasting or telecommunication, and thereby greatly interferes with public administration or with the social order, shall be imprisoned for a term not exceeding ten years'.[125] In *Finland* a working group is reviewing the offences on 'causing public danger' which, after revision, would also comprehend serious acts of computer crime.[126]

c. SUGGESTIONS FOR LEGAL POLICY

In order to achieve an international consensus on computer crime it is *recommended* that the penal codes of all Western countries contain provisions comprising not only damage to tangible property but also *damage to data*. Such a provision should not only address the conventional methods of erasure of data but should also cover other forms of rendering data useless with destructive intent. Yet an overly broad definition of the acts of sabotage is dangerous, since it could lead to a criminalization of labour conflicts in the DP area.

The damaging of hardware and software should only be punished if the perpetrator acts *knowingly*. This element of intent in the field of computer sabotage is of particular importance, since much damage in the DP area is the result of non-punishable acts of recklessness, poorly working software, and other technical errors.

4. The Unauthorized Use of Computers

a. PROBLEMS OF TRADITIONAL LAW

In many countries the unauthorized use of computer services or 'time' is not covered by penal law. These problems are less pronounced in countries such as Belgium, Denmark or Finland, where the *unauthorized or illegal use of another person's property* is penalized (see, for example, section 461, Belgian Penal Code, or section 293, Danish Penal Code). Here the intangible nature of assets stored in DP systems does not create problems because the perpetrator generally uses not only data but also computer hardware. In many American States the theft of service laws also seem to apply in cases of theft of 'computer time'. However, a New York State Court has held that theft of services does not cover the unauthorized use of computers. In some countries, such as Norway and Switzerland, the relevant provisions are restricted to cases in which the victim suffers a loss or inconvenience. Many legal systems, such as those of Austria, West Germany, Japan, and the United Kingdom—do not generally penalize the use of another person's property. According to Austrian, West German, Greek, or Dutch law, for example, the so-called *furtum usus* is only punishable if specific items, such as cars or bicycles, are involved (see, for example, section 248 b, West German Penal Code).[127]

Some legal systems, such as that of France, do not even contain such provisions, and therefore the courts regulated the unauthorized use of cars with *theft* provisions. However, with respect to the unauthorized use of computers such solutions are hardly applicable, since there is usually not substantial deprivation of the computer from the owner and the computer is not 'taken' away. Because of these requirements, section 626 of the Italian Penal Code is also inapplicable, as it regulates the *furtum usus* as some kind of particular, less severe, form ('privilegation') of theft.[128]

The traditional provisions concerning the *unauthorized use of automatic vending machines or public telephone networks* in most legal systems are not able to solve these problems. The Austrian, West German, and Swiss provisions against unauthorized use of automatic machines, for example, are restricted to services offered for a fee (see section 149 (2), Austrian Penal Code; section 265a, West German Penal Code; and section 150, Swiss Penal Code). Similar problems occur in the United Kingdom with section 1 of the English Theft Act 1978, which makes it a crime to obtain services by deception—provided the person rendering the services expects to be paid for them. Similarly, section 42 of the English Telecommunications Act 1984 covers 'a person who dishonestly obtains a service provided by means of a licensed telecommunication system with intent to avoid payment of any charge applicable to the provisions of that service'. In Canada section 287 (1) (b) of the Criminal Code punishes for theft every person 'who fraudulently, maliciously, or without colour of right uses any telecommunication facility or obtains any telecommunication services'. However, in the case *R. v. Michael MacLaughlin*, the Supreme Court held that a telecommunications facility does not include a 'closed' computer system in which terminals are linked directly to the main computer.[129]

In some countries statutes concerning *unlawful use, waste, or withdrawal of electricity* are applicable. This is the case, for example, for section 461, Belgian Penal Code, section 13 of the English Theft Act 1968, or section 287 (1) (a) of the Canadian Criminal Code, according to which one commits a theft who fraudulently, maliciously, or without colour of right abstracts, consumes, or uses electricity or gas, or causes it to be wasted or diverted. In France, section 379 of the Penal Code is applicable as well, since, according to French courts, it is extended to the 'theft' of electricity and applies to 'all other criminal acts' (tout autre procédé coupable'). In other countries, such as West Germany, the respective provisions cannot be applied because they require that energy be withdrawn by an illegally installed connection (section 248c, West German Penal Code). In Australia, the applicability of 'theft of electricity' provisions (such as section 233 of the Tasmania Criminal Code) also is doubted.[130]

In specific cases *additional criminal provisions* have to be considered. The above-mentioned provisions on *breach of trust* can be applied in some countries when employees in certain positions cause damage to their principal.[131] In Canada, a charge of *impersonation* under section 361, Canadian Criminal Code, may result if a person falsely assumes the identity of a lawful computer-user.[132]

Consequently, international regulation of the unauthorized use of computers is not homogeneous.

b. NEW ACTS AND BILLS

In the *United States* the legal situation has improved insofar as many *States* have enacted new laws against theft of computer services. Most States which passed special computer-crime legislation included time-theft in their general provisions on computer crime by prohibiting the unlawful use of or access to DP systems. In some States a specific provision on 'theft of services' was created (see, for example, section 11.46.200 (a), Alaska Statutes, section 53a–251 (c) Connecticut Statutes, or section 933, Delaware Code Annotated). A special approach can be found in the previously mentioned Criminal Code of Virginia (section 18.2.–98.1), where 'computer time or services or data processing services or information or data stored in connection therewith' is defined to be property which may be the object of larceny (sections 18.2–95 or 18.2–96), or embezzlement (section 18.2.–111), or false pretences (section 18.2–178). At the *Federal level* the Federal Computer Systems Protection Bill of 1983 proposed to incriminate in one section the damaging of a computer as well as the 'withholding or denial of the use of a computer, a computer program, or stored information'. The Federal Computer Systems Protection Bill of 1984 suggests the inclusion of the unauthorized use of computers in the general provision on computer crime by including 'computer services' in the definition of protected 'property'. Contrary to these proposals, the above-described Counterfeit Access Device and Computer Fraud and Abuse Act 1984 regulates some forms of 'time-theft' by punishing whoever 'knowingly accesses a computer without authorization . . . , and by means of such conduct knowingly uses, modifies, destroys, or discloses information in, or prevents authorized use of, such computer if such computer is operated for or on behalf of the Government of the United States and such conduct affects such operation'. Section 1030 (a), however, excludes 'the case of a person having accessed a computer with authorization and using the opportunity such access provides for purposes to which such access does not extend, if the using of such opportunity consists only of the use of the computer.'[133]

In *Canada* the Criminal Law Amendment Act 1985 punishes in section 301.2 of the Criminal Code 'anyone who, fraudulently and without colour of right, (a) obtains, directly or indirectly, any computer service, (b) by means of an electromagnetic, acoustic, mechanical or other device, intercepts or causes to be intercepted, directly or indirectly, any function of a computer system, or (c) uses or causes to be used, directly or indirectly, a computer system with intent to commit an offence under paragraph (a) or (b) or an offence under section 387 in relation to data or a computer system'.[134] In *France* the above-mentioned 1986 proposal of the Ministry of Justice covers 'the obtainment or the incitement to obtainment of an illegal gain committed by the fraudulent use of an automatic information processing system'. In *Portugal* sections 42 and 45 of the proposed Data Protection Bill propose criminalizing the unauthorized use of computer data or computer programs committed with the intent to gain profit.[135]

In *West Germany* in a more restricted approach the parliamentarians of the governing coalition parties in 1985 suggested a provision which would punish 'any person who makes unauthorized use of data processing equipment and by so doing causes damage to the person entitled to use it'. However, this provision was then dropped and not implemented in the 'Second Law for the Prevention of Economic Crime'.[136] The *Swiss* Committee of Experts for the Revision of the Penal Code proposes a revised section 150 (formerly section 151) on the 'unauthorized use of services' which applies, among others, to 'any person who knowing that payment is required uses . . . a service which a data processing system applies or which an automat arranges'.[137] Similar proposals are suggested by the *Austrian* Ministry of Justice (proposing an amendment to section 147 of the Penal Code on 'obtaining a service without paying')[138] and by the *Norwegian* Standing Committee on Criminal Law Reform, proposing an amendment to section 403 of the Penal Code.[139]

Contrary to these computer-specific proposals, a number of countries also aim at a *general treatment of unauthorized use of property*. The *Swiss* Committee of Experts for the Revision of the Penal Code, in addition to the above-mentioned provisions on unauthorized use of services requiring payment (section 150), proposes a new section 141 (2) (revising the former section 143) of the Penal Code which punishes 'any person who removes a movable object from its legitimate owner thereby causing him considerable prejudice'.[140] A new *Norwegian* reform proposal states that 'whoever uses or disposes of property belonging to another person without authorization and with the intent to obtain gain for himself or another, or causes considerable loss to the victim, shall be imprisoned for theft of use to a prison term up to three years' (section 261 of the Penal Code).[141] Similarly, the *Finnish* Penal Code Revision Committee advocates the retention of a general provision which, as far as the penalties are concerned, would equate serious cases of unauthorized use with theft of goods, whereas harmless cases would be excluded.[142] The *Swedish* bill contains a deletion in the general provision on 'unlawful use of property' (chapter 10, section 7) which would make this provision applicable in cases of time-theft of computers.[143]

c. SUGGESTIONS FOR LEGAL POLICY

As far as an international consensus concerning rules against computer crime is concerned, one might *recommend* that countries consider penalizing the unauthorized use of computerized information systems. Criminalization would be justified not only by the losses and potential risks of time-theft for the owner of the computer but primarily by the value of the exclusive use of computerized information systems for its owner. Criminalization, however, should be limited to cases in which the perpetrator knowingly infringes security measures. Alternatively, overcriminalization (such as punishing the use of a colleagues' desk-top calculator or minicomputer) could be avoided by requiring the intent to cause other computer-abuses or harm, as illustrated by the Canadian reform proposal. In employer–employee relationships it is particularly important that non-authorized use be defined clearly by internal enterprise regulations.

As far as the *legal technique* is concerned, it should be noted that the problem of *furtum usus* is not a computer-specific problem but a *general problem of penal law*. Apart from the 'property approach' already discussed, two different legal techniques are possible: reform could be effected by introducing a *general provision* against unlawful dispossession or use of another's property, as currently suggested by the Finnish, Norwegian, and Swedish reform proposals, or by introducing a *specific provision* against *furtum usus* of computer systems, which—as comparative law shows—could be incorporated into the penal code in various ways: as a general clause against computer crime, corresponding to most American bills; in combination with a provision against unauthorized access to or interference with DP systems, as suggested by the Canadian reform proposal; as part of a provision against computer-damage, as exemplified by the Federal Computer Systems Protection Bill of 1983; as an amendment to the existing provisions against *furtum usus* of cars; in combination with existing provisions on the unauthorized use of telephone facilities as suggested by the new Austrian bill; or finally, as a distinct provision against *furtum usus* of computers, as suggested by an American bill introduced in the House of Representatives on 3 November 1983.[144]

Computer-specific approaches, however, will have to take great care in deciding which *kinds of information-processing units* and telecommunications facilities (not only consisting of business computers but also of household computers, pocket calculators, word-processing systems, and wrist watches) should be protected. The American and Canadian reform legislations present a variety of possible solutions. According to the Canadian Criminal Code Amendment Act 1985 the term 'computer system' means a device, or a group of interconnected or related devices, one or more of which (a) contains computer programs or other data and (b), pursuant to computer programs, performs logic and control, and may perform any other function.[145] However, at least for Continental law countries, it seems questionable whether it will be necessary or desirable to give an exact definition of the protected computers. As already pointed out, legislation should be functionally oriented and should not overly concentrate on the present state of technical development. If specific and well-defined provisions on *furtum usus* are created, it would therefore be preferable not to refer to technical devices but rather to certain ways of using them.[146]

The best solution for countries not wishing a general provision on *furtum usus* might be a provision against *unauthorized access* to DP systems, which would encompass most of the cases discussed here.

5. Unauthorized Access (Protecting the Integrity of Computer Systems)

Today, the importance of data communication and DP systems is forcing many countries to protect the integrity of these systems independent of the status of secrecy of the information processed. This approach of protecting the *integrity of certain computer and communication systems*, including a 'formal sphere of secrecy' was developed in the field of wiretapping of telephone communications and has now been extended to the interception of data communications and unauthorized access to DP systems.

a. THE PRESENT LEGAL SITUATION

As far as *wiretapping and the interception of data communications* are concerned, the traditional wiretap statutes of most legal systems refer only to the interception of oral communications or conversations. The new section 617 of the Italian Penal Code, for example, is limited to communications 'between persons'. The same applies to section 201, West German Penal Code; sections 139a and 139c, Penal Code of the Netherlands; section 179 bis, Swiss Penal Code; or the United States Federal Wire Tap Act 1968. Similarly, in the United States, title III of the Omnibus Crime Control and Safe Street Act 1968 (18 USC §§2510–20) addresses 'aural acquisition of the contents of any wire or oral communications' and does not refer to digitally transmitted messages. Section 605 of the US Communications Act 1934 (47 USC §605, amended in 1968, 1982, and 1984) prohibits the authorized interception of radio transmissions and wire communications not covered by the Omnibus Control Act, but requires that such communications be broadcast. At the State level, in some American States the legal situation is similar (see, for example, Kansas Statutes Annotated §21–40002), whereas in other States a broader approach could be reached by laws concerning intercepting, recording, or divulging private communications (see, for example, section 631, Californian Penal Code). In Canada, on the other hand, the wiretapping of computer communications is punishable by section 178.11 of the Criminal Code, provided two persons communicate orally or by telecommunication. The Canadian statute, however, does not apply to communications between two computer systems belonging to the same person, two computers communicating with one another rather than with their owners, or one computer system communicating with itself. In Belgium, section 17 of the Law on Telecommunications of 13 October 1930 could be applicable to cases of wiretapping of computer communications. The same is true for section 1 (1) of the English Interception of Communication Act 1985, providing that 'a person who intentionally intercepts a communication in the course of its transmission . . . by means of a public telecommunication system shall be guilty of an offence'.

In all countries the applicability of penal provisions is even more difficult with respect to 'mere' *unauthorized access to DP and storage systems*. 'Mere' unauthorized access to computer systems means the entering into a computer system without causing any damage to the owner other than retrieving information for no particular purpose. This act could be compared with copying a key and/or entering another's property without causing any damage. The traditional provisions protecting domestic peace (such as section 439, Belgian Penal Code; section 123, West German Penal Code; or section 614, Italian Penal Code) or punishing the unauthorized alteration or copying of keys (such as section 399, French Penal Code) obviously do not apply to these modern 'computerized' forms of 'burglary', 'breaking in', or 'entering'. The traditional provisions on breaking open a letter in most cases also cannot be used (see, for example, section 118, Austrian Penal Code, and section 202, West German Penal Code).[147]

b. REFORM PROPOSALS

New legislative proposals covering wiretapping and unauthorized access to data-processing and communication systems represent *various approaches*, ranging from provisions criminalizing 'mere' access to DP systems to those punishing access only in cases where information is obtained, modified, or damaged.

The first law criminalizing *'mere' access* was the *Swedish* Data Act of 2 April 1973, which in the general section 21 punishes, among others, any person who unlawfully procures access to computer-stored data. In the course of the above-discussed reform of the Penal Code, an additional amendment of the provision, which would cover all kinds of wiretapping, has been suggested.[148] Similarly, in the *United States* the proposed Federal Computer Protection Systems Act 1984 provides in section 2(c) that 'whoever intentionally and without authorization accesses a computer . . . or a computer system or computer network including such computer' shall be guilty of a misdemeanour. Though not yet passed, the Federal Computer Protection Systems Act has been the model for several State legislations penalizing mere access (such as section 11.46.484(a), Alaska Statutes; section 502(d)(2) of the new penal Code of California; section 53a–251(b), Connecticut Statutes; section 932, Delaware Statutes; or section 434.850, Kentucky Revised Statutes). Section 502(d)(2) of the new Californian Penal Code (effective since 1 January 1985), for example, penalizes as a misdemeanour 'any person who intentionally accesses any computer system, computer network, computer program, or data, knowing that the access is prohibited by the owner or lessee'; the law is especially interesting, as it does not apply to 'any person acting within the scope of his or her employment'.[149] In *Denmark* the Penal Code Amendment Act on 'Datakriminalitet' (1985) reforms section 263 (2) of the Penal Code, making it a crime to 'obtain access to another person's informations or programs which are meant to be used in a data processing system'. In addition, section 263(3) imposes a more severe punishment if the act is committed 'with the intention to procure or make oneself acquainted with information about trade secrets of a company'.[150]

A more restricted conception of punishment for 'mere access' can be found in the West German, Finnish, and Norwegian reform proposals, which require an *infringement of security measures*. Section 202(3) of the *West German* Penal Code (enacted in 1974), which had equated some pictures and storage devices with letters in order to protect them against unauthorized interception, could only be applied to select cases in the DP area. Therefore the 'Second Law on the Suppression of Economic Crime' deleted the storage devices in section 203 (3) and enacted a new section 203a. This section punishes 'any person who obtains without authorization, for himself or for another, data which are not meant for him and which are specially protected against unauthorized access'.[151] Similarly, in *Norway* an amendment of 16 February 1979 to section 145 of the Penal Code provides that whoever illegally gains access to the contents of a closed communication, or to records which usually are accessible only with the aid of special equipment, will be liable to the same penalty as that applicable to the breaking-open of a letter or another closed document. A new Norwegian reform proposal of the Standing Committee on Criminal Law Reform of 1985 concerning section 145 is based on the same concept, and intends to penalize whoever 'by breaking a protection, obtains unauthorized access to data stored or transmitted by electronical or other technical means'.[152] Similarly, in *Finland* the Working Group on Informational Crimes proposed a new penal provision on 'system-hacking'. The provision applies to all acts of accessing data systems which are committed 'through the unauthorized use of a password or by otherwise breaking the identification control or other similar protection'. The proposed provision is subsidiary to provisions providing a more severe penalty; the damage to or alteration of data as well as interception of telecommunications or trade espionage would therefore not fall under this provision.[153]

Whereas these proposals limit criminalization by establishing certain objective requirements, the Canadian Criminal Law Amendment Act 1985, the proposals of the Swiss Committee of Experts for the Revision of the Penal Code, and the French proposals do so by *demanding a specific intention*. Section 301.2(1)(b) of the new *Canadian* Code punishes 'everyone who fraudulently and without a colour of right . . . by means of an electromagnetic, acoustic, mechanical or other device intercepts or causes to be intercepted, directly or indirectly, any function of a computer system'.[154] The *Swiss* proposals cover 'any person who, with the intent of unlawfully enriching himself or another person, procures without authorization, electronically stored data or programs'.[155] The proposed *French* provision criminalizes 'the fraudulent and surreptitious obtainment of a program, of data or of any other element of an automatic information processing system'.[156]

A *more restricted approach*, primarily found in the *United States* Federal Legislation, demands not only illegal access to DP systems but the obtaining, modifying, or destroying of information. The new American Counterfeit Access Device and Computer Fraud and Abuse Act 1984 (effective since 12 October 1984) which intends to prevent unauthorized access to computers used by the federal government, banks, and credit bureaus, applies to anyone who 'knowingly accesses a computer without authorization, or having accessed a computer with authorization, uses the opportunity such access provides for purposes to which such authorization does not extend', and by means of such conduct (1) obtains certain classified US government information with the intent or reason to believe that such information so obtained is to be used for the injury of the United States, or to the advantage of any foreign nation; (2) obtains information of a financial institution or a consumer reporting agency; or (3) knowingly uses, modifies, destroys, or discloses information in, or prevents authorized use of certain computers (Publ.L.98–473, H.J.Res. 648–354, §1030).[157]

In some countries there are also proposals which *combine* several of these approaches in a provision covering both 'mere' access and, under more severe sanctions, qualified forms of access. This is particularly the case in the legislation of the American States. An example is the *California* Penal Code of 1985, which, in addition to the previously mentioned misdemeanour in sections 502(b), (c) and (c)(1), punishes as a public offence certain forms of access gained for the purpose of, among others, fraud, extortion, obtaining property or certain information, or incapacitating a computer system (for further examples, see section 53a–251(e), Connecticut Statutes or section 935, Delaware Code Annotated.)[158]

c. EVALUATION AND SUGGESTIONS FOR LEGAL POLICY

Because of the potential danger connected with the increasing frequency of wiretapping and unauthorized access to computers, especially by remote DP systems, the general criminalization of *both wiretapping* and *unauthorized access* to computer systems is advisable.

This should not be obtained by an amendment to the provisions concerning private or trade secrets but by a *separate provision* concerning unauthorized access to DP systems. As future technical developments will make it increasingly difficult to distinguish between telecommunications systems and computer systems, it would be suitable to place the wiretap provision in the same (or in close connection with the) provision against unauthorized access of computer systems. This *close connection of wiretap and access statutes* is illustrated by the new Canadian legislation, which does not simply prohibit the interception of computer communication systems but includes the interception of any 'functions of a computer system'. With respect to the scope of application of the new statute, it must be decided whether it is necessary to penalize the pirating of certain data communications from satellites and microwave links, an increasingly popular activity in the United States.

If it is compatible with the representative national legal system, criminal repression could be *reduced or modulated* in specific cases. In order to *avoid the criminalization of minor breaches* (such as overtime use of computers by students) and to improve data security, unauthorized access should be made punishable only in cases in which *data are protected by security measures*. In the field of telecommunications systems such security measures are required by article 22 of the International Telecommunication Convention of 1973, according to which the members agree to take all possible measures, compatible with the system of telecommunication used, with a view to ensuring the secrecy of international correspondences. Alternatively, overcriminalization could be avoided by requiring the intent to cause other computer-abuses or harm.

As 'hackers' often intend to improve data-security, it could be considered to grant a certain *'premium'* in cases in which the perpetrator gives *immediate notice* of his access and of the loopholes used in the data system to the victim or to State authorities. This 'premium' could, for example, be discretion not to prosecute or special consideration of the hacker's collaboration at the time of sentencing. The prosecution of all or of less severe cases upon application only, or only if specifically required by the public interest, is also possible, and is suggested by the Norwegian and Swiss reform proposals. As is the case with all the other provisions suggested here, unauthorized access to computers should be punished only if the perpetrator acts knowingly.

6. Tax Fraud and Customs Offences

As far as computer-specific tax fraud is concerned, three different aspects must be mentioned:
(a) Problems of traditional tax fraud committed with the help of computers;
(b) Specific taxation problems arising from the evaluation of the economic value of software and information; and
(c) Special taxation and customs problems originating from transborder data flow of these data.

a. COMPUTER-ASSISTED 'TRADITIONAL' TAX FRAUD

In many countries *traditional tax fraud* committed with the help of computers does not create computer-specific problems, since the tax-fraud provisions generally apply regardless of whether the fraud is committed by traditional methods or with computer-assistance. Section 370 (1), No. 2 of the West German 'Abgabenordnung', for example, only requires that *false or incomplete facts* relevant for tax purposes be given to the tax agencies. In other countries, however, such as the United Kingdom, the provisions on tax fraud require the *deception of a person*. In a decision concerning the VAT Act 1983 (*R. v. Moritz* (1981)) an English judge held that 'deception' in the sense of the respective statute required that a human mind be deceived. In response, an amendment to the VAT Act 1983 was proposed.

The preceding considerations[159] concerning the general fraud provision also bear on the evaluation and solution of this problem. Like the general fraud provisions, the provisions on tax fraud should not only *comprehend* the deception of a person but also the *manipulation of a computer*.

b. ACCOUNTING PRACTICES AND TAX-EVALUATION WITH RESPECT TO SOFTWARE IN THE NATIONAL AREA

DP-specific questions arise in fields where the evaluation of the new economic values in the DP area is uncertain. This holds true especially for *accounting practices* and *tax-evaluation* of computer software. Accounting practices and policies for software are highly diversified and uncertain in Western countries. There are some countries (e.g. Ireland, Denmark, and Norway) in which software is regarded primarily as an *operating cost*. In others (e.g. Belgium, France, West Germany, and the United States), software can or must be treated as an *investment*, set out as a balance-sheet asset in certain cases, especially for software purchases linked to hardware purchases, for packaged software royalties, and for expenditures on software developed outside the company. Similar uncertainty prevails in the field of *value-added taxes and sales taxes*, which in some countries depend on whether software is considered to be a service or a product.[160]

These problems are primarily problems of *tax law*. However, because in many countries the penal provisions of tax law refer to substantive tax law, they can also become important in the field of *criminal law*. Consequently, legal solutions in the field of software-evaluation and taxation should be precise in order to distinguish clearly between illegal tax fraud and legal tax-circumvention.

c. TAX AND CUSTOMS PROBLEMS CONCERNING TRANSBORDER DATA FLOWS

Special problems could also arise in future in the field of transborder data flow. So far, trade with software and other information has been quite unrestricted since it has been regulated by the liberal legislation covering international trade and investment in the services or technology sales sectors. Customs duty applied only to hardware media (tapes, discs, etc.) and software bound to hardware, and not invoiced separately. However, this situation seemed to be due to uncertainties concerning related questions rather than to an explicit international consensus favouring liberal trade policies. There is a danger that this could change in the future, as in several countries official authorities are considering levying the same customs duties and ad valorum duties on software as on tangible merchandise. A final position has not yet been taken in most countries, since taxing software poses various problems, especially with respect to information flow within transnational enterprises, software transfers through telecommunications networks, international investments in services, and technology transfers. Because of these problems, some countries were demanding an international agreement on the principle of excepting information and software from taxation. On 23 April 1985 the Council of the European Communities adopted Regulation No. 1055/85 (amending Regulation EEC No. 1224/80), which came into force on 1 May 1985. According to article 8a of the new regulation, in the determination of the customs value of imported carrier media bearing data or instructions, only the cost or value of the carrier medium itself shall be taken into account. Therefore the customs value shall not include the cost or value of the data or instructions, provided that this is distinguished from the cost or the value of the carrier medium. The General Agreement on Tariffs and Trade (GATT) Committee on Customs Valuation discussed a similar agreement concerning a 'Decision on the Valuation of Carrier Media Bearing Software for Data Processing Equipment', which was agreed upon on 25 September 1984.[161]

d. RECOMMENDATIONS FOR LEGAL POLICY

It is *recommended* that the *general provisions on tax fraud* not only comprehend the deception of a person but also the manipulation of a computer. As far as the specific questions of evaluation, taxation, and clearance of software are concerned, *different accounting, taxation, and customs practices* with respect to software should be *avoided* in order to create a free international information market.

7. Summary: The Recommendations of the OECD Working Group

The penal coverage of computer-related economic crime was discussed by an *ad hoc* working group of the Organization for Economic Co-operation and Development (*OECD*) from 1983 to 1985. In September 1985 the working group and the ICCP Committee of the OECD recommended that member countries consider the extent to which acts committed knowingly in the field of computer-related crime should be covered by national penal legislation. Based on a comparative analysis of substantive law, which the author has elaborated and which has been the basis of the foregoing considerations, the working group and the ICCP Committee of the OECD suggested the following list of acts which could constitute a common denominator between the different approaches taken by Member Countries:

(1) The input, alteration, erasure, and/or suppression of computer data and/or computer programs made wilfully with the intent to commit an illegal transfer of funds or of another thing of value;

(2) The input, alteration, erasure, and/or suppression of computer data and/or computer programs made wilfully with the intent to commit a forgery;

(3) The input, alteration, erasure, and/or suppression of computer data and/or computer programs, or other interference with computer systems, made wilfully with the intent to hinder the functioning of a computer and/or telecommunications system;

(4) The infringement of the exclusive right of the owner of a protected computer program with the intent to exploit commercially the program and put it on the market;

(5) The access to or interception of a computer and/or telecommunications system made knowingly and without the authorization of the person responsible for the system, either by infringement of security measures or for other dishonest or harmful intentions.

In addition to these acts, the author recommended in his comparative report that a list of criminal 'minimum rules' for fighting computer crime should contain certain intolerable acts in connection with trade and industrial secrets; this additional issue of trade-secret protection of computer-stored data is to be considered by the OECD in 1986 within the broader context of general trade-secret protection. With respect to future harmonization of legislation, the infringement of the rights of the owner of a protected chip design should also be considered for inclusion in the list of criminal 'minimum rules' for fighting computer crime. This question has recently arisen during the work of the OECD and has not been implemented in their work program.

When the Select Committee of Experts on Computer-related Crime of the *Council of Europe* started to discuss the legal problems of computer crime in December 1985 the author therefore recommended the committee to adopt the list of acts elaborated by the OECD working group, to transform the recommendation of the OECD into a legally binding document, and to consider the amendment of the following acts:

(6) The illegal obtaining, disclosing, and/or using of trade and industrial secrets committed *contra bonos mores* (especially by company outsiders and by employees during their employment); and

(7) The infringement of the exclusive right of the owner of a protected chip design with the intent to exploit it commercially and put it on the market.

The Select Committee of Experts on Computer-related Crime of the Council of Europe will discuss the adoption of the OECD list and these amendments in 1986. It is to be expected that the recommendations of the OECD and their taking over and adaptation by other international organizations will help to incorporate the above-mentioned phenomena into the national legislations, thus resulting in a harmonized solution for all Western countries.

B. COMPUTER-RELATED INFRINGEMENTS OF PRIVACY[162]

The extent to which the collection, storage, use, and transmission of personal data is permissible was problematic long before the invention of the computer. However, due to limited methods of using data it was formerly possible for a few offences of defamation and infringements of special secrets (especially in the medical area and other professional fields) to grant sufficient protection. Expanded possibilities of collecting, storing, accessing, comparing, selecting, linking, and transmitting data provided by new technologies since the 1960s have caused new threats which prompted many countries to enact new bodies of administrative, civil, and penal regulations.

Since the legal discussion on the threat to privacy caused by modern computer technology began years before that on computer-related economic crimes, international co-ordination with respect to the former started earlier, and has already led to a certain degree of harmonization of privacy legislation in many Western countries. Therefore the following comparative overview first describes the existing international consensus in this field (*infra*, 1). Since penal regulations in one country often correspond to administrative or civil regulations in others, and since penal provisions covering privacy infringements often refer to administrative regulations, this survey then examines general concepts of privacy legislation (*infra*, 2) before analysing penal provisions on privacy infringements (*infra*, 3). Following this analysis, some suggestions for future action are made (*infra*, 4).

1. The Existing International Framework

International organizations developed a common approach to privacy protection at an early stage in order to prevent the development of different concepts and national regulations that would impede transborder data flow.[163] The main work in this field has so far been done by the OECD, the Council of Europe, and the European Communities.

a. THE OECD GUIDELINES

In 1977 the *OECD* started to elaborate guidelines governing the protection of privacy and transborder flows of personal data. These guidelines were adopted by the Council of the OECD on 23 September 1980 as a recommendation to the member states. At the time of writing, they had been endorsed by 22 member states of the OECD (Austria, Belgium, Canada, Denmark, Finland, France, West Germany, Greece, Iceland, Italy, Japan, Luxembourg, the Netherlands, New Zealand, Norway, Portugal, Spain, Sweden, Switzerland, Turkey, the United Kingdom, and the United States). The guidelines do not legally bind the members and only contain a recommendation to implement the general principles laid down in the text.

The scope of the guidelines relates to physical persons only, applies to both the private and the public sectors, and includes automated and non-automated data processing. They contain the following eight principles for national application:

(1) Collection-limitation, meaning that there should be limits to the collection of personal data and that any such data should be obtained by lawful and fair means and, where appropriate, with the knowledge or consent of the data subject;
(2) Data quality, stipulating that data should be relevant to the purpose for which they are to be used, and, to the extent necessary for those purposes, should be accurate, complete, and kept up-to-date;
(3) Purpose-specification, requiring that the purposes for which personal data are collected should be specified not later than at the time of data collection and that the subsequent use should be respectively limited;
(4) Use-limitation, affirming that personal data should not be disclosed, made available, or otherwise used for purposes other than those previously specified exept with the consent of the data subject or by the authority of the law;
(5) Security safeguards requiring reasonable safety measures;
(6) Openness, claiming a general policy of openness about developments, practices, and policies with respect to personal data and means to establish the existence and nature of personal data;
(7) Individual participation, requiring that the data subject has a right to access and to control the data; and
(8) Accountability, calling for accountability of a data controller for complying with measures giving effect to all these principles.

As far as the international application of privacy laws is concerned, the guidelines in principle request free transborder flow of personal data. However, some interests warrant a restriction of such flow, especially if data are re-exported to circumvent domestic privacy legislation.[164]

b. THE COUNCIL OF EUROPE CONVENTION

A more binding international agreement was achieved by the Council of Europe. On 17 September 1980 the Committee of Ministers of the Council of Europe, which has addressed privacy concerns since 1968, ratified the 'Convention Protecting Individuals with Regard to Automatic Processing of Personal Data'. The convention was opened for signature on 28 January 1981 and has been signed by Austria, Belgium, Denmark, France, West Germany, Greece, Iceland, Italy, Luxembourg, Norway, Portugal, Spain, Sweden, Turkey, and the United Kingdom. It was ratified by France, West Germany, Norway, Spain, and Sweden, and came into force on 1 October 1985. In contrast to the OECD guidelines, which are voluntary in nature, the Council of Europe Convention is a contractual commitment for state parties and is legally binding.

The scope of the Convention is limited to 'natural' persons and to automated files, it applies to automated files in both the private and in the public sectors. The Convention expresses ten basic principles representing minimal standards which must be incorporated into the legislation of the contracting states. Though similar, these principles are narrower and more specific than those of the OECD. They stipulate social justification, collection-limitation, information quality, purpose-specification, limitation of disclosure, security safeguards, openness, time-limitation, accountability, and participation by individuals. Based on the principle of equivalent protection, the main rule of the convention covering transborder data flow between contracting parties is that data flow to a country providing equivalent protection cannot be hindered. However, there are also exceptions of this rule.

In future the Council of Europe will concentrate on adapting these basic principles to specific sectors, such as medical, research, and statistical data.[165]

c. THE RESOLUTIONS AND RECOMMENDATIONS OF THE EUROPEAN COMMUNITIES

Likewise, the European Communities have attempted to harmonize privacy laws since 1976. In its resolutions of 8 April 1979 (relating to the protection of the individual against the technical evolution of informatics), of 8 May 1979 (relating to the rights of the individual in the face of technical developments in data processing), and of 9 March 1982 (relating to the protection of the rights of the individual in the face of technical developments in data processing), the European *Parliament* urged the EC Commission to initiate a community action and recommend to the member states to sign and ratify the Council of Europe Convention.

This was done by the *Commission* of the European Communities on 29 July 1981, when it issued a recommendation to the member states to sign the Council of Europe Convention. In the event that the member states refuse the ratification or the Convention proves to be insufficient the Commission plans to propose an instrument on the basis of the Treaty of Rome. In November 1985 the privacy protection of legal persons was discussed by the '*Legal Observatory*' of the Commission of the European Communities.[166] A policy statement of the International Chamber of Commerce (ICC) on this meeting pleaded against protecting the data of business legal persons by the same legislative provisions which protect the privacy of individuals.[167]

2. The General Concepts and Differences of National Legislations

a. THE PRESENT STATE OF LEGISLATION

The actions by the OECD, the Council of Europe, and the European Communities described above have strongly promoted national privacy legislation. In most Western countries special legislation against infringements of privacy has been passed or prepared:

(1) In *Australia*, the Freedom of Information Act of 9 March 1982, amended by the Freedom of Information Amendment Act 1983 (covering the public sector only without provisions concerning transborder data flow) as well as several state laws (the New South Wales Privacy Committee Act no. 37 of 2 March 1975 being of special interest);

(2) In *Austria*, the Federal Act on the Protection of Personal Data No. 565 of 18 October 1978 (regulating the public and private sector and in principle stipulating administrative authorization for transborder data flows);

(3) In *Canada*, the federal Access to Information Act and the federal Privacy Act (S.C. 1980-81-82-83, c.111), were passed on 28 June 1982 and were put into force on 1 July 1983 (applying to the public sector only without provisions concering transborder data flow), as well as at the provincial level, Quebec's 'An Act Respecting Access to Documents Held by Public Bodies and the Protection of Personal Information' which received the Royal Assent on 23 June 1982 (applying to the public sector only);

(4) In *Denmark*, the Private Registers Act (No. 293) of 8 June 1978 and the Public Authorities' Registers Act (No. 294) of 8 June 1978 (stipulating a license for exporting data in cases where the dissemination of data within Denmark would require a license);

(5) In *France*, the Act No. 78–17 on Data Processing, Data Files, and Individual Liberties on 6 January 1978 (applying to the public and the private sector and demanding that transborder data flow be declared to the National Committee of Data Processing and Freedom;

(6) In *West Germany*, the Federal Data Protection Act of 27 January 1977, which took effect on 1 January 1979 (applying to the federal public sector and the private sector, and allowing transborder data flow if the dissemination of the data is permitted in West Germany) as well as various State Data Protection Acts (applying to the State public sector);

(7) In *Iceland*, Act No. 63/1981 of 25 May 1981 concerning Systematic Recording of Personal Data of 25 May 1981 (applying to the private and the public sector and requiring permission for transborder data flow; the Act expired and was renewed with minor changes in 1985);

(8) In *Israel*, Privacy Act No. 5741–1981 approved by the Knesset on 23 February 1981 and proclaimed on 11 March 1981 (applying to the public and the private sector and requiring registration for transborder data flow);

(9) In *Italy*, Law No. 121 of 1 April 1981 on the Regulation of the State Police Administration (applying to a part of the public sector only);

(10) In *Luxembourg*, the Act of 30 March 1979 Organizing the Identification on Physical and Legal Persons by Number, and the Act of 31 March

1979 Regulating the Use of Nominal Data in Electronic Data Processing (applying to the public and private sector and requiring the permission of the Minister of Informatics for transborder data flow);

(11) In *New Zealand*, the Wanganui Computer Center Act No. 19 of 9 September 1976 (amended by laws no. 83 of 1977, 118 of 1979, and 52 of 1980) and the Official Information Act of 17 December 1982 (covering only the public sector);

(12) In *Norway*, Act No. 48 of 9 June 1978 on Personal Data Registers (effective on 1 January 1980, applying to the public and private sector, and in connection with the Royal Decree of 21 December 1979, requiring only the notification of transborder data flow);

(13) In *Sweden*, the Data Act of 11 March 1973 (Law No. 289), amended by laws no. 334 of 1979 and no. 446 of 1982 (applying to the private and public sector and requiring permission from the Data Inspectorate Board for transborder data flow);

(14) In *Switzerland*, several cantonal laws and a number of municipal regulations covering the public sector only (see especially the Law of the Canton of Geneva of 24 June 1976 on the Protection of Computerized Information, amended by the Law of 17 December 1981; the Law of the Canton of Neuchâtel of 14 December 1982 on the Protection of Privacy; the Law of the Canton of Vaud of May 1981 on Data Banks and the Protection of Personal Data) as well as the guidelines for the processing of personal data in the federal administration of 16 March 1981;

(15) In the *United Kingdom*, the Data Protection Act of 12 July 1984 (applying to the public and private sector and requiring that transborder data flow be registered upon which the Registrator has the power to prohibit the data export).

(16) In the *United States* a variety of specific laws have been enacted, especially the Privacy Act 1974, establishing fair information practices and notification procedures for government agencies (5 USC §552 a); the Fair Credit Reporting Act 1970, covering credit, insurance, and employment information in the private sector (15 USCA §1681–81 t); the Fair Credit Billing Act 1974, protecting privacy in the granting of credit (15 USC §1601); the Freedom of Information Act, including exceptions to the general policy of disclosure of government use of information (4 USCA §5521); the Family Educational Rights and Privacy Act 1974, regulating the information practices of federally funded educational institutions (20 USCA §1232 g); the Right to Financial Privacy Act 1978, permitting government access to customs records of financial institutions for law-enforcement purposes only (12 USCA §§1101–22, 3401–22); the Privacy Protection Act 1980, limiting government officers or employees in searching or seizing work product materials from persons who intend to use them for public communication (42 USC §2000 aa); and the Cable Communications Policy Act

1984, addressing the privacy of cable television subscribers (Pub.L. 98–549, passed 30 October 1984), as well as additional statutes at the State level regulating information-gathering practices or computerized data processing especially addressing government agencies.

In addition to these statutes there are bills pending in many countries to establish or to amend privacy protection. The main ones are:

(1) In *Australia*, a Privacy Bill including the private sector (expected to be passed in 1986);

(2) in *Austria*, an amendment to the Federal Data Protection Act (applying to the private and public sector);

(3) In *Belgium*, a Data Protection Bill presented to Parliament on 10 November 1983 (covering the public and the private sector and containing criminal provisions on eavesdropping and technical optical observation);

(4) In *Canada*, a bill for the revision of the Privacy Act as well as some provincial bills (see, for example, for Ontario Bill 34—An Act to Provide for Freedom of Information and Protection of Individual Privacy; first reading on 12 July 1985);

(5) In *Finland*, a government bill for a Personal Data Register (Data Protection) Act covering the public and private sector (and laid before Parliament on 30 April 1986);

(6) In *West Germany*, various amendments to the Federal Data Protection Act proposed by the Social Democratic Party in 1985, by the Federal Government on 31 January 1986, and by some States on 28 February 1986, as well as several government bills for privacy protection and information flows in the field of prosecution and intelligence agencies;

(7) In *Greece*, a proposal for a bill covering the public and private sector;

(8) In *Italy*, the Data Protection Bill of 5 June 1984 covering the public and private sector;

(9) In *Japan*, a proposal to establish a Data Protection Act;

(10) In the *Netherlands*, a new Data Protection Bill submitted to Parliament in July 1985, covering the public and most of the private sector;

(11) In *Portugal*, the Bill on Data Protection of 16 March 1984, materializing section 35 of the Portuguese Constitution of 2 April 1976, amended 13 August 1982;

(12) In *Spain*, drafts of Data Protection Bills materializing sections 18 and 105 of the Spanish Constitution of 23 December 1978 and covering the public and the private sector (Proposed Resolution No. 13/III of 11 May 1984; Proposed Law No. 64/III of 16 March 1984; Proposed Law No. 110/III of 28 June 1983); and

(13) In *Switzerland*, a proposed Law on the Protection of Personal Data of December 1983 covering the public and the private sector (and supplementing the already existing privacy laws of several cantons).[168]

b. COMPARATIVE ANALYSIS

The work of the OECD, the Council of Europe, and the European Communities has already effected a certain degree of *uniformity* in the general administrative and civil regulations of the various privacy laws. Consequently most of the above-mentioned acts include, for example, provisions covering the limitation of data collection, the individual's right of access to 'his' personal data, and other principles enunciated in the OECD guidelines and in the Council of Europe Convention.

However, as these principles contain general rules only, considerable *differences* remain in general administrative and civil regulations, and as a result in the respective criminal provisions as well. A first major difference between the various privacy legislations can be found in the *legislative rationale*. Whereas the Anglo-American approach is directed at specific solutions to already-recognized rights and specific problems, the Continental law countries prefer comprehensive solutions in general omnibus privacy laws. The reason for this difference in approach does not lie primarily in different evaluations of privacy but mainly in the different legal systems. Whereas the common law evolved in response to specific practical needs, the European legal system tends to create a whole new set of rights and obligations at one point in time.

This difference in thinking and tradition led to the different *scope of application* of privacy legislations, illustrated by the preceding survey on the state of national legislation. Whereas most European laws provide comprehensive coverage of both the public and private sector in a general privacy law, many common-law countries, e.g. the United States, Australia, New Zealand, and Canada (and, until recently, also the United Kingdom), do not have a principal privacy law but more restricted special solutions, especially in the fields of government and consumer credit-reporting agencies. Common-law countries, in addition, do have some special common-law torts protecting privacy (especially 'appropriation', 'false light', 'intrusion', and 'public disclosure'). However, these torts do not, for example, appear to provide a remedy for dissemination of personal information by privately owned computers.

With respect to the scope of application, further differences can be found in the field of the *covered data*. Most laws comprehend name-linked data of individuals or 'natural persons' (such as American, Belgian, British, Canadian, Dutch, Finnish, French, West German, or Swedish law). Nonetheless, some acts and bills also confer rights on *legal persons* and organizations (especially Australia, Austria, Denmark, Iceland, Italy, Luxembourg, New Zealand, Norway, and Switzerland). This question is especially important, as an extension of the general privacy laws to legal persons does not only imply governmental controls of the privacy laws to the data of legal persons but also gives these legal persons a right of access to the data concerning themselves. Additional differences exist with regard to the type of processing of data.

Whereas some laws and bills are only aimed at automatic data processing (especially Austria, Belgium, Italy, Luxembourg, the Netherlands, Portugal, Spain, and the United Kingdom), a considerable number of countries do not specify the form of processing, and hence the legislation also covers certain *manually recorded data* (especially Australia, Canada, Denmark, Finland, France, West Germany, Greece, New Zealand, Norway, Sweden, Switzerland, and the United States).

The *legitimation requirements* for processing personal data also differ, especially in the private sector. Some laws (such as the French and Scandinavian) are based more on formal or *procedural requirements* whereas others (such as the West German) rely more on *substantive rules*. In most countries the procedural and the substantive approach are *combined*.

As far as the *formal requirements* for starting personal DP are concerned, many countries require *registration, declaration, or notification* of all or at least some specific data (see, for example, Austria, Belgium, Denmark, France, Iceland, Italy, the Netherlands, Norway, Spain, and Switzerland). Especially for specific data, some countries even require official *authorization or license* (such as Luxembourg, Portugal, Sweden, and the United Kingdom). The above-described variety in the requirements with respect to transborder data flow is caused primarily by these differences.

The *substantive requirements* for processing personal data also vary. In the *public sector* the use of data is generally admissible when it is needed for the accomplishment of a legitimate agency task (see, for example, sections 6 and 7(2) of the Austrian Data Protection Act or sections 8 and 9 of the West German Federal Data Protection Act). In the *private sector* the use of data is usually permitted and the legal situation is quite clear when the person concerned has given his (written) *consent* or when the use of the data is permitted by *law* (see, for example, section 18 (1) No.1, Austrian Data Protection Act, or section 3 of the West German Federal Data Protection Act). If these two conditions do not apply, the admissibility of using data is in general determined by *balancing the conflicting interests*, that is, the privacy interest of the individual and the legitimate interests of the holder of the information. This is illustrated by section 17 of the Austrian Data Protection Act, which considers the 'legitimate interests' of the processor and the 'interests warranting protection of persons affected', by section 26 of the French Act on Data Processing, Data Files, and Individual Liberties, according to which any natural person is entitled to object, 'for due cause' to the processing of personal data concerning himself, and by sections 23–5, 32 and 33 of the West German Federal Data Protection Act, which allow the use of data if this is necessary to protect the legitimate interests of the holder of the file but only if there is no reason to suppose that it will harm the interests of the person concerned that warrant protection. However, since this balancing of interests is expressed in different legal terms, influenced to a great extent by political evaluations of the importance of privacy protection and applied by different control institutions, it leads not only to different results in the various countries but also to legal uncertainty. In order to ease this uncertainty some countries have created '*absolute*' prohibitions for certain acts and areas, such as the acquisition of data by fraudulent, dishonest, or illegal means (see, for example, section 25, French Act on Data Processing, Data Files, and Individual Liberties, and section 14, Luxembourgian Act Regulating the Use of Nominal Data). Other 'absolute' prohibitions involve the storage of highly sensitive data, concerning, for example, race, religious belief, or political opinions (compare, for example, section 3(2), 17(4), Danish Private Registers Act; section 31, French Act on Data Processing Data Files and Individual Liberties; and section 15, Luxembourgian Act Regulating the Use of Nominal Data). For certain areas or businesses some legal systems also *enumerate those data* which alone can be registered (see, for example, for direct mail agencies, section 17, Danish Private Registers Act).

As already indicated, differences between the various privacy laws can also be found with regard to the *control institutions*. In some European countries *special agencies* for protecting individual freedom are established, such as, for example, in Austria the Data Protection Commission and the Data Protection Council (sections 35–6, Data Protection Act); in France, the National Data Processing and Liberties Commission (sections 6–13, Act on Data Processing, Data Files, and Individual Liberties; or in West Germany, the Commissioner for Data Protection (sections 17–21, Federal Data Protection Act). In other countries, such as the United States, the individual must resort to the *judicial system* to remedy privacy-abuses (the creation of a Privacy Protection Commission is suggested by the Bill of a 'Privacy Protection Act of 1984', H.R. 3743, but this bill is not expected to be passed).

These differences among the general administrative regulations are not only relevant for administrative law but also determine, to a large extent, differences in criminal law, which often refers to these regulations.

3. Penal Concepts and Criminal Offences of Privacy Laws

In most countries computer-related infringements of privacy are covered by two types of criminal provision: the first consists of traditional provisions protecting privacy rights in general (such as the offences of defamation, disclosure of special secrets, or intercepting, recording, and divulging private communications) and the second type involve the new criminal provisions of the privacy acts presented above. Section 189 of the Spanish proposal for a Predraft of a New Criminal Code illustrates that these two types of provision may be linked together. However, since the general offences of defamation do not pose computer-specific problems, and since the protection of special secrets and offences of wiretapping have already been discussed above,[169] the following analysis is confined to the criminal provisions of the new privacy laws.[170] These provisions show considerable differences both in their scope of application and in the offences covered.

a. THE DIFFERENT SCOPES OF APPLICATION

The first difference between the criminal offences found in the various privacy laws concerns the scope of data whose use is prohibited. This is caused by the above-described different fields of application of the respective privacy laws. Legal systems which only have privacy regulations in specific areas, which only cover name-linked data of individuals, or which apply only in cases of automatic data processing generally have penal provisions with a more limited scope of application than those with comprehensive privacy legislation that includes data of legal persons and manually recorded data.[171]

For details of the different scopes of application of privacy legislations, subsection B.2 should be consulted.[172] However, an exception to this general identity of the administrative and the penal scope of application of privacy legislation can be found in a few privacy legislations. An extension of the penal law was adopted especially by the Swedish Data Act, which, in its administrative part, covers personal data of natural persons only, but in section 21 contains a general penal provision applying to all kinds of data.[173] The Portuguese draft of a Privacy Bill also includes penal provisions of a general nature. On the other hand, the penal provisions of the Swiss proposed 'Law on the Protection of Personal Data' of 1983 are limited to the private sector; the public sector is regulated only by administrative law.

b. THE DIFFERENT ACTS COVERED

The main differences among the penal privacy offences, however, do not exist in their general scope of application but in the different illegal acts covered. These differences in penal coverage are mainly caused by a *divergent evaluation* of the *criminal character* of privacy infringements and of the role that penal law should play in this field.

In some countries, especially in North America, criminal law is not widely used for privacy protection. This is illustrated, for example, by the Canadian federal privacy legislation, which only punishes the act of obstructing the work of the Information Commissioner and of the Privacy Commissioner by an administrative fine (see section 67, Access to Information Act, and section 68, Privacy Act). Similarly, in the *United States* at the federal level there are only a few penal provisions concerning computer-related infringements of privacy, and in only a few States have the legislatures recently added special criminal penalties for invasion of privacy involving the use of computer systems, or added privacy sections in the general computer crime laws (such as section 18.2–152.5 of the Code of Virginia). The Data Protection Act of the United Kingdom contains a variety of offences which, however, are mainly formal, with infractions punished by fines only. The new privacy bill of the Netherlands also applies a very restricted penal approach.

Contrary to this, many European privacy laws include *comprehensive lists* of *severely punished criminal offences* which refer to many of the acts

prohibited by administrative law. The criminal provisions of the Belgian
Privacy Bill of 1983, for example, are so voluminous and dispersed through-
out the statute, with extensive references to administrative provisions, that
plans to translate them into English for the appendix of this book were
abandoned. Some legislations—e.g. the Italian privacy bill (sections 23 and
29)—even include punishment for negligent acts. The Spanish proposal for a
Predraft of a new Criminal Code of 1984 (section 189), as well as the
proposals of the Finnish Working Group on Informational Crimes and of the
French Commission for the Revision of the Penal Code, intend to stress the
importance of criminal sanctions of privacy legislations by implementing the
most important infringements in the general Penal Code (in West Germany
specific data of the public sector have been covered since 1974 by section 203,
subsection 2, sentence 2, of the Penal Code).[174]

The following systematization of privacy infringements focuses primarily
on the privacy laws already enacted and demonstrates the wide variety of
penal offences in the various privacy laws.

Infringements of Substantive Privacy Rights

As far as infringements of substantive privacy rights are concerned, most
European privacy laws punish certain cases of illegal *disclosure, dissemination, and obtainment of and/or access to data* (see, for example, sections 48,
49 Austrian Data Protection Act; section 27 (1), no.1 in connection with
section 4 (1) and (2), 9, 12, 16, and 19, Danish Private Registers Act and
section 29 (1), no. 1, Danish Public Authorities' Registers Act; section 43,
French Act on Data Processing, Data Files, and Individual Liberties; section
41 (1), nos 1 and 2, West German Federal Data Protection Act; or section 20
(3) and 21 Swedish Data Act). Some laws go even further, and include the
unlawful use of data (see section 48, Austrian Data Protection Act, which
does not, however, criminalize the mere illegal transmission of data). A
special form of fraudulently obtaining nominal data can be found in the
Luxembourgian law, which punishes the abuse of the right of access by use of
an assumed name (section 35 of the Act Regulating the Use of Nominal
Data).

In contrast to these far-reaching provisions, section 15 of the United
Kingdom Data Protection Act only provides for the imposition of a fine if
personal data in respect of which services are provided by a person carrying
on a computer bureau are disclosed by this person without the prior authority
of the person for whom those services are rendered. In the United States the
Fair Credit Reporting Act 1970 sets out criminal penalties for employees of
consumer-reporting agencies who wilfully disclose information to unauthorized parties and for persons who use fraudulent methods to obtain personal
data from a consumer-reporting agency (15 USC §§1681q–1681r). The
American Privacy Act 1974 also makes punishable the illegal disclosure of
specific individually identifiable information by employees of an agency
(section 3, §552a, paras (1) and (3)). Also at the State level, for example,

California's criminal information statute contains misdemeanour penalties for unauthorized disclosure of private information committed by public officials or employees (sections 81–1117.02 and .03). In some States there exist more far-reaching provisions. According to section 11.46.740 (a) (1), Alaska Statutes, for example, a person commits the offence of criminal use of a computer if he or she, having no right to do so or any reasonable grounds for believing so, accesses a computer and obtains information concerning a person.

In addition to the unlawful dissemination of data a second type of illegal data processing which many privacy legislations also cover is the illegal *entering, modification, and/or falsification of data* with the intent to cause damage (see, for example, section 49, Austrian Data Protection Act, and section 41 (1), no.1, West German Federal Data Protection Act). Section 21 of the Swedish Data Act, which also includes the unlawful alteration of data, shows that these acts can also be covered by general computer-crime statutes.[175] This connection with the above-described general computer sabotage statutes has been illustrated by the new proposals of the Austrian Ministry of Justice (1985).[176] It suggests a general provision against damaging and modifying data, and consequently proposes to omit these acts from section 49 of the Data Protection Act. In the United States the illegal modification of data is covered by general computer-crime statutes in many states.[177]

Whereas some legal systems, such as the West German one, confine punishability to these two main types of acts, many privacy laws also penalize certain acts of unauthorized *collection, recording, and/or storage* of data (see, for example, section 41 in connection with section 26, French Act on Data Processing, Data Files, and Individual Liberties). This is especially the case for data on racial, religious, political, and other highly sensitive matters (section 27 (1), no.1 in connection with sections 3, 9 (2) (3), 17, 21 (1), Danish Private Registers Act; section 42 in connection with sections 30 and 31, French Act on Data Processing, Data Files, and Individual Liberties; section 25 of the Italian bill; and section 33 in connection with sections 16 and 17, Luxembourgian Act Regulating the Use of Nominal Data). It is also true for data acquired by fraudulent, unfair, or illegal means (section 41 in connection with section 25, French Act on Data Processing, Data Files, and Individual Liberties and section 33 in connection with section 14, Luxembourgian Act Regulating the Use of Nominal Data). Further examples of special prohibitions against storing certain information concern data for the purpose of warning persons against doing business with or employing or serving specific persons (section 27 (1), no.1 in connection with section 3 (3), Danish Private Registers Act), or data from direct mailing agencies when the concerned person requests their deletion (section 27 (1), no.1 in connection with section 18, Danish Private Registers Act).

As far as *storage of incorrect data* is concerned, some legal systems rely on the general offences of defamation. Elsewhere, privacy legislation expressly makes it a crime to neglect the updating of data (see, for example, section 27 (1), no.1 in connection with sections 6 (1), (2), 13, Danish Private Registers Act; section 28 of the Italian bill; and section 20 (4), Swedish Data Act). Similarly, the Luxembourgian law makes it punishable not to rectify inaccurate data on request, or not to transmit the correction of such data (section 34 in connection with sections 22 and 23 of the Act Regulating the Use of Nominal Data).

The substantive infringements of privacy rights, however, differ not only in the data covered and the types of acts punished but also according to the extent to which the described acts are *permitted*. As the penal provisions which determine this question either refer to the respective general provisions of the privacy laws or regulate the justification of the use of personal data by general clauses which are similar to those of the administrative provisions, the previously described heterogeneities, inaccuracies, and uncertainties in the field of administrative law can also be found within the respective penal provisions.[178]

Formal Offences Against Supervisory Agencies and Regulations
Because of the uncertainties of the substantive provisions many legal systems rely to a great extent on additional offences against formal legal requirements or against orders of supervisory agencies. This movement away from a substantial to a procedural approach is favoured by a widespread European way of thinking which believes that data-protection laws should not only prevent abuses in the field of privacy but should also provide a general scheme determining the circulation of information in society.[179]

The formal offences against supervisory agencies which are therefore included in most privacy laws generally contain much more precise descriptions of the prohibited acts than do the substantive ones. However, these formal provisions also vary considerably within the various national legislations. The variations between the formal offences are not only based on differences in administrative law concerning the existence, nature, and powers of supervisory agencies and the respective duties of the data processors, but they are mainly caused by different answers to the fundamental question as to whether such 'formal' offences should be criminal in nature. This leads to the result that some countries, such as Denmark or France, punish formal offences against supervisory agencies and regulations with *severe criminal sanctions*, while others, such as West Germany, regard such offences as 'Ordnungswidrigkeiten', 'petty offences', 'irregularities', or 'administrative offences', punished only by (*administrative*) *fines*. A *most interesting compromise* has now been adopted by a new Finnish bill for a Personal Data Register Act of 1986 which, in section 44, requires that the violation of the data-protection rules must cause a *concrete danger* to a data subject's privacy or to other rights.

The main type of formal infraction which is covered by penal law in many States concerns the *infringement of the legal requirements for starting per-*

sonal data processing (such as registration, notification, application for registration, declaration, or licensing), the use of data files for purposes or time limits other than those declared to the authorities in these initial declarations, or the disregard of terms and conditions subject to which a license was given (see, for example, section 27 (1) no.1 in connection with sections 8, 20 (1) and (2), 21 (2), and 27 (2), no. 4, Danish Private Registers Act; sections 41 and 42 in connection with sections 28 and 44, French Act on Data Processing, Data Files, and Individual Liberties; section 32, Luxembourgian Act Regulating the Use of Nominal Data; and section 20 (1) and (2), Swedish Data Act). The Italian bill even provides a punishment for negligent acts of this nature (section 23). Contrary to these severe regulations, in some countries, such as Austria, West Germany, or the United Kingdom, neglect of registration requirements or registration containing incorrect or incomplete particulars is punished only by a fine (section 50 (1) Austrian Data Protection Act; section 42 (1), no.4 West German Federal Data Protection Act; and sections 5 (5) and 6 (6), the United Kingdom Data Protection Act). Similarly, in the United States, for the public sector the Privacy Act 1984 makes it a misdemeanour to maintain a system of records without meeting specified notice requirements (section 552 a para. i (2)).

Additional formal offences which can be found in many European privacy legislations are infringement of certain *regulations, prohibitions, or decisions* of the surveillance authorities (see, for example, section 27 (1), no.2 in connection with sections 5 (1), 15 (2), and 27 (1), no. 5, Danish Private Registers Act; and section 24 of the Italian bill) and the *refusal to give information or the statement of false information* to the surveillance authorities (section 27 (1), no.2 in connection with section 22 (2), Danish Private Registers Act; section 20 (6), Swedish Data Act; and sections 10 (9) and 12 (10), the United Kingdom Data Protection Act). In section 50 (1), Austrian Data Protection Act, and section 42 (1), no.5, West German Federal Data Protection Act, similar acts are punished only with administrative fines. Additional offences concern the *hindering* of the surveillance authorities (section 37, Luxembourgian Act Regulating the Use of Nominal Data), *refusal to grant access* to property, and *refusal to permit inspections* by surveillance authorities (see the administrative fine provided by section 42 (1), no.5, West German Federal Data Protection Act), or obstructing the execution of a warrant (covered by a fine in section 12, schedule 4, the United Kingdom Data Protection Act).

Additional 'Ordnungswidrigkeiten' in the West German Federal Data Protection Act include *failure to appoint a controller of data protection* in the company (section 42 (1), no.2) and *neglect to record* the grounds or means for the dissemination of personal data (section 42 (1), no.3).

Infringement of the Individual's Information Rights
In most European countries it is also an offence not to inform the party registered or to do so falsely, or not to reply to a request regarding a right of

access or to do so falsely (section 2 (1), no. 1 in connection with sections 5 (2), 10 (1), 11 (1), (2), 14, 15, and 24, Danish Private Registers Act; section 34 in connection with section 20, Luxembourgian Act Regulating the Use of Nominal Data; and section 20 (5), Swedish Data Act). In West German law this act is punished only as an 'Ordnungswidrigkeit' (by a fine) (section 42 (1), no.1 of the Federal Data Protection Act).

Neglecting Security Measures
Some countries go even further and punish the *neglect of security measures* by an administrative fine (section 36, Luxembourgian Act Regulating the Use of Nominal Data) or even as a criminal offence (section 27 (1), no.2 in connection with sections 6 (3), (4), and 20 (3), Danish Private Registers Act; section 42 in connection with section 29, French Act on Data Processing, Data Files, and Individual Liberties; or section 26 of the Italian privacy bill).

c. SUMMARY AND CONCLUSIONS

The present survey on criminal privacy offences in Western countries demonstrates that these offences contain considerable differences and heterogeneities. Contrary to the limited concepts of criminal privacy infringements in North American States, many European countries make extensive use of criminal offences which are not only wide in their scope of application but are also often extremely vague. This heterogeneity and vagueness of the penal provisions creates severe legal uncertainty and impedes transborder data flows.

4. Suggestions for Future Action

In order to avoid national transborder data control, which would not only be ineffective but would also hinder free trade and constitute a major threat to privacy, the harmonization of privacy laws should be continued. This should particularly be done in specific areas (such as those of medical data, credit reporting, and personal information systems), as this enables the formulation of more precise regulations as well as the possible harmonization of the different approaches of American and European law systems. A good platform for such solutions is offered by the necessary adaptation of privacy laws to the increasing use of telecommunications networks, of personal computers, and of audiovisual recognition techniques as well as by the considerations on 'second-generation' privacy laws, which are currently being undertaken in various States and international organizations.

Harmonization should not be limited to the field of civil and administrative privacy law but should also extend to *criminal-law provisions* where international comparison and harmonization have not yet really begun. Considering the varying and often imprecise penal provisions in the various countries analysed above and the many countries which can be affected by transborder data flow operations, it would be desirable to limit criminalization to certain intolerable acts to be precisely described. In order to achieve this aim, in December 1985 the author recommended to the Select Committee of Experts on Computer-related Crime of the Council of Europe at its first meeting of placing the harmonization of criminal privacy infringements on its agenda for future work. The Committee agreed to the discussion of this item and will treat the question of criminal privacy protection in 1986.

Taking into account the considerable differences between the national legislations in the field of criminal privacy protection, the author would suggest a two-stage working plan in order to arrive at an international consensus in this field: As a first step, the Council of Europe and/or other appropriate international organizations should try to agree on certain basic principles which should be taken into account by all national legislations in the field of computer-related criminal privacy legislation and which could be laid down in a recommendation or a convention. Based on these principles, a second step would involve the establishment of a list of acts of criminal privacy infringements. This list of acts could be put in the form of a model law and prevent both under- and overcriminalization. As a starting-point for discussion, the author would propose that the fundamental ideas on which this list of acts should be based include the following principles:[180]

(1) The protection of privacy against offences caused by modern computer technology is of great importance. However, this protection should be based primarily on administrative and civil law regulations. Recourse to criminal law should be made only as a last resort. This means that criminal sanctions should be used only in cases of severe offences in which adequate regulation cannot be achieved by administrative or civil law measures (*Ultima Ratio Principle*).

(2) The respective criminal provisions must describe the forbidden acts precisely and should avoid vague general clauses. Precise descriptions of illegal acts can easily be achieved, for example, for specific unfair methods of obtaining data or for specific sensitive data. In cases in which precise descriptions of illegal acts are not possible due to the necessity of a difficult balancing of interests (privacy versus freedom of information), criminal law should decline to incriminate substantive infringements of privacy and adopt a formal approach, based on administrative requirements of notification of potentially harmful DP activities. Failure to complain against these notification requirements and to obey regulations of the data protection authorities could then be criminalized. These formal offences are in accordance with the principle of culpability as long as they can be considered bans *per se* (Gefährdungsdelikte, délits-obstacle), punishing the endangering of privacy rights. In many areas, criminal privacy infringements, therefore, would presuppose both the infringement of formal requirements as well as the endangering of substantive privacy rights (*Principle of Precision and of Formal Guarantees*).

(3) The criminalized acts should be described as clearly as possibly by the respective penal law provisions. Therefore, a too-extensive use of the referral technique (that is, the technique pursuant to which activities regulated outside the penal law provisions are criminalized by reference) makes criminal provisions unclear and incomprehensible and should be avoided. If implicit or explicit references of the criminal law are used, the criminal provision itself should at least give an adequate idea of the forbidden acts (*Clearness Principle*).

(4) Different computer-related infringements of privacy should not be criminalized in one global provision. The principle of culpability requires a differentiation according to the interests affected, the acts committed, the status of the perpetrator, as well as of his intended aims and other mental elements (*Principle of Differentiation*).

(5) In principle, computer-related infringements of privacy should only be punishable if the perpetrator acts with intent. Criminalization of negligent acts requires a special justification (*Principle of Intent*).

(6) Minor computer-related offences against privacy should be punished only on application or instigation of the victim or of the Privacy Protection Commissioner or of the Privacy Protection Authority (*Principle of Application*).

The recommendation and acceptance of these principles by international organizations and national legislators could help to establish an adequate criminal law system in the DP area and facilitate transborder data flows.

C. PROCEDURAL PROBLEMS

Computer crime is not only posing new problems for substantive penal law but for procedural law as well. Since international study of these problems is still in its initial phase, these problems can only be briefly mentioned here.

1. Evidence from Computer Records

a. DIFFERENCES BETWEEN CONTINENTAL AND COMMON-LAW COUNTRIES

The admissibility of evidence from computer records in court depends to a great extent on the underlying fundamental principles of evidence in the respective country. As a result, two main groups of countries must be differentiated.

The *Continental law countries and many others*, such as Austria, Denmark, Finland, West Germany, France, Japan, Norway, Portugal, and Sweden, are based on the principle of *free introduction and free evaluation of evidence*. In these countries the courts, in principle, can use all kinds of evidence and must weigh the extent to which it can be relied on. Legal systems based on these principles, in general, do not hesitate to introduce computer records as evidence. Problems occur only when procedural provisions provide specific regulations for the proof of judicial acts or proof with legal documents. In these cases the content of a document could be regarded as a 'copy', with the consequence that the court may inquire into the underlying data, as it is generally more reliable. In France, in the field of civil law, Law No. 80–525 of 12 July 1980 on Proof of Judicial Acts introduced new possibilities of proof of judicial acts, according to which, under certain conditions, originals can be replaced by reliable copies (see section 1348, Civil Code).[181]

Contrary to the legal situation in Continental law countries, the *common-law countries*, especially Australia, Canada, the United Kingdom, and the United States, are, to a greater extent, characterized by an oral and adversarial procedure. In these countries a witness can only testify concerning his personal knowledge, permitting his statements to be verified by cross-examination. Knowledge from secondary sources, such as other persons, books, or records, is regarded as '*hearsay evidence*', and is, in principle, inadmissible. However, there exist several exceptions to the hearsay evidence rule, such as the 'business records exception', or the 'photographic copies exception'. The business records exception, for example, permits a business record created in the course of everyday commercial activity, to be introduced as evidence even if there is no individual who can testify from personal knowledge.

In these countries the question as to whether computer files and printouts are inadmissible hearsay evidence or fall under one of these exceptions has been subject to extensive debate.[182] Some common-law countries have accepted computer printouts as falling within the business records exception. Others have elaborated laws and bills allowing computer records to be admitted as evidence if certain conditions are met.

b. NEW ACTS AND BILLS IN COMMON-LAW COUNTRIES

The *English* Police and Criminal Evidence Act 1984, which received the Royal Assent on 31 October 1984, provides in section 69 (a) that a statement in a document produced by a computer must satisfy the following conditions in addition to the general requirements for admissibility of documents to be used as evidence:

(1) That there are no reasonable grounds for believing that the statement is inaccurate because of improper use of the computer;

(2) That at all material times the computer was operating properly, or if not, that any respect in which it was not operating properly or was out of operation was not such as to affect the production of the document or the accuracy of its contents; and

(3) That any relevant conditions specified in rules of court under subsection (2) below are satisfied.

Part II of Schedule 3 of the Act, which supplements section 69 by making more detailed provision as to the admissibility of computer evidence, provides in Paragraph 11 that in estimating the weight of a statement admissible under section 69 consideration shall be given to all the circumstances, including contemporaneity and the question as to whether any person who was in a position to do so had any incentive to conceal or misrepresent the facts. The Police and Criminal Evidence Act of 1984 applies to England and Wales only. The Scottish Law Commission intends to produce proposals on that topic in 1986.

Australian law is tackling the problem by using two different approaches, which can be classified as the 'computer-specific' approach and the 'business records approach'; in some jurisdictions both concepts are adopted simultaneously. The 'computer-specific' approach uses legislative provisions that are specifically aimed at the admissibility of computer-produced evidence. Such provisions can be found in the Australian Capital Territory (Part VII of the Evidence Ordinance 1971), in Queensland (section 95 of the Evidence Act 1977), and in South Australia (Part VIA of the Evidence Act 1929–83). On the other hand, the 'business records' approach considers computer-produced evidence only as one aspect in the general question of admissibility of business records. It is used in the Australian Captial Territory (section 29 (2) of the Evidence Ordinance 1971), in the Commonwealth (Part IIIA of the Evidence Act 1905), in New South Wales (Part IIC of the Evidence Act 1898), in Queensland (section 93 of the Evidence Act 1977), in South Australia (section 45a of the Evidence Act 1929–83), and in Victoria (section 55 of the Evidence Act 1958). In 1985, the Australian Law Reform Commission produced an Interim Report on the law of evidence and suggested a Draft Evidence Bill which would be used in the Federal Court. The Bill is currently a topic of public discussion.

In the *United States* several state laws contain provisions which specifically address problems of evidence. In 1983 the Evidence Code of *California* was amended by a new section 1500.5, which is identical to section 3 of the Suggested State Legislation of the State Governments Committee. The new section states that 'computer recorded information or computer programs, or copies of computer recorded information or computer programs, shall not be rendered inadmissible by the best evidence rule'. A printed representation of computer information or computer programs shall be admissible to prove the existence and content of the computer information. The printed representations will be presumed to be accurate representations of the computer information that they purport to present. This presumption, however, only affects the burden of proof of producing evidence. If any party to a judicial proceedings introduces evidence that such a printed representation is inaccurate or unreliable, the party introducing it as evidence will have the burden of proving, by a preponderance of evidence, that the printed representation is the best available evidence of the existence and content of the respective computer information or computer programs. In *Iowa*, the new computer crime law of 1984 in section 716A.16 simply creates a new rule of evidence, saying that 'in a prosecution under this chapter, computer printouts shall be admitted as evidence of any computer software, program, or data contained in or taken from a computer, notwithstanding an applicable rule of evidence to the contrary'.

In *Canada*, a new Evidence Act (Bill S–33) was introduced into the Senate on 18 November 1982.[183] The Bill included provisions relevant to the admissibility of computer printouts and other computer-generated evidence in judicial proceedings. After the change of Parliament the Bill was not reintroduced. Instead, the Canadian Department of Justice consulted with members of the legal profession and held in March 1985 a national conference on the admissibility of computer records in order to make a number of changes to Bill S–33. The new proposals of the Department have not yet been made public.

c. INTERNATIONAL CO-ORDINATION, ESPECIALLY IN CIVIL PROCEDURAL LAW

In *civil procedural law* there exist similar problems. Here, the use of computer-readable data as evidence in court proceedings is discussed at the international level, especially by the United Nations Commission on International Trade Law (UNCITRAL) and by the Customs Co-operation Council (CCC). In February 1985 a draft UNCITRAL recommendation and a draft CCC resolution were elaborated. The UNCITRAL recommendation, which was adopted in June 1985, urges governments to review the legal rules affecting the use of computer records as evidence in ligitation in order to eliminate unnecessary obstacles preventing their admission.[184] The draft CCC recommendation, among others, expresses its full support for the development of an international instrument concerning the requirements that would give an electronic signature or an authentification of computer-transmitted information the same legal effect or status as a traditional signature.[185]

2. Procedural Problems in International Computer-crime Cases

In international computer-crime cases additional procedural problems arise. For example, the possibility of committing a crime by remote DP in one country with results in another may lead to *concurrent claims of jurisdiction* based on the principle of territoriality. In order to avoid double-jeopardy effects, this may necessitate a re-examination of the definitions of the competent jurisdiction (especially of the principle of *territoriality*) and of the international *conventions on the transfer of proceedings*.[186]

The applicability of the conventions concerning *mutual assistance* (see especially the European Convention of 20 April 1959) and *extradition* (see especially the European Convention on Extradition of 13 December 1957) in computer-crime cases is a further example of new procedural law problems caused by computer crime. This issue is closely linked to the problems of substantive penal law mentioned above, since double criminality is one of the basic requirements in extradition conventions and since some countries may make double criminality a condition to give mutual assistance in certain cases (see article 5 (1) of the European Convention on mutual assistance in criminal matters of 1959). For extradition offences containing a list of extraditable offences, the problem is obvious. At its first session in December 1985 the Select Committee of Experts of the *Council of Europe* agreed to deal with these questions during 1986 and 1987.

International prosecution of certain computer crimes is also raising the question as to whether national judicial authorities have to ask for a *rogatory commission* when they can easily *gain access to the database* of a company located abroad via the terminal of a national branch of this company. Further questions concern the admissibility of *wiretapping of computer communications* by judicial authorities, the *secrecy of documents* in mutual assistance procedures, and the *restitution of damages*, especially in cases in which information is copied.

D. THE NEED FOR COMPARATIVE LAW AND INTERNATIONAL CO-OPERATION

The present analysis of the main legal problems caused by computer crime shows that information technology calls for new legislative efforts in various areas of the law. These should be co-ordinated at an international level.

International co-operation is recommended not only in order to profit from foreign legal experiences. As far as *civil and administrative economic law* are concerned, harmonized solutions are also necessary in order to secure equal conditions of competition, to facilitate free transborder data flow, and to avoid the transfer of undesirable or detrimental actions in foreign countries. In many areas of the law relating to computer crime (especially in the field of trade-secret law, copyright law, chip-protection law, tax law, and privacy law) the harmonization of the civil law is also a prerequisite for effecting a uniform penal law which refers to and depends on civil-law regulations. This harmonization of *penal and procedural law* is important, especially in order to protect the international data networks, to enable the functioning of international instruments of co-operation in criminal matters, and to guarantee that evidence gathered in one country is admissible in court in another.

Another solution would cause 'data havens' and 'computer-crime havens', and therefore lead to restrictions in transborder data flow. This would imperil privacy, trade secrets, and the free economic development of an international information market. As data can be transferred in an encoded form in a telephone call of a few seconds' duration, such efforts of limitation and control would also be doomed to failure.

The international information market and international data networks therefore have condemned *national* legal solutions to the archives of the past and made international solutions a necessity. As reform proposals concerning the emerging information market are currently being discussed in most countries, it is not only necessary but also convenient to harmonize or at least co-ordinate the new computer laws at this point in time.

V.

The Security Measures of Computer-users

Empirical analysis shows that most cases of computer crime were caused, enabled, or at least simplified by the victim's inadequate security systems. Furthermore, since detection routines were often missing and measures for risk- and loss-reduction had not been prepared by the companies, in many cases the perpetrators were able to continue their work for a long time, resulting in unnecessary high losses.

Fighting computer crime is therefore first and foremost a question of prevention by the companies and individuals concerned. Thus this chapter will discuss (A) the aims and scope, (B) the establishment, and (C) the main elements of an effective safety strategy.

A. AIMS AND SCOPE OF SAFETY STRATEGIES

1. The Aims to be Achieved

Computer-security strategies have to fulfil five main functions. First, they have to *deter* people from trying to commit any unauthorized acts. Second, because this aim is, in many cases, unachievable, security measures primarily have to *prevent* the successful completion of computer crimes. Third, since such prevention of computer crimes cannot always be attained, especially within reasonable costs, safety strategies have to *detect* computer crime in order to terminate the execution of completed acts, to prevent the completion of attempts, to permit correction and recovery, and to generally deter other potential perpetrators. Fourth, safety strategies have to *minimize the effects and damages* of computer crimes which could not be prevented and to simplify recovery and correction. In addition to these four aims of deterrence, prevention, detection, and risk-minimization, which are in the interest of the computer user, safety measures finally have to *fulfil legal requirements*, especially of privacy, tax, and commercial law, thus also serving social and public interests.

117

2. The Threats to be Covered

The scope of a company's safety strategy must not be restricted to the topic of computer crime. Besides the intentional acts of computer crime (and the above-mentioned legal requirements), consideration must also be given to *threats caused by negligence*, human errors and professional incompetence, to *natural occurrences and environmental forces*, such as extreme temperatures, fire, storms, water, smoke, and living organisms, as well as to air-conditioning breakdowns and power failure. The implications of *labour strikes* should also be taken into account. Organized labour has recognized the strategic importance of DP installations since the early 1970s, and has used it effectively to produce considerable results by small numbers of employees, especially in France and the United Kingdom.

The efficient development of safety strategies should consider all of these threats from the outset. Although this book focuses on the aspect of computer crimes, the organizational approach described in Section B is also applicable to the other above-mentioned threats and many of the security measures described in Section C are also effective in thoses cases.

B. THE ESTABLISHMENT OF A SECURITY STRATEGY

1. The Need for Risk-awareness and Task-force Organization

The inadequate safety measures of a company in most cases are caused by a *lack of awareness* of the problems involved in data security. An essential prerequisite for the establishment of safety measures[1] is therefore to overcome this deficiency by informing potential victims of the dangers inherent in DP. Computer-users must be aware that their DP systems are not only dealing with 'technical' questions but are handling the company's entire assets. They should recognize, for example, the need to apply the same personal security measures to certain key personnel within the DP areas as were formerly applied to accountants, cashiers, or tellers. Companies depending on DP application have to know the risks and consequences of the destruction of their entire computer data in order to produce and update backup copies of all files. Companies storing valuable knowledge in computer files have to measure the risk of appropriation of their secret data by competitors to decide about adequate access control systems or use of telecommunications systems. However, this information concerning potential computer-related crimes is not only necessary for the motivation of people in charge to provide security measures. It is also a prerequisite for the cost–benefit analysis which is necessary before deciding upon safety measures (see subsection 2.c, below).

It is obvious that this general risk-awareness of the companies concerned is an insufficient basis for security management. In order to obtain a more precise conception and control of the problem the companies concerned have to install a *task force responsible* for all further security management. This may comprise representatives from all sections related to computer security, such as the computer, audit, personnel, legal, insurance, plant-protection, and fire departments. The task force should be assisted by an outside consultant specialized in the field of computer crime and security, especially in firms with little experience in computer security. As the subsequent implementation of security masures will have to overcome considerable resistances and hostility, the task force should be led from the beginning by a senior manager with an appropriate reputation and sufficient authority.

2. Safeguard-determination

The question of which safety measures should be implemented in a company should not be decided arbitrarily by the adaptation of external checklists or on the basis of rules of thumb, but in a rational way based on the principles of (a) identification and evaluation of assets, (b) identification and assessment of threats and risks, as well as (c) a cost–benefit analysis.

a. IDENTIFICATION OF ASSETS

Computer-users can only protect themselves effectively against the threats of computer crime if they know which objects must be protected. Consequently, the first step of the task force responsible for security management must be to identify and evaluate those of the company's assets in need of protection. The performance of this *identification and evaluation of assets* primarily must stress the protection of people (a matter of course, which, however, is also of interest to the company aiming at maintaining continuous production), hardware facilities, system programs, application programs, and other internal and external data containing valuable information, money, supplies, and merchandise. The assets, especially the various data, must be evaluated and listed.

b. RISK-EVALUATION

An effective security strategy has to know against what kinds of attack originating from which perpetrators the evaluated assets must be protected. Therefore the task force responsible for computer security management, as a second step, has to identify the potential threats of losses. As was mentioned above, this *risk-analysis* should not only consider the threats of computer crime but also take into account the acts caused by negligence, error, and professional incompetence, as well as strikes and natural disasters. The necessary risk-identification thereby can not only be based on the internal loss-experience of the concerned company but also must utilize the experiences of other companies. One of the main goals of the above systematization of objects, *modi operandi*, and perpetrators of computer crime was to enable this utilization of external loss experience. The phenomenological study of computer crime given in Chapter II should therefore be the basis for the development of any safety strategy. Readers only interested in risk control of computer crime who have not read this chapter are encouraged to first familiarize themselves with this general analysis and systematization of computer crime.

Risk-evaluation must include an assessment of the probabilities of the stated risks. It is obvious that this *risk-assessment* is extremely difficult, and in many areas only a rough estimation can be provided. In some cases, such as the fields of data-keying errors caused by negligence or of fraud against cash-dispenser machines, there may be enough experience to use actuarial methods and formulae. In most areas, however, this is impossible due to the unknown 'dark figure' of computer crime. The estimates concerning the extent and 'dark figures' of such crime given above are intended to provide some orientation. Another approach to risk-assessment could be based on assumptions concerning the number of people who could cause losses.

c. SAFEGUARD-SELECTION

As a third step, the task force should collect information concerning possible safeguards which could form a barrier between the identified assets and the identified threats. The effects of the safety measures should be evaluated. This *collection and evaluation of safeguards* should use, to the greatest extent possible, books, checklists, standards of due care, and information obtainable from consultants. A systematization and an overview of the most important safety measures which should be considered will be given below (Section C).

The compilation and listing of assets, threats, and safety measures will show that there are a wide variety of combinations and various choices of safety strategies which can prevent the identified threats causing losses to the identified assets. The available safeguards and safety strategies should be selected by the criteria of *costs and effectiveness*, especially by comparing the costs and effects of alternative safety strategies and by weighing the potential losses of assets and the assessment of risks against the financial, time, and efficiency costs of the security measures and their effectiveness in *cost–benefit analysis*.

As was previously stated, the selection of safeguards also has to take into account *legal requirements* concerning computer security. In the past few years, in most Western countries computer security has become a requirement imposed by laws and regulations, especially by tax and business law concerning proper book-keeping and by privacy law in order to protect social and public interests. In future these requirements will increase, especially in the field of public-user systems and in the course of the development and recognition of electronic signatures (for criminal provisions requiring a certain protection of DP systems see *supra*, Chapter IV, especially p. 88).

Legal requirements for data protection could even lead to a system which will be able to evaluate the value of security measures (for example, by use of a point system which would maintain the users' freedom to decide on the types of security systems applied). On the other hand, it has also to be considered that an increasing number of laws are limiting the use of certain safeguards, such as the privacy laws limiting investigation into the background of personnel.[2]

3. Testing the System and Implementing Possible Countermeasures

Security systems must not only be *developed in theory* but also be *tested practically*. One of the most important test methods is the application of *cases and 'scenarios'* which match the identified threats to the identified assets. The systematization and the case descriptions given in Chapter II above can be used as such scenarios for testing a developed safety strategy. Another method is the installation of 'tiger teams' which try to break the security system with the consent of senior management but without the knowledge of the DP department.

The most important point for testing and perfecting a security system is the consideration and implementation of possible *countermeasures developed and used by the potential perpetrators*, who will try to circumvent the safety measures installed by the potential victims. In order to evaluate the effects of their safety strategies and to install effective countermeasures, DP-users must therefore be informed about techniques used by perpetrators to bypass security measures. This anticipating of perpetrators' reactions is a prerequisite to winning the current competition between prevention, anti-prevention, and anti-anti-prevention techniques.

The circumvention of DP security measures by perpetrators can take place on several levels, the use of which primarily depends on the perpetrators' functions and skills. Because of the danger of criminal reproduction, only a general outline of practices revealed up to the present will follow.

a. PERPETRATORS' ORGANIZATIONAL COUNTERMEASURES

In many computer-crime cases the perpetrators have been able to circumvent safety measures by simple organizational techniques without any skills in programming or computer technique. An easy and increasingly applied method to circumvent dual controls, for example, is the *collusion* of several perpetrators, which can be achieved by voluntary participation and profit-sharing, bribery, or extortion.

Checks for *plausibility* and upper and lower limits which become known are bypassed by the perpetrators' 'modesty' in staying below the checked sums; perpetrators who know that subsidies for families with more than 10 children are especially checked will not manipulate allowances for one family with 12 children but for two families with six.

Causing an *emergency situation* such as a system breakdown shortly before the execution of an important job tied to specific times is an effective method of forcing management to dispense with segregation of jobs and to allow the programmer direct access to the computer. Similarly, causing of several false alarms can condition the security staff to ignore a true alarm.

Secret *passwords* may, in many cases, be obtained by a search for written notes, by good observation, or by hoax phone calls and questions (such as 'Do you know the *new* password already?').

b. PERPETRATORS' COUNTERMEASURES IN THE FIELD OF OPERATING AND APPLICATION PROGRAMMING

A wide variety of techniques to circumvent safety measures are at the perpetrators' disposal if he has some knowledge of operating and programming. The most frequently used method of circumventing safety controls on the program level has been dealt with above, i.e. the suppression and alteration of *control outputs* and control logs, for example by use of 'Trojan-horse' routines built into regular application programs.

Access-control systems designed to prevent such illegal acts can be wiped out, for example, by inserting into a utility program applied by all users a routine which will obtain special privileges for the perpetrator's password when this program is used by a privileged program.[3] These *'Trojan-horse' routines* can be equipped with programmes which can cause their erasure after execution so that all traces of the illegal activity are destroyed. Another widespread method of providing access to password-protected access-control systems is the insertion of additional *private passwords* in DP systems. This method is particularly favoured by employees in the field of telecommunications about to leave the company in order to guarantee further access to their employer's computer system. The same result can be achieved by the insertion of a program routine which *records* and stores the company's *password alterations* in a perpetrator's *secret mailbox*. Programs which automatically test one password after another or which make an active computer system appear to be inactive in order to capture the user's secret password are further methods of evading password protection.

Another easily applied technique of bypassing access-control systems is the use of privileged *utility programs*, which can copy or destroy privileged data or writeover labels on files. In many computer systems there exist *stand-alone utilities* (such as specific copy functions) which do not need a special operation system and can be used (for example, after the breakdown of the operation system) without a supervisor providing access-control facilities and log-files. Logging procedures and job-accounting routines installed to detect such irregular program applications can also be wiped out by *giving common names* of unsuspicious application programs to the irregularly applied programs, as was done in the above-mentioned West German case of software theft.[4] If dangerous utilities are restricted and locked in the company concerned the perpetrator can still *import utilities* trom other computer centres. Logging procedures as well as restrictions on utility programs can also be circumvented by the *export of data files* to the non-protected environment of another computer centre. An easily practised method in order to circumvent controls of data carriers which are leaving the company is the concealment of information by its *encodement*; as a result of this technique a person who is checking the data file will only register useless data instead of valuable information.

c. PERPETRATORS' COUNTERMEASURES IN THE FIELD OF SYSTEM PROGRAMMING

Considerable extensions of techniques to circumvent safety measures exist for perpetrators with *technical skills*, especially in the field of *operating systems*. Such people, for example, can build in 'Trojan-horse' techniques not only among the often tens of thousands of program routines of application programs but also into an operating system with sometimes up to five or six million instructions, the assembler, the *compiler* and *circuitry*, which are not usually checked by the audit department. Such *changes in the operating system* are not only dangerous because of the resulting possibilities to circumvent access-control systems but also with regard to the virus and sabotage programs discussed above,[5] which can lead to disastrous consequences when implemented in the privileged parts of the operating systems. For example, simple method of inserting such a virus into the operating system could be the mailing of an infiltrated version of the operating system to the user by *pretending to deliver a new version* of the program, originating from its regular producers. Another method would be to *bribe an employee of the supplier* of the operating system to deliver a special version of the software.

Furthermore, programmers with expertise in the operating system can use *system anomalies* as trapdoors. '*Asynchronous attacks*', based on checkpoint restart capabilities of computer systems, for example, permit access to the backup copy of the computer program produced by the system during working hours, and enable production programs, status data, and the method of operation to be changed. In the field of telecommunications systems, methods have been discovered which make it possible to pass terminal commands through the *electronic mail feature* of general communications systems.[6]

d. WIRETAPPING AND OTHER 'TECHNICAL' METHODS

For perpetrators with technical expertise wiretapping offers a wide variety of possibilities of obtaining data and passwords and of interfering with data communication, especially in the field of remote DP. As previously described in Chapter II, subsection A.2, the techniques of wiretapping may range from a coil on a drop-wire to the picking up of stray microwaves or to penetrations of data-switching computers. If the potential victim tries to prevent improper use of wiretapped passwords (for example, by using non-recurrent passwords or transaction codes which are only valid for one-access, transformation passwords or callback procedures), the perpetrator can use techniques of *active infiltration* by intercepting in a communications system a hidden computer which is accessing the main computer when the legitimate terminal is inactive. (These methods are referred to as 'piggy-back-entry', 'between-the-lines-entry', 'line-grabbing', and 'cancel-sign-off-technique').[7]

For additional 'technical' methods one can refer to the above-described cash-dispenser manipulations, which illustrate the construction of special technical devices, the interception of radiation, or the deciphering of codes. As far as protection by 'intelligent' chip cards is concerned, it should be noted that 'analysers' already exist which are able to read out the information stored in the existing 'first generation' of chip cards.

4. Implementation, Control, and Updating of the Safety System

It is obvious that a safety strategy not only has to be written in manuals but also successfully *implemented and maintained* in practice. This can be extremely difficult, because in many cases safeguards are making work more time-consuming and difficult. First, management must approve the plan. Second, staff members must be convinced that the safeguards are in their own and the company's best interests in order to be motivated to accept and practise the security measures. (In a West German company, for example, staff members with no motivation for security aspects installed a program-modification to set control sums to zero in order to avoid the burdensome task of searching for mistakes.) For both purposes, a good explanation of safeguards, especially using scenarios and experiences of loss by other firms, is necessary. As many departments are involved in the field of computer security, the designation of specific persons with the responsibility for iden-tified safeguards is most important in both the implementation and mainten-ance phases of the safety system.

The system has to be *tested by the audit department* after implementation. In the subsequent phase *permanent control* of the maintenance of safeguards is most essential. If safeguards are not continually controlled, laziness and negligence will soon ruin even the best-developed safety system. A good method of control here can be the above-mentioned test attacks by outsiders or insiders ('tiger teams') trying to intrude upon the system with the consent of the senior management or the audit department but without other peoples' knowledge.

This method can also help to provide information for the *updating of the safety system*, which is essential, as assets, threats, and technical developments will be subject to continual changes. Security management presents a con-tinual challenge.

C. THE MAIN ELEMENTS OF AN EFFECTIVE SAFETY SYSTEM

It is obvious that the risk-measurement, cost–benefit analysis, and legal requirements for data protection described above will lead to different results in each individual company. This dependence of safety requirements on the actual situation in the firm concerned does *not* permit the elaboration of *lists of generally adoptable safety measures*. The following overview concerning the main techniques of risk-control can therefore be only a *general systematization of strategies* which should be considered for the prevention of computer crimes.[8]

1. Personal and Educational Safety Measures

Adequate personal safety measures are the starting-point in and one of the main instruments for the prevention of computer crime. The majority of computer-crime cases could have been prevented by taking more care on this point. However, as already indicated, many managers categorize their computer departments as dealing with 'technical' questions and are not aware of the risks which the DP area and DP employees can present for the company's assets. A well-developed safety system in the personal sector should therefore make use of both personnel controls and motivation.

a. CONTROLS

Personnel security controls must begin with *hiring procedures* for DP employees, in which not only technical skills but also security questions should be considered. Thorough pre-employment screening is most important. The revision of references should always be completed by confidential inquiries to former employers, who often fail to include misdemeanours, misconduct, and other negative items in their references in order to avoid judicial conflicts and to make dismissals easier but are willing to talk about these things frankly in a confidential telephone call. The agreement on a probation period can provide for a later release without a detailed stated cause.

During employment, vacation and job-rotation politics should be considered in order to avoid dependency on the exclusive knowledge of one person and to prevent one employee being permanently able to conceal evidence of manipulation. General methods of controlling the correctness of the employee's work, especially by computer-supported plausibility checks, will be dealt with below in connection with the respective organizational measures. In special cases, particularly in the event of suspected acts of sabotage and of cash-dispenser and high-efficiency vending-machine manipulations, additional camera supervision (including television cameras) may be justified. Special peculiarities, such as the non-taking of holidays or excessive spending of employees in highly sensitive jobs should always be investigated. Personal supervision methods should not only be directed towards employees but also extended towards maintenance staff, suppliers, and subcontractors.

The greatest care must be taken with *employment-termination practices*. As more than 50% of all cases of computer sabotage and theft of software committed by employees are committed shortly before the employee leaves the company, it is important to remove employees from the DP and computer areas before or immediately after notice has been given. After releasing an employee, his codes and passwords should be immediately changed, especially in the field of remote DP. Release of staff with possible access to password files should be followed by check and change of all passwords in order to delete possible 'private passwords' and colleagues' passwords installed or obtained by the employee before leaving the company.

b. MOTIVATION, EDUCATION, AND CODES OF ETHICS

Simple control of employees does not constitute sufficient personnel politics. The application of adequate safety measures and the honest behaviour of employees will also be influenced by their *motivation*.

Employee-counselling and security briefings should help to make staff members more aware of the risks for their company in the DP area, thus motivating them to use the often uncomfortable and time-consuming safety measures outlined by their management.

A good business atmosphere, fair practices, and an aura of a privileged elite are prerequisites for a positive motivation of employees. Disgruntlement and fear of redundancy due to a company's rationalization are the main reasons for computer sabotage and similar offences. These concerns should therefore be prevented and removed by procedures airing employees' grievances and by adequate information and participation. Legal alternatives should be offered for people who want to test their technical expertise against perpetrators' desire for a challenge.

Directors of a company should set an example of *moral leadership* for their staff members. A better standard of moral behaviour, especially in the field of unauthorized software copying, should be achieved by *codes of ethics*. This approach should not be restricted to business and industry but also extended to society in general, for example by teaching *computer ethics* in computer courses.[9]

2. Physical Safety Measures

Physical safety measures should not only concentrate on the computer room and data-storage facilities but also include peripheral systems such as terminals or outdoor cash-dispensers as well as air-conditioning systems (favourite targets of terrorists), power stations, fire-detection and suppression systems, and the cabling in the false ceilings of computer centres (for the respective attacks of computer sabotage see above, Chapter II, subsection A.3).

a. ARCHITECTURAL DESIGN

The implementation of physical security measures is not only a task for the plant-protection department but it must begin with the architectural design of DP centres. If buildings containing computer centres are newly constructed, specialist architects with experience in computer security should be consulted. Computer centres must be located in a safe area with respect to the company's environment and the situation of the DP centre within the respective firm. In order to protect the computer system against bombing attacks, an adequate safety zone should separate the computer centre from the public areas. Furthermore, computer centers should be physically separated from the company's other departments. Processing and storage functions must be installed in separate offices. Backup facilities and backup copies should be placed in a distant, safe building and unnecessary doors and windows should be avoided.

b. BUILDING MATERIALS AND EQUIPMENT

Building materials should be protected against intruders, bombing attacks, fire, water, and electronic or accoustic interference. Special attention must be paid to the suppression of compromising emissions of electronic impulses caused by terminals, typewriters, and other facilities (see above, p. 13). Special building materials able to absorb bombing attacks and explosions may be used (especially for walls, doors, and windows). Fire-detection and suppression systems (using Halon gas) must be a matter of course. An overvoltage protection should be able to prevent both accidents and acts of sabotage.

Physical access-control systems equipped with intrusion alarms, television-monitoring, personal identification systems, and automated record-keeping abilities as well as badges for access control in sensitive areas should then keep intruders out of the computer centre. Special control measures may be taken in sensitive areas of the DP department. The computer room and the data library, for example, may be subject to special access controls. Specific devices, such as personal computers, could be locked.

3. Organizational and Technical Safety Measures

Organizational and technical safety measures are among the most important methods of preventing computer crime, and they must be developed and implemented mainly by specialists and auditors, systems and application programmers and analysts, and electronics engineers. Many publications contain long checklists and enumerations of these measures, often leaving the user lost in a multitude of unsystematically listed points. However, as safety systems are only as strong as their weakest point, good systematic design of these measures is most important. A practicable systematization can be achieved by differentiating between *general organizational control principles* for all areas of data processing and *measures to protect special areas and functions* of the DP system.

a. GENERAL CONTROL MEASURES

As far as general control measures for the entire DP system are concerned, it should first be guaranteed that the DP centre is reporting directly to the head of the company, and that the above-mentioned physical separation of the computer centre from the company's other departments corresponds to a clear *separation of functions* performed. In order to prevent one individual from having responsibility for the complete processing of any transaction, this separation of duties and responsibilities should be applied as a general rule for all areas of the company. In the DP department separation of functions should especially concern the functions of original source document-preparation, original source document-approval, database administration, system programming, application program development, program testing, program release, and operating. The separation of functions may go even further and separate sensitive applications and non-classified applications. Such isolated systems not only give better protection against espionage and manipulations but can also prevent virus programs in sensitive areas by providing a 'transitive closure'.

In order to guarantee this separation of functions and to restrict the access to information, the physical access-control systems must be supplemented by a *logical access-control system* which must restrict access to the contents of a computer system. This logical access-control system, which should be implemented in isolated parts of the operating system and in the hardware, is the basis of all other logical security measures. A reasonable, access-control system must not only provide restrictions of access to different people but also restrictions of the type of access these people have (such as limitation of reading, writing, deleting, and altering functions) as well as restrictions on operating times, dates, and uses of software. A restriction of the 'write' function, for example, may provide a protection against the spread of virus programs. The access-control system must also provide extensive logging, recording, and analysing functions. Access-control systems available on the market, such as ACF2, APOS, CA-SENTINEL, RACF, RSS, SECURE, or TOP-SECRET, fulfil these requirements to varying degrees.[10]

A most important point of access-control systems, especially in online systems, is their *identification of the legal user*. The majority of systems employ passwords which vary in their degree of sophistication. However, as was shown above, password protection can be easily beaten in most cases. Machine-readable cards are also a common means of identification but, as demonstrated above, can also be manipulated and copied. Voiceprint registration, machine-readable fingerprints, and signature-verification are possible but they are not commonly used. Like most currently available identification procedures, they also can be circumvented by wiretapping and active infiltration. Therefore satisfying security requirements in many areas will only be achieved by the recently developed *'smart' chip-cards*, which include a microcomputer. These contain an electronically stored personal identification number without which the chips cannot be used. The chips can be programmed to administer transformation password procedures, provide encoding functions for passwords or messages (thus giving protection against wiretapping), and store each transaction in the card (thus permitting management to deal with complaints easily). These chip cards are made in such a way that their programs cannot be read or altered.[11]

Access-control systems will only prevent acts of unauthorized people. In order to prevent manipulations by employees engaged in their regular work, sensitive transactions generally have to be checked by *controls*. Controllers and the controlled subjects should be independent and be selected from different populations. In some areas dual controls by separate people are indispensible. As a general rule, however, controls should be made as independent as possible from humans and be performed to the greatest extent possible by the computer (for examples, see below). The computer is an ideal and cheap instrument for monitoring, accounting, and detecting deviations from normal activities. Computer controls that do not need human manipulation during operation are usually not only much less expensive but, in general, also much more reliable than safeguards which require human involvement and thus are susceptible to negligence and collusion. Therefore extensive use should be made to produce and analyse *logs* with computer support such as computer-operator console logs, processing schedules, computer-utilization, and storage summaries.

The greatest attention should be paid to the monitoring and analysis of *adjustment and error-correction routines*, to exception-item-handling, and to processing steps in emergency situations, as these are often abused or affected by manipulation schemes. Unresolved exceptions and unexplained activities on computer logs, increases in adjustments and error-corrections, customer- or employee-complaints, chronic imbalances of controls (often regarded as mistakes by the computer) as well as missing assets should always lead to special control and audit measures.

All functions, the respective job runs, and the control responsibilities should be clearly described and documented. This *documentation* should also regulate access rights to information. Therefore top-secret, secret, confidential, restricted, and unclassified data must be clearly classified and marked.

Disaster-recovery planning should provide organizational emergency planning for the entire DP systems and secure availability of backup facilities concerning both hardware and up-to-date versions of all programs and data files. Strict administrative policies and controls are necessary in all areas to ensure that safety and control measures are not only documented in manuals but are actually practised. If possible, a system should not rely entirely on automatic DP but also be able to survive for a certain time and/or to a certain degree on a manual basis.

b. SPECIAL INPUT CONTROLS

In the field of input controls special attention must be paid to source document-preparation, validation and approval, and data-conversion and entry, as well as to error-correction controls. Especially in cases in which respective dual controls and authorization techniques cannot be used for reasons of cost, extensive use of *computer-supported automatic checks* should be made. The computer should be used in particular to perform sequence checks, plausibility checks, upper and lower limits checks, and special checks for adjustment corrections and exception item-handling. These should not be made known within the sensitive departments of the company and should be changed regularly. The resulting logs should be analysed by the audit department. In order to control data conversion, entry check totals and accounting check digits should be computed.

c. SPECIAL COMMUNICATIONS CONTROLS

Communications security must include both the protection of physical data-carrier exchange and the protection of telecommunications systems. *Data-carriers* containing sensitive data should always be protected by *electronic sealing methods* or by *encoding* against alteration of data during transport. Companies which exchange data-carriers with other firms or other departments must always consider the necessity for special erasure of data remaining on files which are not completely written out.

Telecommunications systems should provide adequate *log-on procedures*, user-identifications, passwords with adequate length and proper key management, transaction codes, transformation passwords, traps for standard passwords often used by hackers, time delays between invalid input attempts, callback procedures, automatic disconnect facilities, and loggings which are analysed by the DP and audit staff with computer support. In traditional wire connections, satisfactory security against wiretapping and active infiltration in telecommunications systems can only be provided by the *encoding* of the entire data communication (using stream-cipher, block-cipher, or public-key encoding).[12] In future, the risk of wiretapping can also be reduced by the increasing use of *optic fibres* for wide-band, high-speed transmission, because optical signals do not radiate from fibre cables.

In computer systems with *remote diagnostic procedures* special attention should be focused on the protection of this highly sensitive communications point. Top-secret computer applications should, if possible, be executed on separate computer hardware with no connection to telecommunications systems and remote diagnostic procedures.

d. SPECIAL PROCESSING CONTROLS

Processing control is the most critical point in DP security. A comprehensive processing control would, in principle, have to control hardware, operating systems, and application programs. *Hardware and operating system checking* are, in most cases, beyond the scope of normal DP users. However, these should verify that they only use original hardware and system software from their regular suppliers in order to prevent the import of virus programs and other 'Trojan horses'. When hardware or software is delivered in highly sensitive areas, the receiver should try to remain as anonymous as possible to the suppliers. In these cases, the transport of equipment from the supplier to the user also should be safeguarded. In future, special control routines against virus programs may become necessary.

Application-program checking is still one of the most difficult points in DP security. This must include the checking of *new programs* and of *program changes* and guarantee the *integrity* of released, stored, and processed programs against alteration. The control of programs and program-amendments should be simplified by standardized programming instructions and not only be practised by manual methods but, to the greatest extent possible, by the help of special audit software such as automatic flowcharting, program mapping, or embedded audit modules. However, even with a large number of computer-supported audit tools, the control of programs is still one of the most crucial points in DP security. Manipulations of stored and processed programs can be made difficult by storing the program only in the object code. The opportunities of manipulating sensitive programs during their processing stage can be reduced further by temporal and special isolation of these programs, such as by applying serial processing mode.

Considering the difficulties of program-checking and the wide variety of possible manipulations in the field of computer hardware and operating systems it becomes clear that perfect security concerning the exclusion of 'Trojan-horse' routines would only be achievable at great cost. The control of DP processing should therefore always be completed by *application controls* and *checks of the resulting output* which are not based on the company's own DP system. Computer-support for these checks can be obtained by independent DP systems. A bank which is making a company's salary payments, for example, can easily provide a computer printout in which all payments to the same accounts or to the same names are arranged according to decreasing amounts, thus making an effective control of salary payments possible and independent of the manipulations of company-produced printouts.

e. SPECIAL DATA-STORAGE CONTROLS

Stored data primarily have to be protected by the above-described access-control systems and by control of the jobs executed. The *access-control system* should not only prevent unauthorized access but also register each alteration of data and each unsuccessful attempt at access by producing special logs which cannot be switched off, manipulated, or otherwise affected by the perpetrator. The *analysis of these logs* again should be carried out by the audit staff with the help of computer-support which can provide special programmer access listings, programmer work profiles, and supervision of failed access attempts.

Control of data-storage should also prevent the unauthorized export of data files to unprotected environments where manipulations could be made without being recorded by the company's logs. Furthermore, sensitive data files should only be stored in an encoded form. Special attention should be paid to protection against erasure of and sabotage against data files. For example, in highly sensitive areas an activation of degaussers should only be possible by special staff or by the collusion of two people.

f. SPECIAL OUTPUT CONTROLS

Output controls must supervise all *data leaving the DP centre* and the company and all *data remaining accessible* when other people are working with the DP equipment. Control of outgoing data must not only consider all legal ways of output but also possible data leakage, especially via telecommunications facilities, remote diagnostics, electronic emission, or export of data by maintenance staff. Export of data by maintenance staff, for example, can be prevented by copying maintenance discs on company discs which will remain within the company.

Particular care must be taken in the export of encoded data which are difficult to identify. As the copying and taking away of *discs* is difficult to control, disc drives in *personal computers* can be replaced by fixed-disc devices while safety copies are provided on the central host system in highly sensitive areas. An even better protection in the field of personal computers would be possible if the computer hardware could provide for an encoding of all data stored on the discs and if the hardware could be locked and sealed safely.

Used tapes and discs with sensitive data should always be erased with a security degausser before release. Residual data which may remain in temporary storage locations should be erased by well-designed computer systems. All data stored should contain *specific marks*, especially copyright signs, hidden identification marks, and serial numbers to give proof of their origin in cases of search and seizure later on. If the computer system is administering customer addresses, the names and addresses of some managers of the company should be stored on the file with an incorrect spelling. If these managers then receive promotion material from a competitor with their address showing the same misspelling they receive both knowledge and proof of the theft of their company's address data and their transmission to the sender of the letters.

g. SPECIAL PROTECTION OF LICENSED PROGRAMS

If computer programs are licensed to third parties, protection can be sought on three levels. The licensor can try to prevent illegal copying of the program, prevent illegal use of programs, and facilitate proof of illegal use.

The most common means for *preventing* or *discouraging copying* are program routines which make direct disc-to-disc or tape-to-tape copying impossible. The use of this method, however, has the disadvantage that the purchaser of the software cannot make backup copies and that a skilled programmer can 'unlock' the copy protection. There are also a number of programs on the market which are designed to break the protection systems and render the uncopyable programs copyable. The suppliers of these programs claim that they only permit users to make legal backup copies![13]

Illegal use of programs is often hindered by retaining the source code of the program and only giving away the object code in order to prevent changes and adaptation to the product. This method used to work fairly well. Today, however, many computer systems provide debugging tools which permit the recompilation of programs from object to assembler code. In order to prevent illegal use of programs, some people now implement in their software products 'killer routines' which cause the erasure of the programs or the destruction and manipulation of other data in case of illegal applications. These routines, sometimes referred to as 'killer software', can be activated, for example, by counters, calender dates, or hardware specifications. In order to prevent liability for losses caused by the application of such 'killer routines', sophisticated legal counselling is required.[14]

The prudent software-user should always take steps to enable the *detection and proof* of software piracy. In order to detect program piracy in some cases, especially when programs are administering mail features, specific program routines can provide automatic information of the owner of the software in cases of software theft, similar to the above-described method[15] of using misspelled addresses. In order to prove software piracy, it is recommended that the code be 'salted' by adding non-operative lines of coding ('fingerprints') and a unique identification code included in each copy of the program. If records are kept which correlate the identification code with the name of the respective program-purchaser, it is much easier to trace the source of the copy and to find the pirate responsible.[16]

4. Internal Auditing

A strict DP internal audit program can be a most effective countermeasure for preventing, detecting, and deterring computer fraud. Large organizations, both in the private and the public sector, should therefore pay great attention to having a powerful and independent internal audit department. In contrast to external auditing, which is generally practised by accounting firms and auditing corporations and has to certify the accuracy of certain financial statements, DP internal audit primarily has to provide *effectiveness, efficiency, and productivity* of the computer application. This chapter will focus on the DP auditor's role as far as it applies to computer crime.

DP internal auditing concerning computer fraud is one of the most advanced and most difficult areas of the DP profession. The *professional qualifications* of DP auditors, on the one hand, must include all auditing skills. On the other, they should have skills in DP, especially concerning application programming, system programming, hardware, database management, and data communication. Furthermore, DP auditors should be familiar with business knowledge in their area and must keep up to date both on audit practices and on developments in the field of computer technique. The DP auditing department should be independent and equipped, if possible, with a separate computer which cannot be manipulated or controlled by personnel in the DP department.

The *scope of DP auditing* is primarily that of the DP environment but must also extend to non-automated areas that can affect the computerized system. DP auditing pertaining to computer security should begin with its participation in the design and development of the company's security system (see above, subsection B.1). It then should focus on the examination, control, and updating of the company's safety measures, comprising all of the above-mentioned personal, physical, organizational, and technical safeguards. As far as DP audit tools and techniques are concerned, in most countries audit organizations have provided checklists and recommendations. The American Institute of Internal Auditors, for example, lists the following seventeen main items: test data method, base-case system-evaluation, integrated test facility, parallel simulation, transaction selection, embedded audit data collection, extended records, generalized audit software, snapshot, tracing, mapping, control flowcharting, job-accounting data-analysis, system development life-cycle, system acceptance and control group, code comparison, and disaster testing. There is a considerable amount of literature concerning the methods of DP auditing.[17]

Internal auditing must be highly visible and highly *unpredictable* in order to deter people from committing criminal acts. Since many computer criminals are managers, even they must be subject to surprise audits to the greatest degree possible. No-one should be able to predict accurately when and where auditors will look next and which methods they will use.

5. Insurance Against Computer Crime

An overall safety strategy must also consider protection given by insurance companies. As insurance policies against computer crime and losses vary considerably in different countries and can easily be obtained from insurance companies, they will not be presented here in detail.[18]

In order to assess the value of insurance against computer crime in a global safety concept it should be stated that insurance against computer crime is an important means of reducing the effects of and losses caused by computer crimes which a company cannot prevent. However, it must also be pointed out that protection through insurance policies can be claimed only after the crimes have been detected. Insurance protection is useless for victims who do not know about the alteration or theft of their data by manipulated control printouts. Protection through insurance policies should therefore be considered an additional means only. The focal point of internal prevention of computer crime must be in the field of personal, organizational, and technical safety measures.

6. Formulation of Contracts

A good safety system should make the best use of all available legal protection (for the protection of computer assets by the penal code, patents, copyright, trade secrets, trademarks and contracts, see above, Chapter IV, Section A). Proper formulation of contracts, especially with employees, licensees, vendors, and customers, should therefore be included in the company's safety strategy. As was explained above,[19] such a formulation of contracts can not only provide the company with rights which are important in litigation but also legal certainty which will prevent actions in dubious, 'grey' zones and reduce the risk of future lawsuits. Furthermore, civil sanctions laid down in contracts can deter perpetrators from committing certain acts leading to civil remedies. Obligation to give information and disputed programs to expert witnesses for comparison can also facilitate the preparation of a lawsuit.

Contracts with employees, software package contracts, or software development contracts should, for example, always consider clauses of non-disclosure of information and non-removal of data-carriers, rights concerning specified uses, and licensing of programs, rights to modify sources, moral rights of copyright, and admissibility of security measures built into computer programs. If the purchaser of software does not receive the source code, an escrow agreement should be settled in order to provide the availability of the source code in cases of the vendor's bankruptcy. Because of the high risks inherent in DP, contract development and, if possible, contract negotiation should be carried out with the support of a legal consultant specialized in computer law.

7. Proceedings and Legal Action in Cases of Suspicion and Loss

Finally, tactical methods in cases of suspicion and loss is an important point in a company's safety strategy.[20] In such cases the main focus should be on three often-conflicting aims: to *minimize further losses*, to *investigate an unknown perpetrator*, and to *secure legal evidence*.

In cases in which there is no threat of additional loss, suspicions should not be made public in order to prevent countermeasures by the perpetrator, such as the destruction of evidence. Especially in cases in which the perpetrator has not yet been investigated or where evidence is insufficient, traps should be set, particularly if continued criminal activities are possible. This could be done, for example, in cases of manipulation by providing for additional control printouts or of sabotage by installing secret cameras in a false ceiling in the computer centre. In a number of cases, however, immediate action must be taken to prevent further losses, such as the dismissal of an employee under suspicion, even if this suspicion is thus made public. In such cases, before the action is announced or executed, all relevant data should be copied in order to make manipulation and destruction of data by an undiscovered perpetrator or a potential accomplice ineffective.

As far as the investigation of an unknown perpetrator is concerned, victimized enterprises are facing the same problems as the investigation authorities. The explanations in Chapter VI can therefore be referred to as far as these points are concerned. In order to overcome their problems and to obtain evidence, the company can rely on *private investigation*, *civil remedies*, and *penal procedures*. Private investigation, for example, in the field of software theft can provide a 'test purchase' or a recompilation of a competitor's program. However, private investigations are often limited because they cannot investigate information in other people's homes or offices. The possibilities of obtaining evidence by civil proceedings, especially by preliminary injunctions and civil seizure, vary considerably in various countries, as the differences between the pre-trial discovery procedures and Anton Piller orders in common-law countries, the 'saisie-contrefaçon' in France, or the application of section 809, Bürgerliches Gesetzbuch, in the Federal Republic of Germany demonstrate. In most cases a criminal prosecution is advantageous because of the greater search and seizure powers of investigation authorities. Data and other legal evidence which have been seized by the investigating authorities during penal search procedures can often be used in civil proceedings. However, in practice criminal proceedings are often not pursued due to fears of destroying the company's reputation when it becomes known that a computer manipulation has taken place.

If penal or civil actions are intended, an appropriate *time management* is most important. On the one hand, the time-limits of the respective national legal systems must be considered. For example, in the Federal Republic of Germany requests for penal prosecution of software thefts must be made within three months after knowledge of the offence and the offender apprehended since many penal offences in copyright law and the law on unfair competition are prosecutable only at the request of the injured party. Civil claims based on the law of unfair competition become statute-barred after six months and compensation claims based on the copyright law after three years. On the other hand, both in interim-injunction proceedings as well as in normal principal-proceedings civil claims should not be prosecuted before sufficient evidence is at hand. The weighing of the risk of having legal time-limits expire and of not having enough evidence can create severe problems. Similar dilemmas arise from the decision whether or not civil remedies should be sought on an ordinary basis or on the basis of a preliminary injunction. Preliminary remedies have the advantage of being rapid but also bear the risk of being liable for damages if the main proceedings cannot be won.

With regard to the considerable risks of losing a case, especially in cases of software theft, the decision concerning legal actions and the evaluation of the available evidence should only be made in co-operation with a legal adviser who has *special knowledge* of the issues. As far as possible, legal actions should be taken before investigating authorities and courts with specialized knowledge in the field of computer crime and computer law. American criminology has good reason to compare the particular difficulties arising in the field of computer crime with those existing in the field of forensic medicine, where the use of specialists has become widespread.

D. INTERNATIONAL ASPECTS

If the different limitations of personal safety measures caused by the national privacy laws are put aside, the security strategies of companies do not differ in the various countries. The future development of safety measures can therefore easily be continued at an international level, thus profiting from foreign experiences. In some areas such international co-operation is essential, especially for the standardization of security measures such as in the fields of cash-dispenser cards, electronic signatures, or telecommunications networks which work on an international basis.

VI.

The Prosecution of Computer Crime

1. Difficulties of Discovery and Detection

The correct and concise application of the law and the prosecution of computer crimes, especially by investigating authorities and courts, is complicated by particular difficulties of discovery and detection in the DP area.[1]

a. DISGUISE OF CRIME

To begin with, the prosecution of computer crime in many cases is hindered by the fact that the criminal acts are disguised by the perpetrators. Computer fraud, for example, is often concealed by the manipulation of DP printouts. Computer espionage committed by copying data files as well as 'time-theft' *per se* do not appear as crimes in victimized companies which often do not have an opportunity to discover and prove unauthorized use of their data in an opponent's well-guarded firm. Computer sabotage is often made to appear a system failure or a mistake. In many cases privacy infringements cannot be discovered by victims and by State authorities as the acts take place in well-protected computer centres.

> In American criminology the possibility of disguising a crime by manipulation of data has led to the term 'second-hand nature of computer printouts'. The resulting problem for auditors and prosecutors can be illustrated by a report made by the head of a computer centre who described to the author how his colleague removed the data concerning critical business procedures from the data memory before the company's audit, thus preventing a check of these data on the subsequent printouts.

b. HIDDEN TRACES

In many cases the investigation and prosecution of computer crime is aggravated by the fact that program and data alterations do *not leave traces* comparable with classic document forgeries. Handwriting-analysis is no longer possible in electronic data banks. To reduce the problem of proving

139

authorship of data entries, an attempt should be made to identify the people inputting and processing data by loggings and other kinds of recordings. Another possibility of investigation is to follow the traces of the embezzled money, which in most cases must finally be transferred to the perpetrators.

> The problem of following electronic traces was colourfully illustrated in a West German case. The perpetrators had replaced the name and address of one of their employer's suppliers with that of a fictitious firm on the master data file which was connecting account numbers with suppliers' addresses to check the payment of invoices. As a result of this alteration, the subsequent invoice of the respective supplier resulted in a cheque made out, not to the supplier, but to the perpetrators' fictitious firm. This payment of about DM135 181 to an unknown supplier caused suspicion and the cheque was stopped. In the investigation that followed, traces of the perpetrators were sought by analysing the logs concerning the master-file changes. However, as the logs for certain periods of time were missing, the author of the address changes could not be discovered. Investigations into the address written on the cheque did not initially lead to success either, since the perpetrators had chosen the address of a large house in which they had just installed an additional mail box bearing the name of their fictitious firm. Surveillance of the mailbox at first proved unsuccessful, as the perpetrators had become aware of the detection of their attempted fraud and did not try to obtain the cheque. However, some weeks later a letter from the bank where the perpetrators had opened an account for the fictitious firm in order to cash the cheque was delivered to the mail-box. Comparison of the handwriting appearing in the papers filled out for the opening of the bank account with that of about 100 employees finally led to a programmer, who was convicted of the offence. His alleged accomplice, however, could not be proved guilty.[2]

c. NON-VISIBILITY OF EVIDENCE

The investigation and prosecution of computer crime requires a great deal of checking computer data. Most of these data are no longer stored in a visible, human-readable form but in an invisible and only machine-readable highly concentrated form in electronic storage devices. One of the main problems in the discovery and detection of computer crime by prosecution agencies and courts therefore consists of a *lack of visual and understandable evidence* caused by the anonymity, compression, and often even encoding of electronically stored data. These problems are especially serious in the case of program manipulations, because a complete check of a computer program and a discovery of inadmissible hidden program routines require a great deal of work which is often not economically justifiable. However, the lack of visual evidence of electronically stored data is also a considerable hindrance in detecting manipulations in the field of any DP-stored data. Representatives of specialized departments and auditing offices as well as accountants and investigating officials are often unable to directly check suspicious data.

> The effect of the lack of visual and comprehensible evidence, even in very simple cases, can be illustrated by a West German case in 1971, in which 300 000 customer-addresses stored on magnetic tapes were stolen from a mail-order

firm. The injured company had succeeded in obtaining a court injunction for the restoration of all address data from the competitor, who had bought the addresses from the perpetrators. The bailiff, who wanted to carry out his duty, was politely afforded entry to the competitor's premises, led to the computer centre, and pleasantly requested to do his task. However, he was confronted with a multitude of magnetic tapes and discs, the contents of which he could not discover, and was therefore obliged to leave the computer centre empty-handed. While the address data were voluntarily surrendered a few days later by the company, it certainly cannot be ruled out that the magnetic tapes concerned had previously been duplicated, thus negating the success of the court injunction.[3]

d. ENCODING OF EVIDENCE

The perpetrator can make these problems even worse and expected search-and-seizure procedures more difficult by *protecting* his *data* with some of the above-mentioned safety measures, especially with passwords, hindering instructions, and cryptographic techniques. These techniques would also be a major hindrance for control of transborder data flows because effective control here is inconceivable when anyone who wishes not to conform to legal requirements can, in an encoded telephone call of only a few seconds' duration, complete an unauthorized transfer. Also, in the field of privacy infringements cryptographic techniques can make effective control of stored data, especially in the field of small personal computers, very difficult.

> Cryptographic techniques used by perpetrators have already caused considerable problems in a number of West German cases, especially in the field of fixed-storage devices which were difficult to seize. A much simpler trick was used by some juvenile software thieves, who had stored bars of music at the beginning of their cassettes before the illegally copied programs started.[4]

e. ERASURE OF EVIDENCE

Additional difficulties of discovery and detection result from the fact that the perpetrators can easily *avoid proof by erasing data*. Methods of rapid erasure of data have been dealt with above. Perpetrators' explanations of such acts as mistakes in computer handling have also been previously mentioned.

> A sophisticated 'automatic' method of such destruction of proof was disclosed in a Dutch proceedings against an illegal arms dealer. A gun-runner, who had stored the addresses of his clients in a small computer, had changed the regular commands in the operating system so that the input of a copy- or print-command via the computer's keyboard would execute the erasure of all data. This trap, especially programmed for expected search-and-seizure procedures, was, however, detected by the DP specialists of the Dutch 'Fraudecentrale', who sensed that something had been changed in the computer's operating system and therefore produced copies of the seized discs in their own computer system.[5]
> In a West German case the perpetrator had constructed a data safe which was built to erase all data by an electric field when opened by an unauthorized person.[6]

f. LARGE NUMBERS OF DATA

If computer data are checked by prosecution agencies further problems result from the *large numbers of single processes* usually handled by DP which cannot be controlled perfectly. However, it must be pointed out that these detection difficulties are not caused by the computer but can be reduced by DP, which offers the possibility of systematic checks and system checking in addition to individual case checking. As mentioned above, auditors and prosecutors can use the computer and special audit software to assist prosecution.

g. INEXPERIENCE OF PROSECUTORS

The problems of prosecution in the field of DP described above are seriously aggravated by the fact that many *auditors, investigation officers, judges, and attorneys* are *not familiar* with information media and cannot deal properly with the technical problems of computer crime. In view of the new nature of these problems, this is not surprising. The unsatisfactory attempt at tackling problems of computer crime illustrated in the above-mentioned[7] case in 1971 is still typical for many prosecution authorities and government agencies. For example, a whole series of stayed prosecution proceedings and case dismissals in court, as well as various court decisions on civil law, can only be explained by the wish of the responsible official not to have to deal with the specific problems of the case.[8]

> This book will not go into the details of the many stayed proceedings. The problem of State agents unfamiliar with DP may be illustrated by a report of a DP specialist describing to the author how he crossed the West German/Swiss border with a number of magnetic tapes containing valuable data. When he was asked by the customs officials whether the tapes were empty or not and truthfully declared their valuable contents, he received the answer: 'Then you don't need to pay any duty, as *used* tapes are worthless.'

h. LEGAL UNCERTAINTIES AND NATIONAL FRONTIERS

The *legal uncertainties and shortcomings*, especially in the field of substantive penal law and the law of evidence which have already been dealt with in chapter IV, are further hindrances for prosecution. In cases of transnational computer crime, the *national frontiers* often create additional difficulties, especially in the areas of mutual assistance and extradition (see section IV.C.2).

2. Measures to be Taken

Analysis of problems in the field of prosecution shows that a reform of penal and procedural law is not sufficient to make adequate prosecution of computer crime possible. In order to overcome these hindrances, one of the most important measures for combatting computer crime is therefore an appropriate training of auditors, accountants, and investigating officials.[9]

a. SPECIAL INVESTIGATION TRAINING IN VARIOUS COUNTRIES

The first country concerned with special DP training for prosecution agencies was the *United States*, where the Federal Bureau of Investigation is trying to make a high proportion of agents literate in computers. Up to the present, hundreds of special agents have gone through the courses at the FBI Academy in Quantico, Virginia. The above-mentioned Hitachi/IBM case[10] showed that the FBI and victims of computer crime are also using special undercover investigators, especially in the field of espionage and program piracy. This case involved a computer-consulting firm in Silicon Valley, which was initially intended to be used as a front to catch people sending high technology to Eastern bloc countries.[11] In order to obtain more information about 'hacking', several United States' law-enforcement officials have begun to consult public bulletin-boards. In Phoenix, for example, this led to the prosecution of a 16-year-old boy who had posted a message offering to install a device on television sets which would allow customers to access pay-TV stations without payment.[12]

Since June 1980 thorough Computer Crime Investigation Techniques Courses are given by the Royal *Canadian* Mounted Police at the Canadian Police College in Ottawa. The Royal Canadian Mounted Police is also serving as a centralized agency for dealing with complicated cases of computer crime.

In *Japan* the police have also reached a high level of specialization. The National Police Agency set up a 'workshop to study counter measures against new-type crimes such as abuses of computer system' in 1980 and a 'task force to study legislation on computer system protection' in 1982. In July 1982 the National Police Agency also held a 'National Conference for Investigators against Computer Crime'. In addition, the Tokyo Metropolitan Police Department in December 1982 conducted an opinion poll among 500 computerized companies ('Questionnaire on crime prevention measures against computer crime'). The success of the Japanese efforts can be clearly seen in their crime statistics: in 1983, for example, the Japanese police could clear 508 of the 642 cash dispenser manipulations which had been made known to them in that year.

As a model for specialization of investigation agencies in the field of computer crime, one should also refer to the *Dutch* 'Fraudecentrale—Centrale Recherche Informatiedienst', whose agents have been participating in the Canadian Police College's courses and have successfully proved their experience in the above-described gun-runner case[13] and others.

In the Federal Republic of Germany, where similar efforts directed by a central agency are lacking, the author has tried to overcome this deficiency by giving lectures and courses to inform judges, public prosecutors, and investigating officers about the new cases, problems, and legal questions. This work has contributed to some improvement in the situation in the Federal Republic in recent years, at least with respect to the activities of specialized prosecution authorities. Thus, today most criminal investigation departments in the West German States have special branches with experts in the detection of computer offences.

> In a case of software theft which the author dealt with, the accused persistently maintained that the computer program used by him was completely different from that stolen from the injured party. However, as a result of a search carried out by the Baden-Württemberg State Criminal Investigation Department, he is faced today with the report of an expert witness indicating that the programs are almost completely identical. On the evidence of this report, he has been instructed in parallel civil proceedings to refrain from using this program and to pay damages to the injured party.

b. NECESSARY CONTENT OF COMPUTER-CRIME INVESTIGATION COURSES

The necessary *content of special computer crime investigation courses* for prosecution agents is shown by the Royal Canadian Mounted Police courses. These are divided into five major areas:
(1) Computers and electronic data-processing fundamentals;
(2) Introduction to computer programming;
(3) Computer security;
(4) The law and evidence; and
(5) Computer crime.

In addition, special attention should be paid to
(6) The field of search and seizure;
(7) The issue of using the computer as an instrument to audit and prosecute, and
(8) The field of international prosecution and co-operation.

In the field of search and seizure, for example, in many (especially in unclear) cases it may be appropriate for policemen to take original data-carriers but leave copies with the respective firm, thus enabling the firm to carry out its work in order to reduce the risks of claims of damage against the police should the proceedings be stayed. The opposite procedure—i.e. to take copies away and leave the original data-carriers with the firm—once caused problems in West German proceedings because the perpetrator had protected his data by passwords and hindering instructions. Because of these safety measures the policemen had been successful in copying only a small part of the data and when the result was discovered weeks later, it was too late to repair the fault. In addition, as the above-mentioned Dutch case indicated, it should be recommended that the prosecutors call in technical experts and produce copies only on computer systems with which they are familiar, if possible by using their own (safe) operating system.

As an example of computer-assisted prosecution, the above-described audit techniques can be referred to. They may be directly or indirectly applied by prosecutors in most cases. A West German case of software theft provides a special example concerning computer-assisted prosecution. In this, the prosecution agencies first intended to stay the proceedings because the costs and problems of comparing voluminous programs seemed to be too high. In co-operation with the injured party, which the author was representing, a program was developed through which the largest part of the comparative work could be done by a computer. The program was handed over to the police, who continued the proceedings successfully within a short time and with little cost. This case is a good example of the fact that special efforts to deal with computer crime will always pay.

Because transborder data flow, especially by telecommunications facilities, will offer new possibilities for 'transnational computer crime', special emphasis should also be given to the field of international investigation, mutual assistance, and extradition. All of the described organizational improvements should be pursued in *close international co-operation*, as was initiated by the First Interpol Seminar for the Investigation of Computer Crime, organized by the Norwegian expert, Stein Schjolberg, in 1981. Present experience in dealing with computer crime is too limited to allow valuable international experience to be neglected.

VII.

Summary: The Need for Further Research, Action and International Co-operation

The protection of computer-administered money, stock levels of goods, balance sheets, company secrets, and other paperless stored property against the new threat of computer crime is of great importance for Western countries. To solve the new problems involved in computer crime, special efforts are necessary, especially in criminological research, the clarification and the reform of prevailing legal provisions, the development of security measures for companies, and the training of investigating officers and judges. These efforts cannot be restricted to a national level but must be carried out through international co-operation; since all Western countries are threatened by the same acts, transborder data processing makes computer crime international and transnational phenomena, many security measures should be standardized internationally, prosecution must not be prejudiced by national frontiers, and the national laws should be harmonized in order to facilitate free transborder data flow and avoid the establishment of computer-crime havens.

147

Notes

CHAPTER I

1. See Bell, *The Coming of Post-Industrial Society* (1980); Freese, *Informations-samhallet* (1983); Freese, Verletzlichkeit des Individuums und der Gesellschaft. In *Der Bundesminister fuer Forschung und Technologie, 1984 und danach—Konferenzdokumentation* (1984), pp. 154 *et seq.*; Häfner, *Der 'Grosse Bruder'* (1980); Häfner, *Mensch und Computer im Jahre 2000* (1984); Lamberton (ed.), *Economics of Information and Knowledge* (1971); Machlup, *The Production and Distribution of Knowledge in the United States* (1962); Masuda, *The Information Society as Post-Industrial Society* (Institute for Information Society, Tokyo, 1980); Toffler, *The Third Wave* (1980); Weizenbaum, *Computer Power and Human Reason* (1976).

2. See Sieber, *Informationstechnologie und Strafrechtsreform* (1985), pp. 12 *et seq.*

3. For the work of the OECD in the field of computer crime, see *infra*, chapter IV, note 1 and section IV. A.7 (pp. 92 et seq., 156).

4. For a detailed discussion of the definition of the term 'computer crime' and its functions, see Sieber, *Computerkriminalität und Strafrecht* (2nd edn, 1980), pp. 29 *et seq.*, 184 *et seq.*, 2/137 et seq.

5. For the appropriateness and final adoption of the definition, see *infra*, section II. C. 3 (p. 27).

CHAPTER II

· 1. For a detailed overview of these phenomena, see Sieber, *Computerkriminalität und Strafrecht* (2nd edn, 1980), pp. 39 et *seq.* For further references, see Appendix 1.

2. For a detailed description of electronic funds transfer systems, see Bequai, *The Cashless Society* (1981); Parker, *Fighting Computer Crime* (1983), pp. 267 *et seq.*

3. This case was verified by inspecting the court records. For more details see, for example, Becker, Rifkin—a documentary history. (1980) **2** *Computer and Law Journal* 471.

4. This case was verified by inspecting police records.

149

5. This case was verified by inspecting police records.

6. See Hitomi (1982) **35** *Horitsu-no-Hiroba* No 12, 5; Japanese National Police Agency, *Report for Investigators of Computer Crime* (1982, photocopied); *Japanese White Paper on Police 1983; Japanese White Paper on Police 1984.*

7. See *Japanese White Paper on Police 1983.*

8. See *infra*, section III. 2 (pp. 33 *et seq.*).

9. This case was verified by an interview by Peter Hohl, editor of the journal *KES—Zeitschrift für Kommunikations- und EDV-Sicherheit*, with a representative of the victim.

10. This case was verified by inspecting police records. For a detailed case description, see Sieber, *Computerkriminalität, supra*, note 1, pp. 153 *et seq.*

11. For details, see Parker, *Fighting Computer Crime, supra*, note 2, pp. 75 *et seq.* See also *infra*, section V. B. 3. b and c (pp. 122 *et seq.*).

12. For verified case descriptions see, for example, Sieber, *Computerkriminalität, supra*, note 1, pp. 80 *et seq.*

13. This case was verified by inspecting the court records. For a detailed case description see Sieber, *Computerkriminalität, supra*, note 1, pp. 58 *et seq.*

14. This case was verified by inspecting the court records and interviewing the perpetrator. For more details of the case, see Sieber, *Informationstechnologie und Strafrechtsreform* (1985) pp. 15, 23; Zimmerli and Liebl (eds), *Computermissbrauch—Computersicherheit* (1984), pp. 45 *et seq.*

15. This case was verified by information given by the official receiver. For a detailed case description, see Sieber, *Computerkriminalität, supra*, note 1, pp. 61 *et seq.*

16. This case was verified by inspecting the court records. For more details, see Parker, *Crime by Computer* (1976), pp. 59 *et seq.*; Sieber, *Computerkriminalität, supra*, note 1, pp. 52 *et seq.*

17. See *Japanese White Paper on Police 1984.*

18. This manipulation technique caused several civil suits by customers against banks in the United States.

19. For a detailed description of the French case, which is based on inspection of the French court records, see Sieber, *Computerkriminalität, supra*, note 1, pp. 128 *et seq.* The Italian case was verified by information obtained by attorney Dr Lorenzo Picotti, University of Bologna, and Dr Carlo Sarzana, Ministry of Justice, Rome.

20. For the Japanese case, see *Japanese White Paper on Police 1983.*

21. The West German cases were verified by an interview with the journalists and by checking parts of the police records.

22. *See Japanese White Paper on Police 1983.*

23. For verified case descriptions see Sieber, *Computerkriminalität, supra*, note 1, pp. 69 *et seq.*

24. See von zur Muehlen, *Computer-Kriminalität* (1972), p. 25; Sieber, *Computerkriminalität, supra*, note 1, pp. 133 *et seq.*; Tiedemann, *Wirtschaftsstrafrecht und Wirtschaftskriminalität*, Vol. 2 (1976), p. 152. For the characteristics of computer crime see also Solarz, *Computer Technology and Computer Crime*, Report

No. 8 of the Research and Development Division (Stockholm, 1983), pp. 13 *et seq.*; Wong, *Computer Fraud in the U.K.—Case Analysis* (photocopied, BIS Applied Systems, Manchester, 1983).

25. For a description of the case, which is based on inspection of the court records, see Sieber, *Computerkriminalität, supra*, note 1, pp. 137 *et seq.*

26. See Parker, *Fighting Computer Crime, supra*, note 2, pp. 90 *et seq.*

27. See Sieber, *Computerkriminalität, supra*, note 1, pp. 127 *et seq.*

28. The most detailed criminological study in the field of perpetrators has now been published by Artur Solarz, *Datorteknik och brottslighet* (1985). Another most interesting study was presented by Jay Bloombecker, Secure computing. (1985) **1** *Conscience in Computing* No. 1, p. 1 *et seq.* For a detailed overview on empirical studies in the field of computer crime, see *infra*, section III. 1. a (pp. 29 *et seq.*).

29. For the challenge motive see Parker, Nycum and Oura, *Computer Abuse* (1973), pp. 5, 49 *et seq.*; Parker, *Crime by Computer, supra*, note 16, pp. 46 *et seq.*

30. For more details concerning the object of computer espionage, see Sieber, *Computerkriminalität, supra*, note 1, pp. 98 *et seq.*; Sieber, Urheberrechtliche und wettbewerbsrechtliche Erfassung der unbefugten Softwarenutzung. (1981) *Betriebs-Berater* 1547 *et seq.* See also *infra*, p. 63 *et seq.*, 74.

31. For a detailed description of this case, see the civil opinions of the Landgericht Mannheim, (1981). *Betriebs-Berater* 1543, Oberlandesgericht Karlsruhe, (1983) *Betriebs-Berater* 986, Bundesgerichtshof, (1985) *Betriebs-Berater* 1747.

32. For a further description of the methods of computer espionage, see Parker, *Fighting Computer Crime, supra*, note 2, pp. 57 *et seq.*, 78 *et seq.*; Sieber, *Computerkriminalität, supra*, note 1, pp. 108 *et seq.*, 2/115 *et seq.*; Sieber, *supra*, note 30, (1981) *Betriebs-Berater* 1548 *et seq.* See also *infra*, section V. B. 3 (pp. 121 *et seq.*).

33. For references of this case see Bloombecker, Computer crime update: the view as we exit 1984. (1985) **7** *Western New England Law Review* 627, 630 *et seq.*

34. For more details and references of this case, see, for example, Bloombecker, *supra*, note 33, (1985) **7** *Western New England Review* 641.

35. For computer espionage by Eastern bloc countries, see Bequai, *How to Prevent Computer Crime* (1983), pp. 234 *et seq.*; Sieber, *Computerkriminalität, supra*, note 1, pp. 116 *et seq.*, 119 *et seq.*, 2/116 *et seq.*

36. This case description is based on police and company statements.

37. See, for example *AZ—Andere Zeitung* (Frankfurt) No. 95, January 1984; *Chips und Kabel* (Berlin) September 1984, p. 34; *Subversion* (Zurich) No. 7, July 1983; *Wechselwirkung* (Berlin) No. 11, September 1984.

38. This case was verified by inspecting the court records.

39. See, for example, *Die Bayerische Hackerpost*, April 1983, pp. 1 *et seq.*

40. For more details, see Cohen, Computer viruses—theory and experiments (University of Southern California, Paper of 31 August, 1983); Dierstein, Computer-Viren. (1985) *KES-Zeitschrift für Kommunikations- und EDV-Sicherheit*, pp. 77

et seq., 125 *et seq.*; as well as the report *Viren im Uni-Rechner.* (1986) *KES-Zeitschrift für Kommunikations- und EDV-Sicherheit* no. 1, p.22.

41. This case is reported, for example, by Parker, *Fighting Computer Crime, supra*, note 2, pp. 144 *et seq.*

42. For verified case descriptions, see Sieber, *Computerkriminalität, supra*, note 1, pp. 87 *et seq.*, 2/121 *et seq.*

43. See, for example, the references in notes 37 and 39.

44. This case was verified by an interview with the security officer of the firm concerned.

45. For the bombing attack on the computer centres of SCS and MBP see (1985) *KES—Zeitschrift für Kommunikations- und EDV-Sicherheit* 113. For an overview, see Sieber, *Computerkriminalität, supra*, note 1, pp. 91 *et seq.*, 2/121 *et seq.*

46. See Bequai, *How to Prevent Computer Crime, supra*, note 35, pp. 245 *et seq.*

47. This case was verified by interviewing the public prosecutor in charge.

48. See Sieber, *Computerkriminalität, supra*, note 1, pp. 124 *et seq.*, 2/124.

49. This case was verified by inspecting the court records.

50. For the phenomena of unauthorized access and 'hacking', see Ammann and Lehnhardt, *Die Hacker sind unter uns* (1985); Heine, *Die Hacker* (1985); Parker, *Fighting Computer Crime, supra*, note 2, pp. 130 *et seq.*; Sieber, *Computerkriminalität, supra*, note 1, pp. 2/100 *et seq.*; Sieber, *Informationstechnologie, supra*, note 14, pp. 18 *et seq.*; Wong, The Hakers and Computer Crime, in *SECURICOM 86* (Congress Proceedings edited 1986 by SEDEP Paris), p. 11. Samociuk, Hacking: A Practical Look at the risks and controls in: *SECURICOM 86* (Congress Proceedings edited 1986 by SEDEP Paris), p. 453.

51. This case was verified by interviewing the perpetrators and the supplier of the videotex software.

52. For the use of the computer as a tool for traditional business offences, see Sieber, *Computerkriminalität, supra*, note 1, pp. 183, 2/125 *et seq.*

53. This case was verified by inspecting parts of the court records. For a detailed description, see Parker, *Crime by Computer, supra*, note 16, pp. 118 *et seq.*; Sieber, *Computerkriminalität, supra*, note 1, pp. 141; Soble and Dallos, *The Impossible Dream* (1975).

54. For an overview, see Herb, *Mangelnde Normenklarheit im Datenschutz-Strafrecht* (University of Tübingen, Dissertation, 1984); Sieber, *Computerkriminalität, supra*, note 1, pp. 24 *et seq.* (especially note 111).

55. Sections II. A. 1 and 3 (pp. 4 *et seq.*, 15 *et seq.*).

56. See *Thompson* v. *San Antonio Retail Merchants Association*, **682** *Federal Reporter* (F. 2d) 509 (5th Cir. 1982). The present case description is based on the summary of Mandell, *Computer, Data Processing, and the Law* (1984), pp. 190 *et seq.*

57. This case has been verified by checking the court records. For a detailed description, see Sieber, *Informationstechnologie, supra* note 14, pp. 19 *et seq.*

58. The information on this case was provided by Dr Carlo Sarzana, Ministry of Justice, Rome.

59. This description was verified by interviewing Swiss state prosecuters and by inspecting the court records. The information given here has also been reported in the public press.

60. See Oberster Gerichtshof, Decision of 22 November 1979. (1980) *Österreichische Richterzeitung* 40.

61. *Jaffess* v. *Secretary of Health, Education, and Welfare*, **393** *Federal Supplement (F. Supp.)* 626. The present case description is based on the summary of Mandell, *supra*, note 56, pp. 188 *et seq.*

62. For this case, see Commission Nationale de l'Informatique et des Libertés, Délibération no. 84 du 3 avril 1984, 5è rapport d'activité. 1985, Annex 18, p. 217. For a further case concerning infringements of formalities of privacy law, see Bayerisches Oberstes Landesgericht (1981) *Juristenzeitung* 410.

63. See Sieber, *Computerkriminalität, supra*, note 1, p. 28.

64. See Dammann, *Datenschutz und Zugang zu Planungsinformationssystemen* (1974); Häfner, *Der 'Grosse Bruder'* (1980); Weizenbaum, *Computer Power and Human Reason* (1976).

65. The case was verified by inspecting the court records.

66. The case was verified by inspecting the court records. For a detailed description, see Sieber, *Computerkriminalität, supra* note 1, pp. 148 *et seq.*

67. *Japanese White Book on Police 1983.* See also Jaburek and Schmölzer, *Computer-Kriminalität* (1985), p. 59.

68. The malfunction was investigated by the US Comptroller-General. See US Comptroller-General, General Accounting Office, NORAD's missile warning system: what went wrong? *GAO Report MASAD 81—30* (1981); for additional references see Bloombecker, *supra*, note 33. (1985) **7** *Western New England Review* 629 *et seq.*

CHAPTER III

1. See Becker, *The Investigation of Computer Crime* (edited by the US Department of Justice, 1980), pp. 6, 43.

2. For the empirical studies of the Stanford Research Institute International, see Parker, *Computer Abuse Assessment* (1975); Parker, *Computer Abuse, Perpetrators and Vulnerabilities of Computer Systems* (1975); Parker, *Computer Security Management* (1981); Parker, Computer abuse research update. (1980) **2** *Computer and Law Journal* 329; Parker, *Crime by Computer* (1976); Parker, *Fighting Computer Crime* (1983); Parker Nycum and Oüra, *Computer Abuse* (1973). A critical examination of the studies is given by Taber, A survey of computer crime studies. (1980) **2** *Computer and Law Journal* 275.

3. See General Accounting Office, *Computer Related Crimes in Federal Programs* (1976).

4. See Bloombecker, Secure computing. (1985) **1** *Conscience in Computing* No. 1, 1; Bloombecker, Computer crime update: the view as we exit 1984. (1985) **7** *Western New England Review* 627, 645.

5. See American Institute of Certified Public Accountants, *Report on the Study of EDP-Related Fraud in the Banking and Insurance Industries* (1984), p. 5.

6. See American Bar Association, *Report on Computer Crime* (1984); American Bar Association, *Statement of Joseph B. Tompkins* (1984).

7. See Von zur Mühlen, *Computer-Kriminalität, Gefahren und Abwehr* (1973).

8. For the author's empirical studies at the Institute for Criminology and Economic Criminal Law of the University of Freiburg, see Sieber, *Computerkriminalität und Strafrecht* (2nd edn, Köln, 1980); Sieber, Gefahr und Abwehr der Computerkriminalität. (1982) *Betriebs-Berater* 1433; Sieber, Urheberrechtliche und wettbewerbsrechtliche Erfassung der unbefugten Softwarenutzung. (1981) *Betriebs-Berater* 1547; Sieber, *Informationstechnologie und Strafrechtsreform* (1985).

9. See Liebl, in Zimmerli and Liebl (eds), *Computermissbrauch— Computersicherheit* (1984), esp. p. 18; Poerting and Pott, *Computer-Kriminalität* (edited 1986 by the German Bundeskriminalamt), pp. 31 *et seq.*

10. For the inquiry of the West German Federal Investigation Bureau see Poerting and Pott, supra note 9; Steinke, Die Kriminalität durch Beeinflussung von Rechnerabläufen. (1984) *Neue Zeitschrift für Strafrecht* 295.

11. See Herb, *Mangelnde Normenklarheit im Datenschutz-strafrecht* (Dissertation, University of Tübingen, 1984).

12. For the empirical studies of the Computer Abuse Research Bureau at the Caulfield Institute for Technology see CIT-CARB/The Computer Abuse Research Bureau at Chisholm Institute of Technology, *Profiling and Encouraging the Prevention of Computer Abuse*; CIT-CARB, *Computer Control Quarterly Newsletter* December 1985; Fitzgerald, *The Computer Abuse Profile in Australia* (1982); Fitzgerald, *Computer Related Crime in Australia 1984* (1985); Lewens, Australian computer abuse profile. In *Computer Abuse—Risks, Security and Control*, Proceedings of a CIT-CARB conference (1979).

13. See Local Government Audit Inspectorate, *Computer Fraud Survey* (photocopied 1981); Audit Commission for Local Authorities in England and Wales, *Computer Fraud Survey* (1985); Scottish Law Commission, Computer crime. *Consultative Memorandum* No. 68 (1986), pp.35 *et seq.*

14. For the empirical studies of private security consultant Wong, see Wong, Computer crime in the UK—are you vulnerable? (1984) *Datenschutz und Datensicherung* 34; Wong, Computer-related fraud. (1983) **5** *Information Age*, No. 1, 16; Wong, *Computer Fraud in the UK—Case Analysis* (photocopied *BIS* Applied Systems, Manchester, 1983); Wong, *Computer Related Fraud Casebook* (BIS Applied Systems, Manchester, 1981); Wong, *Risk Analyses and Control* (photocopied, BIS Applied Systems, Manchester, 1981).

15. See Commission of the European Communities/Information Technology Task Force, *The Vulnerability of the Information Conscious Society—European Situation, Summarized Conclusions* (June 1984).

16. See Kainomaa, Tietoturva sekä vahingot ja väärinkäytökset atk:ssa (Data security, losses and abuses in the field of automatic data processing). *Tutkimus-Raportti* 3/84 (published by Tietotekniikan Kehittämiskeskus—Center for the Development of Data Technology/Helsinki, 1984); Lehtimaja, Atk-turvallisuus ja lainsäädäntö (Data security and legislation). (1984) *Suomen Poliisilehti* 40.

17. For the studies of Artur Solarz see Solarz, *Datortekniken och brottsligheten in Brottsutvecklingen* (National Council for Crime Prevention, 1981); Solarz, *Computer Technology and Computer Crime*, Report No. 8 of the Research and Development Division (National Council for Crime Prevention, 1981); Solarz (ed.), *Datorteknik, brottslighet och ADB-saekerhet* (National Council for Crime Prevention, 1982).

18. See Organization for Economic Co-operation and Development (OECD) (ed.), *Computer-related Criminality*, Report DSTI/ICCP/84.22 of 30 August 1985, p. 7.

19. See Jaburek and Schmëlzer, *Computer-Kriminalität* (1985).

20. See Jaburek and Schmölzer, *supra*, note 19, 29; Zima, Computerkriminalität. (1980) *Journal für Betriebswirtschaft* No. 2, 82.

21. See OECD (ed.), *supra*, note 18, pp. 5 *et seq.*

22. Japanese National Police Agency, *Report for Investigators of Computer Crime* (photocopy, 1982); *Japanese White Paper on Police 1983*; *Japanese White Paper on Police 1984*.

23. Information obtained by Dr Erwin Zimmerli, head of the respective police division. See also Zimmerli and Angst, in Zimmerli and Liebl (ed.), *supra*, note 9, pp. 333 *et seq.*

24. For a detailed discussion of the 'dark figure' in the DP area see Sieber, *Computerkriminalität*, *supra*, note 8, pp. 168 *et seq.*, 2/129 *et seq.*

25. Ontario Provincial Police, *Computer Crime and Security Surrey* (approximately 1981).

26. For this investigation, see note 11.

27. See *supra*, note 8.

28. See *supra*, note 2.

29. See *supra*, note 3.

30. See *supra*, note 4.

31. See *supra*, note 12.

32. See *supra*, note 14.

33. See *supra*, note 22.

34. See *supra*, note 17.

35. See *supra*, note 15.

36. p. 11.

37. pp. 12 *et seq.*

38. pp. 14 *et seq.*

39. For the future development of computer crime see also Sieber, *Informations-technologie, supra*, note 8, p. 21.

40. pp. 5, 9 *et seq.*

CHAPTER IV

1. Chapter IV, Section A is based on a report which the author has prepared for the *Organization for Economic Co-operation and Development (OECD)* in Paris. See Sieber, Analysis of substantive penal law and recommendations for legal policy. Chapter III of the OECD report *Computer-related Criminality: Analysis of Legal Policy in the OECD Area*, Report DSTI/ICCP 84.22 of 15 November 1984 (first version), 30 August 1985 (second version), and 18 April 1986 (final version). The complete OECD report will be published in 1986. For their most valuable contributions the author is very much indebted to Martine Briat, Hans-Peter Gassmann, and Paul Kenneth from the OECD ICCP Secretariat.

2. For these empirical changes, see especially *supra*, p. 4 *et seq.*

3. See Sieber, Internationale Erforschung und Bekämpfung der Wirtschaftskriminalität. In Albrecht and Sieber (eds), *20 Jahre Südwestdeutsche Kriminologische Kolloquien*, Kriminologische Forschungsberichte aus dem Max-Planck-Institut für ausländisches und internationales Strafrecht Freiburg, Vol. 18 (1984), pp. 29, 46 *et seq.*, 59 *et seq.*, 62 *et seq.*

4. As far as civil law is concerned, the study is confined to the question adjacent to comprehension of computer crime. Further civil law problems (such as liability for software or validity of contracts accomplished via active videotex systems) are not dealt with.

5. For the legal comprehension of CD manipulations see, for example, for **Australia**, Kirby, *Paper on the Legal Aspects of Information Technology*, Presented at the First Session of the ICCP on 27 September 1982; for **Austria**, Oberlandesgericht Wien, Decision of 22 May 1984, *Österreichische Juristenzeitung Leitsatzkartei*, section 129 Z3 StGB (Strafgesetzbuch), 1985/24; Höpfel, Die 'Bankomat'-Karte: Werttraeger? Schlüssel? Urkunde? (1983) *Österreichische Juristenzeitung* 234; for **Belgium**, Erkelens, La délinquance informatique belge et le droit pénal belge. In Annexe *à (1985) Droit de l'Informatique* No. 6, p.21, 22 *et seq.*; Spreutels, Infractions liées à l'informatique en droit belge. (1985) *Revue de Droit Pénal et de Criminologie* 357, 367 *et seq*; for **France**, Cour de Cassation, Decision of 24 November 1983, No. 82/90.672 B.R.A., (1985) wistra (*Zeitschrift für Wirtschaft, Steuer, Strafrecht*) 156; Massé, Infractions contre l'ordre financier. (1985) *Revue de science criminelle et de droit comparé* 101; Pradel and Feuillard, Les infractions commises au moyen de l'ordinateur. (1985) *Revue de Droit Pénal et de Criminologie* 307, 312 *et seq*; for the **Netherlands** de Schraaf, Computermisdaad. (1984) *Informatie* No.2 (February) 99, 100 *et seq.*; de Schraaf, GEA en het strafrecht. (1985) *Bank-en effectenbedrijf* (March) 96 *et seq.*; for **West Germany** Amtsgericht Berlin Tiergarten. (1984) wistra 114; *Amtsgericht Kulmbach* (1985) *Neue Juristische Wochenschrift* 2282; Gropp, Die Codecarte: Der Schlüssel zum Diebstahl. (1983) *Juristenzeitung* 487; Lenckner and Winkelbauer, Strafrechtliche Prob-

leme im modernen Zahlungsverkehr. (1984) wistra 83, 84 *et seq.*; Tiedemann, Computerkriminalität und Missbrauch von Bankomaten. (1983) *Wertpapier Mitteilungen* 1326, 1330 *et seq.*, for **Switzerland**, Zürcher Obergericht (1971) Blätter für Zürcherische Rechtsprechung 21. (1971) *Schweizerische Juristenzeitung* 224; Schmid, *Missbräuche im modernen Zahlungs- und Kreditverkehr* (1982), pp. 32 *et seq.*; for the **United Kingdom**, Scottish Law Commission, *Computer Crime* (Consultative Memorandum No. 68, 1986), pp. 40 *et seq.*

6. For the applicability of theft and embezzlement with respect to deposit money see, for **Belgium**, Erkelens, *supra*, note 5, Annexe à (1985) *Droit de l'Informatique* No. 6, 24; for **West Germany** Oberlandesgericht München. (1977) *Juristenzeitung* 408 with commentary by Sieber; Sieber, *Computerkriminalität und Strafrecht* (2nd edn, 1980), pp. 194 *et seq.*; for **Luxembourg**, Jaeger, La fraude Informatique. (1985) *Revue de Droit Pénal et de Criminologie* 323, 340 *et seq.*; for the **Netherlands** Kaspersen and Keijzer, Het Nederlandse Strafrecht en Computermisbruik, in: Kaspersen (ed.), *Strafrecht in de Informatiemaatschappij* (1986), 35, 46, *et seq.*; for **Switzerland**, (1961) **87** *Entscheidungen des Schweizerischen Bundesgerichts* IV, 115; Eidgenössisches Justiz- und Polizeidepartement, Bericht zum Vorentwurf über die Änderung des Strafgesetzbuches und des Militärstrafgesetzes betreffend die strafbaren Handlungen gegen das Vermögen und die Urkundenfälschung (1985), p. 7; Schubarth, *Die Systematik der Aneignungsdelikte* (Dissertation, Basel, 1968), pp. 18 *et seq.*, for the **United Kingdom**, Kielwein, *Die Straftaten gegen das Vermögen im englischen Recht* (1955), p. 53; Scottish Law Commission, *supra*, note 5, 46 *et seq.*, 51 *et seq.*; for the **United States,** Bequai, *How to Prevent Computer Crime* (1983), pp. 153, 155;

7. For the provision of fraud, see, for example, for **Austria,** Jaburek and Schmölzer, *Computer-Kriminalität* (1985), pp. 81 et *seq.*; for **Belgium**, Erkelens, *supra*, note 5, *Annexe à (1985) Droit de l'Informatique* No. 6, 23 *et seq.*, for **France**, Massé *supra*, note 5, (1985) *Revue de science criminelle et de droit comparé* 103, 106 *et seq.*; Pradel and Feuillard, *supra*, note 5 (1984) *Revue de Droit Pénal et de Criminologie* 311 *et seq.*; for **West Germany**, Oberlandesgericht München. (1977) *Juristenzeitung* 408 with commentary by Sieber; Lenckner, *Computerkriminalität und Vermögensdelikte* (1981), pp. 25 *et seq.*; Sieber, *Computerkriminalität, supra*, note 6, pp. 1/198 *et seq.*, 2/2 *et seq.*; Tiedemann, *supra*, note 5, (1983) *Wertpapier Mitteilungen* pp.1329 *et seq.*; for **Luxembourg**, Jäger, *supra*, note 6, (1985) *Revue de Droit Pénal et de Criminologie* 342 *et seq.*; for **Switzerland,** Eidgenössisches Justiz- und Polizeidepartement, *supra*, note 6, p. 20; Rohner, *Computerkriminalität* (1976), pp. 81 *et seq.*; Stratenwerth, Computerbetrug. (1981) **98** *Schweizerische Zeitschrift für Strafrecht* 229; for the **United Kingdom**, *D.P.P.* v. *Ray* (1973) **3** *All England Law Reports* 131; Scottish Law Commission, *supra*, note 5, pp. 41 *et seq.*; Tettenborn, Some legal aspects of computer abuse. (1980) **2** *The Company Lawyer* 147, 148; for the **United States,** Bequai, *How to Prevent Computer Crime, supra*, note 6, pp. 152 *et seq.* For similar problems in **Australia** and a restrictive interpretation of section 252A of the Tasmanian Criminal Code on 'Dishonestly obtaining a financial advantage' see Briscoe, *Research Paper on Computer Misuse* (Law Reform Commission of Tasmania), pp. 61 *et seq.*, 88.

8. For the questions of credit-card fraud see, for example, for **West Germany**,

Bundesgerichtshof, (1985) *Neue Juristische Wochenschrift* 2280; Otto, *Bargeld-loser Zahlungsverkehr und Strafrecht* (1978), pp. 93 *et seq.*; for **Switzerland**, Schmid, *supra*, note 5, pp.56 *et seq.*

9. For the provisions of breach of trust or 'abus de confiance' in the DP area, see, for **Austria**, Jaburek and Schmölzer, *supra*, note 7, pp. 83 *et seq.*; for **Belgium**, Erkelens, *supra*, note 5, Annexe à (1985) *Droit de l'Informatique* No. 6, 24 *et seq.*, 27; for **France**, Pradel and Feuillard, *supra*, note 5, (1985) *Revue de Droit Pénal et de Criminologie* 313, 317; for **West Germany**, Bundesgerichtshof, (1979) *Goltdammers Archiv für Strafrecht* 143; Oberlandesgericht München (1977) *Juristenzeitung* 408 with commentary by Sieber; Labsch, *Untreue* (1983), pp. 257 *et seq.*; Lenckner, *supra*, note 7, pp. 28 *et seq.*; Sieber, *Computerkriminalität, supra*, note 6, pp. 1/238 *et seq.*, 2/13 *et seq.*; Tiedemann, *supra*, note 5, (1983) *Wertpapier Mitteilungen* 1330; for **Luxembourg**, Jäger, *supra*, note 6, (1985) *Revue de Droit Pénal et de Criminologie* 349 *et seq.*; for the **United Kingdom**, Scottish Law Commission, *supra* note 5, pp. 69 *et seq.*

10. For the provisions of forgery and other provisions of falsification see, for **Australia**, Briscoe, *supra*, note 7, pp.83 *et seq.*; for **Austria**, Jaburek and Schmölzer, *supra* note 7, pp. 69 *et seq.*; for **Belgium**, Erkelens, *supra*, note 5, Annexe à (1985) *Droit de l'Informatique* No. 6, 25; Spreutels, *supra*, note 5, (1985) *Revue de Droit Pénal et de Criminologie* pp. 360 *et seq.*; for **France,** Massé, *supra*, note 5, (1985) *Revue de science criminelle et de droit comparé* 102 *et seq.*; Pradel and Feuillard, *supra*, note 5 (1985) *Revue de Droit Pénal et de Criminologie* 310 *et seq.*; for **West Germany**, Sieber, *Computerkriminalität, supra*, note 6, 1/251 *et seq.*, 2/20 *et seq.;* Tiedemann, *supra*, note 5 (1983) *Wertpapier Mitteilungen* 1330; Winkelbauer, Computerkriminalität und Strafrecht. (1985) *Computer und Recht* 40, 41 *et seq.;* for **Italy**, Picotti, Problemi penalistici in tema di falsificazione di dati informatici. (1985) *Il diritto dell'Informazione dell'Informatica* 939; for **Luxembourg**, Jäger, *supra*, note 6, (1985) *Revue de Droit Pénal et de Criminologie* 345 *et seq*; for the **Netherlands** Kaspersen and Keijzer, *supra*, note 5, in Kaspersen (ed.), 42 *et seq.*; de Schraaf, *supra*, note 5, (1984) *Informatie* No 2, p.101; for **Switzerland**, Rohner, *supra*, note 7, 59 *et seq.;* Zweifel, *Buchführungsdelikte mittels EDV und Massnahmen zu deren Verhinderung* (1984), pp. 117 *et seq.*; for the **United Kingdom**, Scottish Law Commission, *supra*, note 5, pp. 43 *et seq.* (concerning the Scots crime of uttering); for the **United States**, US Appellate Court, **18** *American Criminal Law Review* 377; Bequai, *How to Prevent Computer Crime, supra*, note 6, p. 157.

11. See, for the provisions on false accounting, for example, Briscoe, *supra*, note 7, p. 121; for the provisions on counterfeiting, Bequai, *How to Prevent Computer Crime, supra*, note 6, p.157.

12. For a **comparative overview** on the international computer crime law problems, see Briat, La fraude informatique. (1985) *Revue de Droit Pénal et de Criminologie* 287; Schjolberg, *Computers and Penal Legislation* (1983); Sieber, in OECD, *supra*, note 1; Sieber, New legislative responses to computer related economic crimes and infringements of privacy, in Kaspersen (ed.) *Strafrecht in de Informatiemaatschappij* (1986), p. 75.

13. For the law reform in **Sweden** see Schjolberg, *Computers and Penal Legislation,*

supra, note 12, p. 32; Sieber, *Computerkriminalität, supra,* note 6, p. 358; Solarz, *Datorteknik och brottslighet* (1985). For the other **Nordic countries**, see *infra,* notes 22 and 23.

14. In addition to the Acts described, the 'Small Business Computer Security and Education Act of 1984' was passed by the US Senate on 29 June 1984. This Act does not contain penal provisions but establishes a 'Computer Security and Education Advisory Council' which, in addition to other tasks, shall advise the Administration in questions concerning computer crimes against small businesses. For the legal situation in the **United States**, see, for example, Bequai, *Computer Crime* (1978), especially pp. 25 *et seq*; Bloombecker, *Criminal Informatics Law*, Paper written for the Intergovernmental Bureau for Informatics (1983); Bloombecker, *The Computer Crime Law Reporter* (looseleaf, 1984; amended 1986); Couch, A suggested legislative approach to the problem of computer crime. (1981) **38** *Washington and Lee Law Review* 1173; Mandell, *Computers, Data Processing, and the Law* (1984); Mendes, La législation pénale en matière d'ordinateurs et les mesures de sécurité aux Etats-Unis. Annexe à *Droit de l'Informatique* 1985–6, p.39; Möhrenschlager, *Neue bundesstrafrechtliche Regelung gegen die Fälschung und den Missbrauch von Kreditkarten in den USA* (1985) wistra 216; National Criminal Justice Information and Statistics Service, *Criminal Justice Resource Manual* (1979); Nycum, The criminal law aspects of computer abuse: Part I State penal law, Part II Federal criminal code. **5** (1976) *Rutgers Journal of Computers and Law* 271, 297; Parker, *Fighting Computer Crime* (1983), especially pp. 227 *et seq.*; Sokolik, Computer crime—the need for deterrent legislation. (1980) **2** *Computer and Law Journal* 353; US Department of Justice, *Computer Crime— Legislative Resource Manual* (1980). For further references see *infra*, Appendix 1.

15. For the legislative situation in the **United Kingdom**, see The Forgery and Counterfeiting Act 1981, *Halsbury's Statutes of England*, Vol. 51 (3rd edn, 1982), pp. 707 *et seq.*; Scottish Law Commission, *supra*, note 5, 44 *et seq.*, 88 *et seq*; Tapper, *Computer Law* (3rd edn, 1983), pp. 96 *et seq.*; Tettenborn, *supra*, note 7. (1980) **2** *The Company Lawyer* 147.

16. For the law reform in **Australia**, see Briscoe, *supra*, note 7, pp. 45 *et seq.*; McNiff and Juris, *Criminal Liability for Australian Computer Abuse* (ed. 1980 by the Computer Abuse Research Bureau at the Caulfield Institute of Technology, Melbourne); Scottish Law Commission, *supra*, note 5, 135 *et seq.*; Working Party of the National Companies and Securities Commission, Draft Working Paper on Computer Crime—Substantive Law Aspects (1982).

17. For the legal situation in **Canada**, see Department of Justice, *Response of the Government of Canada to the Report of the Parliamentary Sub-Committee on Computer Crime* (1983); Hertz, Protecting computer systems with the criminal law. (1983) *Computer Law* 1; Institute of Law Research and Reform of the University of Alberta, Background Paper on Improper Interference with Computers and the Misappropriation of Commercial Information; Piragoff, Combatting computer crimes with criminal laws, in: Kaspersen (ed.), *Strafrecht in de Informatiemaatschappij* (1986), p. 103; Piragoff, Les projets législatifs canadiens visant à la protection de l'intégrité des systèmes informati-

ques. In: Annexe à (1985) *Droit de l'Informatique* No. 6, p. 33 (updated version of Computers. (1984) *Ottawa Law Review* 306; Sub-Committee on Computer Crime of the Standing Committee on Justice and Legal Affairs, Final Report, 14, 16, and 21 June 1983 (House of Commons, Issue No. 18).

18. For the legal situation in **Denmark**, see Greve, *EDB-strafferet* (1984); Hog, EDB og EDB-Kriminalitet. In *Anklagemyndighedens arsberetning* (edited by the Danish Director of Public Prosecutions, 1981), p. 58; Meilby and Hog, Mandatsvig. (1985) *Juristen* 41.

19. See Zweites Gesetz zur Bekämpfung der Wirtschaftskriminalität of 15 May 1986, *Bundesgesetzblatt* I, p. 721. The first official reform proposals in **West Germany** were worked out in 1978 by the Commission of Experts for Combatting Economic Crime, initiated by the West German Ministry of Justice. The recommendation of this group, including the opinions of Lampe and Sieber, are published in: Bundesministerium der Justiz (ed.), *Tagungsberichte der Sachverständigenkommission zur Bekämpfung der Wirtschaftskriminalität* (Vol. 12, 1977), pp.59 *et seq.* For an overview on the legal situation, see, for example, Deutscher Bundestag, Beschlussempfehlung und Bericht des Rechtsausschusses, Bundestagsdrucksache 10/5058 of 19 February 1986; Hartmann, La criminalité informatique et sa répression par les réformes pénales en République Féderale d'Allemagne. In Annexe à (1985) *Droit de l'Informatique* No. 6, p. 11; Lampe, Die strafrechtliche Behandlung der sogenannten Computerkriminalität. (1975) *Goltdammers Archiv für Strafrecht* 1; Lenckner, *Computerkriminalität und Vermögensdelikte* (1981); Möhrenschlager, *Der Regierungsentwurf eines Zweiten Gesetzes zur Bekämpfung der Wirtschaftskriminalität* (1982) wistra 201; Sieber, *Computerkriminalität und Strafrecht* (2nd edn, 1980); Sieber, *Informationstechnologie und Strafrechtsreform* (1985); Tiedemann, *supra*, note 5 (1983) *Wertpapier Mitteilungen* 1326; Winkelbauer, *supra*, note 10. (1985) *Computer und Recht* 41 *et seq.* For further references, see Appendix 1.

20. For the legal situation in **Switzerland**, see Egli, *Grundformen der Wirtschaftskriminalität* (1985), p. 150; Eidgenössisches Justiz- und Polizeidepartement, *supra*, note 6, pp. 2 et *seq.*; Rohner, *Computerkriminalität* (1976); Stratenwerth, *supra*, note 7. (1981) **98** *Schweizerische Zeitschrift für Strafrecht* 229; Schmid, *Wirtschaftskriminalität in der Schweiz* (Schweizerischer Juristenverein, Referate und Mitteilungen No. 2, 1985), pp. 254 *et seq.* For further references, see Appendix 1.

21. For the legal situation in **Austria**, see Zima, Computerkriminalität (1980) *Journal für Betriebswirtschaft* No.2, 82; Jaburek and Schmölzer, *Computer-Kriminalität* (1985).

22. For the legal situation in **Sweden**, see the references *supra*, note 13.

23. For the legal situation in **Norway**, see Andenaes, Fonger, Oug, Origstad, Drolsum, Schjolberg and Selmer, Datakriminalitet. *Norges Offentlige Utredvinger* No. 31 (1985); Schjolberg, Computer-Assisted Crime in Scandinavia. (1980) **2** *Computer and Law Journal* 457; Schjolberg, Computer crime in Norway. In: Bing and Selmer (eds), *A Decade of Computers and Law* (1980), p. 440; Schjolberg, *Computers and Penal Legislation* (1983); Schjolberg, *Computers and Penal Legislation—A study of the legal politics of a new technology*, Complex 2/83 (Universitetsforlaget, Oslo).

24. For the situation in **Finland**, see Hämäläinen, Atk-rikollisuus ja rikoslain-säädänto (Computer crime and penal legislation). (1984) *Suomen Poliisilehti* 38; Kainomaa, Tietoturva sekä vahingot ja väärinkäytökset atk:ssa (Data security, losses and abuses in the field of automatic data processing), *Tutkimus-Raportti* 3/84 (published by Tietotekniikan Kehittämiskeskus—Center for the Development of Data Technology, Helsinki, 1984); Lehtimaja, Atk-turvallismus ja lainsäädäntö (Data security and legislation). (1984) *Suomen Poliisilehti* 40; Lehtimaja, Om databrott ur finländsk synvinkel (Finnish perspective on computer crime). (1979) *Tidskrift, utgiven av Juridiska Föreningen i Finland* 668; Lehtimaja, Tietokonerikollisuuteen liittyviä oikeudellisia ongelmia (Legal problems of computer crime). (1983) *Defensor Legis* 54; Lehtimaja, Laki ei tunne atk-rikoksia. (1984) *Lakimiesuutiset* No. 10, 5; Stenlund and Lampola, Tietotekniikka, hallinto ja oikeus (Information technology, administration and the law), *Jyväskylä* 1985.

25. For the legal situation in **France** see Aupecle-Guicheney, Les infractions pénales favorisées par l'informatique (Thèse de doctorat de 3è cycle, 1984); Chaigneau, La délinquance télématique. In *Télématique et communication— un nouveau droit, Actes des Troisièmes Entretiens de Nanterre de Droit de l'Informatique* (1985), p.91; Pitrat, Fraude informatique et pouvoirs publics. In: Annexe à *(1985) Droit de l'Informatique* No. 6, 46; Pradel and Feuillard, *supra*, note 5 (1985) *Revue de Droit Pénal et de Criminologie* 307.

26. For law reform in **Portugal**, see also *infra*, p. 99 and Appendix 2.

27. See also the report of the Australian Working Party, *supra*, note 16, at 3 *et seq.*, 51 *et seq.*, 57 *et seq.*, Briscoe, *supra*, note 7, 73 *et seq.*, Canadian Sub-Committee, *supra*, note 17, 17 *et seq.*; Tettenborn, *supra*, note 7 (1980) **2** *The Company Lawyer* 151.

28. See also Schjolberg, Computer and penal legislation. In *SECURICOM 1984* (Congress Proceedings edited by SEDEP, Paris), 23 *et seq.;* Sieber, *Informationstechnologie, supra*, note 19, 33 *et seq.*

29. See, for example, for **Belgium,** Erkelens, *supra*, note 5. Annexe à (1985) *Droit de l'Informatique* No. 6, 26 *et seq.*; Spreutels, *supra*, note 5. (1985) *Revue de Droit Pénal et de Criminologie* 362 *et seq;* for **West Germany** Sieber, *Computerkriminalität, supra*, note 6, 1/190.

30. See Chambre Criminelle de la Cour de Cassation, Decision of 8 January 1979. (1979) **175** *Bulletin des Arrêts de la Cour de Cassation* 32; Pradel and Feuillard, *supra*, note 5, (1985) *Revue de Droit Pénal et de Criminologie* 317.

31. See Jaburek and Schmölzer, *supra*, note 7, 45 *et seq.*

32. Court of Appeals of Arnhem, Decision of 27 October 1983, (1984) *Nederlandse Jursprudentie* 80; (1984) *Computerrecht* No. 1, 31; (1984) *Droit de l'informatique* No.2, 22. The same opinion was adopted in a similar case by the Court of Appeals of Antwerpen Decision of 13 December 1984, (1985–1986) *Rechtskundig Weekblad* 244. For critics see Vandenberghe, Computermisbruik, beveiliging en strafrecht, in Kaspersen (ed.) *Strafrecht in de Informatiemaatschappij* (1986) p.25, 28 *et seq.*; Vandenberghe, Diefstal van computergegevens, revolutie in het strafrecht, (1986) *Computerrecht*, No. 1, p.39.

33. See, for example, for **Belgium**, Erkelens, *supra*, note 5. Annexe à (1985) *Droit de l'Informatique* no. 6, 26 *et seq*.; for **Finland**, Decision of the Supreme Court (1955) *KKO* I 1 (in the meantime, in Finland the Electricity Act passed in 1979 includes an express reference to the offence of theft).

34. For the **United Kingdom**, see Theft Act 1968, sections 4 and 6 (*Halsbury's Statutes of England*, 3rd edn, vol. 8, 1969, pp.784 *et seq*., 786); *Oxford* v. *Moss*. (1979) **68** *Criminal Appeal Reports* 183 with commentary by Smith in (1979) *Criminal Law Review 119; R.* v. *Lloyd and Others*. (1985) **2** *All England Law Reports* 661; Briscoe, *supra*, note 7, 59; Hammond, Quantum physics, econometric models and property rights to information. (1981) **27** *McGill Law Journal* 47, 66 *et seq*.; Schjolberg, *Computers and Penal Legislation*, *supra*, note 12, pp. 71; Scottish Law Commission, *supra*, note 5, pp. 51 *et seq*.; Tapper, *Computer Law, supra*, note 15, pp. 216; Tettenborn, The function of the law in industrial espionage. (1979/80) **1** *The Company Lawyer* 267 *et seq*. See also the references *infra*, note 43.

35. For **Australia**, see Briscoe, *supra*, note 7, 54 *et seq*.; Working Party of the National Companies and Securities Commission, *supra*, note 26, 61, 75.

36. For the protection of trade secrets, especially in the DP area, in the **United States** see *Hancock* v. *State*. **402** *South Western Reporter* 906 (Texas Criminal Appeal Court, 1966); *Ward* v. *The Superior Court of California*. **3** *CLSR* 206 (Calif. Super. Court, 1972); *People* v. *Home Insurance Company*. **591** *Pacific Reporter* 1036 (Colo., 1979); *Dowling* v. *US*. **30** *BNA's Patent, Trademark & Copyright Journal* (PTCJ) 241, (1985) Gewerblicher Rechtsschutz und Urheberrecht Internationaler Teil (*GRUR Int*.) 610; Baker, *Scuttle the Computer Pirate—Software Protection Schemes* (1984), pp.32 *et seq*.; Bequai, *Computer Crime, supra*, note 14, pp. 28 *et seq*.; Bequai, *How to Prevent Computer Crime, supra*, note 6, 155; Dessemontet, *The Legal Protection of Know-how in the United States of America* (2nd edn, 1976); Keet, *Preventing Piracy—A Business Guide to Software Protection* (1985), pp. 69 *et seq*.; Mandell, *supra*, note 14, 130 *et seq*.; Mantle, Trade secret and copyright protection of computer software (1984) **IV** *Computer/Law Journal* 669, 673 *et seq*.; National Criminal Justice Information and Statistics Service, *supra*, note 14, 142 *et seq*.; Saumweber, Der Schutz von Know-how im deutschen und amerikanischen Recht (Munich dissertation, 1978), pp. 177 *et seq*., 265 *et seq*.; Stern, Patent and trade secret protection of computer software under United States law. In: Brett and Perry (eds), *The Legal Protection of Computer Software* (1981), pp. 65 *et seq*., 71 *et seq*.; US Department of Justice, *Computer Crime Legislative Resource Manual, supra*, note 14, 3 *et seq*.

37. For the protection of trade secrets in **Canada**, see *R.* v. *Stewart* (1982), High Court of Justice, Decision of 25 June 1982, **38** *Ontario Reports* (2nd) p. 84, (1982) **68** *Canadian Criminal Cases (CCC* 2d) 305; *R.* v. *Stewart* (1983), Ontario Court of Appeal. **42** *Ontario Reports* (2d) 225; Alberta Institute of Law Research and Reform, Improper Interference with Computers and the Misappropriation of Commercial Information, Background Paper (1983); Alberta Institute of Law Research and Reform, Protection of Trade Secrets, Report for Discussion No.1 (1984); Piragoff, Computers. (1984) **16** *Ottawa Law Review* 305, 311 *et seq*., Sub-Committee on Computer Crime of the Standing Committee on Justice and Legal Affairs, *supra*, note 17, 15.

38. The applicability of the provisions punishing the acts of receiving or trading with stolen goods is controversially disputed in many countries. See, for example, for **West Germany** Rupp, *Zur strafrechtlichen Verantwortung des 'bösgläubigen' Softwareerwerbers* (1985) wistra 137; for the **United States,** see the decision *US* v. *Dowling* cited in note 36. The new **Danish** Penal Code Amendment Act on 'Datakriminalitet' of 1985 in section 284 of the Penal Code now states that the same punishment applies to the illegal receiving of computer programs as to receiving stolen goods.

39. See also the Canadian Sub-Committee on Computer Crime, *supra*, note 17, 15; Hammond, *supra*, note 34. (1981) *27 McGill Law Journal* 47 *et seq.*; Schjolberg, *supra*, note 28, In: *SECURICOM 1984*, p. 19.

40. For trade-secret protection and unfair competition protection of computer software and data see, for **Austria**, Jaburek and Schmölzer, *supra*, note 7, 48 *et seq.*, 64 *et seq.;* for **Belgium**, Erkelens, *supra*, note 5. Annexe à (1985) *Droit de l'Informatique* No. 6, 27 *et seq.;* for **France**, Bertrand, *Protections du Logiciel* (1984), pp. 151 *et seq.;* Pradel and Feuillard, *supra*, note 5 (1985) *Revue de Droit Pénal et de Criminologie* 318; Thunis, Les modes de protection juridique du logiciel. (1983) *9/1 Droit de Pratique du Commerce International (DPCI)* 121, 140 *et seq.;* for **West Germany** see von Gamm, Der urheber- und wettbewerbsrechtliche Schutz von Rechenprogrammen. (1969) *Wettbewerb in Recht und Praxis* 96; Kolle, Der Rechtsschutz der Computersoftware in der Bundesrepublik Deutschland. (1982) *Gewerblicher Rechtsschutz und Urheberrecht (GRUR)* 443, 456 *et seq.*; Krüger, Der strafrechtliche Schutz des Geschäfts- und Betriebsgeheimnisses im Wettbewerbsrecht. (1984) *European University Studies* **405**; Lampe, Der strafrechtliche Schutz des Know-how gegen Veruntreuung durch den Vertragspartner. (1977) *Betriebs-Berater* 1477; Sieber, *Computerkriminalität, supra*, note 6, 2/72 *et seq.*, Sieber, Urheberrechtliche und wettbewerbsrechtliche Erfassung der unbefugten Softwarenutzung. (1981) *Betriebs-Berater* 1547, 1553 *et seq.*; for **Italy**, Introvigne, Case comment. (1983) *European Intellectual Property Review* 347; for **Luxembourg**, Jäger, *supra*, note 6, (1985) *Revue de Droit Pénal et de Criminologie* 348; for the **Netherlands**, Supreme Court of the Netherlands, decision of 26 June 1953. (1954) *Dutch Law Reports* No. 90; Supreme Court of the Netherlands, Decision of 23 June 1961. (1961) *Dutch Law Reports* No. 423; Ministry for Foreign Affairs of the Netherlands, Letter to the Acting Commissioner of Patents and Trademarks of the USA. (1985) **50** *Federal Register* 24796, 24798; Kaspersen and Keijzer, *supra,* note 6, in: Kaspersen (ed.), p.62 *et seq.*; for **Norway** and the **Nordic countries**, see Bull, Legal protection of computer programs. In: Bing and Selmer (eds), *A Decade of Computers and Law* (1980), 410, 416 *et seq.* A **comparative overview** of trade-secret protection in the European countries is given by Oehler (ed.), *Der strafrechtliche Schutz des Geschäfts- und Betriebsgeheimnisses in den Ländern der europäischen Gemeinschaft sowie in Österreich und in der Schweiz*, Vol. I (1978), Vol. II (1981); Tiedemann, Literaturbericht. (1982) **94** *Zeitschrift für die gesamte Strafrechtswissenschaft* 299.

41. See the references *supra*, note 36.

42. See the references *supra*, note 37.

43. For the protection of trade secrets in the **United Kingdom** see the references *supra*, note 34 as well as *Saltman Engineering Company* v. *Campbell Engineering Company*. (1948) Reports of Patent Designs and Trade Mark Cases 203; and Scottish Law Commission, *supra*, note 5, p. 85. For the issue of breach of confidence in relation to computer systems see *Format Communications Manufacturing Ltd* v. *ITT (UK) Ltd*. (1983) *Fleet Street Reports* 473. For an overview, see Brett and Perry (eds), *The Legal Protection of Computer Software* (1981), pp. 23 *et seq.*; Pearson, *Computer Contracts* (1984), pp. 224 *et seq.*; Wilson, The protection of computer programs under common law. In: Brett and Perry (eds), *The Legal Protection of Computer Software* (1981), p. 75. For **Australia**, see Briscoe, *supra*, note 7, pp. 60, 103 *et seq.*

44. For **Japan**, see Osaka District Court Decision of 18 December 1979. (1981/8) No.70 *Kogyoshoyn-Kenho Kenkyu* 17, (1981/2) *Patents & Licensing* 14.; Kawashia and Greguras, Software protection in Japan. (1982) *Computer Fraud & Security Bulletin* 10; SIA Japan Software Industry Association/Software Legal Protection Committee, A Report on Japanese Legal Protection of Software (May 1983), pp. 18 *et seq.*

45. See the references supra, note 19; and *Bundestags-Drucksache* 9/1707 of 1 June 1982; Möhrenschlager, *Ergänzender Nachtrag*. (1984) wistra 171; Sieber, *Informationstechnologie, supra*, note 19, pp. 49 *et seq.*

46. The regulations of the **Swedish** Unfair Competition Act of 1931 are a modification of legislation passed in 1919, which was based upon the German law on unfair competition. The new Protection of Trade Secrets Acts requires that the perpetrator obtains access to a trade secret by certain means and utilizes or discloses the trade secret; attempts and acts in preparation are also subject to penal sanctions.

47. For the use of court injunctions in the field of computer crime, see *infra*, p. 136.

48. See the references *supra*, note 37.

49. See the references *supra*, note 36.

50. Resolution no. 571 of 3 July 1974.

51. For the phenomenological description and cases of illegal exports of computer hardware and software see Sieber, *Computerkriminalität, supra*, note 6, 1/119 *et seq.*

52. For law reform in **France**, see *supra* note 25; for **Portugal**, *infra*, p. 99 and Appendix 1; for **Italy**, *infra*, Appendix 2; for **Finland**, *supra*, note 24.

53. Concerning computer contracts see, from an **international level**, Marella, Contratto unitario e collegamento negoziale nella 'vendita' di hardware & software. (1985) *Rivista Critica del Diritto Privato* 81; Pearson, *Computer Contracts* (1984); for **France**, Bertrand, *Contracts informatiques* (1983); Bertrand, *supra*, note 40, 135 *et seq.*; de Bellefonds and Hollande, *Les Contrats informatique* (1984); Coipel and Cruysmans *et al.*, *Le droit des contrats informatiques* (1983); de Lamberterie, *Les contrats en informatique* (1983); for **West Germany**, Ellenberger and Müller, *Zweckmässige Gestaltung von Hardware-, Software- und Projektverträgen* (2nd edn, 1984); Kilian, Vertrags-

gestaltung und Mängelhaftung bei Computer-software. (1986) *Computer und Recht* 187; Kindermann, Vertrieb und Nutzung von Computersoftware aus urheberrechtlicher Sicht. (1983) *Gewerblicher Rechtsschutz und Urheberrecht (GRUR)* 150; Kindermann, Das Nutzungsrecht am Computerprogramm. (1984) *Neue Zeitschrift für Arbeits- und Sozialrecht* 209; Kindermann, Der angestellte Programmierer. (1985) *GRUR* 1008; Koch, *Computer-Vertragsrecht* (1985); Link, Die Auswirkungen des Urheberrechts auf die vertraglichen Beziehungen bei der Erstellung von Computerprogrammen. (1986) *GRUR* 141; Sieber, *Computerkriminalität, supra*, note 6, 2/90 *et seq.*; Sieber, Copyright protection of computer programs in Germany. (1984) *European Intellectual Property Review* 214, 220 *et seq.*; Zahrnt, *Datenverarbeitungsverträge* (2nd edn., 1981) and *DV-Verträge* (1985); for **Italy**, Alpa, *I contratti di utilizzazione del computer* (1984); Marella, Vendita di 'hardware' con 'software' e risoluzione del contratto per inadempimento. (1985) *Il Foro Italiano* part I 2718;; for **Japan**, see SIA Japan Software Industry Assocation, *supra*, note 44, 23 *et seq.*; for **Switzerland**, Fuchs, *Der Erwerb von Computern* (1978); Wasser, *Der Computerwartungsvertrag* (1980); for the **United Kingdom**, Chappatte, Specific problems involved in licensing software. (1985) **2** *Computer Law & Practice* 16; Tapper, *Computer Law, supra*, note 15, 42 *et seq.*, 205 *et seq.*; for the **United States,** see Brandon and Segelstein, *Data Processing Contracts* (2nd edn, 1984); Keet, *supra*, note 36, 97 *et seq.;* Mandell, *supra*, note 14, 1 *et seq.*, 134 *et seq.*, Remer, *Legal Care for Your Software* (1982).

54. According to a definition worked out by the WIPO Working Group on Technical Questions Relating to the Legal Protection of Computer Software during a meeting in Canberra in April 1984, a computer program can be defined as a well-formed set of instructions capable of directing automatic information-handling machines to perform some functions, in a specific way. For more details see WIPO Working Group on Technical Questions Relating to the Protection of Computer Software, Canberra 2–6 April 1984, Report published 30 April 1984.

55. See *supra*, pp. 12 *et seq.*

56. For statistical data concerning the value of computer software see Bertin and Lamberterie, *La Protection du Logiciel* (1985), p. 39; Organization for Economic Co-operation and Development/Committee for Information, Computer and Communications Policy, *Software: A New Industry*, Document ICCP (84) 4 of 2 October 1984, especially pp. 17 *et seq.*, 63 *et seq.*, 81 *et seq.*, 180 *et seq.*; (1985) *BIT-Nachrichten* No.22/23, April 1985, p. 13.

57. Nevertheless, names of programs protected as trade marks can be of considerable commercial value, since a memorable and distinctive name can identify the program with a particular trader and assure a purchaser or licensee that he is getting a certain quality of program. For trade-mark protection of computer programs, see Baker, *supra*, note 36, 64 *et seq.*; Bertrand, *supra*, note 40, 115 *et seq.*; Betten, Zum Rechtsschutz von Computerprogrammen. (1983) *Mitteilungen der deutschen Patentanwälte* 62; Betten, Der Rechtsschutz von Computer-Software. (1986) *Mitteilungen der deutscheu Patentanwälte* 10;

Hannemann, *The Patentability of Computer Software* (1985), p. 10; Keet, *supra* note 36, 113 *et seq.*; Mandell, *supra*, note 14, 132 *et seq.*; Niblett, A good name is valuable–protect it. *Computer Weekly* 18 March 1982; Pearson, *Computer Contracts, supra*, note 43, 215 *et seq.*, 271 *et seq.*

58. Concerning patent protection of computer programs, see, for **Austria**, Jaburek and Schmölzer, *supra*, note 7, 50; for **Belgium,** Erkelens, *supra*, note 5. Annexe à (1985) *Droit de l'Informatique* No. 6, 29; for **France,** Schlumberger v. *Director of INPI*, Paris Court of Appeals, Decision of 15 June 1981. (1981) *Propriété industrielle—Bulletin documentaire* 285, iii–175; Bertrand, *supra*, note 40, 31 *et seq.*; Hannemann, *supra*, note 57, 158 *et seq.*; République Française/Ministère de l'Industrie et de la Recherche, *Vers une Protection des Logiciels Informatiques—Situation actuelle et propositions* (Rapport Combaldieu, 15 December 1983), pp.10 *et seq*; Thunis, *supra*, note 40. (1983) 9 *DPCI* 134 *et seq.*; for **West Germany** *Siemens AG* v. *AEG-Telefunken.* (1977) *Gewerblicher Rechtsschutz und Urheberrecht (GRUR)* 96, (1977) 8 *International Review of Industrial Property and Copyright Law (IIC)* 558; Licentia Patent-VerwaltungsGmbH. (1977) *GRUR* 657, (1978) **9** *IIC* 459; *Siemens AG* v. *AEG-Telefunken.* (1978) *GRUR* 102, (1978) **9** *IIC* 363; *Burroughs Corp.* v. *AEG-Telefunken.* (1978) *GRUR* 420, (1979) **10** *IIC* 489; Hannemann, *supra*, note 57, 229; Kindermann, Zur Lehre von der technischen Erfindung. (1979) *GRUR* 443, 501; Kolle, *supra*, note 40, (1982) *GRUR* 445; Ulmer and Kolle, Copyright Protection of Computer Programs, (1983) **14** *IIC* 159; Gall, Computerprogramme und Patentschutz. (1985) *Mitteilungen der deutschen Patentanwälte* 183; for **Italy**, Pretura di Milano, Decision of 16 May, 1983. (1985) *Rivisto di Diritto Industriale* parte II, 67; Afferni, Brevettabilità del software. In: Alpa, *La tutela giuridica del software* (1984), p. 1; Ghidini, I programmi per computers fra brevetto e diritto d'autore. In: Alpa, *supra* cited, p. 17 *et seq.*; Introvigne, Case comment. (1983) *European Intellectual Property Review (EIPR)* 347, 348; for the **Netherlands**, Netherlands Board of Appeals Patent Office, Decision of 19 January 1983. (1983) *Bijblad bij Industriele Eigendom (BIE)* No.104; Hannemann, De octrooieerbaarheid van software uitvindingen in Nederland. (1983) *BIE* 317; Hannemann, *supra*, note 57, 229; for **Switzerland** Dimensional Synthesis. (1974) *IIC* 448; Hannemann, *supra*, note 57, 214; for the **United Kingdom**, see Slee and Harris's applications. (1966) *Reports of Patent, Designs and Trade Mark Cases (RPC)* 194; International Business Machines Corp. application. (1980) *Fleet Street Reports (FSR)* 564; Gever's application. (1970) *RPC* 91; Badger Co. Inc.'s application. 1970 *RPC* 36; Burroughs Corporation (Perkins') application. (1974) *RPC* 147; Hannemann, *supra*, note 57, 131 *et seq.*; Pearson, *supra*, note 43, 242 *et seq.* For a *comparative overview* see Bertrand, *supra*, note 40, 34 *et seq*; Hannemann, supra, note 57, pp. 28 *et seq.*

59. For the European Patent Convention and the new guidelines of the European Patent Office see Notices Dated 6 and 26 March 1985 Concerning Amendments to the Guidelines for Examination in the European Patent Offices, (1985) *Official Journal EPO* 173; Bauer, Rechtsschutz von Computerprogrammen in der Bundesrepublik Deutschland. (1985) *Computer und Recht* 5, 6; Gall, Computerprogramme und Patentschutz. (1985) *Mitteilungen der deutschen Patentanwälte* 181; Gall, European Patent Office Guidelines 1985 on the

protection of inventions relating to computer programs. (1985) *Computer Law & Practice* No. 1, 2; Hannemann, *supra*, note 57, 242 *et seq.*; Kolle, The Patentability of Computer Software in Europe and under the International Patent Treaties. In: Brett and Perry (eds), *supra*, note 43, pp 30 *et seq.*

60. For patent protection of computer programs in the **United States**, see *Gottschalk* v. *Benson* (1972). **409** *United States Supreme Courts Reports (US)* 63; *Parker* v. *Flook* (1978). **437** *US* 584; *Diamond* v. *Diehr* (1981). **450** *US* 175. (1981) *Gewerblicher Rechtsschutz und Urheberrecht Internationaler Teil* 646; Hannemann, *supra*, note 57, 28 *et seq.*; Keet, *supra*, note 36, 41 *et seq.*; Mandell, *supra*, note 14, 126 *et seq.*; Mantle, *supra*, note 36, (1984) **VI** *Computer and Law Journal* 670 *et seq.*; Pearson, *supra*, note 43, 244 *et seq.*; Stern, The legal protection of computer software and computer-related innovations in the United States. (1982) *Industrial Property* 152, 176, 162 *et seq.*; World Intellectual Property Organization (WIPO), Committee of Experts on the Legal Protection of Computer Software, Second Session Geneva, 13–17 June 1983, Report LPCS/II/6 of 17 June 1983, p. 3.

61. For patent protection of computer programs in **Canada**, see *Schlumberger Canada Ltd.* v. *Commissioner of Patents* (1981). **56** *Canadian Patent Reporter* (*CPR* 2d) 204; Hannemann, *supra*, note 57, 115 *et seq.*; Pearson, *supra*, note 43, 248 *et seq.* For an overview concerning **Canada**, the **United Kingdom** and the **United States**, see Tapper, *supra*, note 15, 18 *et seq.*

62. For patent protection of computer programs in **Australia**, see Context Systems Incoporated's application. (1978) *Australian Official Journal of Patents* 1093; Hannemann, *supra*, note 57, 147 *et seq.*

63. For patent protection of computer programs in **Japan**, see note 44 and Hannemann, *supra*, note 57, pp. 221 *et seq.*

64. For copyright protection of computer programs in the **United States**, see Federal Law No.96/517 of 12 December 1980 altering section 101 of the Copyright Act, Public Law No. 96–517 94 Stat. 3015, 3028; US Courts of Appeals, *Williams Electronic Inc.* v. *Artic International, Inc.* **685** *Federal Reporter* (*F.* 2d) 870, (1984) Gewerblicher Rechtsschutz und Urheberrecht Internationaler Teil (*GRUR Int.*) 191; US Court of Appeals, *Apple Computer Inc.* v. *Franklin Computer Corp.* **714** *F.* 2d 1240, **26** *BNA's Patent, Trademark & Copyright Journal (PTCJ)* 433; US Court of Appeals, *Apple Computer Inc.* v. *Formula International Inc.* **27** *PTCJ* 414, **221** *United States Patent Quarterly (USQ)* 762; Baker, *supra*, note 36, 15 *et seq.*, Bauer, Urheberrechtsschutz von Computerprogrammen in den USA. (1984) *GRUR Int.* 136; Keet, *supra*, note 36, 51 *et seq.*; Mantle, *supra*, note 14, (1984) *Computer Law Journal* 677 *et seq.*; National Commission on New Technological Uses of Copyrighted Works (CONTU), Final Report, 31 July 1978, especially pp. 9 *et seq.*; Pearson, *supra*, note 43, 242 *et seq.*; Stern, *supra*, note 60, (1982) *International Review of Industrial Property and Copyright Law* 152.

65. For the copyright protection of computer programs in **Australia**, see *Apple Computer Inc.* v. *Computer Edge Pty Ltd.* (1984) *Fleet Street Reporter* 481, (1984) *Australian Trade Practices Reports* No.40–453; Briscoe, *supra*, note 7, 98 *et seq.*; Pearson, *supra*, note 43, 258 *et seq.*

66. For the copyright protection of computer programs in the **United Kingdom**, see *Gates* v. *Swift*. (1982) *Reports of Patent, Design, and Trade Mark Cases (RPC)* 339; *Sega Enterprises* v. *Alca Electronics*. (1982) *Fleet Street Reporter (FSR)* 516, (1984) *Gewerblicher Rechtsschutz und Urheberrecht Internationaler Teil* 111; *Sega Enterprises* v. *Richards*. (1983) *FSR* 73; *Systematica Ltd* v. *London Computer Centre Ltd*. (1983) *FSR* 313; *Thrustcode Ltd* v. *VW Computing Ltd*. (1983) *FSR* 502; *Format Communications MFG Ltd* v. *ITT (UK) Ltd*. (1983) *FSR* 473; Carr, Copyright protection for computer software—a UK perspective. (1982) *European Intellectual Property Review* 88; Committee to Consider the Law on Copyright and Designs (Whitford Committee), *Report on Copyright and Design Law*, HMSO 1977 (Cmnd.6732); *Reform of the Law relating to Copyright, Designs and Performers' Protection*, HMSO 1981 (Cmnd. 8302), pp. 33 *et seq.*; Pearson, *supra*, note 43, 250 *et seq.*; Scottish Law Commission, *supra*, note 5, p. 83; Wilson, *supra*, note 43. In: Brett and Perry (eds), pp. 78 *et seq.*

67. For the copyright protection of computer programs in **Canada**, see *IBM Corp.* v. *Ordinateurs Spirales Inc.* (1984) **80** *Canadian Patent Reporter (CPR 2d)* 187, (1985) *Gewerblicher Rechtsschutz und Urheberrecht Internationaler Teil* 124; Canadian Department of Consumer and Corporate Affairs/Department of Communications, *From Gutenberg to Telidon, A White Paper on Copyright* (1984), pp. 79 *et seq.*; Pearson, *supra*, note 43, 259; Sub-Committee on Computer Crime, *supra*, note 16, 19.

68. For copyright protection of computer programs in **West Germany**, see Gesetz zur Änderung von Vorschriften auf dem Gebiet des Urheberrechts of 24 June 1985, *Bundesgesetzblatt I* of 27 June 1985; Beschlussempfehlung und Bericht des Rechtsausschusses zum Entwurf eines Gesetzes zur Änderung auf dem Gebiet des Urheberrechts (Drucks. 10/837), *Bundestags-Drucksache* 10/3360 of 17 April 1985; Bundesgerichtshof (1985) *Betriebs-Berater* 1747, (1985) *Computer und Recht* 22; Bundesarbeitsgericht (1984) *Gewerblicher Rechtsschutz und Urheberrecht (GRUR)* 429 with commentary by E. Ulmer, 429; Oberlandesgericht Karlsruhe (1983) *Betriebs-Berater* 986 *et seq.*; Oberlandesgericht Koblenz (1983) *Betriebs-Berater* 992; Oberlandesgericht Frankfurt (1983) *Betriebs-Berater* 1745; Bauer, Rechtsschutz von Computerprogrammen in der Bundesrepublik Deutschland. (1985) *Computer und Recht* 5; Betten, *supra*, note 57, (1983) *Mitteilungen der deutschen Patentanwälte* 62; Erdmann, *Neue höchstrichterliche Rechtsprechung zum Urheberrecht und Geschmacksmusterrecht* (1985), pp. 47 *et seq.*; Flechsig, Die Novelle zur Änderung und Ergänzung des Urheberrechts. (1985) *Neue Juristische Wochenschrift* 1991; Kolle, *supra*, note 40, (1982) *GRUR* 443; Schmidt and Knorr, Die Werkhöhe bei Software. (1986) *Informatik und Recht* 7; Sieber, Copyright protection of computer programs in Germany. (1984) *European Intellectual Property Review* 214, 253; Ulmer and Kolle, *supra*, note 58, (1983) **14** *International Review of Industrial Property and Copyright Law* 159.

69. For the copyright protection of computer programs in **France**, see Cour d'Appel de Paris, Decision of 2 November 1982, *Gazette du Palais* 2–3 mars 1983 with commentary by J.R. Bonneau, (1983) *Gewerblicher Rechtsschutz und Urheberrecht Internationaler Teil* 60 with commentary by Stana, (1983) *European Intellectual Property Review* 222; Tribunal de Grande Instance de Paris,

Decision of 14 June 1983, *Gazette du Palais*, 26–30 August, 1983 with commentary by Bonneau; Bertin and Lamberterie, *La protection du Logiciel* (1985); Bertrand, *supra*, note 40, 61 *et seq.*; Dietz, Das Problem des Rechtsschutzes von Computerprogrammen in Deutschland und Frankreich. (1983) *Bijblad bij de Industriele Eigendom* 305; Knorr, Der Schutz der Computersoftware in Frankreich. (1986) *Computer und Recht* 52; République Française/Ministère de l'Industrie et de la Recherche, *supra*, note 58, 13 *et seq.*; Röttinger, Zur Neuregelung des Softwareschutzes in Frankreich. (1985) *Gewerblicher Rechtsschutz und Urheberrecht Internationaler Teil* 808; Thunis, *supra*, note 40, (1983) *DPCI* 138.

70. For the copyright protection of computer programs in **Italy**, see Tribunal of Turin, Decision of 14 July 1983; Pretore di Milano, Decision of 1 June 1983, (1983) Foro Italiano parte II 389; Pretore di Padova, Decision of 15 December 1983, (1985) Il diritto dell'informazione e dell'informatica 728; Pretura di Pisa, Decision of 11 April 1985, (1985) *Rivista di Diritto Industriale* parte II p. 67; Alpa (ed.), *La tutela giuridica del software* (1984) (with contributions by Ghidini, pp. 9, 35 *et seq.* and Spolidoro, pp. 103 *et seq.*); Ciampi, La proteggibilità dei programmi elettronici e dei relativi manuali applicativi. (1984) *Il diritto dell'informazione e dell'informatica* 258; Floridia, La protezione giuridica del software. (1986) *Il Corriere Giuridico* no. 2 p. 209; Introvigne, Case comment. (1983) *European Intellectual Property Review* 347; Rossello, La tutela giuridica del 'software' nei primi orientamenti giurisprudenziali italiani. (1985) Il *diritto dell'informazione e dell'informatica* 103.

71. For the copyright protection of computer programs in the **Netherlands**, see the various court decisions printed in (1983) *Bijblad bij de Industriele Eigendom (BIE)* 328 *et seq.*; Governmental Working Group on Piracy, Piracy of Works Protected by Copyright (Interim Report 1984); Verkade, Anmerkung to the Decision of the Arrondissementsrechtbank te's Hertogenbosch. (1983) *Gewerblicher Rechtsschutz und Urheberrecht Internationaler* Teil 669; Verkade, Bescherming van computer programmatur in Nederland. (1983) *BIE* 298; Vandeberghe, *Bescherming van Computer-software* (1984); Woltring, Computer-programmatuur. (1966) *Computerrecht* No. 1, p.27.

72. For the copyright protection of computer programs in the **Nordic countries** with its special 'catalogue rule', see Bull, Legal protection of computer programs. In Bing and Selmer, *supra*, note 23, pp. 410 *et seq.*; Swedish Committee on the Revision of the Copyright Law, Copyright and Computer Technology (1985, SOU 51). For **Finland**, see *supra*, note 24.

73. For the protection of computer programs see, for **Austria**, Hodik, *Der Schutz von Software im österreichischen Recht* (1984); Jaburek and Schmölzer, *supra*, note 7, 51 *et seq.*; for **Belgium**, Erkelens, *supra*, note 5, Annexe à (1985) *Droit de l'informatique* No. 6, 29; see also the comparative report by Vandenberghe, *Bescherming van Computersoftware, Een rechtsvergelijkend onderzoek* (1984).

74. For the protection of computer programs in **Switzerland**, see Troller, Der Rechtsschutz von Computerprogrammen in der Schweiz (1986) *Computer und Recht* 232; Wittmer, *Der Schutz von Computersoftware—Urheberrecht oder Sonderrecht?* (1981).

75. For the copyright protection of computer programs in **Japan**, see Tokyo District Court, Decision of 24 May 1982. (1982/6) *Patents and Licensing* 13; Tokyo District Court, Decision of 6 December 1982 (1983) **482** *Hanrei Times* 65, (1983) **8** *Patents and Licensing* 16, **25** BNA's *Patent, Trademark & Copyright Journal (PTCJ)* 139; Yokahama District Court, Decision of 30 March 1983, (1983) *Hanrei Jiho* No. 1081, 125, (1983) European Intellectual Property Review *(EIPR)* 138; Osaka District Court, Decision of 26 January 1984; SIA/Japanese Software Industry Association, *supra*, note 44, 4 *et seq.*; Borking, Bescherming van Software in Japan. (1983) *Bijblad bij de Industriele Eigendom* 311; Kawashia and Greguras, *supra*, note 44, (1982) *Computer Fraud & Security Bulletin* 10; Rahn, Sonderschutzgesetz für Computerpogramme in Japan? (1984) *Gewerblicher Rechtsschutz und Urheberrecht Internationaler Teil (GRUR Int.)* 217.

76. For a **comparative overview** on copyright protection of computer programs in most of the countries mentioned, see Association Internationale pour la Protection de la Propriété Industrielle, Annuaire 1984/III, Conseil des Présidents—Athènes 1983, *Protection juridique du logiciel*, pp. 83 *et seq.*; Betten, Der internationale Programmschutz. (1985) *Computer und Recht* 120; Keplinger, Authorship in the information age—protection for computer programs under the Berne and Universal Copyright Conventions. (1985) *Copyright* 119; Keplinger, Legal Protection for Computer Programs, UNESCO/WIPO/ GE/CCS/2 Document of 17 December 1984; Kindermann, Special protection systems for computer programs—a comparative study. (1976) *International Review of Industrial Property and Copyright Law* 301; Kindermann, Computer software and copyright conventions. (1981) *European Intellectual Property Review* 6; Kolle, Der Urheberrechtsschutz von Computerprogrammen und Videospielen im Ausland. (1985) *Zeitschrift für Urheber- und Medienrecht/ Film und Recht* 15; Ploman and Hamilton, *Copyright* (1980), pp. 167 *et seq.*; SIA/Japan Software Industry Association, *supra*, note 44, 38 *et seq.*; United Nations Educational Scientific and Cultural Organization/World Intellectual Property Organization, Documents UNESCO/WIPO/GE/CCS Nos 1 and 2 of 17 December 1984 and No. 3 of 15 March 1985; Vandenberghe, *Bescherming van Computersoftware, Een rechtsvergelijkend onderzoek* (1984).

77. For the Commission of the European Communities, see note verbale of the Delegation of the Commission of the European Communities, stated in Tokyo on 15 March 1984; for WIPO/UNESCO, *supra*, note 76; for the OECD, *supra*, notes 1 and 56.

78. See also *infra*, note 80.

79. See the references *supra*, note 76, especially Kolle, (1985) *Zeitschrift für Urheber- und Medienrecht/Film und Recht* 25 *et seq.* In addition, see Kolle, Internationale Vereinigung für gewerblichen Rechtsschutz — Bericht der deutschen Landesgruppe. (1985) *Gewerblicher Rechtsschutz und Urheberrecht Internationaler Teil (GRUR Int.)* 29, 32.

80. For **West Germany**, see Bundesgerichtshof (1985) *Betriebs-Berater* 1747. 1750 and the references *supra*, note 68; for **France**, see Bertin and Lamberterie, *supra*, note 69, 27 *et seq.* and the references *supra*, note 69; for the **United States**, see the references *supra*, note 64. For a detailed discussion of the subject matter of copyright, see Sieber, *supra*, note 68, (1984) *EIPR* 217 *et seq.*; for a

comparative overview, see Kolle, *supra*, note 76, (1985) *Zeitschrift für Urheber- und Medienrecht/Film und Recht* 21 *et seq.*

81. See WIPO Working Group on Technical Questions, *supra*, note 54, 5. For further discussion, see Betten, Urheberrechtsschutz von Computerprogrammen. (1984) *Mitteilungen der Deutschen Patentanwälte* 201, 203 *et seq.*; Kolle, *supra*, note 79, (1985) *GRUR Int.* 29, 31.

82. See, for example, for **West Germany** Sieber, *supra*, note 68, (1984) *EIPR* 224; for the *Netherlands* District Court of Hertogenbosch (1983) *Gewerblicher Rechtsschutz und Urheberrecht Internationaler Teil* 663 (affirming copyright infringement in a case in which 16% of the actual program statements were found to be identical; for a **comparative overview**, see Kolle, *supra*, note 76, (1985) *Zeitschrift für Urheber- und Medienrecht*/Film und Recht 24 *et seq.*

83. See the references *supra*, note 53.

84. See, for example, for **France** Bertrand, *supra*, note 40, 71 *et seq.*; for **West Germany** Bauer, *supra*, note 68, (1985) *Computer und Recht* 8 *et seq.*

85. See Sieber, *supra*, note 68, (1984) *EIPR* 222 *et seq.*

86. See references *supra*, note 64.

87. See references *supra*, note 65.

88. See references *supra*, note 66.

89. See references *supra*, note 68.

90. See references *supra*, note 69.

91. See references *supra*, note 75.

92. See references *supra*, note 72.

93. For general references, see *supra*, notes 68–74. For **Finland**, see, in addition, the legislation printed in (March 1985) *Copyright* 105 *et seq.*; the report in (1984) *Gewerblicher Rechtsschutz und Urheberrecht Internationaler* Teil 373; and Liedes and Lahtinen, Letter from Finland, development of copyright legislation in Finland from 1982 to 1984. (March 1985) *Copyright* 129 *et seq.*

94. For general references see *supra*, notes 64–7 and 76.

95. For the requirements of such legislation see Deutsche Vereinigung für gewerblichen Rechtsschutz und Urheberrecht. (1984) *Gewerblicher Rechtsschutz und Urheberrecht* 419, 423; Flechsig (ed.), *Rechtspolitische Überlegungen zum Urheberstrafrecht* (1982); Sieber, *Informationstechnologie, supra*, note 19, p.58.

96. For the Work of WIPO and UNESCO see the references *supra*, notes 54 and 76.

97. For the *Japanese* legislative proposals see the references *supra*, note 75.

98. For the *French* legislative proposals see the references *supra*, note 69, especially Republique Francaise, pp. 24 *et seq.*, and Thunis, (1983) *DPCI* 160 *et seq.*

99. See the above (note 76) cited document UNESCO/WIPO/GE/CCS 3 of 15 March 1985.

100. Subsection IV A.2c is based on a report which the author has prepared for the Select Committee of Experts on Computer-related Crime of the Council of Europe as an addition to the OECD report cited *supra*, note 1. See Sieber,

Proposal for a Council of Europe Initiative in the Field of Computer-related Economic Crime, Council of Europe Doc. No. PC—R—CC(86) 10 of 26 March 1986, pp. 5 et seq. (Appendix).

101. For the economic background see Organization for Economic Co-operation and Development (OECD), *L'industrie des semi-conducteurs* (1985).

102. For patent law see *supra*, pp. 64 *et seq.* For the law on registered design see, for example for **West Germany**, Kolle, *supra* note 79, (1985) *GRUR Int.* 33.

103. See above, pp. 65 *et seq.*

104. For the legal protection of computer chips in the United States see the references *infra*, note 107.

105. See, for **Australia**, *Ancher Mortlock, Murray and Woolley Pty Ltd and Others v. Hooker Homes Pty Ltd.* (1971) **2** *New South Wales Law Reports* 278; *L.A. Randell Pty Ltd* v. *Millman Services Pty Limited.* (1977) **17** *Australian Law Reports (ALR)* 140; *Ogden Industries Pty Ltd and Others* v. *Kis (Australia) Pty Ltd.* (1982) **45** *ALR* 129; *Edwards Hot Water Systems* v. *S.W. Hart and Co. Pty Ltd.* (1983) **49** *ALR* 605; for **West Germany** Kolle, *supra*, note 79, (1985) *GRUR Int.* 33; for the **Netherlands**, Zwolle District Court, Decision of 22 July 1983, (1983) *Bijblad bij de Industriele Eigendom* No. 102; Minister for Foreign Affairs of the Netherlands, letter to the Acting Commissioner of Patents and Trademark of the USA. (1985) **50** *Federal Register* 24796, 24797 *et seq.*; for the **United Kingdom**, see *Dorling* v. *Honnor Marine Ltd.* (1964) *Reports of Patent, Design and Trade Mark Cases (RPC)* 103; *British Northrup* v. *Texteam Blackburn Ltd.* (1974) RPC 57; *Solar Thomson Engineering Co. Ltd* v. *Barton.* (1977) *RPC* 537; *LB* (Plastics) Ltd v. *Swish Products.* (1979) *FRC* 551; *Hoover* v. *George Hulme (Stockport) Ltd.* (1982) *Fleet Street Reporter* 565; *British Leyland Motor Corporation Ltd* v. *Armstrong Patents Company Ltd.* (1984) **3** *Common Market Law Reports* 102; Pearson, *supra*, note 43, 233 *et seq.*, 238 *et seq.*

106. See *supra*, pp. 56 *et seq.*

107. For the protection of integrated circuits under **United States** law see the Semiconductor Chip Protection Act of 1984, Pub.L. 98–620 (8 November, 1984), 17 USC §101, (1984) **28** *BNA's Patent, Trademark and Copyright Journal* (PTCJ) 90; Copyright Office's Interim Regulations on Mask Work Protection. (1985) **29** *PTCJ Copyright Journal* 254; Copyright Office, Mask work protection—implementation of the Semiconductor Chip Protection Act 1984. (1985) **50** *Federal Register* No. 125, 26714, (1985) **30** PTCJ 248, (1985) *Gewerblicher Rechtsschutz und Urheberrecht Internationaler Teil* (GRUR Int.) 511; Beise, Copyright für Computerchips in den USA. (1984) *Recht der internationalen Wirtschaft* 68; Hein, Der US Semiconductor Chip Protection Act von 1984. (1985) *GRUR Int.* 81; Pearson, *supra*, note 43, 233 *et seq.*, 238 *et seq.*

108. See, for **Australia**, **560** *Federal Register (FR)* 24665 and 26818 (26820); for *Canada*, **50**, *FR* 25288; for *Japan*, 1053 US Patent and Trademark Office, *Official Gazette (TMOG)* 23 April 1985, p.105; **49** *FR* 12 355; **49** *FR* 44517; **50** *FR* 14277; **50** *FR* 16530; **50** *FR* 24668; for the *Netherlands*, **50** *FR* 24795; **50** *FR* 26818 (26820); for *Sweden*, 50 *FR* 25618; Committee on the Revision of the Copyright Law, *supra*, note 72; for the *United Kingdom* and *Northern Ireland*, **50** *FR* 25666; **50** *FR* 26810; for the *European Communities* **50** *FR* 26821; (1985)

Gewerblicher Rechtsschutz und Urheberrecht Internationaler Teil 700.

109. Ministry of International Trade and Industry, A Bill for 'An Act Concerning the Circuit Layout of a Semiconductor Integrated Circuit' of April 1985.

110. See Commission of the European Communites, Proposal for a Council Resolution on a Community Framework for the Legal Protection of the Topographies of Semiconductor Products, Document COM (85) 280 final, of 31 May 1985.

111. WIPO, Committee of Experts on Intellectual Property in Respect of Integrated Circuits, Draft Treaty, Document IPIC/CE/I/2 of 28 June 1985.

112. See, for **Australia** (State of Tasmania), Briscoe, *supra*, note 7, 61, 121; for **Austria**, Jaburek and Schmölzer, *supra*, note 7, 33 *et seq.*, 53 *et seq.*, 67; for *Belgium,* Erkelens, *supra*, note 5, Annexe à (1985) *Droit de l'Informatique* No. 6, 28 *et seq.*; Spreutels, *supra*, note 5, (1985) *Revue de Droit Pénal et de Criminologie,* 359 *et seq.*; for **Canada,** *R. v. Christensen et al.* (1978). **26** *Chitty's Law Journal* 348; Piragoff, *supra*, note 17, (1984) *Ottawa Law Review* 308; Sub-Committee on Computer Crime, *supra*, note 17, 12, 14; for the **Netherlands** Kaspersen and Keijzer, *supra*, note 6, in: Kaspersen (ed.) pp. 53 *et seq.*; de Schraaf, *supra*, note 5, (1984) Informatie, No. 2, 103; for **West Germany** Sieber, *Computerkriminalität, supra*, note 6, 1/191 *et seq.*, 2/2; Tiedemann, *supra*, note 5, (1983) *Wertpapier Mitteilungen* 1329; for **Switzerland**, Eidgenössisches Justiz- und Polizeidepartement, *supra*, note 6, 16; for the **United Kingdom,** Scottish Law Commission, *supra*, note 5, pp. 74 *et seq.*, 79 *et seq.*; for the **United States,** US Department of Justice, *Legislative Resource Manual, supra*, note 14, 2.

113. For the admissibility of computerized record-keeping see, for example, in **West Germany**, sections 44 *Handelsgesetzbuch*, 147 Abgabenordnung; in **Switzerland**, sections 957 *et seq.* Obligationenrecht; Zweifel, *supra*, note 10, 38 *et seq.*

114. For law reform in the **United States,** see *supra*, note 14.

115. See *infra*, p. 99 and Appendix 2.

116. For law reform in **Switzerland**, see *supra*, note 20.

117. For law reform in **Finland**, see *supra*, note 24.

118. For law reform in **Canada**, see *supra*, note 17.

119. For law reform in **Switzerland**, see *supra*, note 20.

120. For law reform in **Finland**, see *supra*, note 24.

121. For law reform in **West Germany**, see *supra*, note 19.

122. For law reform in **Austria**, see *supra*, note 21.

123. For law reform in **France,** see *supra*, note 25.

124. For law reform in **Denmark**, see *supra*, note 18.

125. For law reform in **Norway**, see *supra*, note 23.

126. For law reform in **Finland**, see *supra*, note 24.

127. For the unauthorized use of another person's property see for **Australia**, Briscoe, *supra*, note 7, 62 *et seq.;* for **Belgium**, Spreutels, *supra*, note 5, (1985) *Revue de Droit Pénal et de Criminologie,* 364 *et seq.*; for **West Germany** Sieber, *Computerkriminalität, supra*, note 6, 1/191; for the **Netherlands**, Kaspersen and

Keijzer, *supra*, note 6 in: Kaspersen (ed.), 58 *et seq.*; for Switzerland, Noll, Die Sachentziehung im System der Vermögensdelikte. (1968) **84** *Zeitschrift für Strafrecht* 344; Rohner, *supra, note 7, 17 et seq.*; for the **United Kingdom,** Briscoe, *supra*, note 7, 64; Scottish Law Commission, *supra*, note 5, 65 *et seq.*; for the **United States,** Bequai, *How to Prevent Computer Crime*, supra, note 6, 156.

128. For the various provisions on theft see also *supra*, notes 29–37.

129. For the provisions on unauthorized use of automatic vending machines or public telephone networks and for similar provisions see, for example, for **Canada, R. v.** *Michael McLaughlin*, (1980) *Supreme Court Reports (SCR)* 331, (1980) **18** *Criminal Reports (CR)* (3d) 339; Parker, *Fighting Computer Crime, supra,* note 14, 157 *et seq.*; Schjolberg, *Computers and Penal Legislation, supra*, note 12, 82 *et seq.*; for **West Germany** Sieber, *Computerkriminalität, supra*, note 6, 236 *et seq.*; for **Switzerland**, Rohner, *supra*, note 7, 30 *et seq.*; for the **United Kingdom**, Briscoe, *supra*, note 7, 88; Scottish Law Commission, *supra*, note 5, 73; for a **comparative survey**, Falkenbach, *Die Leistungserschleichung* (1983), pp. 288 *et seq.*, 329 *et seq.*

130. For the provisions of unlawful use, waste or withdrawal of electricity see for **Australia**, Briscoe, *supra*, note 7, 79 *et seq.*; for **Belgium**, Erkelens, *supra*, note 5, Annexe à (1985) *Droit de l'Informatique* No. 6, 27, 29; for **West Germany** Sieber, *Computerkriminalität, supra*, note 6, 191; for **Switzerland**, Eidgenössisches Justiz- und Polizeidepartement, *supra*, note 6, 13; Rohner, *supra*, note 7, 29 *et seq.*, for the **United Kingdom**, Tettenborn, *supra*, note 7, (1980) **2** *The Company Lawyer* 149.

131. See *supra*, note 9.

132. See Piragoff, *supra*, note 17, Annexe à (1985) *Droit de l'Informatique* No.6, 35.

133. For law reform in the **United States,** see *supra*, note 14.

134. For law reform in **Canada**, see *supra*, note 17.

135. For law reform in **France** and **Portugal,** see *supra* notes 25 and 26.

136. For law reform in **West Germany**, see *supra*, note 19.

137. For law reform in **Switzerland**, see *supra*, note 20.

138. For law reform in **Austria,** see *supra*, note 21.

139. For law reform in **Norway**, see *supra*, note 23.

140. For law reform in **Switzerland**, see *supra*. note 20.

141. For law reform in **Norway**, see *supra*, note 23.

142. For law reform in **Finland**, see *supra*, note 24.

143. For law reform in **Sweden**, see *supra*, note 13.

144. 98th Congress 1st Session, House of Representatives 4301 of 3 November 1983 (introduced by Mr Coughlin).

145. For law reform in the **United States** and **Canada**, see *supra*, notes 14 and 17.

146. See supra, note 28.

147. For the penal comprehension of wiretapping of computer communications and accessing computer systems see, for **Austria**, Jaburek and Schmölzer, *supra*, note 7, 65 *et seq.*; for **Belgium**, Erkelens, *supra*, note 5, Annexe à (1985) *Droit de l'Informatique* No. 6, 29 *et seq.;* for **Canada,** Piragoff, *supra* note 16, (1984) **16** *Ottawa Law Review* 309 *et seq.*; for **West Germany** Sieber, *Informationstechnologie, supra*, note 19, 51 *et seq.*; Winkelbauer, *supra*, note 10, (1983) *Computer und Recht* 44; for the **Netherlands,** Kaspersen and Keijzer, *supra*, note 6, in: Kaspersen (ed.), 59 et seq.; for the **Nordic countries**, Schjolberg, *Computers and Penal Legislation, supra,* note 23, 23 *et seq.*, 37 *et seq.*, 100 *et seq.*; for the **United Kingdom,** Scottish Law Commission, *supra*, note 5, 47 *et seq.*

148. For law reform in **Sweden,** see *supra*, note 13.

149. For law reform in the **United States,** see *supra*, note 14.

150. For law reform in **Denmark**, see *supra*, note 18.

151. For law reform in **West Germany**, see *supra*, note 19.

152. For law reform in **Norway**, see *supra*, note 23.

153. For law reform in **Finland**, see *supra*, note 24.

154. For law reform in **Canada**, see *supra*, note 17.

155. For law reform in **Switzerland**, see *supra*, note 20.

156. For law reform in **France**, see *supra*, note 25.

157. For law reform in the **United States,** see *supra*, note 14.

158. *Ibid.*

159. pp. 39 *et seq.*

160. See the *comparative report* by Sennes, Régimes d'imposition des logiciels. (1985) *Droit de l'informatique* No. 7, 2. For **West Germany** see Reuther, Software in der Handels- und Steuerbilanz. In: Koelsch *et al.* (eds), *Wirtschaftsgut Software* (1985), p. 31.

161. See General Agreement on Tariffs and Trade, Committee on Customs Valuation, Document VAL/8 of 10 October 1984 (Restricted); Amory, Nouvelles des Communautés européennes. (1985) *Droit de l'informatique* No. 7, 41; Borking, Import duties on the value of software from EEC countries. *Computer Law & Practice* No. 1, 10; Franceus, Rapport sur la journée d'études import-export de progiciel. (1985) *Droit de l'Informatique* No. 7, 39.

162. Chapter IV, Section B is based on a report which the author has prepared for the Select Committee of Experts on Computer-related Crime of the Council of Europe. See Sieber, *Proposal for a Council of Europe Initiative in the Field of Computer-related Infringements of Privacy*, Council of Europe. Doc. No. PC-R-CC (86) 11 of 26 March 1986.

163. For the possible implications of the diverging privacy legislations to the free flow on transborder data see, for example, Bergmann, *Grenzüberschreitender Datenverkehr* (1985); Bing, Forsberg and Nygaard, Problèmes juridiques posés par les flux transfrontières de données. *OECD report DSTI/ICCP/81.9* (1981);

Frosini, Banche dei dati e tutela della persona. In Camera dei Deputati (ed.), *Banche dati e tutela della persona* (2nd edn, 1983), pp. 3, 14 *et seq.*; de Houwer, *Privacy and Transborder Data Flows* (Vrije Universiteit, Brussels, 1984), pp. 9 *et seq.*; International Chamber of Commerce (ICC), Information Flows—An International Business Perspective, Policy statement adopted by the Council at its 144th session, 21 June 1983, Doc. no.373–22/4 Rev. 5; Organization for Economic Co-operation and Development, *Transborder Data Flows*, Proceedings of an OECD Conference held December 1983 (1985); Wochner, *Der Persönlichkeitsschutz im grenzüberschreitenden Datenverkehr* (1981).

164. For the **OECD** Guidelines, see OECD, *Guidelines on the Protection of Privacy and Transborder Flows of Personal Data* (1980); OECD, *Transborder Data Flows and the Protection of Privacy* (1979); OECD, Transborder Data Flows: An Overview of Issues, *Report DSTI/ICCP/83.29,* 11 October 1983; Bergmann, *Grenzüberschreitender Datenverkehr, supra,* note 163, 143 *et seq.*; de Houver, *Privacy and Transborder Data Flows, supra,* note 163, 9 *et seq.*; Sarzana, L'attività delle istituzioni internationali in materia dei tutela dell privacy. In: Camera dei Deputati (ed.), *Banche dati e tutela della persona* (2nd ed, 1983), p. 502.

165. For the work of the **Council of Europe** in the field of privacy protection, see Council of Europe, Protection of the Privacy of Individuals *vis-à-vis* Electronic Data Banks in the Private Sector, Resolution No. (73) 22, adopted by the Committee of Ministers of the Council of Europe on 26 September 1973 (1974) and Resolution No. (74) 29 adopted by the Committee of Ministers of the Council of Europe on 20 September 1974 (1975); Council of Europe, Explanatory Report on the Convention for the Protection of Individuals with regard to Automatic Processing of Personal Data, convention opened for signature on 28 January 1981 (1981); Council of Europe/Committee of Ministers, Recommendation No. R (80) 13 of the Committee of Ministers to Member States on Exchange of Legal Information Relating to Data Protection (adopted by the Committee of Ministers on 18 September 1980, Recommendation No. R (81) 1 of the Committee of Ministers to Member States on Regulations for Automated Medical Data Banks (adopted by the Committee of Ministers on 23 January 1981, Recommendation No. R (83) 10 of the Committee of Ministers to Member States on the Protection of Personal Data used for Scientific Research and Statistics (adopted by the Committee of Ministers on 23 September 1983). In addition, see Bergmann, *Grenzüberschreitender Datenverkehr, supra,* note 163, 152 *et seq.*; Buguicchio, The work of the Council of Europe in the field of data protection. In Council of Europe/Camera dei Deputati, *Legislation and Data Protection*, Proceedings of the Rome Conference on Problems Relating to the Development and Application of Legislation on Data Protection (1983), pp. 229 *et seq.*; de Houwer, *supra,* note 163, 15 *et seq.*; Sarzana, *supra* note 164, in Camera dei Deputati (ed.), *Banche dati e tutela della persona* (2nd ed, 1983), pp. 498 *et seq.*

166. For the initiatives of the **European Communities**, see Bergmann, *supra*, note 163, 160 *et seq.*; de Houwer, *supra*, note 163, 24 *et seq.*; Sarzana, *supra*, note 164, in: Camera dei Deputati (ed.), *Banche dati e tutela della persona* (2nd edn., 1983), 504 *et seq.* For the work of the Legal Observatory see the report in (1985) *Computer und Recht* 191.

167. See International **Chamber of Commerce** (ICC), Privacy Legislation, Data Protection and Legal Persons, Policy Statement adopted by the ICC Council at its 146th session in June 1984, Document No. 373/25 Rev.

168. For a **comparative overview,** see Bergmann, *supra*, note 163, 74 *et seq.*, 101 *et seq.*; Bing, Personal data systems—a comparative perspective. In:Bing and Selmer, A Decade of Computers and Law (1980), pp.72 *et seq.*; Burkert, *Data Security and Confidentiality—Item F, Freedom of Information and Data Protection*, Final Report of August 1983 (edited by Gesellschaft für Mathematik und Datenverarbeitung mbH, Bonn, 1983); Herb, Mangelnde Normenklarheit im Datenschutz-Strafrecht (University of Tübingen Dissertation 1984), 7 *et seq.*, 16 *et seq.*; de Houwer, *supra*, note 163, 27 *et seq.*; Pagano, Panorama of personnel data protection laws. In Council of Europe/Camera dei Deputati, *Legislation and Data Protection*, Proceedings of the Rome Conference on Problems relating to the Development and Application of Legislation on Data Protection (1983), pp. 236 *et seq.*; Pagano, Tutela dei dati personali: evoluzione della legislazione europea. In: *Bolletino di informazioni constituzionali e parlamentari* (Camera dei Deputati, 1985) 109; Wilk, *Selected Foreign National Data Protection Laws and Bills* (edited by the US Department of Commerce, 1978).

169. See *supra*, pp. 60 *et seq.*, 86 *et seq.*

170. For the specific penal apects of privacy legislation see for a **comparative overview** Sieber, *supra*, note 12, in: Kaspersen (ed.), 89 *et seq.*; for **Austria** Jaburek and Schmölzer, *supra* note 7, 57 *et seq.*, 65, 67; for **West Germany** Haft, Zur Situation des Datenschutzstrafrechts. (1979) *Neue Juristische Wochenschrift (NJW)* 1194; Herb, *supra*, note 168, 25 *et seq.*; Tiedemann, Datenübermittlung als Straftatbestand. (1981) *NJW* 945; for **Luxembourg**, Jaeger, *supra*, note 6, (1985) *Revue de Droit Pénal et de Criminologie* 328 *et seq.*

171. For these problems originating from the referral technique of privacy legislations, see Haft, *supra*, note 170, (1979) *NJW* 1194; Herb, *supra*, note 168, 25 *et seq.*; Tiedemann, *supra*, note 170, (1981) *NJW* 945.

172. See pp. 100 *et seq.*

173. See p. 42.

174. For law reform in **Finland** and **France**, see *supra*, notes 23 and 25.

175. See *supra*, p. 42.

176. See *supra*, p. 49.

177. For computer-crime legislation in the **United States**, see *supra*, note 14.

178. For critics of the imprecise laws, see Haft, *supra*, note 170, (1979) *NJW* 1194; Herb, *supra*, note 168, 25 *et seq.*; Schünemann, Der strafrechtliche Schutz von Privatgeheimnissen. (1978) **90** *Zeitschrift für die gesamte Strafrechtswissenschaften* 23, Tiedemann, *supra*, note 170, (1981) *NJW* 945.

179. See Frosini, *supra*, note 163, in: Camera dei Deputati (ed.), *Banche dati e tutela della persona* (2nd edn, 1983) 3 *et seq.*; Rodotà, Data protection—some problems for newcomers. In Council of Europe/Camera dei Deputati, *Legislation and Data Protection*, Proceedings of the Rome Conference on Problems

Relating to the Development and Application of Legislation on Data Protection (1983), pp. 186 *et seq.*; Rodotà, Policies and perspectives for data protection. In: Council of Europe, *Beyond 1984: The Law and Information Technology in Tomorrow's Society*, Proceedings of the Fourteenth Colloquy on European Law (1985), pp. 13 *et seq.*; Simitis, Data protection—a few critical remarks. In: Council of Europe/Camera dei Deputati, *supra* cited, pp. 172 *et seq.*; Simitis, General report. In: Council of Europe, *Beyond 1984*, *supra* cited, pp. 109 *et seq.*

180. For general principles of economic criminal law see the resolutions of the XIII Congress for International Criminal Law on 'Concept and Principles of Economic and Business Criminal Law' of the Association Internationale de Droit Pénal. See Sieber, Report, (1983) **54** *Revue Internationale de Droit Pénal* 81.

181. Law No. 80–525 of 12 July 1980 on Proof of Judicial Acts.

182. See for example The Australian Law Reform Commission, Evidence Volume 1, Interim Report No. 26 (1985) pp. 356 *et seq.*; Bequai, *How to Prevent Computer Crime*, *supra*, note 6, 97 *et seq.*; Brown, *Computer-Produced Evidence in Australia*. (1984) **8** *University of Tasmania Law Review* 48; Canadian Sub-Committee, supra note 17, 17 *et seq.*; Kelman and Sizer, *Computer Generated Output as Admissible Evidence* (1982); Sieber, *supra*, note 12, in: Kaspersen (ed.), 96 *et seq.*; Tapper, *Computer Law*, *supra*, note 15, 16 *et seq.*; Staniland, *Computer Evidence in South Africa* (1985) **2** *Computer Law & Practice* No. 1, 21; US Department of Justice, *Computer Crime, Legislative Resource Manual*, *supra*, note 14, 17 *et seq.*

183. Canada Evidence Act, S.33, *An Act to give effect, for Canada, to the Uniform Evidence Act* adopted by the Uniform Law Commission of Canada, first session, 32nd Parliament, 29–30–31 Elizabeth II 1980–81–82. (Introduced by the Government on 18 November 1982, second reading on 7 December 1982, and on 28 June 1983.)

184. See United Nations Commission on International Trade Law, *Legal Value of Computer Records* (Report A/CN 9/265 of 21 February 1985 prepared by the Secretary General), pp. 9 *et seq.*; United Nations Economic and Social Council/ Economic Commission for Europe/Committee on the Development of Trade, *Legal Aspects of Trade Data Interchange*, Report TRADE/WP.4/R. 298/Rev. 1 of 6 August 1984 and Report TRADE/WP.4/R. 330 of 25 February 1985.

185. See Customs Co-operation Council, *Customs Applications of Computers*, Draft CCC Resolution concerning the use of computer-readable data as evidence in court proceedings, Document 32.562 E/T7–387 of 7 June 1985.

186. For a general overview, see Olmstead, *Extra-territorial Application of Laws and Responses Thereto* (1984); de Schutter, Grensoverschrijdende computercriminaliteit—Nood aan harmoniserende aanpak, in: Kaspersen (ed.), Strafrecht in de Informatiemaatschappij (1986), 143; as well as Chapter IV of the OECD report cited (note 1).

CHAPTER 5

1. For the organizational steps to establish a company's security system, see Bequai, *How to Prevent Computer Crime* (1983), pp. 180 *et seq.*; Carrol,

Computer Security (1977), pp. 39 *et seq.*; Norman, *Computer Insecurity* (1983), pp. 311 *et seq.*; Parker, *Computer Security Management* (1981), pp. 107 *et seq.*; Wong, *Computer Crime—Risk Management and Computer Security* (photo-copied, BIS Applied Systems, Manchester, 1985), pp. 9 *et seq.*

2. For these legal aspects, see Chapter 4, Section B, and the case description supra, p. 23 *et seq.*

3. See Parker, *supra*, note 1, 231 *et seq.*

4. See *supra*, p. 13 note 31.

5. pp. 16 *et seq.*

6. See Parker, Computer Security Management, *supra* note 1, 31.

7. See Beker and Piper, *Cipher Systems: The Protection of Communication* (1982); Parker, *Fighting Computer Crime* (1983), pp. 78 *et seq.*; Sieber, *Computerkriminalität und Strafrecht* (2nd edn, 1980), pp.2/102 *et seq.*

8. For the security measures available see also Aalders, Herschberg and Van Zanten, *Handbook for Information Security* (1985); Bequai, *How to Prevent Computer Crime, supra*, note 1, p. 196 *et seq.*; Breuer, *Computer-Schutz durch Sicherung und Versicherung* (1984), pp. 19 *et seq.*; Buss and Salerno, Common sense and computer security. (1984) *Harvard Business Review* 113; Carrol, *Controlling White-Collar Crime* (1982); Carroll, *Computer Security* (1977); Droux, Physische EDV-Sicherheit. In: Zimmerli and Liebl (eds), *Computermissbrauch—Computersicherheit* (1984), pp. 195 *et seq.*; Highland, Security for microcomputers. In: *SECURICOM 86* (Congress Proceedings edited 1986 by SEDEP Paris), p. 437; Highland and Highland, A Guide to NBS Computer Security Literature. (1982) **1** *Computer and Security* 164; Hütte and Pohl, Requirements to personal computer processing sensitive data, in: *SECURICOM 86* (Congress Proceedings edited 1986 by SEDEP Paris), 347; Krauss and MacGahan, *Computer Fraud and Countermeasures* (1979); Martin, *Security, Accuracy and Privacy in Computer Systems* (1973); Norman, *supra*, note 1, 247 *et seq.*; Poerting and Pott, *Computerkriminalität* (ed. 1986 by the German Bunderkriminalamt Wiesbaden), pp. 65 *et seq.*; Schönberg, Organisatorische und softwaregestützte EDV-Sicherheit. In: Zimmerli and Liebl (eds), *Computermissbrauch—Computersicherheit* (1984), pp. 83 *et seq.*; Sieber, Gefahr und Abwehr der Computerkriminalität. (1982) *Betriebs-Berater* 1433; US Department of Justice/Bureau of Justice Statistics, *Computer Crime—Computer Security Techniques* (1982); Weck, *Datensicherheit* (1984); Zweifel, Buchführungsdelikte mittels EDV und Massnahmen zu deren Verhinderung (1984).

9. For these issues, see especially the new journal *Conscience in Computing* (edited by the National Center for Computer Crime Data, Los Angeles).

10. For an overview, see Friessem, *Zugriffskontrollsysteme für MVS-Anlagen* (Gesellschaft für Mathematik und Datenverarbeitung, Bonn, 1980); Schönberg, *supra*, note 8, in: Zimmerli and Liebl (eds), 154 *et seq.*, 187 *et seq.*

11. See Schönberg, *supra*, note 8, in Zimmerli and Liebl (eds), 165 *et seq.*; Weinmann, Security problems concerning chip-card applications. In: *SECURICOM 1984* (Congress Proceedings edited by SEDEP, Paris, 1984), p. 141; Weinmann and Heidt, *Zusammenfassung der Studie 'Einsatz von Chipkarten-Systemen bei der Deutschen Bundespost'* (edited by SCS GmbH, Essen, 1983).

12. See, for example, Beker and Piper, *supra*, note 7; Meyer and Matyas, Installation and distribution of cryptographic variables in an EFT/POS network with a large number of terminals. In: *SECURICOM 86* (Congress Proceedings edited 1986 by SEDEP Paris), p. 231; Schönberg, *supra*, note 8, in: Zimmerli and Liebl (eds) 167 *et seq.*; Weck, *Datensicherheit, supra*, note 8, 283 *et seq.*

13. In *West Germany* the Landgericht Düsseldorf in a decision of 28 November 1984 (12 0 403/84) held that the distribution of such a program constitutes an infringement of copyright. See also von Gravenreuth, Unterlassungsanspruch gegen Software-Kopierprogramme. (1985) *Gewerblicher Rechtsschutz und Urheberrecht* 504.

14. For *West Germany* see the decision of the Bundesgerichtshof, (1981) *Neue Juristische Wochenschrift* 2684.

15. p. 132.

16. For the technical measures to protect computer programs, see Keet, *Preventing Piracy—A Business Guide to Software Protection* (1985), pp. 117 *et seq.*; Pearson, *Computer Contracts* (1984), pp. 273 *et seq.*; Sieber, *Computerkriminalität, supra*, note 7, 2/90 *et seq.*; Sieber, Urheberrechtliche und wettbewerbsrechtliche Erfassung der unbefugten Softwarenutzung. (1981) *Betriebs-Berater* 1555 *et seq.*

17. See Bequai, *How to prevent Computer Crime, supra*, note 1, 104 et seq.; Deutsches Institut für Interne Revision, *Revision der elektronischen Datenverarbeitung* (4th edn, 1982); Glazer and Jaenicke, *A Framework for Evaluating the Internal Audit Function* (Institute for Internal Auditors, Research Foundation, 1980); Hofmann. Die externe Revision als Teil der Abwehrmassnahmen. In: Zimmerli and Liebl (eds), *Computermissbrauch—Computersicherheit* (1984), pp. 307 *et seq.*; Institute for Internal Auditors Inc., *Systems Auditability and Control* (1977); Krauss and MacGahan, *supra*, note 8, 222; Meyer zu Loesebeck, *Unterschlagungsverhütung und Unterschlagungsprüfung* (1983); Parker, *Computer Security Management, supra*, note 1, 271 *et seq.*; Schröder, *Steuerliche Betriebsprüfung EDV-gestützer Buchführungssysteme* (1983).

18. See, for example, in **France** the 'Globale Fraude Informatique'; in **West Germany**, the 'Computer-Missbrauchs-Versicherung' (Colonia, Gerling, Hermes Kreditversicherungs AG); in **Japan** the 'Financial Institute Computer Crime Coverage'; in **Sweden**, the 'EDP Insurance' (Skandia); in the **United Kingdom** the 'Electronic and Computer-crime Policy' (Lloyd's) and the 'Computer-Crime Policy' (Trident General Insurance). For an overview, see Breuer, *supra*, note 8, 273 *et seq.*; Briat, Les assurances et le logiciel. (1984) 3 *Droit de l'informatique* 9; Heidinger, *Die Computer-Missbrauchs-Versicherung* (1980).

19. See *supra*, p. 63 with further references note 53.

20. See Sieber, *Computerkriminalität, supra*, note 7, 2/90 and *supra*, note 16, (1981) *Betriebs-Berater* 1556.

CHAPTER VI

1. For the difficulties in detecting computer offences and the respective training of the police see Becker, The trial of a computer crime. (1980) **2** *Computer Law Journal* 441; Becker, *The Investigation of Computer Crime* (1980); Bequai, *How to Prevent Computer Crime* (1983), pp. 118 *et seq.*; Brandenburg, *Kriminalistik en Computer* (Graduation Thesis Police Academy of Apeldoorn, 1984); Holzner, Täglich 500 Milliarden Dollar-Transaktionen über EDV. (1985) *Kriminalistik* 590 *et seq.*; Paul, Computerkriminalität. (1980) *Kriminalistik* 410, 535; Schabeck, *Computer Crime Investigation Manual* (looseleaf, 1979); Sieber, *Computerkriminalität und Strafrecht* (2nd edn, 1980), pp. 146 *et seq.*; US Department of Justice/Bureau of Statitstics, *Computer Crime—Expert Witness Manual* (1980); Zimmerli and Angst, Die Aufdeckung von Computerdelikten. In: Zimmerli and Liebl (eds), *Computermissbrauch—Computersicherheit* (1984), pp. 333 *et seq.*

2. This case was verified by inspecting the court records. For a detailed case description see Sieber, *Computerkriminalität, supra*, note 1, 150 *et seq.*

3. This case was verified by inspecting the court records.

4. See von Gravenreuth, *Das Plagiat in strafrechtlicher Sicht* (to be published in 1986).

5. This case was verified by interviewing the Dutch prosecutors.

6. Information given by the public prosecutor.

7. p. 140 *et seq.* note 3.

8. For details and verified case descriptions see Sieber, *Computerkriminalität, supra*, note 1, 99 *et seq.*

9. See also Council of Europe, Teaching, Research and Training in the Field of 'Computers and Law', Recommendation No. R (80) 3 adopted by the Committee of Ministers of the Council of Europe on 30 April 1980 and Explanatory Memorandum (1981).

10. See above, p. 14 note 34.

11. See Bloombecker, Computer crime update: the view as we exit 1984. (1985) **7** *Western New England Review* 641 *et seq.*

12. See Bloombecker, *supra*, note 11, (1985) **7** *Western New England Review* 636 *et seq.*

13. p. 141 note 5.

Appendix 1

International Select Bibliography

This bibliography contains the main general literature on computer crime. Special literature concerning specific items (such as tradesecret, copyright, or privacy protection, security strategies, or prosecution) is cited in the respective notes.

AUSTRALIA

Briscoe, W.G., *Law Reform Commission of Tasmania—Research Paper on Computer Misuse* (Hobart/Tasmania, approximately 1984).

CIT-CARB—The Computer Abuse Research Bureau at Chisholm Institute of Technology, Profiling and encouraging the prevention of computer abuse. *Computer Control Quarterly Newsletter* December 1985.

Fitzgerald, Kevin J., *The computer abuse profile in Australia* (edited by the Computer Abuse Research Bureau at Chisholm Institute of Technology, Caulfield, Victoria, 1982).

Lewens, Alan, Australian computer abuse profile. In: *Computer Abuse—Risks, Security and Control*, Proceedings of a CIT-CARB conference at Chisholm Institute of Technology, Caulfield, Victoria, July 1982.

McNiff, Francine, and Juris, B., *Criminal Liability for Australian Computer Abuse* (edited by the Computer Abuse Research Bureau, Caulfield Institute of Technology, Melbourne, 1980).

Working Party of the National Companies and Securities Commission, Draft Working Paper on Computer Crime—Substantive Law Aspect (1984).

AUSTRIA

Zima, Herbert, Computerkriminalität. (1980) *Journal für Betriebswirtschaft*, No.2, p.82.

Jaburek, Walter, Software für Großsysteme—Ist Computerkriminalität eingeplant? In: Koelsch, Raimund, Schmid, Werner, and Schweiggert, Franz (eds), *Wirtschaftsgut Software* (Stuttgart, 1985), p.83.

Jaburek, Walter and Schmölzer, Gabriele, *Computer-Kriminalität* (Wien, 1985).

BELGIUM

Cools, Marc, Het fenomeen computercriminaliteit. In: Cools, Marc, De Houwer, Joke, Erkelens, Catherine, Vanderhoydonck, Francis, and De Schutter, Bart, *Soft- en hard, ware het niet om de fraude—Bedenkingen over computercriminaliteit* (7 JUS Interuniversitaire Studenten Reeks, Antwerpen, 1985), p.11.

Cools, Marc, Beschouwingen over computerbeveiliging of preventieve maatregelen inzake computercriminaliteit in een ondernemingsgerichte context. In: Cools, Marc, De Houwer, Joke, Erkelens, Catherine, Vanderhoydonck, Francis, and De Schutter, Bart, *Soft- en hard ware het niet om de fraude—Bedenkingen over computercriminaliteit* (7 JUS Interuniversitaire Studenten Reeks, Antwerpen, 1985), p.25.

Cools, Marc, Computerkriminaliteit en het Belgisch strafrecht. (1984) **4** Politieblad 248.

Crombe, Yves, and Warton, Luis, *La Sécurité des Systèmes Informatiques* (edited by

Université Catholique de Louvain, Institut d'Administration et de Gestion, 1982).

Erkelens, Catherine, Beteugeling van computer-criminaliteit. (1985) *Panopticon* 334.

Erkelens, Catherine, Computercriminaliteit en het begrip 'vermogensdelict'. In: Cools, Marc, De Houwer, Joke, Erkelens, Catherine, Vanderhoydonck, Francis, and De Schutter, Bart, *Soft- en hardware het niet om de fraude—Bedenkingen over computercriminaliteit* (7 JUS Interuniversitaire Studenten Reeks, Antwerpen, 1985), p.63.

Erkelens, Catherine, La délinquance informatique belge et le droit pénal belge. In: Annexe à (1985) *Droit de l'Informatique* No. 6, p.21.

Houwer, Joke de, *Privacy and Transborder Data Flows* (Vrije Universiteit Brussel, Centrum voor International Strafrecht, 1984).

Houwer, Joke de, Privacy en grensoverschrijdend dataverkeer: een vergelijkende studie van internationale en nationale reglementeringen. In: Cools, Marc, De Houwer, Joke, Erkelens, Catherine, Vanderhoydonck, Francis, and De Schutter, Bart, *Soft-en hard, ware het niet om de fraude—Bedenkingen over computercriminaliteit* (7 JUS Interuniversitaire Studenten Reeks, Antwerpen, 1985), p. 87.

Schutter, Bart de, La criminalité liée à l'Informatique, (1985) *Revue de Droit Pénal et de Criminologie* 383.

Schutter, Bart de, Computerfraude, In: *Acten van het RUG-seminarie over Computer en recht* (Ter Perse).

Spreutels, Jean P, Infranctions liées à l'informatique en droit Belge. (1985) *Revue de Droit Pénal et de Criminologie* 357.

Vanderhoydonck, Francis, Juridische kanttekeningen bij het beheer van risico's verbonden aan het electronisch geldverkeer. In: Cools, Marc, De Houwer, Joke, Erkelens, Catherine, Vanderhoydonck, Francis, and De Schutter, Bart, *Soft- en hard, ware het niet om de fraude—Bedenkingen over computercriminaliteit* (7 JUS Interuniversitaire Studenten Reeks, Antwerpen, 1985), p.123.

CANADA

Department of Justice, *Response of the Government of Canada to the Report of the Parliamentary Sub-Committee on Computer Crime* (1983).

Hertz, Allen Z., Protecting computer systems with the criminal law. (1983) *Computer Law* 1.

Institute of Law Research and Reform of the University of Alberta, Background Paper on Improper Interference with Computers and the Misappropriation of Commercial Information (Edmonton/Alberta, 1983).

Sub-Committee on Computer Crime of the Standing Committee on Justice and Legal Affairs, Final Report, 14, 16, and 21 June 1983, House of Commons, Issue No.18.

Piragoff, Donald K., Combatting computer crime with criminal laws. In: H.W.K. Kaspersen (ed.), *Strafrecht in de Informatiemaatschappij* (Congress Proceedings of the Symposium of the Vrije Universiteit Amsterdam of 22 April 1986, Amsterdam, 1986), p.103.

Piragoff, Donald K., Les projets législatifs canadiens visant à la protection de l'intégrité des systèmes informatiques. In: Annexe à (1985) *Droit de l'Informatique* No. 6, p. 33 (updated version of 'Computers'. (1984) *Ottawa Law Review* 306).

DENMARK

Greve, Vagn, *EDB-strafferet* (Kobenhagen, 1984).

Hog, Ulla, EDB og EDB-Kriminalitet. In *Anklagemyndighedens arsberetning* (edited by the Danish Director of Public Prosecutions, 1981), p.58.

Meilby, Finn and Hog, Ulla, Mandatsvig. (1985) *Juristen* 41.

FEDERAL REPUBLIC OF GERMANY

Ammann, Thomas and Lehnhardt, Matthias, *Die Hacker sind unter uns* (München, 1985).

Betzl, Karl-Michael, *Sicherung des Rechnungswesens* (Köln, 1974).

Bull, Hans-Peter, *Datenschutz oder die Angst vor dem Computer* (München, 1984).

Breuer, Roland, *Computer-Schutz durch Sicherung und Versicherung* (Neubiberg b. München, 1984).

Gravenreuth, Günter Freiherr von, *Das Plagiat in strafrechtlicher Sicht* (Köln, 1986).

Haft, Fritjof, Stellungnahme in der öffentlichen Anhörung des Deutschen Bundestages zu den Entwürfen eines 2. WiKG. In: Deutscher Bundestag, Protokoll Nr. 26 über die 26. Sitzung des Rechtsausschusses vom 6.6.1984, Appendix p. 201.

Haft, Fritjof, Zur Situation des Datenschutzstrafrechts. (1979) *Neue Juristische Wochenschrift* 1194.

Hartmann, Wolfram, La criminalité informatique et sa répression par les réformes pénales en République Féderale d'Allemagne. In: Annexe à (1985) *Droit de l'Informatique* No. 6, 11.

Herb, Armin, Mangelnde Normenklarheit im Datenschutz-Strafrecht (University of Tübingen Dissertation, 1984).

Lampe, Ernst-Joachim, Die strafrechtliche Behandlung der sogenannten Computerkriminaliät. (1975) *Goltdammers Archiv für Strafrecht* 1.

Lenckner, Theodor, *Computerkriminalität und Vermögensdelikte* (Karlsruhe, 1981).

Möhrenschlager, Manfred, Der Regierungsentwurf eines Zweiten Gesetzes zur Bekämpfung der Wirtschaftskriminalität. (1982) wistra (*Zeitschrift für Wirtschaft, Steuer, Strafrecht*), p. 201.

Mühlen, Rainer A.H. von zur, *Computer-Kriminalität—Gefahren und Abwehr* (Neuwied, 1973).

Poerting, Peter, and Pott, Ernst, *Computerkriminalität* (edited 1986 by the German Bundeskriminalamt, Wiesbaden).

Polizei-Führungsakademie Hiltrup, *Erscheinungsformen der Computerkriminalität und der Manipulation von technischen Anlagen* (Hiltrup, 1975).

Rupp, Wolfgang, Computersoftware und Strafrecht (University of Tübingen Thesis 1985).

Sieber, Ulrich, *Computerkriminalität und Strafrecht* (2nd edn, Köln, 1980).

Sieber, Ulrich, Copyright protection of computer programs in Germany. (1984) *European Intellectual Property Review* 214, 253.

Sieber, Ulrich, Gefahr und Abwehr der Computerkriminalität. (1982) *Betriebs-Berater* 1433.

Sieber, Ulrich, *Informationstechnologie und Strafrechtsreform* (Köln, 1985).

Sieber, Ulrich, De la nécessité d'une législation internationale contre la fraude informatique. In: Annexe à (1985) *Droit de l'Informatique* No. 6, 4.

Sieber, Ulrich, Der urheberrechtliche Schutz von Computerprogrammen. (1983) *Betriebs-Berater* 977.

Sieber, Ulrich, Urheberrechtliche und wettbewerbsrechtliche Erfassung der unbefugten Softwarenutzung. (1981) *Betriebs-Berater* 1547.

Steinke, Wolfgang, Die Kriminalität durch Beeinflussung von Rechnerabläufen. (1984) *Neue Zeitschrift für Strafrecht* 295.

Tiedemann, Klaus, Computerkriminalität und Missbrauch von Bankomaten. (1983) *Wertpapier Mitteilungen* 1326.

Tiedemann, Klaus, Datenübermittlung als Straftatbestand. (1981) *Neue juristische Wochenschrift* 945.

Tiedemann, Klaus, *Wirtschaftsstrafrecht und Wirtschaftskriminalität* Vol. 2 (Reinbek/Hamburg, 1976).

Weck, Gerhard, *Datensicherheit* (Stuttgart, 1984).

Winkelbauer, Wolfgang, Computerkriminalität und Strafrecht. (1985) *Computer und Recht* 40.

Zimmerli, Erwin, and Liebl, Karlhans (eds), *Computermissbrauch—Computersicherheit* (Ingelheim/Küsnacht, 1984).

FINLAND

Hämäläinen, Erkki, Atk-rikollisuus ja rikoslainsäädäntö (Computer Crime and Penal Legislation). 1984 *Suomen Poliisilehti* 38.

Kainomaa, Seppo, Tietoturva sekä vahingot ja väärinkäytökset atk:ssa (Data security, losses and abuses in the field of automatic data processing), *Tutkimus-Raportti* 3/84 (published by Tietotekniikan Kehittämiskeskus ry.:n—Centre for the Development of Data Technology, Helsinki, 1984).

Lehtimaja, Lauri, Om databrott ur finländsk sysuinkel (Finnish Perspective on

Computer Crime). (1979) *Tidskrift, uutgiven av Juridiska Föreningen i Finland* 668.

Lehtimaja, Lauri, Tietokonerikollisuuteen liittyviä oikeudellisia ongelmia (Legal problems of computer crime). (1983) *Defensor Legis* 54.

Lehtimaja, Lauri, Atk-turvallisuus ja lainsäädäntö (Data security and legislation). (1984) *Suomen Poliisilehti* 40.

Lehtimaja, Lauri, Laki ei tunne atk-rikoksia. (1984) *Lakimiesuutiset* No. 10, 5.

Stenlund, Heikki and Lampola, Markku, *Tietotekniikka, hallinto ja oikeus* (Information Technology, Administration and the Law) (Jyväskylä, 1985).

FRANCE

Aupecle-Guicheney, Nadine, Les infractions pénales favorisées par l'informatique (Thèse de doctorat de 3è cycle Montpellier, 1984).

Bertin, G. and Lambertine, I. de, *La protection du logiciel—Enjeux juridiques et économiques* (Paris, 1985).

Chaigneau, Anne, La délinquance télématique. In: *Télématique et communication— un nouveau droit, Actes des Troisièmes Entretiens de Nanterre de Droit de l'Informatique* (Paris, 1985), p.91.

Chamoux, Françoise and Chamoux, Jean-Pierre, Adaption du Droit à la Vulnerabilité de l'Informatique en Europe. In: *SECURICOM 1984* (Congress Proceedings, edited by SEDEP) (Paris, 1984), p. 7.

Cosson, Jean, *Les grands escrocs en affaires* (Paris, 1979).

Grissonnanche, La securité des données dans les systèmes informatiques et l'assurance. (1983) **34** *L'argus international,* January—February (Sécurité et informatique), p.17.

Pitrat, Charlotte Marie, Fraude Informatique et pouvoirs publics. In: Annexe à (1985) *Droit de l'Informatique* No. 6, p. 46.

Pradel, Jean and Feuillard, Christian, Les Infractions commises au moyen de l'ordinateur. (1985) *Revue de Droit Pénal et de Criminologie* 307.

Thunis, Xavier, Les modes de protection juridique du logiciel. (1983) **9** *Droit et pratique du commerce international* 121.

République Française—Ministère de l'Industrie et de la Recherche, *Vers une protection des Logiciels informatiques* (Paris, 1983).

ITALY

Alpa, Guido, *La tutela giuridica del software* (Milano, 1984).

Alpa, Guido and Bessone, Mario, *Banche dati, telematica e tutela della persona* (Padova, 1984).

Catalini, Gianpiero, Alcune considerazioni in materia di protezione giuridica dei programmi per ordinatori. (1981) *Il diritto d'autore* 292.

Catania, Nino, Security and privacy, the state of Italian legislation and the effects of harmonization of rules on the European problem. In: *SECURICOM 1984* (Congress Proceedings, edited by SEDEP) (Paris, 1984), p. 34.

Figone, Alberto, Sulla tutela penale del 'software'. (1984) *Giurisprudenza Italiana*, part II, 351.

Giannantonio, Ettore, *Introduzione all'informatica giuridica* (Milano, 1984).

Nuvolone, Pietro, La trasmissione elettronica dei fondi e la tutela dell'utente. (1985) *Il diritto dell'informazione e dell'informatica* 593.

Picotti, Lorenzo, Appendice a Criminalità da Computer. (1984) *Politica del diritto* 629.

Picotti, Lorenzo, Criminalità da computer e diritto penale dell'impresa. In: *Il diritto penale dell'impresa* (Atti del convegno, Siracusa, 7–9 December, 1984.

Picotti, Lorenzo, Problemi penalistici in tema di falsificatione di dati informatici. (1985) *Il diritto dell'informazione e dell'informatica* 939.

Rodotà, Stefano, *Elaboratori elettronici e controllo sociale* (Bologna, 1973).

Rodotà, Stefano, Protezioni dei dati e circolazione dell'informazione. (1984) *Rivista critica del diritto privato* 721.

Rossello, Carlo, La tutela giuridica del 'software' nei primi orietamenti giurisprudenziali italiani. (1985) *Il diritto dell'informazione e dell'informatica* 103.

Russo, Licia, Informatica e criminalità. (1984) *Rivista italiana di diritto e procedura penale* 324.

Santini, Gerardo, La tutela giuridica della programmazione elettronica. (1968) *Giurisprudenza Italiana*, part IV, 225.

Sarzana, Carlo, Criminalità e tecnologia: il caso dei computer-crimes. (1979) *Rassegna penitenziaria e criminologica* 53.

Sarzana, Carlo, Note sul diritto penale dell'informatica. (1984) *La giustizia penale*, part I, 21.

Sarzana, Carlo, Victims of crime. Contribution to the Seventh United Nations Congress on the Prevention of Crime and the Treatment of Offenders (edited by the Italian Ministry of Justice, June 1985).

Tria, Lucia, Osservazioni in tema di reati elettronici. (1984) *Archivio penale* 283.

JAPAN

(A) Literature Available in the English Language

National Police Agency, *Report for Investigators of Computer Crime* (Tokyo, 1982).

White Paper on Police (Tokyo, 1983).

White Paper on Police (Tokyo, 1984).

(B) Additional Literature in Japanese (Concerning Japan Only; Titles Translated)

Hirohata, Shiro, Application of penal law for computer crime. (1982) **35** *Keisatsu-gaku Ronshu* (The Journal of Police Science) No. 35, 9.

Hirohata, Shiro, The present situation of computer crime and its countermeasures, (1985–4) *Jurist* No. 834, 25.

Hitomi, Nobuo, The present state of occurrence of computer crime. (1982) *Keisatsu-gaku Ronshu* (The Journal of Police Science) No. 35, 9.

Iga, Okikazu, The widespread use of computers and criminal law. (1985–10) *Jurist* No. 846, 53.

Itakura, Hiroshi, Computer crime and criminal law. (1980) *Jurist* No. 707, 144.

Itakura, Hiroshi, Computer crime and criminal law. (1982) *Hogaku-Seminar* (Judicial Seminar) No. 329, 100.

Kobayashi, Michio, The countermeasures for computer crime prevention. (1982) **35** *Keisatsugaku Ronshu* (The Journal of Police Science) No. 35, 61.

Matoba, Sumio, Computer crime and the problems of criminal law. (1985–10) *Jurist* No. 846, 6.

Mikami, Kazuyuki, Propulsion of countermeasures for computer crime. (1982) *Keisatsugaku Ronshu* (The Journal of Police Science) No. 35, 1.

Nishihara, Haruo, The use of computers and criminal law problems. (1971) *Jurist* No. 484, 35.

Ohya, Minoru, Computer crime. (1985) *Hogaku-Seminar* (Judicial Seminar) No. 363 p. 20, no. 363, p. 66.

Ohya, Minoru, Furuta, Yuki and Nishida, Noriyuki, On computer crime and the task of penal legislation. (1985–10) *Jurist* No. 846, 16.

Takeuchi, Naoto, A study about the legislation of the protection of computer-systems. (1984) *Keisatsugaku Ronshu* (The Journal of Police Science) No. 37, 67.

Toda, Nobuhisa, Prevention of computer crime. (1982) **53** *Keisatsu-Kenkyu* (The Journal of Police Study) No. 9, 27.

Yonezawa, Keiji, Computer and criminal law. (1985) *Hanrei* (Jurisprudence) *Times* No. 559, 53.

LUXEMBOURG

Jaeger, Marc, La fraude informatique. (1985) *Revue de Droit Pénal et de Criminologie* 323.

NETHERLANDS

Brandenburg, Koos, *Kriminalistiek en Computer* (Graduation Thesis of the Police Academy of Apeldoorn, 1984).

Dijken, Pieter van, *Computer en Boekhouding* (1981).

Dijken, Pieter van, Computer en criminaliteit. (1983) *Algemeen Politieblad* 487.

Kaspersen, H.W.K., and Keijzer, Nico, Het Nederlandse strafrecht en computer-misbruik. In: H.W.K. Kaspersen (ed.) *Strafrecht in de Informatiemaatschappij* (Congress Proceedings of the Symposium of the Vrije Universiteit Amsterdam of 22 April 1986, Amsterdam, 1986), p. 35.

Schraaf, H.A. van de, Computermisdaad, (1984) 26 *Informatie* No. 2 (February), 99.

Vandenberghe, Guy P.V. *Berscherming van Computersoftware, Een rechtsvergelijkend onderzoek* (Antwerpen, 1984).

Vandenberghe, Guy P.V., Computermisbruik, beveiliging en strafrecht. In: H.W.K, Kaspersen (ed.) *Strafrecht in de Informatiemaatschappij* (Congress Proceedings of the Symposium of the Vrije Universiteit Amsterdam of 22 April 1986, Amsterdam, 1986), p. 25.

NORWAY

Andenaes, Johs, Fongner, Else Bugge, Oug, Thor, Qrigstad, Lasse, Drolsum, Ruth, Schjolberg, Stein, and Selmer, Knut S., Datakriminalitet. *Norges Offentlige Utredvinger* No. 31 (Oslo, 1985).

Schjolberg, Stein, Computer-assisted crime in Scandinavia. (1980) **2** *Computer and Law Journal* 457.

Schjolberg, Stein, Computer crime in Norway. In: Bing, Jan, and Selmer, Knut (eds), *A Decade of Computers and Law* (Oslo, 1980), p. 440.

Schjolberg, Stein, *Computers and Penal Legislation* (Oslo, 1983).

Schjolberg, Stein, *Computers and Penal Legislation—A study on the Legal Politics of a New Technology*, Complex 2/83 (Universitesforlaget, Oslo).

Schjolberg, Stein, Computer and penal legislation. In: *SECURICOM 1984* (Congress Proceedings edited by SEDEP) (Paris, 1984), p. 15.

SPAIN

Madrid, Conesa F., *Estudo de Derecho, Informàtica y derecho penal* (Valencia, 1983).

Morales, Fermin Prats, *La tutela Penal de la Intimidad: Privacy e Informatica* (Barcelona, 1984).

SWEDEN

Solarz, Artur, *Computer Technology and Computer Crime*, Report No. 8 of the Research and Development Division, National Council for Crime Prevention (Stockholm, 1981).

Solarz, Artur (ed.), *Datorteknik, brottslighet och ADB-saekerhet* (National Council for Crime Prevention, Stockholm, 1982).

Solarz, Artur, *Datorteknik och brottslighet* (National Council for Crime Prevention, Stockholm, 1985).

Solarz, Artur, *Datortekniken och brottsligheten in Brottsutvecklingen* (National Council for Crime Prevention, Stockholm, 1981).

Swedish Ministry of Defence, *The Vulnerability of the Computerized Society* (Stockholm, 1979).

Swedish Ministry of Defence, Datorer, Sårbarhet, Säkerhet, *Statens Offentliga Utredningar* (SOU) No. 1986, 12 (Stockholm, 1986).

SWITZERLAND

Antognazza, G., Computerkriminalität: Stellenwert überschätzt. (1983) *Kriminalistik* 389.

Bauknecht, Computer-Kriminalität. In: Neutra Treuhand AG (ed.), *Wirtschafts-Kriminalität* (Zurich, 1982), p. 99.

Bollag, Thierry G., *Computer-Kriminalität und Möglichkeiten ihrer Bekämpfung* (Diploma Thesis of the Hochschule St Gallen für Wirtschafts- und Sozialwissenschaften, 1985).

Egli, Heinz, *Grundformen der Wirtschaftskriminalität* (Heidelberg, 1985), p. 144.

Eidgenössisches Justiz- und Polizeidepartement (ed.), *Bericht zum Vorentwurf über die Änderung des Strafgesetzbuches und des Militärstrafgesetzes betreffend die strafbaren Handlungen gegen das Vermögen und die Urkundenfälschung* (Bern, 1985).

Fischer, Thomas, Computer-Kriminalität, Gefahren und Abwehrmassnahmen. **71** *Betriebswirtschaftliche Mitteilungen* (Bern, 1979).

George, André, *Les risques de pertes Indirectes induites par les systèmes informatiques*, The Geneva Papers on Risk and Insurance (edited by Association Internationale pour l'Etude de L'Economie de L'Assurance, 1979), p. 56.

Rohner, Louis, *Computerkriminalität—Strafrechtliche Probleme bei 'Zeitdiebstahl' und Manipulationen* (Zürich, 1976).

Stratenwerth, Günter, Computerbetrug. (1981) **98** *Schweizerische Zeitschrift für Strafrecht* 229.

Zimmerli, Erwin and Liebl, Karlhans (eds), *Computermissbrauch—Computersicherheit* (Ingelheim/Küsnacht, 1984).

Zweifel, Sibylle, *Buchführungsdelikte mittels EDV und Massnahmen zu deren Verhinderung* (Zurich, 1984).

UNITED KINGDOM

Local Government Audit Inspectorate, *Computer Fraud Survey* (photocopied 1981).

McKnight, Gerald, *Computer Crime* (London, 1973).

Norman, Adrian R.D., *Computer Insecurity* (London, 1983).

Saxby, Stephen, Computers and the law: old statutes for new problems?, In: *SECURICOM 1986* (Congress Proceedings edited 1986 by SEDEP, Paris), p. 133.

Scottish Law Commission, Computer crime. *Consultative Memorandum* No. 68 (Edinburgh, 1986).

Tettenborn, Andrew, Some legal aspects of computer abuse. (1980) **2** *The Company Lawyer* 147.

Wong, Ken, *Computer Crime Casebook* (photocopied, BIS Applied Systems, Manchester, 1983).

Wong, Ken, *Computer Crime—Risk Management and Computer Security* (photocopied, BIS Applied Systems, Manchester, 1985).

Wong, Ken, Computer-related fraud. (1983) *Information Age* 16.

Wong, Ken, *Computer Related Fraud Casebook* (photocopied, BIS Applied Systems, Manchester, 1983).

Wong, Ken, Computer-related Fraud in the UK. (1983) *Information Age* 238.

Wong, Ken, The hackers and computer crime, *SECURICOM 1986* (Congress Proceedings edited 1986 by SEDEP, Paris), p. 11.

UNITED STATES

Allen, Brandt, The biggest computer frauds. (May 1977) *The Journal of Accountancy* 52.

American Bar Association, *Report on Computer Crime* (Washington, DC, 1984).

American Institute of Certified Public Accountants, *Report on the Study of EDP-Related Fraud in the Banking and Insurance Industries* (New York, 1984).

Becker, Jay J., *The Investigation of Computer Crime* (edited by the US Department of Justice, Law Assistance Administration, Washington, DC, 1980).

Becker, Jay J., The trial of a computer crime. (1980) **2** *Computer and Law Journal* 441.

Bequai, August, *Computer Crime* (Massachusetts, 1978).

Bequai, August, *How To Prevent Computer Crime* (Toronto, 1983).

Bequai, August, *The Cashless Society* (New York, 1981).

Bloombecker, Jay J., *Computer Crime, Computer Security, Computer Ethics* (edited by the National Center for Computer Crime Data, Los Angeles, 1986).

Bloombecker, Jay J., *The Computer Crime Law Reporter* (loosleaf, amended 1985, edited by the National Center for Computer Crime Data, Los Angeles).

Bloombecker, Jay J., Computer crime update: the view as we exit 1984. (1985) **7** *Western New England Law Review* 627.

Bloombecker, Jay J., Criminal informatics law. Paper written for the Intergovernmental Bureau for Informatics (Washington DC, 1983).

Bloombecker, Jay J., *Introduction to Computer Crime* (edited by the National Center for Computer Crime Data, Los Angeles, 1985).

Bloombecker, Jay J., Secure computing—who are the computer criminals? (1985) **1** *Conscience in Computing* 1.

Carrol, John M., *Computer Security* (Los Angeles, 1977).

Couch. Robert, A suggested legislative approach to the problem of computer crime. (1981) **38** *Washington and Lee Law Review* 1173.

General Accounting Office, *Computer Related Crimes in Federal Programs* (Washington, 1976).

Kling, Rob, Computer abuse and computer crime as organizational activities. (1983) **2** *Computer and Law Journal* 403.

Kraus, Leonard and MacGahan, Aileen, *Computer Fraud and Countermeasures* (Englewood Cliffs/New York, 1979).

Leibholz, Stephan W. and Wilson, Louis D., *Users' Guide to Computer Crime* (Radnor, Pennsylvania, 1974).

Mandell, Steven L., *Computers, Data Processing, and the Law* (St Paul, 1984).

Mantle, Ray, A., Trade secret and copyright protection of computer software. (1984) *Computer and Law Journal* 669.

McKnight, Gerald, *Computer Crime* (London, 1973).

Mendes, Meredith, W., La législation pénale en matiére d'ordinateurs et les mesures de sécurité aux Etats-Unis. Annexe à (1985–6) *Droit de l'Informatique* 39.

Möhrenschlager, Manfred, Neue bundesstrafrechtliche Regelung gegen die Fälschung und den Missbrauch von Kreditkarten in den USA. (1985) *wistra (Zeitschrift für Wirtschaft, Steuer, Strafrecht)* 216.

National Criminal Justice Information and Statistics Service (Law Enforcement Assistance Administration, US Department of Justice), *Criminal Justice Resource Manual* (Washington, 1979).

Nycum, Susan, The criminal law aspects of computer abuse: Part I State penal law, Part II Federal criminal code. (1976) **5** *Rutgers Journal of Computers and Law* 271, 297.

Parker, Donn B., *Computer Abuse Assessment* (Stanford Research Institute, Menlo Park, California, 1975).

Parker, Donn B., *Computer Abuse, Perpetrators and Vulnerabilities of Computer Systems* (Stanford Research Institute, Menlo Park California, 1975).

Parker, Donn B., Computer abuse research update. (1980) **2** *Computer and Law Journal* 329.

Parker, Donn B., *Computer Security Management* (Reston/Virginia, 1981).

Parker, Donn B., *Crime by Computer* (New York, 1976).

Parker, Donn B., *Ethical Conflicts in Computer Science and Technology* (Reston, AFIPS Press, 1979).

Parker, Donn B., *Fighting Computer Crime* (New York, 1983).

Parker Donn B., Nycum, Susan, and Oüra, S. Stephan, *Computer Abuse* (Stanford Research Institute, Menlo Park, California, 1973).

Schabeck, Tim A., *Computer Crime Investigation Manual* (looseleaf, Madison, 1979).

Sokolik, Stanley L., Computer crime—the need for deterrent legislation. (1980) **2** *Computer and Law Journal* 353.

Stern, Richard H., The legal protection of computer software and computer-related innovations in the United States. (1982) *International Review of Industrial Property and Copyright Law*, 152, 176.

Taber, John K., A survey of computer crime studies. (1980) **2** *Computer and Law Journal* 275.

US Department of Justice, *Computer Crime—Expert Witness Manual* (Washington, DC, 1980).

US Department of Justice, *Computer Crime—Legislative Resource Manual* (Washington, DC, 1980).

US Department of Justice, *Computer Security Techniques* (Washington, DC, 1981).

US Department of Justice, *Criminal Justice Resource Manual* (Washington, DC, 1979).

White collar crime—computer crime. (1980) **18** *American Criminal Law Review* 370.

Whiteside, Thomas, *Computer Capers* (New York, 1978).

INTERNATIONAL AND COMPARATIVE STUDIES

Briat, Martine, La fraude informatique: une approche de droit comparé, (1985) *Revue de Droit Pénal et de Criminologie* 287.

Camera dei Deputati (ed.) *Banche Dati e tutela della persona* (2nd edn, Rome, 1983).

Commission of the European Communities—Information Technology Task Force, *The Vulnerability of the Information-Conscious Society—European Situation, Summarized Conclusions* (June 1984).

OECD (Organization for Economic Co-operation and Development) (ed.), Computer-related Criminality: Analysis of Legal Policy in the OECD Area, *Report DSTI/ICCP/84.22* of 15 November 1984 (first version) and 30 August 1985 (second version) and 18 April 1986 (final version) (by Martine Briat and Ulrich Sieber).

Schutter, Bart de, Grensoverschrijdende computercriminaliteit-Nood aan harmoniserende aanpak, in: H.W.K. Kaspersen (ed.), *Strafrecht in de Informatiemaatschappij* (Congress Proceedings of the Symposium of the Vrije Universiteit Amsterdam of 22 April 1986 (Amsterdam, 1986), p.143.

Sieber, Ulrich, New legislative responses to computer-related economic crimes and infringements of privacy In: H.W.K. Kaspersen (ed.), *Strafrecht in de Informatiemaatschappij* (Congress Proceedings of the Symposium of the Vrije Universiteit Amsterdam of 22 April 1986, Amsterdam, 1986), p.75.

Sieber, Ulrich, Proposal for a Council of Europe Initiative in the Field of Computer-related Economic Crime, Council of Europe Doc.no. PC-R-CC (86) 10 of 26 March 1986 (Strasbourg, 1986).

Sieber, Ulrich, Proposal for a Council of Europe Initiative in the Field of Computer-related Infringements of Privacy, Council of Europe Doc. no. PC-R-CC (86) 11 of 26 March 1986 (Strasbourg, 1986).

Appendix 2

International Corpus Juris of Computer Crime Statutes

This compilation contains the most important computer-crime acts and bills discussed above. **All translations are unofficial.** Countries with a variety of different state laws are only represented by exemplary statutes. In cases in which law amendments are not understandable without the altered law, the whole new body of law is provided (amendments are then printed in italic). For further acts and bills as well as explanations of the civil and administrative statutes to which the criminal offences refer (especially in the fields of copyright and privacy legislation) see Chapter IV.

AUSTRALIA

Computer-related Economic Crimes

THE NORTHERN TERRITORY CRIMINAL CODE ACT (No. 47), 1983

Section 276. Making False Data Processing Material, etc.

(1) Any person who unlawfully alters, falsifies, erases or destroys any data processing material with any fraudulent intention is guilty of a crime and is liable to imprisonment for 3 years.

(2) If he does so with the intent that an incorrect data processing response will be produced and with the intent that it may in any way be used or acted upon as being correct, whether in the Territory or elsewhere, to the prejudice of any person, or with intent that any person may, in the belief that it is correct, be induced to do or refrain from doing any act, whether in the Territory or elsewhere, he is liable to imprisonment for 7 years.*

CRIMES (AMENDMENT) ORDINANCE (NO. 4) NO. 44, 1985 AMENDING THE NEW SOUTH WALES CRIMES ACT 1900 IN ITS APPLICATION TO THE AUSTRALIAN CAPITAL TERRITORY

Section 93. Interpretation.
In this Part, unless the contrary intention appears— . . .

'gain' means a gain of any property, whether temporary or permanent, and includes the keeping by a person of any property that he or she already has; . . .

'property' means any real or personal property and includes—
(a) a chose in action and any other intangible property, other than an incorporeal hereditament;
(b) a wild animal that is tamed or ordinarily kept in captivity; and
(c) a wild animal that is not tamed nor ordinarily kept in captivity but that is—
  (i) reduced into the possession of a person who has not lost or abandoned that possession; or
  (ii) in the course of being reduced into the possession of a person;

Section 115. Dishonest Use of Computers.

'(1) A person who, by any means, dishonestly uses, or causes to be used, a computer or other machine, or part of a computer or other machine, with intent to obtain by that use a gain for himself or herself or another person, or to cause by that use a loss to another person, is guilty of an offence punishable, on conviction, by imprisonment for 10 years.

'(2) In this section, 'machine' means a machine designed to be operated by means of a coin, bank-note, token, disc, tape or any identifying card or article.

DRAFT PROVISIONS TO AMEND THE AUSTRALIAN CAPITAL TERRITORY LAW

Section 137 C. Forgery and the Use of Forged Instruments

'(1) A person shall not make a false instrument with the intention that he or she, or another person, shall use it to induce another person to accept it as genuine, and by reason of so accepting it to do or not to do some act to that other person's, or to another person's, prejudice.

'(2) A person shall not use an instrument which is, and which he or she knows to be, false, with the intention of inducing another person to accept it as genuine and by reason of so accepting it to do or not to do some act to that other person's, or to another person's, prejudice.

'(3) A person shall not make a copy of an instrument which is, and which he or she knows to be, a false instrument, with the intention that he or she, or another person, shall use it to induce another person to accept it as a copy of a genuine instrument and by reason of so accepting it to do or not to do some act to that other person's prejudice.

'(4) A person shall not use a copy of an instrument which is, and which he or she knows to be, a false instrument, with the intention of inducing another person to accept it as a copy of a genuine instrument and by reason of so accepting it to do or not to do some act to that other person's, or to another person's, prejudice.

Penalty: Imprisonment for 10 years.

Section 137 D. Possession of False Instrument

'A person shall not have in his or her custody, or under his or her control, an instrument which is, and which he or she knows to be, false, with the intention that the person or another shall use it to induce another person to accept it as genuine, and by reason of so accepting it to do or not to do some act to that other person's, or to another person's prejudice.

Penalty: Imprisonment for 10 years.**

---

* Section 1 of the Code provides that unless the contrary intention appears—
'alters' includes adds to;

'data processing material' means all information and programmes used in or with a DP system;

'data processing response' means any printout, response, or result obtained from the operation of a DP system.

** Section 93 of the Act provides that unless the contrary intention appears 'instrument' means—
  (a) a document, whether of a formal or informal character;
  (b) a card by means of which property or credit can be obtained; and
  (c) a disc, tape, sound track or other device on or in which information is recorded or stored by mechanical, electronic, or other means;

AUSTRIA

(A) Computer-related Economic Crimes

THE PROVISIONS OF THE CRIMINAL CODE AS AMENDED BY THE PROPOSALS OF THE MINISTRY OF JUSTICE FOR A PENAL CODE AMENDMENT ACT OF 1985

Section 126a. Damage to Stored Data

(1) Any person who suppresses, alters, erases or otherwise renders useless electronic, magnetic or otherwise invisible or not directly readable stored data, without being authorized to dispose of the data or to dispose of them alone, is liable to imprisonment for a term not exceeding six months or to a fine not exceeding 360 daily rates.

(2) If the damages caused by the offence exceed 10 000 Schillings, the penalty shall be imprisonment for a term not exceeding two years or a fine not exceeding 360 daily rates. If the damages caused by the offence exceed 200 000 Schillings, the penalty shall be imprisonment for a term from six months to five years.

Section 147a. Computer Fraud

(1) Any person who, with the intention of procuring an unlawful gain for himself or for a third person, causes prejudice to another's property by influencing the result of data processing records through incorrect arrangement of the program, through interference with the flow of the records or through the feeding of wrong or incomplete data, is liable to imprisonment for a term not exceeding three years.

(2) If the damages caused by the offence exceed 200 000 Schillings, the penalty shall be imprisonment for a term not exceeding ten years.

Section 149. Obtaining a Service Without Payment

(1) . . .

(2) Any person who, without paying, obtains for himself or for a third person a service, other than goods, from an automat, is liable to imprisonment for a term not exceeding six months or to a fine not exceeding 360 daily rates.

Moreover, any person who obtains for himself or for a third person, without the consent of the authorized person, a service from a data processing facility without offering reasonable payment, is also liable to punishment.

Section 166. Commission Within Family Circle

(1) Any person who damages property or *stored data*, commits theft, . . . [there follows a list of various other offences], to the detriment of his or her spouse, a relative in direct line, a brother or sister or to the detriment of another relative is, if he lives together with the said person, liable to imprisonment for a term not exceeding 3 months or to a fine not exceeding 180 daily rates. If the offence would otherwise be punishable by imprisonment for a term equal to or exceeding 3 years, the penalty is imprisonment for up to 6 months or a fine of up to 360 daily rates.

Section 227a. Falsification of Stored Data

(1) Any person who alters without authority any electronic, magnetic or otherwise invisible or not directly readable stored data with the intention of using them in a legal transaction as evidence of a right, a legal relationship or a fact or to influence a data processing facility, is liable to imprisonment for a term not exceeding two years.

(2) Moreover, any person who uses stored data which has been altered without authority (subsection 1) in a legal transaction as evidence of a right, a legal relationship or a fact or to influence a data processing facility, is also liable to punishment.

(3) Section 226 applies *mutatis mutandis.*

Section 229a. Suppression of Stored Data

(1) Any person who deletes or suppresses stored data (section 227a) without being authorized to dispose of the data or to dispose of them alone, with the intention of preventing their use in a legal transaction as evidence of a right, a legal relationship or a fact or to influence a data processing facility, is liable to imprisonment for a term not exceeding one year.

(2) Section 229 (2) applies *mutatis mutandis.*

(B) Infringements of Privacy

PENAL PROVISIONS OF THE FEDERAL DATA PROTECTION ACT OF 18 OCTOBER 1978

Section 48. Breach of Confidentiality

(1) Any person who unlawfully divulges or makes use of data with which he has been entrusted or to which he has been given access solely for the purposes of his employment in the data processing field, the disclosure and use of which is likely to prejudice a legitimate interest of the person affected, shall, where not liable to a greater penalty under another provision, be liable to imprisonment for a period not exceeding one year.

(2) Such person may only be prosecuted on the application of a person whose interest in the continued confidentiality of the data has been prejudiced or on application by the Data Protection Commission.

(3) The trial may be held *in camera*
  1. on application by the prosecution agency, the accused or by a private party to the proceedings; or
  2. where the court deems it necessary in the interests of persons who are not parties to the proceedings.

Section 49. Unauthorized Interference with Data Processing

Any person who unlawfully interferes with the rights of another with intent to cause damage, in that he erases, falsifies or otherwise alters computerised or computer-aided data or in that he procures computerised or computer-aided data shall, where not liable to a greater penalty under another provision, be liable to imprisonment for a period not exceeding one year.

Section 50. Administrative Penalties

(1) Any person who processes data by automatic means without having fulfilled the information or registration requirements imposed under this Act, or discloses data in violation of the provisions of section 47(4), commits an administrative offence punishable by a fine of up to 150 000 Schillings.

(2) The attempt to commit such an offence is punishable.

(3) Data media and programs which form part of an offence under subsection 1 may be confiscated pursuant to sections 10, 17, 18 of the Act of Administrative Penalties 1950.

(4) Jurisdiction for decisions under subsections 1 to 3 shall lie with the head of the government of the State.

(5) Appeals against decisions under subsection 4 shall be heard by the Data Protection Commission.

(6) The Data Protection Comission shall be notified of legally binding decisions under subsection 4.

SECTION 49 OF THE FEDERAL DATA PROTECTION ACT AS AMENDED BY THE PROPOSALS OF THE MINISTRY OF JUSTICE FOR A PENAL CODE AMENDMENT ACT OF 1985

Section 49. Unauthorized Interference with Data Processing

Any person who unlawfully and intentionally causes prejudice to another person's rights by obtaining automatically processed data, is to be punished by imprisonment for a term not exceeding 1 year, unless the offence is subject to a greater penalty under another provision.

CANADA

(A) Computer-related Economic Crimes

CRIMINAL LAW AMENDMENT ACT, 1985
(AMENDMENTS TO THE CRIMINAL CODE)

43. The definition 'document' in section 282 of the said Act is repealed and the following substituted therefor:

'credit card'
'carte de crédit'

' 'credit card' means any card, plate, coupon book or other device issued or otherwise distributed for the purpose of being used

    (a) on presentation to obtain, on credit, money, goods, services or any other thing of value, or

    (b) in an automated teller machine, a remote service unit or a similar automated banking device to obtain any of the services offered through the machine, unit or device;

'document'
'document'

'document' means any paper, parchment or other material on which is recorded or marked anything that is capable of being read or understood by a person, computer system or other device, and includes a credit card, but does not include trade marks on articles of commerce or inscriptions on stone or metal or other like material;'

46. The said Act is further amended by adding thereto, immediately after section 301.1 thereof, the following section:

Unauthorized
use of
computer

"**301.2** (1) Every one who, fraudulently and without colour of right,

    (*a*) obtains, directly or indirectly, any computer service,

    (*b*) by means of an electromagnetic, acoustic, mechanical or other device, intercepts or causes to be intercepted, directly or indirectly, any function of a computer system, or

    (*c*) uses or causes to be used, directly or indirectly, a computer system with intent to commit an offence under paragraph (*a*) or (*b*) or an offence under section 387 in relation to data or a computer system

is guilty of an indictable offence and is liable to imprisonment for a term not exceeding ten years, or is guilty of an offence punishable on summary conviction.

Definitions

    (2) In this section,

'computer
program'
*'programme
d'ordinateur'*

'computer program' means data representing instructions or statements that, when executed in a computer system, causes the computer system to perform a function;

'computer
service'
*'service
d'ordinateur'*

'computer service' includes data processing and the storage or retrieval of data;

'computer
system'
'ordinateurs'

'computer system' means a device that, or a group of interconnected or related devices one or more of which,

    (a) contains computer programs or other data, and

    (b) pursuant to computer programs,

        (i) performs logic and control, and

        (ii) may perform any other function;

'data'
'donnée'

'data' means representations of information or of concepts that are being prepared or have been prepared in a form suitable for use in a computer system;

'electromagnetic
acoustic,
mechanical
or other
device'
'dispositif

'electromagnetic, acoustic, mechanical or other device' means any device or apparatus that is used or is capable of being used to intercept any function of a computer system, but does not include a hearing aid used to correct subnormal hearing of the user to not better than normal hearing;

'function'
'fonction'
'function' includes logic, control, arithmetic, deletion, storage and retrieval and communication or telecommunication to, from or within a computer system;

'Intercept'
'intercepter'
'intercept' includes listen to or record a function of a computer system, or acquire the substance, meaning or purport thereof.'

58. (1) Section 387 of the said Act is amended by adding thereto, immediately after subsection (1) thereof, the following subsection:

Mischief in relation to data
'(1.1) Every one commits mischief who wilfully
(a) destroys or alters data;
(b) renders data meaningless, useless or ineffective;
(c) obstructs, interrupts or interferes with the lawful use of data; or
(d) obstructs, interrupts or interferes with any person in the lawful use of data or denies access to any person who is entitled to access thereto.'

1972,c,13. s.30
(2) Subsections 387(3) to (5) of the said Act are repealed and the following substituted therefor:

Idem
'(3) Every one who commits mischief in relation to property that is a testamentary instrument or the value of which exceeds one thousand dollars
(a) is guilty of an indictable offence and is liable to imprisonment for a term not exceeding ten years; or
(b) is guilty of an offence punishable on summary conviction.

Idem
(4) Every one who commits mischief in relation to property, other than property described in subsection (3),
(a) is guilty of an indictable offence and is liable to imprisonment for a term not exceeding two years; or
(b) is guilty of an offence punishable on summary conviction.

Idem
(5) Every one who commits mischief in relation to data
(a) is guilty of an indictable offence and is liable to imprisonment for a term not exceeding ten years; or
(b) is guilty of an offence punishable on summary conviction.

Offence
(5.1) Every one who wilfully does an act or wilfully omits to do an act that is his duty to do, if that act or omission is likely to constitute mischief causing actual danger to life, or to constitute mischief in relation to property or data,
(a) is guilty of an indictable offence and is liable to imprisonment for a term not exceeding five years; or
(b) is guilty of an offence punishable on summary conviction.'

(3) Section 387 of the said Act is further amended by adding thereto the following subsection:

Definition of 'data'
'(8) In this section, "data" has the same meaning as in section 301.2.'

(B) Infringements of Privacy

PENAL PROVISION OF THE FEDERAL 'PRIVACY ACT' OF 1982 (SC 1980/81/82/83, c.111, as amended)

Offences

Obstruction
68. (1) No person shall obstruct the Privacy Commissioner or any person acting on behalf or under the direction of the Commissioner in the performance of the Commissioner's duties and functions under this Act.

Offence and punishment
(2) Every person who contravenes this section is guilty of an

offence and liable on summary conviction to a fine not exceeding one thousand dollars.

PENAL PROVISION OF THE FEDERAL 'ACCESS TO INFORMATION ACT' OF 1982

(SC 1980/81/82/83, c.111, as amended)

Offences

Obstruction   **67.** (1) No person shall obstruct the Information Commissioner or any person acting on behalf or under the direction of the Commissioner in the performance of the Commissioner's duties and functions under this Act.

Offence and punishment   (2) Every person who contravenes this section is guilty of an offence and liable on summary conviction to a fine not exceeding one thousand dollars.

PENAL PROVISIONS OF QUEBEC'S 'AN ACT RESPECTING ACCESS TO DOCUMENTS HELD BY PUBLIC BODIES AND THE PROTECTION OF PERSONAL INFORMATION' OF 1982

Section 158.
Every person who knowingly denies or impedes access to a document or information to which access is not to be denied under this Act is guilty of an offence and is liable, in addition to costs, to a fine of $100 to $500, and, for every subsequent offence within two years, to a fine of $250 to $1 000.

Section 159.
Every person who knowingly gives access to a document or to information which, under this Act, is not to be disclosed or to which, according to law, a public body denies access, is guilty of an offence and is liable, in addition to costs, to a fine of $200 to $1 000, and, for every subsequent offence within two years, to a fine of $500 to $2 500.

Section 160.
Every person who impedes the progress of an inquiry or examination of a request or application by the Commission by knowingly providing it with false or inaccurate information, or otherwise, is guilty of an offence and is liable, in addition to costs, to the fine established in section 159.

Section 161.
Every person who impedes the progress of an inquiry or examination of a request or application by the Commission by knowingly omitting to provide it with the information it requires is guilty of an offence and is liable, in addition to costs, to a fine of $50 for each day or part of day during which the offence continues.

Section 162.
Every person who contravenes this Act, the regulations of the government, or an order of the Commission, is guilty of an offence and is liable to the fine prescribed in section 158.

Section 163.
An error or omission made in good faith does not constitute an offence within the meaning of this Act.

Section 164.
Proceedings under this division are instituted by the Commission or by a person generally or specially authorized by it for that purpose.
    The Summary Convictions Act (R.S.Q., chapter P–15) applies to proceedings instituted under this division.

Section 165.

Fines collected under this Act form part of the consolidated revenue fund and, consequently, are to be remitted to the Minister of Finance.

(C) Procedural Law

BILL S 33 OF 1982: 'AN ACT TO GIVE EFFECT, FOR CANADA, TO THE UNIFORM EVIDENCE ACT ADOPTED BY THE UNIFORM LAW CONFERENCE OF CANADA'

Recorded Evidence

Interpretation

Definitions
'duplicate'

'original'

'photograph'

130. In this section and sections 131 to 159,

'duplicate' means a reproduction of the original from the same impression as the original, or from the same matrix, or by means of photography, including enlargements and miniatures, or by mechanical or electronic re-recording, or by chemical reproduction or by other equivalent technique that accurately reproduces the original

'original' means

(*a*) in relation to a record, the record itself or any facsimile intended by the author of the record to have the same effect,

(*b*) in relation to a photograph, the negative and any print made from it, and

(*c*) in relation to stored or processed data or information, any printout or intelligible output that reflects accurately the data or information or is the product of a system that does so;

'photograph' includes a still photograph, photographic film or plate, microphotographic film, photostatic negative, x-ray film and a motion picture.

Best Evidence Rule

Best evidence
rule

131. Subject to this Act, the original is required in order to prove the contents of a record.

Admissibility of
duplicates

132. A duplicate is admissible to the same extent as an original unless the court is satisfied that there is reason to doubt the authenticity of the original or the accuracy of the duplicate.

Admissibility of
copies

133. Where an admissible duplicate cannot be produced by the exercise of reasonable diligence, a copy is admissible in order to prove the contents of a record in the following cases:

(*a*) the original has been lost or destroyed;

(*b*) it is impossible, illegal or impracticable to produce the original;

(*c*) the original is in the possession or control of an adverse party who has neglected or refused to produce it or is in the possession or control of a third person who cannot be compelled to produce it;

(*d*) the original is a public record within the meaning of section 145 or is recorded or filed as required by law;

(*e*) the original is not closely related to a controlling issue; or

(*f*) the copy qualifies as a business record within the meaning of section 152.

Other evidence

134. Where an admissible copy cannot be produced by the exercise of reasonable diligence, other evidence may be given of the contents of a record.

Voluminous records

135. (1) The contents of a voluminous record that cannot conveniently be examined in court may be presented in the form of a chart, summary or other form that, to the satisfaction of the court, is a fair and accurate presentation of the contents.

Examination and copies

(2) The court may order the original or a duplicate of any record referred to in subsection (1) to be produced in court or made available for examination and copying by other parties at a reasonable time and place.

Written explanation

136. (1) Where a record is in a form that requires explanation, a written explanation by a qualified person accompanied by an affidavit setting forth his qualifications and attesting to the accuracy of the explanation is admissible in the same manner as the original.

Examination of person making explanation

(2) A party, with leave of the court, may examine or cross-examine a person who has given a written explanation under subsection (1) for the purpose of determining the admissibility of the explanation or the weight to be given to it.

Testimony, deposition or written admission

137. The contents of a record may be proved by the testimony, deposition or written admission of the party against whom they are offered, without accounting for the non-production of the original or a duplicate or copy.

Condition of admissibility

138. The court shall not receive evidence of the contents of a record other than by way of the original or a duplicate where the unavailability of the original or a duplicate is attributable to the bad faith of the proponent.

Notice

Notice and production

139. (1) No record other than a public record to which section 146 applies and no exemplification or extract of such a record or affidavit relating to such a record shall be received in a party's evidence in chief unless the party, at least seven days before producing it, has given notice of his intention to produce it to each other party and has, within five days after receiving a notice for inspection given by any of those parties, produced it for inspection by the party who gave the notice.

Notice and production in civil proceeding

(2) In a civil proceeding, the provisions of subsection (1) apply only to a business record within the meaning of section 152 or a record to which section 79, 147, 149, 150 or 151 applies.

Authentication

Authentication

140. The proponent of a record has the burden of establishing its authenticity and that burden is discharged by evidence capable of supporting a finding that the record is what its proponent claims it to be.

Self-authentication

141. There is a presumption of authenticity in respect of the following:

(a) a record bearing a signature purporting to be an attestation or execution and bearing a seal purporting to be a seal mentioned in the *Seals Act* or a seal of province or political subdivision, department, ministry, officer or agency of Canada or a province;

(b) a record purporting to bear the signature in his official capacity of a person who is an officer or employee of any entity described in paragraph (a) that has no seal, if a public officer having a seal and official duties in the same political subdivision certifies under seal that the person has the official capacity claimed and that the signature is genuine;

(c) a copy of an official record or report or entry in it, or of a record authorized by law to be recorded or filed in a public office, including a compilation of data, purporting to be certified as correct by the custodian or other person authorized to make a certification;

(d) a publication purporting to be issued by any person, body or authority empowered to issue the publication by or pursuant to an enactment;

(e) a formally executed document purporting to be produced from proper custody and executed twenty years or more before the time it is tendered in evidence;

(f) any printed material purporting to be a newspaper or periodical;

(g) any inscription, sign, tag, label or other index of origin, ownership or control purporting to have been affixed in the course of business;

(h) a document purporting to be attested or certified under oath, solemn affirmation, affidavit or statutory declaration administered, taken or received in Canada by a person authorized to do so;

(i) a document purporting to be executed in a state other than Canada by a person authorized to do so and purporting to bear the seal of the appropriate minister of that state or his lawful deputy or agent;

(j) a document purporting to be executed or attested in his official capacity by a person authorized to do so by the laws of a state other than Canada, accompanied by a certification under section 143.

DENMARK

(A) Computer-related Economic Crimes

PROVISIONS OF THE PENAL CODE AS AMENDED BY THE PENAL CODE AMENDMENT ACT OF 6 JUNE 1985*

Section 193.

(1) Any person who, in an unlawful manner, causes major disturbances in the operation of public means of communication, of the public mail service, of *telegraph- or telephone systems, radio- or television systems, data processing systems,* or of installations for the public supply of water, gas, electricity or heating, shall be liable to simple detention or to imprisonment for a term not exceeding *4* years or, in mitigating circumstances, to a fine.

(2) If such an act has been committed through negligence, the punishment shall be a fine or simple detention.

Section 263.

(1) Any person who, in an unlawful manner,

1. deprives someone of or opens someone's letter, telegram or other sealed communication or note, or acquaints himself with its content,
2. obtains access to the places where another person keeps his personal things,
3. with the help of equipment, secretly listens to or records statements made in private, telephone conversations or other conversations between others or dealings in a closed meeting in which he himself is not taking part or to which he has obtained unauthorized access, shall be liable to a fine, to simple detention or to imprisonment for a term not exceeding 6 months.

(2) *Any person who, in an unlawful manner, obtains access to another person's information or programs which are meant to be used in a data processing system, shall be liable to a fine, to simple detention or to imprisonment for a term not exceeding 6 months.*

(3) *If an act of the kind described in subsection 1 or 2 is committed with the intent to procure or make oneself acquainted with information concerning trade secrets of a company or under other extraordinary aggravating circumstances, the punishment shall be increased to imprisonment for a term not exceeding 2 years.*

Section 264.

(1) Any person who, in an unlawful manner,

1. obtains access to another person's house or any other place not freely accessible,
2. fails to leave another person's land, having been requested to do so,

shall be liable to a fine, to simple detention or to imprisonment for a term not exceeding 6 months.

(2) *If an act of the kind described in subsection 1 no.1 is committed with the intent to procure or make oneself acquainted with information concerning trade secrets of a company or under other extraordinary aggravating circumstances, the punishment shall be increased to imprisonment for a term not exceeding 2 years.*

Section 279a.

Any person who, with the intention of procuring an unlawful gain for himself or for a third party, in an unlawful manner alters, adds or erases data processing programs or by other unlawful means tries to influence the result of such data processing, shall be liable for computer fraud.

Section 280.
Any person who, with the intention of procuring an unlawful gain for himself or for a third party, causes prejudice to the property of another person,
1. by abusing an authority conferred on him to act with power of attorney on behalf of the latter,
2. by acting against the interests of the person concerned in respect of property held in trust by him on behalf of that person,
shall, provided the act is not covered by sections *276–279a* of this act, be liable for breach of trust.

Section 284.
Any person who accepts or obtains for himself or for others a share in profits acquired by theft, unlawful detention of objects found, embezzlement, fraud, *computer fraud*, breach of trust, extortion, misappropriation of funds or robbery, and any person who, by hiding the articles thus acquired, by assisting in selling them or in any other similar manner helps to ensure for the benefit of another person the profits of these offences, shall be liable for receiving.

Section 285.
(1) The offences referred to in section 276, 278–281 and 283 of this Act as well as receiving in connection with such offences or with robbery shall be punished with imprisonment for a term not exceeding 1 year and 6 months.
. . .

Section 286.
(1) . . .
(2) The punishment for embezzlement, fraud, *computer fraud*, breach of trust, or misappropriation of funds may, in the event the offence is not of an especially aggravated nature or where a large number of such offences has been committed, be increased to imprisonment for a term not exceeding 8 years.
(3) . . .

(B) Infringements of Privacy

PENAL PROVISIONS OF THE PRIVATE REGISTERS ETC.
ACT NO. 293 OF 8 JUNE 1978

Section 27
(1) Unless another enactment prescribes more severe punishment, any person who commits an offence as stated in the list set out below shall be liable on conviction to a fine or to lenient imprisonment:—
1. infringement of section 3(2) and (3); section 4(1) and (2); section 5(2) clause 2; section 6; sections 8 and 9; section 10(1); section 11(1), (2) and (4); sections 12–14; section 15(1), (2) clause 2, and (3); sections 16–20; and section 21(1) and (2),
2. failure to comply with a decision made by the DSA pursuant to section 5(1) or section 15(2) clause 1,
3. failure to meet demands made by the DSA pursuant to section 22(2),
4. disregard of a stipulation or of terms and conditions subject to which a licence is given pursuant to the provisions of this Act or to any rule laid down by virtue of this Act, or
5. failure to comply with a mandatory or prohibitory order given pursuant to the provisions of this Act or to any rule laid down by virtue of this Act.
(2) Any directive laid down by virtue of this Act may provide that contravention of any provision of such directive shall be punishable either by a fine or by a fine and a lenient imprisonment.
(3) When an above-mentioned offence is committed by a limited liability company, a co-operative society or the like, the fine may be imposed on the company etc. as such.

Section 28.

Any person who carries on or is employed by an enterprise as referred to in subsection (3) of section 3, in sections 8 and 20 of this Act, may, when convicted of an offence, be deprived of the right to carry on or be employed by such enterprise, provided that the offence committed gives reasonable grounds to fear that it will lead to abuse. Otherwise, subsection (1) clause 3, and subsections (2) and (3) of section 79 of the Danish Penal Code shall apply.

PENAL PROVISIONS OF THE PUBLIC AUTHORITIES' REGISTERS ACT NO. 294 OF 8 JUNE 1978

Section 29.

(1) Unless another enactment prescribes more severe punishment, any person who commits an offence as stated in the list set out below shall be liable on conviction to a fine or to lenient imprisonment:—

1. disregard of terms and conditions stipulated in any consent given pursuant to section 16(2),
2. infringement of section 17 clause 2 or section 18(2) clause 2,
3. disregard of conditions stipulated by virtue of section 18 (3) or section 19.

(2) Any directive laid down by virtue of Part 2 of this Act may provide that infringement of any provision of such directive shall be punishable by a fine.

(3) When an above-mentioned offence is committed by a limited liability company, a co-operative society or the like, the fine may be imposed on the company, etc. as such.

FEDERAL REPUBLIC OF GERMANY

(A) Computer-Related Economic Crimes

PROVISIONS OF THE PENAL CODE AS AMENDED BY THE 'SECOND LAW FOR THE PREVENTION OF ECONOMIC CRIMES' OF 1986

Section 202a. Data Espionage
(1) Any person who obtains without authorization, for himself or for another, data which are not meant for him and which are specially protected against unauthorized access, shall be liable to imprisonment for a term not exceeding three years or to a fine.
(2) Data within the meaning of subsection 1 are only such as are stored or transmitted eletronically or magnetically or in any other form not directly visible.

Section 263a. Computer Fraud
(1) Any person who, with the intention of procuring an unlawful gain for himself or for a third party, causes loss to another by influencing the result of data processing by improper programming, by the use of incorrect or incomplete data, by the unauthorized use of data, or by otherwise interfering without authorization with the processing, shall be liable to imprisonment for a term not exceeding five years or to a fine.
(2) Subsections (2) to (5) of section 263 shall apply *mutatis mutandis*.

Section 269. Falsification of Data of Evidentiary Significance
(1) Any person who, for purposes of deception in a legal transaction, stores or alters data of evidentiary significance such that, when preceived, they would yield an ungenuine or falsified document, or who uses data thus stored or altered, shall be liable to imprisonment for a term not exceeding five years or to a fine.
(2) The attempt shall be punishable.
(3) Subsection 3 of section 267 shall be applicable.

Section 270. Deception in Legal Transactions Involving Data Processing
Wrongfully interfering with data processing in legal transactions shall constitute deception in legal transactions.

Section 271. Constructive False Certification
(1) Any person who wilfully causes declarations, negotiations or matters of fact, which are material to rights or legal relationships, to be recorded *or stored* in public documents, books, *data files* or registers as having been made or as having happened, although they have either not at all been made or happened or else in another manner or by a person in a non-entitled capacity or by some different person, shall be liable to imprisonment for a term not exceeding one year or to a fine.
(2) The attempt shall be punishable.

Section 273. Making Use of False Certifications
Any person who, for the purpose of deception, makes use of a false certification or stored false data of the kind specified in *section 271*, shall be liable to punishment in accordance with the provisions of that section and, if the intent was directed to procuring material gain for himself or another, in accordance with the provisions of section 272.

Section 274. Suppression of a Document; Altering Boundary Indicators
(1) Any person who, with intent to cause prejudice to another,
1. destroys, damages or suppresses a document or technical drawing which either does not belong to him at all or does not belong to him exclusively,
2. *deletes or conceals stored data within the meaning of section 269, which are not or are not exclusively at his disposal, or*

3. removes, destroys, renders unrecognizable, displaces or falsely sets up a boundary stone or any other mark intended to indicate a boundary or waterline
shall be liable to imprisonment for a term not exceeding five years or to a fine.
   (2) The attempt shall be punishable.

Section 303a. Alteration of Data
   (1) Any person who unlawfully erases, suppresses, renders useless, or alters data (section 202a (2)) shall be liable to imprisonment for a term not exceeding two years or to a fine.
   (2) The attempt shall be punishable.

Section 303b. Computer Sabotage
   (1) Imprisonment not exceeding five years or a fine shall be imposed on any person who interferes with data processing which is of essential importance to anothers business, anothers enterprise or an administrative authority by
   1. committing an offence under section 300a (1) or
   2. destroying, damaging, rendering useless, removing, or altering a computer system or a data carrier.
   (2) The attempt shall be punishable.

Section 303c. Prosecution upon Request
The offences of sections 303 to 303b shall be prosecuted only upon request. This shall not apply in the cases where the prosecuting authority deems an intervention of its own motion necessary in view of the special public interest in prosecution.

Section 348. Falsification of Public Documents by an Official
   (1) An official who, being authorized to draw up public records, within his competence certifies falsely or falsely enters in *or feeds* into public registers, books *or data files* any legally significant matter, shall be liable to imprisonment for a term not exceeding five years or to a fine.
   (2) The attempt shall be punishable.

THE PROVISIONS OF THE UNFAIR COMPETITION ACT AS AMENDED BY THE 'SECOND LAW FOR THE PREVENTION OF ECONOMIC CRIME' OF 1986

Section 17. Disclosure of Trade or Industrial Secrets
   (1) A punishment of imprisonment not exceeding three years or a fine shall be imposed upon any employee, workman, or apprentice of a business enterprise, who during the term of his employment relationship, without authorization, communicates to another a trade or industrial secret that has been confided to him or made available to him by virtue of his employment relationship, if he does so for purposes of competition or for personal gain *or for the benefit of a third party* or with the intention of damaging the proprietor of the business
   (2) *The same punishment shall be imposed upon anyone who for purposes of competition or for personal gain or for the benefit of a third party or with the intention of damaging the proprietor of the business*
   1. *obtains or secures without authorization a trade or industrial secret by*
      a) *the application of technical means,*
      b) *the creation of a corporeal reproduction of the secret or*
      c) *the removal of an object in which the secret is incorporated,*
         or
   2. *makes unauthorized use of or communicates to another a trade or industrial secret that he has acquired or otherwise obtained or secured without authorization through a communication of the kind described in subsection 1 or through an act as set out in number 1 of the present subsection done by himself or a third party.*
   (3) *The attempt shall be punishable.*
   (4) *In particularly serious cases the punishment shall be imprisonment not exceeding five years. A case shall, as a rule, be particularly serious if the offender knows at the*

time of the communication that use is to be made of the secret abroad or if he himself makes use of it abroad.

Section 20. Inducement and Offer to Disclose
(1) Anyone who for purposes of competition or for personal gain attempts to induce another to violate sections 17 or 18, or accepts the offer of another to commit such a violation, shall be liable to imprisonment for a term not exceeding two years or to a fine.
(2) The same punishment shall be imposed on anyone who for purposes of competition or for personal gain offers to commit an act in violation of section 17 or 18, or at the suggestion of another declares himself willing to commit such an act.
(3) *Sectiom 31 of the Criminal Code shall apply mutatis mutandis.*

Section 22. Requirements for Prosecution
(1) With the exception of the cases arising under section 4 *and 6c*, criminal prosecution shall be instituted only upon request. *This shall not apply to the cases arising under sections 17, 18 and 20 where the prosecuting authority deems an intervention of its own motion necessary in view of the special public interest in prosecution . . .*

(B) Infringements of Copyright

PENAL PROVISION OF THE TRADITIONAL COPYRIGHT ACT

Section 106. Forbidden Use of Works Protected by Copyright
Any person who, without the consent of the authorized person, reproduces, distributes or publicly communicates a work or an adaption or a transformation of a work, in situations other than those permitted by law, will be liable to imprisonment for a term not exceeding one year or to a fine.

PENAL PROVISIONS OF THE COPYRIGHT AMENDMENT ACT 1985

Section 108a. Forbidden Use for Material Gain
(1) If, in cases of reproduction or distribution pursuant to sections 106 or 108, the offender acts with the intent of procuring a material gain, he will be liable to imprisonment for a term not exceeding five years or to a fine.
(2) The attempt shall be punishable.

Section 109. Prosecution Upon Request
The offences in sections 106 to 108 shall only be prosecuted upon request unless, due to the special public interest in the prosecution the prosecuting authority deems it appropriate to take action of its own motion.

(C) Infringement of Semiconductor Chip Products

PENAL PROVISION OF THE MINISTRY OF JUSTICE'S UNOFFICIAL PRE-DRAFT OF PROVISIONS FOR THE PROTECTION OF THE TOPOGRAPHIES OF SEMICONDUCTOR CHIP PRODUCTS OF 1985

Section 14
Any person who, without the required consent of the bearer of the protective right, in situations other than those permitted by law, reproduces a protected topography

or offers or brings into circulation semiconductor chip products or means of production which contain an unlawful reproduction, will be liable to imprisonment for a term not exceeding . . . years or to a fine. The importation (section 4 subsection 1) of semiconductor chip products or means of production for these purposes is also punishable.

(D) Infringements of Privacy

PENAL PROVISIONS OF THE FEDERAL DATA PROTECTION ACT OF 27 JANUARY 1977

Section 41. Criminal Offences
  (1) Any person who, without authorization
  1. transmits or alters or
  2. retrieves or procures for himself, from information storage systems locked in depositories, personal data protected by this Act, which are not publicly known,
shall be liable to a term of imprisonment not exceeding one year, or to a fine.
  (2) *If* the offender commits the offence in exchange for payment or with the intention of enriching himself or another person or of harming another person, he shall be liable to a term of imprisonment not exceeding two years, or to a fine.
  (3) The offence shall only be prosecuted upon application.

Section 42. Ordnungswidrigkeiten
  (1) Any person who, whether intentionally or negligently
  1. contrary to section 26 (1), section 34 (1), fails to notify the person concerned;
  2. contrary to section 28 (1), section 38 in conjunction with section 28 (1), fails to appoint a controller of data protection or fails to do so within the prescribed time-limit;
  3. contrary to section 32 (2), clause 2, fails to record the grounds or means referred to in that section:
  4. contrary to section 39 (1) or (3), fails to notify the competent supervisory authority or fails to do so within the prescribed time-limit or, contrary to section 39 (2) or (3) fails, when registering, to provide the required particulars, or provides incorrect or incomplete particulars;
  5. contrary to section 30 (2), clause 1, section 40 (2) in conjunction with section 30 (2), clause 1, provides incorrect or incomplete information or fails to provide such information, or fails to do so within the prescribed time-limit or, contrary to section 30 (3), clause 2, and section 40 (2) in conjunction with section 30 (3), clause 2, refuses to grant access to property or premises or refuses to permit checks or inspections or the inspection of documents
commits an 'Ordnungswidrigkeit'.
  (2) The 'Ordnungswidrigkeit' shall be punished with a fine not exceeding DM 50,000.

FINLAND

(A) Computer-Related Economic Crime and Infringements of Privacy

AMENDMENTS TO THE PENAL CODE AS PROPOSED BY THE DRAFT OF A 1986 GOVERNMENT BILL

Chapter 30: Trade and Business Offences

Section 3. Trade Espionage
(1) Anyone who, without authorization, gains access to a trade secret which belongs to another party and concerns methods of production, research and development, economic planning or economic commitment, by means of
   1. unauthorized entry into a depository closed for outsiders, or a data processing system or a data transmission network, which is protected against outsiders;
   2. making a copy of a document or through any method comparable to it; or
   3. spying with the help of a technical device,
with the intent to unlawfully disclose or utilize such a secret, shall be guilty of trade espionage, and upon conviction, shall, insofar as the act is not elsewhere subject to a more severe penalty, be sentenced to a fine or to imprisonment for a term not exceeding two years.
(2) The attempt is punishable.

Section 4. Breach of Trade Secret
(1) Anyone who discloses or utilizes a trade secret, as mentioned under section 3, without authorization and with the intent to either obtain unlawful economic gain for himself or another party or to inflict harm upon another party, provided that the trade secret was
   1. entrusted to him in his capacity as another's employee;
   2. assigned to him for the purpose of performing a task on behalf of another; or
   3. made available to him in his capacity as a member of the board of directors or the supervisory board of a corporation or a foundation, or as the managing director, auditor or receiver of the same, or in any function comparable to these,
shall be guilty of breach of trade secret, and upon conviction, shall, insofar as the act is not elsewhere subject to a more severe penalty, be sentenced to a fine or to imprisonment for a term not exceeding two years.
(2) This provision does not apply to such acts committed by persons mentioned under subsection 1 after the expiration of the period of service.

Section 5. Misappropriation of Trade Secret
Anyone who, without authorization,
   1. in the course of his business, makes use of a trade secret, such as mentioned under section 3, provided it had been obtained through an offence punishable under the Penal Code, or
   2. discloses such a secret, with the intent to obtain economic gain for himself or another party
shall be guilty of misappropriation of trade secret, and upon conviction, shall be sentenced to a fine or to imprisonment for a term not exceeding two years.

Chapter 33: Forgery

Section 1. Forgery
(1) Anyone who makes a false document or other device or falsifies such items with the intent to either put such misleading evidence to the disposal of other parties

or to personally use such false or falsified items as misleading evidence, shall be guilty of forgery, and upon conviction, shall be sentenced to a fine or to imprisonment for a term not exceeding two years.

(2) For the purpose of this provision, 'device' applies to a writing or its fascimile, stamp, token, license plate, sound or video recording, any recording produced by a plotter, a calculator or other similar device, or any magnetic or other data carrier used in automatic data processing, provided that it is admissible as legally relevant evidence of rights, obligations or factual circumstances.

(3) A device is considered to be 'false', if, when used as evidence, it is liable to bring about a misleading impression concerning its origin or the identity of its author.

(4) A device is considered to be 'falsified', if its contents, insofar as any information relevant for proof is concerned, have been altered without authorization.

Section 2. Aggravated Forgery

If

1. the device subject to forgery is kept by an authority for purposes of public records or register and is of importance from a public point of view, or if the proof value of the device otherwise makes it especially weighty, or
2. the perpetrator employed a printing or copying device, a computer or other similar instruments, provided that the acquisition of such instruments was for the purpose of committing forgeries, or if the course of action was otherwise especially deliberate,

and the offence of forgery, as it is manifested in the instances mentioned above, appears as gross when judged in its entirety, the perpetrator shall be guilty of aggravated forgery, and upon conviction, shall be sentenced to imprisonment for at least four months and at most four years.

[There are special provisions for petty cases of forgery and for unauthorized possession of forged documents and on tools suspected to be used for the purpose of committing forgeries.]

Chapter 35: *Inflicition of Damage*

Section 1. Inflicition of Damage

(1) Anyone who, without authorization, destroys or damages property belonging to another party, shall be guilty of inflicition of damage, and upon conviction, shall be sentenced to a fine or to imprisonment for a term not exceeding one year.

(2) The same shall apply to anyone who, without authorization and with the intent to inflict harm upon another party, destroys, spoils, supresses or conceals a writing or other devices, belonging either entirely or in part to another party, or data stored on such devices.

[There are special provisions for petty and aggravated inflicition of damage.]

Chapter 36: *Fraud and Other Dishonesty*

Section 1. Fraud

(1) Anyone who, with the intent to obtain unlawful economic gain for himself or another party or with the intent to inflict harm upon another party by misleading this party or by exploiting errors, causing the party to act or fail to act in a certain way, thus bringing about economic loss to the party deceived or to another party whose interests were to be represented by the party deceived, shall be guilty of fraud, and upon conviction, shall be sentenced to a fine or to imprisonment for a term not exceeding two years.

(2) The same applies to anyone who with the intent mentioned above and without authorization, distorts the final results of data processing by feeding false data into a data processor or otherwise by interfering with data processing, thereby bringing about economic loss to another party.

(3) The attempt is punishable.

[There are special provisions for petty and aggravated fraud.]

Chapter 37: Offences Against Instruments of Payment

Section 8. Fraud Involving Instrument of Payment
(1) Anyone who, with the intent to obtain unlawful economic gain for himself or another,
1. uses a bank card, credit card, payment card, check, or any other instrument of payment comparable to these, without being authorized thereto by the legal holder of the said instrument or in excess of his authority, or otherwise without a legal right, or
2. conveys the instrument of payment or a form for such an instrument to another, with the intent of getting it to be used without a legal right, shall be guilty of fraud involving instrument of payment, and upon conviction, shall be sentenced to a fine or to imprisonment for a term not exceeding two years.
(2) The same applies to anyone who misuses an instrument of payment by overdrawing the cover or the agreed credit limit of his account, thus bringing about economic loss to another party. This, however, is not applicable, should the accused party have had at the moment of using the instrument of payment the intention of reimbursing the loss without delay.

AMENDMENTS TO THE IMPROPER BUSINESS PRACTICES ACT, AS PROPOSED BY THE DRAFT OF A GOVERNMENT BILL OF 1986
Misappropriation of Technical Prototype or Instruction

Prohibition: (1) No one, who has been entrusted with a technical prototype or technical instructions for the purpose of performing a certain labour or a task, or other commercial activities, is allowed to disclose or utilize it without authorization.
(2) No one, who has been informed by another party about a technical prototype or technical instructions, and who is aware of the fact that the party providing the information had obtained or disclosed it without authorization, is allowed to disclose or utilize it without authorization.
Penal sanction: Anyone who, in violation of the prohibitions mentioned above, knowingly utilizes or discloses a technical prototype or technical instructions, shall be guilty of misappropriation of a technical prototype or technical instructions, and upon conviction, shall, insofar as the act is not elsewhere subject to a more severe penalty, be sentenced to a fine.

(B) Infringements of Copyright

PENAL PROVISIONS OF THE ACT RELATING TO COPYRIGHT IN LITERARY AND ARTISTIC WORKS (AS AMENDED BY THE AMENDMENT ACT 1984)

Section 56
Anyone who, for gain, wilfully
1. produces a copy of a work or makes a work available to the public in violation of the present Act; or
2. imports into the country a copy of a work for distribution to the public, which copy has been produced outside the country under such circumstances that such production in Finland would have been punishable under the present Act,
shall, if the act shall be regarded as being gross due to the large number of copies of the work, the extent of the activity, or other comparable reason, be sentenced for a *copyright crime* to a fine or to an imprisonment of a maximum of two years.

Section 56a

Anyone who

1. wilfully or out of gross negligence violates a provision issued for the protection of copyright in the present Act or acts in violation of an instruction issued under section 41, second paragraph, of a provision of sections 51 or 52, or of a prohibition referred to in section 53, first paragraph; or

2. imports into the country a copy of a work for distribution to the public, which he knows or has well-founded reason to suspect to have been produced outside the country under such circumstances that such production in Finland would have been punishable under the present Act,

shall, unless the act is punishable under section 56, be sentenced for a *copyright offense* to a fine or to an imprisonment of a maximum of six months.

Section 56b

Anyone who wilfully violates the provision of section 26d, third paragraph, shall be sentenced for *breach of confidentiality under the Copyright Act* to a fine or to an imprisonment of a maximum of six months, unless a more severe punishment has been provided for the act elsewhere in law.

Section 62

A copyright crime and a violation of any provision of section 51 or 52 shall be subject to public prosecution. In other cases a criminal action for a crime referred to in the present Act shall not be prosecuted by a public prosecutor, unless the injured party has reported it for the purpose of prosecution.

FRANCE

(A) Computer-Related Economic Crime

PROVISIONS OF THE CRIMINAL CODE AS PROPOSED BY THE FRENCH MINISTRY OF JUSTICE IN 1986

Section 307–1
The fraudulent and surreptitious obtainment of a program, of data or of any other element of an automatic information processing system is punishable by imprisonment for a term not exceeding three years and a fine of up to 1 million francs.

Section 307–2
The use, communication or reproduction of a program, of data or of any other element of an automatic information processing system, which infringes upon the right of another, is punishable by imprisonment for a term not exceeding three years and a fine of up to 1 million francs.

Section 307–3
The destruction or alteration of an automatic information processing system or a part of it, or any hindering or falsification of its functioning, is, if the act is committed knowingly and infringes upon the right of another person, punishable by imprisonment for a term not exceeding five years and a fine of up to 2.5 million francs.

Section 307–4
The obtainment or the incitement to obtainment of an illegal gain committed by the fraudulent use of an automatic information processing system is punishable by imprisonment for a term not exceeding five years and a fine of up to 2.5 million francs.
[The following sections 307–5 to 307–8 concern special sanctions for infractions against the above provisions.]

(B) Infringements of Copyright

PENAL PROVISIONS OF THE LAW ON AUTHORS' RIGHTS AND ON THE RIGHTS OF PERFORMERS, PRODUCERS OF PHONOGRAMS AND VIDEOGRAMS AND AUDIOVISUAL COMMUNICATION ENTERPRISES NO. 85–660 OF 3 JULY 1985

Section 52
Publishing, reproduction, distribution, sale, rental or exchange activities in respect of videograms intended for the private use of the general public shall be subject to supervision by the National Cinematographic Center.

Those persons whose activity it is to publish, reproduce, distribute, sell, rent or exchange videograms intended for the private use of the general public shall be required to keep up-to-date documents enabling the origin and destination of videograms to be established as well as the exploitation revenue from such videograms. The sworn agents of the National Cinematographic Center shall be entitled to demand such documents of an accounting or other than accounting nature.

The lack of such documents, the refusal to supply information, the supply of false information and acts for the purpose of dissimulating the origin or the destination of videograms or of revenue from the exploitation of videograms shall be liable to the penalties laid down by section 18 of the Cinematographic Industry Code, subject to the conditions laid down therein.

Section 53
In addition to the reports of police officers or agents, proof of the existence of any infringement of this law may be provided by the statements of sworn agents designated by the National Cinematographic Center and by the societies referred to in Title IV. Such agents.shall be approved by the Minister responsible for culture.

Section 54
Publication of the acts and agreements entered into for the production, distribution performance or exploitation of audiovisual works in France, shall be given by entering them in the register referred to in Title III of the Cinematographic Industry Code.

However, the filing of a title under section 32 of the above-mentioned Code shall be provisional for audiovisual works other than cinematographic works.

Section 55
Indirect communication to the public in the form of videograms of an audiovisual work shall require the formality of statutory deposit of a videogram as stipulated by Law No. 43–341 of 21 June, 1943, amending the statutory deposit arrangements.

Section 56
There shall be inserted after section 426 of the Penal Code a section 426–1 worded as follows:

'*Section 426–1.* Any fixation, reproduction, communication or making available to the public, on payment or free of charge, or any television broadcasting of a performance, a phonogram, a videogram or a program made without authorization, where such is required, of the performer, the producer of phonograms or videograms and the audiovisual communication enterprise shall be punishable by imprisonment of between three months and two years and a fine of between 6,000 francs and 120,000 francs or one of the two penalties.

Any importation or exploitation of phonograms or videograms made without the authorization of the producer or the performer, where such is required, shall be subject to the same penalties.

Failure to pay the remuneration due to the author, the performer or the producer of phonograms or videograms with respect to private copying or public communication or of the television broadcasting of phonograms shall be subject to the fine laid down in the first paragraph.'

Section 57.
Once the offenses under section 426–1 of the Penal Code have been established, the competent police officers may effect seizure of the unlawfully reproduced phonograms and videograms, of the copies and articles manufactured or imported unlawfully and of the equipment specially installed for the purpose of such acts.

Section 58.
The second to last paragraph of section 425 of the Penal Code shall be worded as follows:

'Infringement in France of works published in France or abroad shall be punishable by imprisonment of between three months and two years and a fine of between 6,000 francs and 120,000 francs or by one of these penalties.'

Section 59.
The first two paragraphs of section 427 of the Penal Code shall be worded as follows:

'In the event of repetition of the infringements specified in the three preceding sections, the penalties involved shall be doubled.

In addition, the court may order, either definitively or temporarily, for a period not exceeding five years, the closure of the establishment operated by the convicted person.'

Section 60
Section 428 of the Penal Code shall be worded as follows:
    '*Section 428.* In the cases referred to in the four preceding sections, the court may order confiscation of all or part of the revenue obtained through the infringement and confiscation of all phonograms, videograms, articles or copies that are infringing or have been unlawfully reproduced and of the equipment specifically installed for the purpose of committing the offense.
    It may also order, at the cost of the convicted person, posting of the judgment in compliance with the conditions and subject to the penalties laid down by section 51, and its publication in full or in extract in such newspapers as it may designate, without however the costs of such publication exceeding the maximum amount of the fine incurred.'

Section 61
1. The beginning of section 429 of the Penal Code shall read as follows:
    'In those cases set out in the five preceding sections, the equipment, the infringing articles and the revenues that have been confiscated shall be remitted to the victim or his successors in title to compensate the prejudice they have suffered; the surplus . . . '
    2. Consequently, at the end of this section, the word 'infringed' shall be replaced by the word 'infringing.'

Section 62
There shall be inserted after the fourth paragraph (3) of section 97 of the above-mentioned Law No. 82–652 of 29 July, 1982, two additional paragraphs worded as follows:
    '4. Any infringement of the provisions on time limits for disseminating cinematographic works contained in the authorizations, assignment contracts, work specifications and decrees mentioned in sections 32, 78, 79, the third paragraph of section 83 and section 89.
    Once an infringement of section 89 has been established, the police officers may proceed with the seizure of the mediums unlawfully made available to the public.'

(C) Infringements of Privacy

PENAL PROVISIONS OF ACT NO. 78–17 OF 6 JANUARY 1978 ON DATA PROCESSING, DATA FILES, AND INDIVIDUAL LIBERTIES

Section 41
Any person who engages in the automatic processing of personal data, or holds such data so processed without publication of the official decisions provided for in section 15 or without filing the declaration as provided in section 16, shall be imprisoned for a term of six months to three years, or fined 2,000 to 200,000 francs, or both.
    Moreover, the court may order publication of the judgement in full or in part in one or more newspapers, and public posting thereof at the expense of the convicted party.

Section 42
Any person who records or causes to be recorded, stores or causes to be stored personal data contrary to section 25, 26 and 28–31 shall be imprisoned for a term of one to five years, or fined 20,000 to 2,000,000 francs, or both.
    Moreover the court may order publication of the judgement in full or in part in one or more newspapers and public posting thereof at the expense of the convicted party.

Section 43
Any person who, in connection with recording, filing, transmitting or any other form of processing, has obtained personal data, disclosure of which would prejudice the

reputation or esteem of a person or invade his privacy, and who knowingly and without the authorization of the person concerned discloses such data to any party not authorized to receive them under this or any other Act, shall be imprisoned for a term of two to six months, or fined 2,000 to 20,000 francs, or both.

Section 44
Any person who, holding personal data in connection with recording, filing, transmitting or other processing, uses the same for a purpose other than that specified in the regulation as provided under section 15, or in the declarations made pursuant to sections 16 and 17, or in a statutory provision, shall be imprisoned for a term of one to five years, and fined 20,000 to 2,000,000 francs.

ITALY

(A) Infringements of Intellectual Property Rights

PENAL PROVISIONS OF THE LAW NO. 406 OF 29 JUNE 1981 ON URGENT MEASURES AGAINST THE ABUSIVE AND ILLEGAL DUPLICATION, REPRODUCTION, IMPORT, DISTRIBUTION, AND SELLING OF PHONOGRAPHIC PRODUCTS

Section 1.
Any person who for material gain, copies or, without being responsible for the reproduction, brings into circulation, offers to sell or imports for material gain into state territory, records, tapes or similar devices, will be liable to imprisonment for a term from 3 months to 3 years and to a fine from 500 000 to 6 million Lire. In serious cases the penalty shall be at least 6 months imprisonment and a fine of at least 1 million Lire.

Section 2
A conviction for the offence in section 1 shall be published in at least one daily newspaper and in a technical journal.

(B) Infringements of Privacy

LAW NO. 121 OF 1 APRIL 1981 ON THE REGULATION OF THE STATE POLICE ADMINISTRATION

Section 12
A state officer who, contrary to the provisions and purposes of this Act, discloses or uses data or information, shall be punished by imprisonment of 1 to 3 years, if the act is not punished more severely by another law.
   If the act is committed negligently, the punishment is imprisonment for a term not exceeding six months.

PENAL PROVISIONS OF THE MINISTRY OF JUSTICE'S DRAFT OF A PRIVACY ACT OF 1984

Section 22. Administrative and Jurisdictional Protection
In case of inobservance of the obligations provided for by this Act, the interested party may lodge a petition with the Office pursuant to section 6.
   Independently from the proposition and results of the petition lodged with the Control Office, the interested party may ask the regular judicial authority for the sentencing of persons and bodies, referred to in section 1, to order the performance of the operations due and to award damages. The interested party may also request the provisional remedies provided by laws of procedure.
   Jurisdiction for these requests belongs to the tribunal in the court of appeal district of the judge who would be competent pursuant to ordinary norms.
   The record-office gives notice of the decisions and provisions to the Control Office.
   The control office is also appointed to assume the functions of the Public

Administration under the terms and for the purposes of section 612 (2) Code of Civil Procedure.

Section 23. Omitted or Defective Notification

Any person who forms or holds a computerised bank of personal data, or manages data contained in such banks without providing for notifications prescribed in sections 1 and 20 of this Act, is punishable with imprisonment for a term of between six months and three years and with a fine from 200 000 to 2 million lire.

Anyone who omits to inform the competent office of any amendment of the aim or submits an untruthful notification, in violation of section 8 (3), is subject to the same penalties, unless the fact, in the latter case, constitutes a more serious crime.

The penalties set forth in the preceding subsections are increased if the perpetrator acts with the aim of obtaining an advantage for either himself or others or of causing others damage.

If the facts contemplated in the preceding subsection are committed through negligence, the penalties are reduced by up to half.

If the notification lacks one or more of the items of information set forth by numbers 6, 7 and 8 of section 4, the penalty is imprisonment for a term of between six months and one year.

Section 24. Non-observance of Provisions of the Control Office

Any person who fails to observe, though obliged thereto, one of the provisions lawfully issued by the Control Office pursuant to section 6, numbers 4 and 7, is punishable with either imprisonment for a term of between six months and one year or a fine from 1 to 5 million lire.

Section 25. Unlawful Collection

Any person who inserts data, collected in violation of sections 9, 10 and 11 of this Act, or has it inserted, in a computerised databank, is punishable with imprisonment for a term of between one and three years.

Section 26. Failure to Take Care of Data

Any person who, having inserted personal data in computerised databanks, does not take care to prevent such data from being used contrary to the aim of collection, or to prevent the loss or the alteration of such data in prejudice of the person to whom the data refers, is punishable with imprisonment for a term of between six months and two years.

The offence is punishable by action of the offended party.

Section 27. Unlawful Communication

Any person who, in the exercise of his or her duties or as a consequence thereof, has become acquainted with data contained in a computerised databank and communicates it to others in violation of sections 16, 17, 19, 20 (3), is punishable with imprisonment for a term of between six months and two years.

Section 28. Failure to Cancel or Correct

The person responsible who does not provide for the cancellation or correction of the data in accordance with section 14, numbers 3 and 4, is punishable with imprisonment for a term of between six months and one year.

The offence is punishable by action of the offended party.

Section 29. Violation of Official Secret

The disclosure of the secret set forth in the last paragraph of section 6 is punishable with imprisonment for a term of between one and three years provided the act does not constitute a more serious offence.

If the act is committed through negligence, the penalty is imprisonment for a term of up to six months.

Section 30. Accessory Penalties
Except as provided in the following section, the conviction for one of the offences referred to in sections 23, 25, 28 and 29 entails the exclusion from public offices for a term of between one and five years.

Section 31. Procedural Provisions
Jurisdiction for the offences referred to in the preceding sections belongs to the tribunal, which is to proceed summarily in all cases, notwithstanding sections 502–504 of the Code of Criminal Procedure.

In passing sentence, the judge orders, at the request of the injured party, the publication of the decision, entirely or in excerpts, in one or more daily newspapers and establishes other eventual forms of publicity.

A copy of the decision is transmitted to the Control Office under the responsibility of the record-office.

JAPAN

Infringements of Chip Protection Law

PENAL PROVISIONS OF THE ACT CONCERNING THE CIRCUIT LAYOUT OF A SEMICONDUCTOR INTEGRATED CIRCUIT OF 1985

Section 51
(1) Any person who infringes on a circuit layout right or a sole use right shall be punished with imprisonment and forced labour for a term not exceeding three years or a fine not exceeding 1 million Yen.
(2) The offence referred to in the preceding subsection shall be prosecuted only upon complaint.

Section 52
Any person who has obtained registration for establishment by fraud shall be punished for a term not exceeding one year or a fine not exceeding 300 000 Yen.

Section 53
Any person who violates the provision of section 38 (1) shall be punished for a term not exceeding one year or a fine not exceeding 300 000 Yen.

Section 54
In the case where an order of suspension of the registration procedure under the provisions of section 41 is violated, the officer or staff member of the designated registration organ who committed the act of violation shall be punished for a term not exceeding one year or a fine not exceeding 300 000 Yen.

Section 55
If any of the following events occurs, the officer or staff member of the designated registration organ who committed the violation shall be punished with a fine not exceeding 200 000 Yen:
  (1) if the whole registration procedure is abolished without obtaining the permission referred to in section 34,
  (2) if a report under the provisions of section 39 (1) is not filed or a false report is filed, or if the inspection under the provisions of the said subsection is refused, hindered or avoided, or if a statement answering the questions presented in accordance with the said subsection is not rendered or a false statement is rendered,
  (3) if books are not kept or entries are not made in the books, or false entries are made in the books, in violation of the provision of section 42 (1) or if the books are not maintained in violation of the provisions of subsection 2 of the said section.

Section 56
In the event that a representative of a legal person, an agent representing a legal person or an individual, or an employee or any other working staff member thereof commits an act referred to in section 51 (1), or section 52 in connection with the business of such legal person or individual, the legal person or the individual shall, in addition to the punishment of the violator, be subject to a fine as provided for in each corresponding provision.

LUXEMBOURG

Infringements of Privacy

PENAL PROVISIONS OF THE ACT OF 31 MARCH 1979 REGULATING THE USE OF NOMINAL DATA IN ELECTRONIC DATA PROCESSING

Section 32
Any person who establishes, operates or uses a data bank without holding a valid authorization pursuant to Part 2 of the present Act, or fails to comply with the terms of the Act, shall be punished by eight days to six months imprisonment and by a fine of Frs. 2 501 to Frs. 500 000 or by only one of these penalties.

The same penalties shall apply to anyone who operates or uses a data bank after the authorization referred to in the preceding section has been withdrawn.

The same penalties shall apply to the holder of nominal data who, in the course of storage, filing, transmission or other form of processing, has diverted the data from their purpose as defined in the authorization provided for in Part 2 of the present Act or in the statutory provisions under which the data bank operates, or if the holder of nominal data has, without authorization by the person concerned, knowingly transmitted such data or allowed them to be transmitted to third parties.

Section 33
Any person who collects, records or stores nominal data or arranges the collection, recording or storage of nominal data contrary to the provisions of section 14, 15, 16 and 17, shall be punished by one month to one year imprisonment and by a fine of Frs. 10 000 to Frs. 500 000 or by only one of these penalties.

Moreover, the court may order publication of the judgement in full or in part in one or more newspapers and public posting thereof in such manner as the court shall decide, at the expense of the convicted party.

Section 34
Any person who fails to supply the information requested by virtue of section 20 within the time limit prescribed by law, who knowingly provides inaccurate information or who fails to comply with the obligations set out in sections 22 and 23, shall be punished by eight days to one month imprisonment and by a fine of Frs. 2 501 to Frs. 100 000 or by only one of these penalties.

Section 35
Any person who uses an assumed name or a false title for the purpose of obtaining disclosure of nominal data pursuant to section 20, shall be punished by eight days to one year imprisonment and by a fine of Frs. 2 501 to Frs. 300 000, or by only one of these penalties.

Section 36
Any person who fails to comply with the provisions of sections 26 and 28 or Grand-Ducal Regulations issued under section 27, shall be punished by a fine of Frs. 2 501 to Frs. 100 000.

Section 37
Any person who deliberately prevents or hinders in any way whatsoever, the performance of the functions of the Minister responsible for the register of data banks or of the Advisory Board, shall be punished by eight days to six months imprisonment and by a fine of Frs. 2 501 to Frs. 500 000 or by only one of these penalties.

The refusal to allow bodies entrusted with an enquiry access to premises and documents or to supply the information requested, shall be deemed to constitute deliberate hindrance or prevention of the performance of the Minister's functions.

Section 38
The confiscation and destruction without compensation of all or part of the data bank in respect of which the offences provided for in sections 32 and 33 were committed shall in all cases be ordered in the event of conviction. They may also be ordered in respect of offences provided for in sections 34, 36 and 37.

Section 39
Book 1 of the Penal Code and the Act of 18 June 1979 enabling the courts to make allowances for extenuating circumstances, as amended by the Act of 16th May 1904, shall apply to offences provided for in the present Act.

NETHERLANDS

Infringements of Privacy

PENAL PROVISIONS OF THE DATA PROTECTION BILL NO. 19 095 OF 1985

Section 50

    (1) Any person who
    a) runs a personal register by infringing sections 19, 24, or 25; or
    b) is the owner of a personal register as described in subsection a); or
    c) infringes section 49 subsection 2
is liable to a fine of the second category. (5 000 gilders)

    (2) Any person who purposely commits an act as described in subsection 1 is liable to imprisonment for a term not exceeding 6 months or a fine of the third category. (10 000 gilders)

    (3) The acts punishable pursuant to subsection 1 are petty misdemeanors. The acts punishable pursuant to subsection 2 are felonies.

    (4) In addition to the agents competent under the Penal Code, the agents of the secretariat of the registration office nominated by our minister are also competent for the prosecution of the acts of this section.

NORWAY

(A) Computer-related Economic Crimes

PROVISIONS OF THE PENAL CODE AS AMENDED BY THE PROPOSALS OF THE NORWEGIAN STANDING COMMITTEE ON CRIMINAL LAW REFORM

Section 145

(1) Any person who, without authorization, opens a letter or other sealed writing *or in a similar manner acquaints himself with its content* or obtains access to another person's locked hiding places, shall be liable to a fine or to imprisonment for a term not exceeding 6 months.

(2) *The same punishment shall apply to any such person who, by breaking a protection, obtains unauthorized access to data stored or transmitted by electronical or other technical means.*

(3) If prejudice is caused through unauthorized knowledge acquired thereby, or if the act is committed with the intention to procure somebody an unlawful gain, the punishment may be increased to imprisonment for a term not exceeding 2 years.

(4) *Complicity and assistance shall be punished in the same way.*

(5) *Public prosecution shall only take place if required due to public interest in the prosecution.*

Section 151b

(1) Any person who, by destroying, damaging or putting out of operation data files or equipment for energy supply, broadcasting, telecommunication or communication, causes extensive interruption in public administration or to the society otherwise, shall be liable to imprisonment for a term not exceeding 10 years.

(2) Complicity and assistance shall be punished in the same way.

Section 261

(1) Any person who, by unlawful means, uses or disposes of property belonging to another person, thereby obtaining for himself or for a third party considerable gains or causes considerable prejudice to property of the victim, shall be guilty of theft and liable to imprisonment for a term not exceeding 3 years. Complicity and assistance shall be punished in the same way. By extraordinary extenuating circumstances a fine may be used.

(2) The offence shall be prosecuted only upon the victim's request unless public interest in the prosecution requires public prosecution.

Section 270

(1) Any person who, with the intention of procuring an unlawful gain for himself or for a third party,

1. by bringing about, confirming or exploiting an error in an unlawful manner, induces a person to an act which causes prejudice of property or the risk of prejudice of property to him or to the person he is acting for, or
2. *by using incorrect or incomplete information, by altering computer programs or by other means in an unlawful manner influences the result of data processing, and thereby causes prejudice of property or the risk of prejudice of property,*

is liable for fraud.

(2) Punishment for fraud shall be a fine or imprisonment for a term not exceeding 3 years or both. *Complicity or assistance shall be punished in the same way.*

Section 403

Any person who, without paying the fixed payment, attempts to obtain access to a performance, an exhibition or a meeting in a closed room, or to the transport by ship, by railway *or by other transport facilities, or to the use of a telephone, television, data processing system* or similar facilities, shall be liable to a fine or to imprisonment for a term not exceeding 3 months. Complicity or assistance shall be punished in the same way.

(B) Infringements of Privacy

PENAL PROVISIONS OF THE ACT NO. 48 OF 9 JUNE 1978 ON PERSONAL DATA REGISTER, ETC.

Section 38
Anyone who wilfully or negligently
1. fails to obtain permission pursuant to sections 9, 13 (3), 14, 22, 25, 31 or 36
2. violates the rules or terms and conditions laid down in pursuance of sections 11, 14, 22, 25, 31 or 36
3. utilizes information in violation of the rules in sections 16, 18, 23, 26, 27, 32, or 33
4. fails to comply with requirements from the Data Inspectorate in pursuance of section 5 or section 8
5. fails to comply with requests for information in accordance with section 7 or section 20 or requests for deletion in accordance with section 28
6. fails to provide notification in accordance with section 19 to the person to whom the information applies,
shall be punished by fines or by imprisonment for a term not exceeding one year or both.
Aiding and abetting therein shall be punished in a similar manner.
Regulations issued in pursuance of this Act, may provide that violations of such regulations shall be punished by fines or by imprisonment for a term not exceeding one year or both.

Section 39
If a violation, referred to in section 38, is committed by anyone acting on behalf of an enterprise, fines may be imposed on the enterprise itself, even though no one is punishable under the provisions of section 38.
When imposing a sentence in pursuance of this section, due weight shall be given to the question whether the violation has been committed to promote the interests of the enterprise and whether the enterprise has derived any benefit from the said violation.
Section 28 of the General Civil Penal Code shall not apply to fines imposed in pursuance of this section.

Section 40
If an enterprise, operating a service as referred to in section 13, has provided information in violation of the provisions prescribed in, or issued in pursuance of, this Act, or has provided information which proves to be erroneous or obviously misleading, the said enterprise shall compensate any losses incurred by the person to whom the information applies. This applies irrespective of whether anyone, acting on behalf of or in the service of the enterprise, has been guilty of negligence.

PORTUGAL

Infringements of Privacy and General Computer-Related Crimes

PENAL PROVISIONS OF THE DATA PROTECTION BILL OF 1984

Section 37
Anyone who, in violation of the present law, creates or maintains an automated file of personal data, shall be liable to a fine of up to 60 daily rates.

Section 38
    (1) Anyone who, without legal justification,
        a) violates professional secrecy without causing detriment to the State or to third parties;
        b) does not supply the information that may be required under the terms of the present law or violates the regulations of section 33 (1),
shall be liable to a fine of up to 60 daily rates.
    (2) Prosecution shall be instituted upon request only.

Section 39
    (1) Any state agent who, in violation of the provisions of this law, violates the professional secrecy with the intention of procuring an unlawful gain for himself or for a third party, or of causing damage to the public interest or to third parties, shall be liable to imprisonment for a term not exceeding 2 years or to a fine of 50 to 150 daily rates.
    (2) The attempt shall also be punishable.

Section 40
A punishment of imprisonment not exceeding one year and a fine of up to 120 daily rates shall be imposed upon anyone who
    a) violates professional secrecy to the detriment of the State or of third parties;
    b) gives false information in a request for the authorization to create or maintain an automated file of personal data, or makes alterations not permitted in the document or authorization;
    c) modifies, suppresses or adds personal information in an undue manner in an automated file of personal data;
    d) uses non-public personal data for a purpose other than that legally permitted.

Section 41
Anyone who, in violation of the present law, processes personal data described in sections 3 and 4 or orders such data to be processed, shall be liable to imprisonment for a term not exceeding 2 years.

Section 42
    (1) Anyone who, with the intention of procuring an unlawful gain for himself or for a third party, uses, without authorization, automatically stored data or programs, shall be liable to imprisonment for a term not exceeding 2 years and a fine of up to 120 daily rates.
    (2) The punishment shall be imprisonment for a term not exceeding one year or a fine of up to 60 daily rates if the perpetrator acts without the intention of procuring a gain.
    (3) In the case of the preceding subsection, prosecution shall be instituted only upon request.

Section 43
    (1) Anyone who illegally modifies or erases automatically stored data or programs

shall be liable to imprisonment for a term not exceeding 2 years or a fine of up to 120 daily rates.

(2) The punishment shall be imprisonment of 2 to 6 years or a fine of up to 200 daily rates, if the perpetrator, by acting according to the preceding subsection, causes a considerably high damage.

(3) Prosecution shall be instituted upon request only, except when the act is committed in a public riot.

Section 44
The same punishment applying to qualified theft applies to anyone who, with the intention of procuring an unlawful gain for himself or for a third party, institutes or influences automated data processing or automated data transmission, which usually leads to correct results, and by doing so causes a transfer of values detrimental to a third party.

Sections 45
(1) Anyone who, without the necessary legal authorization, uses for his own profit, a computer or a data network, shall be liable to a fine of up to 50 daily rates.

(2) The punishment shall be imprisonment for a term not exceeding one year, if the perpetrator, by illegally using a computer or a data network, gains access to personal data protected by professional secrecy.

(3) The punishment shall be imprisonment for a term of 2 to 6 years or a fine, if the perpetrator transmits the information to which he had access, and by doing so, causes damage to the State or other third parties.

(4) The attempt is also punishable.

(5) Prosecution shall be instituted only upon request, except in the case of subsection 3, when the transmission causes an especially serious damage.

REPUBLIC OF CHINA

Infringements of Intellectual Property

PENAL PROVISIONS OF THE COPYRIGHT LAW OF 1985

Section 38
Any person who reproduces, without authorization, the intellectual work of another shall be liable to imprisonment for not less than six months but not more than three years and may, in addition thereto, be fined not more than 30 000 Yuan. The same applies to a person who undertakes such reproduction on behalf of another.

Any person who sells or rents, or displays or possesses with intent to sell or lease, an intellectual work as referred to in the preceding paragraph shall be liable to imprisonment for not more than two years and may, in addition thereto, be fined not more than 20 000 Yuan. This shall also apply to one who delivers for profit an intellectual work as referred to in the preceding paragraph.

Section 39
Any person who by imitation or any other means infringes the copyright of another, shall be liable to imprisonment for not more than two years and may, in addition thereto, be fined not more than 20 000 Yuan. The same applies to a person who undertakes such reproduction on behalf of another.

Any person who sells or leases, or displays or possesses with the intent to sell or lease, an intellectual work referred to in the preceding paragraph shall be liable to imprisonment for not more than one year and may, in addition thereto, be fined not more than 10 000 Yuan. This shall also apply to one who delivers for profit an intellectual work as referred to in the preceding paragraph.

Section 40
Any person who commits any of the offences specified in the preceding two sections as a profession shall be liable to imprisonment for not less than six months but not more than five years and may, in addition thereto, be fined not more than 50 000 Yuan.

Section 41
Any person who violates the provisions of paragraph 2 of sections 13, 18 or 19 shall be fined not more than 10 000 Yuan.

Section 42
Any person who reproduces printing plates, the plate-rights of which have been registered, shall be liable to imprisonment for not more than one year and may, in addition thereto, be fined not more than 10 000 Yuan.

Section 43
Any person who violates the provisions of sections 25 or 27 shall be liable to imprisonment for not more than six months and may, in addition thereto, be fined not more than 5 000 Yuan.

Section 44
Any person who violates the provisions of section 26 shall be liable to imprisonment for not more than one year and may, in addition thereto, be fined not more than 10 000 Yuan.

Section 45
Any person who marks with the word 'registered' or a synonym thereof, an unregistered intellectual work or a printing plate shall, in addition to being prohi-

bited by the competent authority from selling such work, be fined not more than 8 000 Yuan.

Section 46
When a person is punished in accordance with sections 38 through 44 hereof, all reproduced, imitated or copied works, and the machines or tools, printing plates, negatives or modes used by him/her exclusively in committing the offences shall be confiscated.

Section 47
Prosecution of any of the offences specified in sections 38 through 43 hereof shall be instituted only upon complaint, provided that this provision shall not apply to cases where the offence committed is that specified in section 43 and the author or the person whose name is unlawfully used is dead.

Section 48
If the representative of a legal person, or the agent, employee or other operative of a legal person or natural person who, in the performance of his/her functional duties, commits any of the offences specified in section 38 through section 45 hereof, in addition to punishing the infringer according to the foregoing sections, such legal person or natural person shall also be fined as specified in the applicable section.

SPAIN

Infringements of Privacy and Honour

PROPOSAL FOR A PREDRAFT OF A NEW CRIMINAL CODE OF 1984

Section 189

(1) Anyone who infringes the legal provisions on the use of computer processing and collects data concerning the honour or the personal or familiar privacy of third parties or manipulates lawfully or unlawfully obtained information and thereby damages these interests, will be liable to imprisonment from 12 to 24 weekends and to a fine equivalent to 6 to 12 months, if the act does not constitute a more severe offence.

(2) A more serious penalty will be imposed if the information obtained is divulged.

SWEDEN

(A) Computer-Related Economic Crimes

AMENDMENTS TO THE PENAL CODE AS PROPOSED BY THE GOVERNMENTAL BILL OF 1985

Chapter 9 Section 1.
Any person who, by deception, induces someone to do or not to do something which involves gain for the offender and loss for the dupe or someone he represents, shall be guilty of fraud and liable to imprisonment for a term not exceeding two years.

Any person who, by presenting incorrect or incomplete information, by altering a program or a recording or otherwise without permission affects the result of an automatic information processing or a similar automatic process in a way which involves gain for the offender and loss for someone else, shall likewise be guilty of fraud.

Chapter 10 Section 7.
If a person unlawfully uses something (in his possession)* which belongs to another and thereby causes loss or inconvenience, he shall be guilty of unlawful use and liable to a fine or to imprisonment for a term not exceeding six months.

(2) . . .

(3) If the crime referred to in subsection 1 is grave, a term of imprisonment not exceeding two years shall be imposed.

(B) Infringements of Trade Secrets

PROPOSALS OF THE COMMISSION ON THE PROTECTION OF TRADE SECRETS OF 1983 FOR AMENDMENTS TO THE UNFAIR COMPETITION ACT (THE PROPOSALS ARE PRELIMINARY AND STILL UNDER DISCUSSION)

Section 2. Industrial Espionage
A person who, without authority, obtains access to a trade secret through:
— unauthorized entry or taking;
— wire-tapping or overhearing, reading, reproducing, copying or investigation;
— deception or offering improper rewards; or
— acts similar to those stated above;
and utilizes or discloses the trade secret, shall be guilty of industrial espionage, and upon conviction, shall be sentenced to imprisonment for not more than two years or to pay a fine, if the act is intentional.**

Section 3. Misuse of Trade Secrets in Commercial Relationships
A person who, without authorization, exploits or discloses to another person a trade secret that he has received in confidence in a bidding procedure, commercial negotiation, or other business relationship, shall be liable for criminal penalties, if the act was intentional.

---

* The words in brackets are deleted by the bill.
**Attempts and acts in preparation are also subject to penal sanctions according to provisions in the Penal Code.

(C) Infringements of Privacy and Computer-Related Economic Crimes

PENAL PROVISIONS OF THE DATA PROTECTION ACT NO. 289 OF 1973 AMENDED 1 JULY 1982

Section 20
(1) Any person who wilfully or negligently
1. establishes or maintains a register of persons without licence or permission under this Act, when such is required,
2. violates a regulation or prohibition issued pursuant to sections 5, 6 or 18,
3. divulges personal data in violation of section 11,
4. violates section 12,
5. delivers incorrect information in performance of his duty to deliver information pursuant to section 10, or
6. delivers incorrect information in a case referred to in section 17,
shall be sentenced to a fine or to imprisonment for a term not exceeding one year.
(2) A person who wilfully or negligently violates section 7a (1) or (3), shall be sentenced to a fine.

Section 21
(1) Any person who unlawfully procures access to records for automatic data processing or who unlawfully makes alterations in or deletions from such records in a file, shall be sentenced for data trespass to a fine or to imprisonment for a term not exceeding two years, unless the offence is punishable under the Penal Code.
(2) The attempt or preparation to commit a crime referred to in subsection 1 shall be punished according to chapter 23 of the Penal Code. Such punishment shall not be imposed if the crime would have been regarded as petty in the event that it would have been carried out.

Section 22
If a register of persons has been established or maintained without the licence or permission required under this Act, the register shall by judgement be declared forfeited unless this is manifestly inequitable. The same applies if a register of persons has been maintained contrary to a prohibition issued pursuant to section 18(2).

Section 23
If a person suffers damage because a register contains incorrect information about him, the responsible registrar shall pay compensation to him. When assessing whether and to what extent damage has been incurred, consideration shall also be paid to suffering and circumstances of other than a purely pecuniary significance.

SECTION 21 (1) OF THE DATA ACT AS PROPOSED BY THE GOVERNMENT BILL OF 1985 (SECTION 21 (2) REMAINING UNCHANGED)

Any person who unlawfully procures access to a record for automatic data processing or who unlawfully makes alterations in, deletions from or entries in such a record in a file, shall be guilty of data trespass and liable to a fine or to imprisonment for a term not exceeding two years, unless the offence is punishable under the Penal Code. *Data which are transmitted electronically or in a similar way for the purpose of automatic data processing, shall also be considered a recording.*

SWITZERLAND

(A) Computer-Related Economic Crimes

AMENDMENTS TO THE PENAL CODE AS PROPOSED BY THE COMMITTEE OF EXPERTS FOR THE REVISION OF THE PENAL CODE (PUBLISHED IN 1985)

Section 141. Removal of Property

(1) Any person who, without the intent to enrich himself, appropriates a foreign movable object shall, upon application, be liable to punishment of imprisonment or of a fine.

(2) Any person who removes a movable object from its legitimate owner, thereby causing him considerable prejudice, shall also be punished.

(3) In cases of self-help, the competent authority may refrain from prosecuting, from transferring the case to the court or from punishing the offender.

Section 143. Unauthorized Procuring of Data

(1) Any person who, with the intent of unlawfully enriching himself or another person, procures without authorization electronically stored data or programs, is liable to punishment of penal servitude for a term not exceeding five years or of imprisonment.

(2) If the offender acts without the intent of enriching himself or another, he is, upon application, liable to punishment of imprisonment or of a fine.

Section 144. Damage to Property

(1) Any person who damages, disturbs or renders useless an object which is subject to another person's rights of property, of possession or of usufruct shall, upon application, be liable to punishment of imprisonment or of a fine.

(2) *Any person who, without authorization, alters or erases electronically stored data or programs shall also, upon application, be liable to punishment.*

(3) If the perpetrator commits the damage in connection with a public riot, he will be prosecuted without request.

(4) If the offender caused considerable damage, penal servitude for a term not exceeding five years may be imposed. The prosecuting authority may decide to take action of its own motion.

Section 147. Fraudulent Misuse of a Data Processing System

Any person who, with the intent of unlawfully enriching himself or another person, induces a data processing or data transmission record, the result of which is incorrect, or prevents such a record, the result of which would have been correct, and thus procures a transfer of value to the disadvantage of another, shall be liable to punishment of penal servitude for a term not exceeding ten years or of imprisonment.

Section 148. Misuse of Check and Credit Cards

Any person who employs a check or credit card or similar instrument of payment, thereby obliging the drawer to pay a third party although he is insolvent, is liable to imprisonment for a term not exceeding five years.

Section 150. Unauthorized Use of Services

Any person who, knowing that payment is required, uses without paying a service such as public transportation, admittance to a performance, an exhibition or a similar event, or

a service which a data processing system supplies or which an automat arranges, shall upon application, be liable to punishment of imprisonment or of a fine.

Section 162 bis. Violation of Manufacturing or Business Secrets
   Any person
— who betrays a manufacturing or business secret which he had the statutory or contractual obligation to protect,
— who takes advantage of the betrayal for himself or for another person,
shall, upon application, be liable to punishment of imprisonment or of a fine.

Section 251. Falsification of Documents
   (1) Any person who, for purposes of deceit in a legal transaction,
— falsifies or forges a document, uses the signature or manual sign of another for the production of a false document,
— *produces a paper of legal significance which creates the impression that it is the result of an independent data processing record,*
— uses a document or paper of this kind,
shall be liable to punishment of penal servitude for a term not exceeding five years or of imprisonment.
   (2) In especially minor cases, punishment may consist in imprisonment or in a fine.

Section 251 bis. False Bookkeeping
   (1) Any person who, for purposes of deceit in a legal transaction, violates a duty imposed by commercial law and keeps false business books, especially by making a false entry in the books or by incorrectly preparing an inventory, a bill or a balance sheet, shall be liable to punishment of penal servitude for a term not exceeding five years or of imprisonment.
   (2) *Visual or data recordings are equivalent to writing.*
   (3) Any person who uses a document or record of this kind for purposes of deceit in a legal transaction, shall also be punished.

Section 317. Falsification of Documents by Holder of Public Office
   (1) Members of a public agency, public officials or 'persons of public faith' who, for purposes of deceit in a legal transaction,
— falsify or forge a document,
— use the signature or manual sign of another for the production of a false document,
— *produce a paper of legal significance which creates the impression that it is the result of an independent data processing record,*
— incorrectly record a legally relevant fact, such as a false signature or manual sign or an incorrect copy, as being authentic,
shall be liable to punishment of penal servitude for a term not exceeding five years or of imprisonment.
   (2) If the offender acts negligently, he shall be liable to punishment of imprisonment for a term not exceeding six months or of a fine.

(B) Infringements of Privacy

DRAFT PROPOSALS OF THE MINISTRY OF JUSTICE AND POLICE FOR A FEDERAL LAW ON THE PROTECTION OF PERSONAL DATA

Section 61. Offences Against the Registration and Reporting Duty
   (1) Any person who intentionally maintains a data bank which is subject to the registration provision of section 28 without having the data bank entered in the register of data banks, is liable to imprisonment or to a fine.
   (2) Any person who intentionally disregards the reporting duty described in section 30 and transmits personal data abroad or to an international agency, is liable to imprisonment or to a fine.

Section 62. Continued Unlawful Processing Notwithstanding Valid Judicial Ruling

Any person who intentionally continues to process personal data although a valid judicial ruling has determined the unlawfulness of this processing, will, upon application, be liable to imprisonment or to a fine.

Section 63. Offences Against the Duty to Supply Information

(1) Any person who, being legally obliged to provide information or corroborations, intentionally gives false information will, upon application, be liable to imprisonment for a term not exceeding 6 months or to a fine.

(2) If false information is the result of arrangments made by the perpetrator in order to falsely inform an unspecified large number of affected people, the penalty is imprisonment.

Section 64. Unauthorized Procuring of Personal Data

Any person who intentionally and without authorization takes personal data which are not freely accessible,

any person who processes data or divulges them to third persons, which he knows or must suppose have been procured by means of a criminal act pursuant to subsection 1,

will, upon application, be liable to imprisonment or to a fine.

Section 65. Breach of Secrecy

(1) Any person who exercises a profession requiring knowledge of secret personal data and who, without authorization, intentionally divulges data entrusted to him or which he obtained in exercising his profession will, upon application, be liable to imprisonment or to a fine.

(2) Any person who is employed by or being trained by a person bound to secrecy is subject to the same penalty.

UNITED KINGDOM

(A) Computer-Related Economic Crimes

THE FORGERY AND COUNTERFEITING ACT 1981

PART I

FORGERY AND KINDRED OFFENCES

Offences

1. The offence of forgery
A person is guilty of forgery if he makes a false instrument, with the intention that he or another shall use it to induce somebody to accept it as genuine, and by reason of so accepting it to do or not to do some act to his own or any other person's prejudice.

2. The offence of copying a false instrument
It is an offence for a person to make a copy of an instrument which is, and which he knows or believes to be, a false instrument, with the intention that he or another shall use it to induce somebody to accept it as a copy of a genuine instrument, and by reason of so accepting it to do or not to do some act to his own or any other person's prejudice.

3. The offence of using a false instrument
It is an offence for a person to use an instrument which is, and which he knows or believes to be, false, with the intention of inducing somebody to accept it as genuine, and by reason of so accepting it to do or not to do some act to his own or any other person's prejudice.

4. The offence of using a copy of a false instrument
It is an offence for a person to use a copy of an instrument which is, and which he knows or believes to be, a false instrument, with the intention of inducing somebody to accept it as a copy of a genuine instrument, and by reason of so accepting it to do or not to do some act to his own or any other person's prejudice.

5. Offences relating to money orders, share certificates, passports, etc
(1) It is an offence for a person to have in his custody or under his control an instrument to which this section applies which is, and which he knows or believes to be, false, with the intention that he or another shall use it to induce somebody to accept it as genuine, and by reason of so accepting it to do or not to do some act to his own or any other person's prejudice.
(2) It is an offence for a person to have in his custody or under his control, without lawful authority or excuse, an instrument to which this section applies which is, and which he knows or believes to be, false.
(3) It is an offence for a person to make or to have in his custody or under his control a machine or implement, or paper or any other material, which to his knowledge is or has been specially designed or adapted for the making of an instrument to which this section applies, with the intention that he or another shall make an instrument to which this section applies which is false and that he or another shall use the instrument to induce somebody to accept it as genuine, and by reason of so accepting it to do or not to do some act to his own or any person's prejudice.
(4) It is an offence for a person to make or to have in his custody or under his control any such machine, implement, paper or material, without lawful authority or excuse.
(5) The instruments to which this section applies are—
    (a) money orders;
    (b) postal orders;
    (c) United Kingdom postage stamps;

(d)   Inland Revenue stamps;
(e)   share certificates;
(f)   passports and documents which can be used instead of passports;
(g)   cheques;
(h)   travellers' cheques;
(j)   cheque cards;
(k)   credit cards;
(l)   certified copies relating to an entry in a register of births, adoptions, marriages or deaths and issued by the Registrar General, the Registrar General for Northern Ireland, a registration officer or a person lawfully authorized to register marriages; and
(m)   certificates relating to entries in such registers.

(6) In subsection (5) (e) above 'share certificate' means an instrument entitling or evidencing the title of a person to a share or interest—

(a)   in any public stock, annuity, fund or debt of any government or state, including a state which forms part of another state; or
(b)   in any stock, fund or debt of a body (whether corporate or unincorporated) established in the United Kingdom or elsewhere.

6. Penalties for offences under Part I

(1) A person guilty of an offence under this Part of this Act shall be liable on summary conviction—

(a)   to a fine not exceeding the statutory maximum; or
(b)   to imprisonment for a term not exceeding six months; or
(c)   to both.

(2) A person guilty of an offence to which this subsection applies shall be liable on conviction on indictment to imprisonment for a term not exceeding ten years.

(3) The offences to which subsection (2) above applies are offences under the following provisions of this Part of this Act—

(a)   section 1:
(b)   section 2;
(c)   section 3;
(d)   section 4;
(e)   section 5(1); and
(f)   section 5(3).

(4) A person guilty of an offence under section 5(2) or (4) above shall be liable on conviction on indictment to imprisonment for a term not exceeding two years.

(5) In this section "statutory maximum", in relation to a fine on summary conviction means the prescribed sum, within the meaning of section 32 of the Magistrates Courts Act 1980 (£1,000 or another sum fixed by order under section 143 of that Act to take account of changes in the value of money); and those sections shall extend to Northern Ireland for the purposes of the application of this definition.

7. Powers of search, forfeiture, etc

(1) If it appears to a justice of the peace, from information given him on oath, that there is reasonable cause to believe that a person has in his custody or under his control—

(a)   any thing which he or another has used, whether before or after the coming into force of this Act, or intends to use, for the making of any false instrument or copy of a false instrument, in contravention of section 1 or 2 above; or
(b)   any false instrument or copy of a false instrument which he or another has used, whether before or after the coming into force of this Act, or intends to use, in contravention of section 3 or 4 above; or
(c)   any thing custody or control of which without lawful authority or excuse is an offence under section 5 above,

the justice may issue a warrant authorizing a constable to search for and seize the object in question, and for that purpose to enter any premises specified in the warrant.

(2) A constable may at any time after the seizure of any object suspected of falling within paragraph (a), (b) or (c) of subsection (1) above (whether the seizure was effected by virtue of a warrant under that subsection or otherwise) apply to a magistrates' court for an order under this subsection with respect to the object; and the court, if it is satisifed both that the object in fact falls within any of those paragraphs and that it is conducive to the public interest to do so, may make such order as it thinks fit for the forfeiture of the object and its subsequent destruction or disposal.

(3) Subject to subsection (4) below, the court by or before which a person is convicted of an offence under this Part of this Act may order any object shown to the satisfaction of the court to relate to the offence to be forfeited and either destroyed or dealt with in such other manner as the court may order.

(4) The court shall not order any object to be forfeited under subsection (2) or (3) above where a person claiming to be the owner of or otherwise interested in it applies to be heard by the court, unless an opportunity has been given to him to show cause why the order should not be made.

Interpretation of Part I

8. Meaning of "instrument"

(1) Subject to subsection (2) below, in this Part of this Act "instrument" means—
   (a) any document, whether of a formal or informal character;
   (b) any stamp issued or sold by the Post Office;
   (c) any Inland Revenue stamp; and
   (d) any disc, tape, sound track or other device on or in which information is recorded or stored by mechanical, electronic or other means.

(2) A currency note within the meaning of Part II of this Act is not an instrument for the purposes of this Part of this Act.

(3) A mark denoting payment of postage which the Post Office authorize to be used instead of an adhesive stamp is to be treated for the purposes of this Part of this Act as if it were a stamp issued by the Post Office.

(4) In this Part of this Act "Inland Revenue stamp" means a stamp as defined in section 27 of the Stamp Duties Management Act 1891.

9. Meaning of "false" and 'making'

(1) An instrument is false for the purposes of this Part of this Act—
   (a) if it purports to have been made in the form in which it is made by a person who did not in fact make it in that form; or
   (b) if it purports to have been made in the form in which it is made on the authority of a person who did not in fact authorise its making in that form; or
   (c) if it purports to have been made in the terms in which it is made by a person who did not in fact make it in those terms; or
   (d) if it purports to have been made in the terms in which it is made on the authority of a person who did not in fact authorise its making in those terms; or
   (e) if it purports to have been altered in any respect by a person who did not in fact alter it in that respect; or
   (f) it it purports to have been altered in any respect on the authority of a person who did not in fact authorise the alteration in that respect; or
   (g) if it purports to have been made or altered on a date on which, or at a place at which, or otherwise in circumstances in which, it was not in fact made or altered; or
   (h) if it purports to have been made altered by an existing person but he did not in fact exist.

(2) A person is to be treated for the purpose of this Part of this Act as making a false instrument if he alters an instrument so as to make it false in any respect (whether or not it is false in some other respect apart from that alteration).

10. Meaning of prejudice and "induce"

(1) Subject to subsections (2) and (4) below, for the purposes of this Part of this Act an act or omission intended to be induced is to a person's prejudice if, and only if, it is one which, if it occurs—

    (a) will result—

        (i) in his temporary or permanent loss of property; or

        (ii) in his being deprived of an opportunity to earn remuneration or greater remuneration; or

        (iii) in his being deprived of an opportunity to gain a financial advantage otherwise than by way of remuneration; or

    (b) will result in somebody being given an opportunity—

        (i) to earn remuneration or greater remuneration from him; or

        (ii) to gain a financial advantage from him otherwise than by way of remuneration; or

    (c) will be the result of his having accepted a false instrument as genuine, or a copy of a false instrument as a copy of a genuine one, in connection with his performance of any duty.

(2) An act which a person has an enforceable duty to do and an omission to do an act which a person is not entitled to do shall be disregarded for the purposes of this Part of this Act.

(3) In this Part of this Act references to inducing somebody to accept a false instrument as genuine, or a copy of a false instrument as a copy of a genuine one, include references to inducing a machine to respond to the instrument or copy as if it were a genuine instrument or, as the case may be, a copy of a genuine one.

(4) Where subsection (3), above applies, the act or omission intended to be induced by the machine responding to the instrument or copy shall be treated as an act or omission to a person's prejudice.

(5) In this section 'loss' includes not getting what one might get as well as parting with what one has.

(B) Infringements of Copyright

PENAL PROVISION OF THE TRADITIONAL COPYRIGHT ACT 1956

Penalties and summary proceedings in respect of dealings which infringe copyright

21.—(1) Any person who, at a time when copyright subsists in a work,—

    (a) makes for sale or hire, or

    (b) sells or lets for hire, or by way of trade offers or exposes for sale or hire, or

    (c) by way of trade exhibits in public, or

    (d) imports into the United Kingdom, otherwise than for his private and domestic use,

any article which he knows to be an infringing copy of the work, shall be guilty of an offence under this subsection.

(2) Any person who, at a time when copyright subsists in a work, distributes, either—

    (a) for purposes of trade, or

    (b) for other purposes, but to such an extent as to affect prejudicially the owner of the copyright,

articles which he knows to be infringing copies of the work, shall be guilty of an offence under this subsection.

(3) Any person who, at a time when copyright subsists in a work, makes or has in his possession a plate, knowing that it is to be used for making infringing copies of the work, shall be guilty of an offence under this subsection.

    (4) The preceding subsections shall apply in relation to copyright

subsisting in any subject-matter by virtue of Part II of this Act, as they apply in relation to copyright subsisting by virtue of Part I of this Act.

(5) Any person who causes a literary, dramatic or musical work to be performed in public, knowing that copyright subsists in the work and that the performance constitutes an infringement of the copyright, shall be guilty of an offence under this subsection.

(6) The preceding provisions of this section apply only in respect of acts done in the United Kingdom.

(7) A person guilty of an offence under subsection (1) or subsection (2) of this section shall on summary conviction—

(a) if it is his first conviction of an offence under this section, be liable to a fine not exceeding forty shillings for each article to which the offence relates;

(b) in any other case, be liable to such a fine, or to imprisonment for a term not exceeding two months:

Provided that a fine imposed by virtue of this subsection shall not exceed fifty pounds in respect of articles comprised in the same transaction.

(8) A person guilty of an offence under subsection (3) or subsection (5) of this section shall on summary conviction—

(a) if it is his first conviction of an offence under this section, be liable to a fine not exceeding fifty pounds;

(b) in any other case, be liable to such a fine, or to imprisonment for a term not exceeding two months.

(9) The court before which a person is charged with an offence under this section may, whether he is convicted of the offence or not, order that any article in his possession which appears to the court to be an infringing copy, or to be a plate used or intended to be used for making infringing copies, shall be destroyed or delivered up to the owner of the copyright in question or otherwise dealt with as the court may think fit.

(10) An appeal shall lie to a court of quarter sessions from any order made under the last preceding subsection by a court of summary jurisdiction; and where such an order is made by the sheriff there shall be a like right of appeal against the order as if it were a conviction.

PENAL PROVISION OF THE COPYRIGHT ACT 1956 (AMENDMENT) ACT 1982

1. Amendment of section 21 of Copyright Act 1956

In section 21 of the Copyright Act 1956 (penalties and summary proceedings in respect of dealings which infringe copyright) after subsection (4) there shall be inserted the following new subsection—

'(4A) Any person who, at a time when copyright subsists in a sound recording or in a cinematograph film, by way of trade has in his possession any article which he knows to be an infringing copy of the sound recording or cinematograph film, as the case may be, shall be guilty of an offence under this section.';

and in subsection (7) the word 'or' where it first occurs shall be omitted and the words 'or subsection (4A)' shall be added after the words 'subsection (2)'.

PENAL PROVISIONS OF THE COPYRIGHT (AMENDMENT) ACT 1983

1. Amendments of section 21 of Copyright Act 1956

(1) Section 21 of the Copyright Act 1956 (offences relating to infringing copies of works in which copyright subsists) shall have effect subject to the following amendments.

(2) In subsection (7) (penalties for offences under subsections (1) and (2) and subsection (4A) (inserted by section 1 of the Copyright Act 1956 (Amendment) Act

1982)) for the words 'subsection (2) or subsection (4A) of this section' there shall be substituted the words 'or subsection (2) of this section, other than an offence for which a penalty is provided by subsection (7A) or (7B) of this section'.

(3) The following subsections shall be inserted after subsection (7)—

'(7A) A person guilty of an offence under subsection (1)(b) or (c) or (4A) of this section relating to an infringing copy of a sound recording or cinematograph film shall be liable on summary conviction to a fine not exceeding level 5 on the standard scale or imprisonment for a term not exceeding two months or to both.

(7B) A person guilty of an offence under subsection (1)(a) or (d) or (2) of this section relating to an infringing copy of a sound recording or cinematograph film shall be liable—

    (a)   on summary conviction, to a fine not exceeding the statutory maximum;

    (b)   on conviction on indictment, to a fine or to imprisonment for a term not exceeding two years or to both.

(7C) In subsection (7A) of this section 'the standard scale' has the meaning given by section 75 of the Criminal Justice Act 1982 and for the purposes of that subsection—

    (a)   section 37 of that Act; and

    (b)   an order under section 143 of the Magistrates' Court Act 1980 which alters the sums specified in subsection (2) of the said section 37.

shall extend to Northern Ireland and the said section 75 shall have effect as if after the words 'England and Wales' there were inserted the words 'or Nothern Ireland'.

(7D) In subsection (7B) of this section 'statutory maximum' has the meaning given by section 74 of the Criminal Justice Act 1982 and for the purposes of that subsection—

    (a)   section 32 of the Magistrates' Courts Act 1980; and

    (b)   an order made under section 143 of that Act which alters the sum specified in the definition of 'the prescribed sum' in subsection (9) of the said section 32,

shall extend to Northern Ireland and subsection (1) of the said section 74 shall have effect as if after the words 'England and Wales' there were inserted the words 'or Northern Ireland'.

2. Search warrants etc

The following sections shall be inserted in the Copyright Act 1956 after section 21—

"21A *Search warrants*

(1) Where, on information on oath given by a constable, a justice of the peace is satisfied that there are reasonable grounds for believing—

    (a)   that an offence under subsection (1)(a) or (d) or (2) of section 21 of this Act relating to an infringing copy of a sound recording or a cinematograph film has been or is about to be committed in any premises, and

    (b)   that evidence that the offence has been or is about to be committed is in those premises,

he may issue a warrant authorizing a constable to enter and search the premises, using such reasonable force as is necessary.

(2) A warrant under this section may authorize persons to accompany any constable who is executing it and must be executed within twenty-eight days from the date of its issue.

(3) In executing a warrant issued under this section a constable may seize any article if he reasonably believes that it is evidence that an offence under subsection (1), (2) or (4A) of section 21 of this Act relating to an infringing copy of a sound recording or a cinematograph film has been or is about to be committed.

(4) In this section 'premises' includes land, buildings, moveable structures, vehicles, vessels, aircraft and hovercraft.

(5) This section shall have effect in Northern Ireland as if in subsection (1)—

    (a)   for the reference to an information there were substituted a reference to a complaint, and

    (b) for the reference to a justice of the peace there were substituted, a reference to a resident magistrate.

(6) This section shall not extend to Scotland.

21B. *(Applies to Scotland)."*

PENAL PROVISION OF THE COPYRIGHT (COMPUTER SOFTWARE) AMENDMENT ACT 1985

Section 3. Offences and Search Warrants

Where an infringing copy of a computer program consists of a disc, tape or chip or of any other device which embodies signals serving for the impartation of the program or part of it, sections 21 to 21B of the Copyright Act 1956 (offences and search warrants) shall apply in relation to that copy as they apply in relation to an infringing copy of a sound recording or cinematograph film.

(C) INFRINGEMENTS OF PRIVACY

PROVISIONS OF THE DATA PROTECTION ACT OF 12 JULY 1984 CONTAINING PENAL OFFENCES*

Prohibition of unregistered holding etc. of personal data.

5.—(1) A person shall not hold personal data unless an entry in respect of that person as a data user, or as a data user who also carries on a computer bureau, is for the time being contained in the register.

(2) A person in respect of whom such an entry is contained in the register shall not—

    (a) hold personal data of any description other than that specified in the entry:

    (b) hold any such data, or use any such data held by him, for any purpose other than the purpose or purposes described in the entry:

    (c) obtain such data, or information to be contained in such data, to be held by him from any source which is not described in the entry;

    (d) disclose such data held by him to any person who is not described in the entry: or

    (e) directly or indirectly transfer such data held by him to any country or territory outside the United Kingdom other than one named or described in the entry.

(3) A servant or agent of a person to whom subsection (2) above applies shall, as respects personal data held by that person, be subject to the same restrictions on the use, disclosure or transfer of the data as those to which that person is subject under paragraphs *(b), (d)* and *(e)* of that subsection and, as respects personal data to be held by that person, to the same restrictions as those to which he is subject under paragraph *(c)* of that subsection.

(4) A person shall not, in carrying on a computer bureau, provide services in respect of personal data unless an entry in respect of that person as a person carrying on such a bureau, or as a data user who also carries on such a bureau, is for the time being contained in the register.

---

* Penal provisions are printed in italic.

(5) Any person who contravenes subsection (1) above or knowingly or recklessly contravenes any of the other provisions of this section shall be guilty of an offence.

Applications for registration and for amendment of registered particulars.

6.—(1) A person applying for registration shall state whether he wishes to be registered as a data user, as a person carrying on a computer bureau or as a data user who also carries on such a bureau, and shall furnish the Registrar, in such form as he may require, with the particulars required to be included in the entry to be made in pursuance of the application.

(2) Where a person intends to hold personal data for two or more purposes he may make separate applications for registration in respect of any of those purposes.

(3) A registered person may at any time apply to the Registrar for the alteration of any particulars included in the entry or entries relating to that person.

(4) Where the alteration would consist of the addition of a purpose for which personal data are to be held, the person may, instead of making an application under subsection (3) above, make a fresh application for registration in respect of the additional purpose.

(5) A registered person shall make an application under subsection (3) above whenever necessary for ensuring that the entry or entries relating to that person contain his current address; and any person who fails to comply with this subsection shall be guilty of an offence.

(6) Any person who, in connection with an application for registration or for the alteration of registered particulars, knowingly or recklessly furnishes the Registrar with information which is false or misleading in a material respect shall be guilty of an offence.

(7) Every application for registration shall be accompanied by the prescribed fee, and every application for the alteration of registered particulars shall be accompanied by such fee, if any, as may be prescribed.

(8) Any application for registration or for the alteration of registered particulars may be withdrawn by notice in writing to the Registrar at any time before the applicant receives a notification in respect of the application under section 7(1) below.

Supervision

Enforcement notices.

10.—(1) If the Registrar is satisfied that a registered person has contravened or is contravening any of the data protection principles he may serve him with a notice ('an enforcement notice') requiring him to take, within such time as is specified in the notice, such steps as are so specified for complying with the principle or principles in question.

(2) In deciding whether to serve an enforcement notice the Registrar shall consider whether the contravention has caused or is likely to cause any person damage or distress.

(3) An enforcement notice in respect of a contravention of the fifth data protection principle may require the data user—

    (a) to rectify or erase the data and any other data held by him and containing an expression of opinion which appears to the Registrar to be based on the inaccurate data; or

    (b) in the case of such data as are mentioned in subsection (2) of section 22 below, either to take the steps mentioned in paragraph *(a)* above or to take such steps as are specified in the notice for securing compliance with the

requirements specified in that subsection and, if the Registrar thinks fit, for supplementing the data with such statement of the true facts relating to the matters dealt with by the data as the Registrar may approve.

(4) The Registrar shall not serve an enforcement notice requiring the person served with the notice to take steps for complying with paragraph *(a)* of the seventh data protection principle in respect of any data subject unless satisfied that the person has contravened section 21 below by failing to supply information to which the data subject is entitled and which has been duly requested in accordance with that section.

(5) An enforcement notice shall contain—

    (a)   a statement of the principle or principles which the Registrar is satisfied have been or are being contravened and his reasons for reaching that conclusion; and

    (b)   particulars of the rights of appeal conferred by section 13 below.

(6) Subject to subsection (7) below, the time specified in an enforcement notice for taking the steps which it requires shall not expire before the end of the period within which an appeal can be brought against the notice and, if such an appeal is brought, those steps need not be taken pending the determination or withdrawal of the appeal.

(7) If by reason of special circumstances the Registrar considers that the steps required by an enforcement notice should be taken as a matter of urgency he may include a statement to that effect in the notice; and in that event subsection (6) above shall not apply but the notice shall not require the steps to be taken before the end of the period of seven days beginning with the date on which the notice is served.

(8) The Registrar may cancel an enforcement notice by written notification to the person on whom it was served.

(9) *Any person who fails to comply with an enforcement notice shall be guilty of an offence; but it shall be a defence for a person charged with an offence under this subsection to prove that he exercised all due diligence to comply with the notice in question.*

Transfer prohibition notices.

12.—(1) If it appears to the Registrar that—

    (a)   a person registered as a data user or as a data user who also carries on a computer bureau; or

    (b)   a person treated as so registered by virtue of section 7(6) above,

proposes to transfer personal data held by him to a place outside the United Kingdom, the Registrar may, if satisfied as to the matters mentioned in subsection (2) or (3) below, serve that person with a notice ('a transfer prohibition notice') prohibiting him from transferring the data either absolutely or until he has taken such steps as are specified in the notice for protecting the interests of the data subjects in question.

(2) Where the place to which the data are to be transferred is not in a State bound by the European Convention the Registrar must be satisfied that the transfer is likely to contravene, or lead to a contravention of, any of the data protection principles.

(3) Where the place to which the data are to be transferred is in a State bound by the European Convention the Registrar must be satisfied either—

    (a) that—

        (i) the person in question intends to give instructions for the further transfer of the data to a place which is not in such a State; and

(ii) that the further transfer is likely to contravene, or lead to a contravention of, any of the data protection principles; or

(b) in the case of data to which an order under section 2(3) above applies, that the transfer is likely to contravene or lead to a contravention of, any of the data protection principles as they have effect in relation to such data.

(4) In deciding whether to serve a transfer prohibition notice the Registrar shall consider whether the notice is required for preventing damage or distress to any person and shall have regard to the general desirability of facilitating the free transfer of data between the United Kingdom and other states and territories.

(5) A transfer prohibition notice shall specify the time when it is to take effect and contain—

(a) a statement of the principle or principles which the Registrar is satisfied are likely to be contravened and his reasons for reaching that conclusion; and

(b) particulars of the rights of appeal conferred by section 13 below.

(6) Subject to subsection (7) below, the time specified in a transfer prohibition notice pursuant to subsection (5) above shall not be before the end of the period within which an appeal can be brought against the notice and, if such an appeal is brought, the notice shall not take effect pending the determination or withdrawal of the appeal.

(7) If by reason of special circumstances the Registrar considers that the prohibition should take effect as a matter of urgency he may include a statement to that effect in the transfer prohibition notice; and in that event subsection (6) above shall not apply but the notice shall not take effect before the end of the period of seven days beginning with the date on which the notice is served.

(8) The Registrar may cancel a transfer prohibition notice by written notification to the person on whom it was served.

(9) No transfer prohibition notice shall prohibit the transfer of any data where the transfer of the information constituting the data is required or authorised by or under any enactment or required by any convention or other instrument imposing an international obligation on the United Kingdom.

(10) *Any person who contravenes a transfer prohibition notice shall be guilty of an offence; but it shall be a defence for a person charged with an offence under this subsection to prove that he exercised all due diligence to avoid a contravention of the notice in question.*

(11) For the purposes of this section a place shall be treated as in a State bound by the European Convention if it is in any territory in respect of which the State is bound.

Unauthorised disclosure by computer bureau.

15.—(1) Personal data in respect of which services are provided by a person carrying on a computer bureau shall not be disclosed by him without the prior authority of the person for whom those services are provided.

(2) Subsection (1) above applies also to any servant or agent of a person carrying on a computer bureau.

(3) *Any person who knowingly or recklessly contravenes this section shall be guilty of an offence.*

Prosecutions
and penalties.

19.—(1) No proceedings for an offence under this Act shall be instituted—

(a) in England or Wales except by the Registrar or by or with the consent of the Director of Public Prosecutions;

(b) in Northern Ireland except by the Registrar or by or with the consent of the Director of Public Prosecutions for Northern Ireland.

(2) A person guilty of an offence under any provision of this Act other than section 6 or paragraph 12 of Schedule 4 shall be liable

(a) on conviction on indictment, to a fine; or

(b) on summary conviction, to a fine not exceeding the statutory maximum (as defined in section 74 of the Criminal Justice Act 1982).

(3) A person guilty of an offence under section 6 above or the said paragraph 12 shall be liable on summary conviction to a fine not exceeding the fifth level on the standard scale (as defined in section 75 of the said Act of 1982).

(4) Subject to subsection (5) below, the court by or before which a person is convicted of an offence under section 5, 10, 12 or 15 above may order any data material appearing to the court to be connected with the commission of the offence to be forfeited, destroyed or erased.

(5) The court shall not make an order under subsection (4) above in relation to any material where a person (other than the offender) claiming to be the owner or otherwise interested in it applies to be heard by the court unless an opportunity is given to him to show cause why the order should not be made.

Liability of
directors etc

20.—(1) Where an offence under this Act has been committed by a body corporate and is proved to have been committed with the consent or connivance of or to be attributable to any neglect on the part of any director, manager, secretary or similar officer of the body corporate or any person who was purporting to act in any such capacity, he as well as the body corporate shall be guilty of that offence and be liable to be proceeded against and punished accordingly.

(2) Where the affairs of a body corporate are managed by its members subsection (1) above shall apply in relation to the acts and defaults of a member in connection with his functions of management as if he were a director of the body corporate.

SCHEDULE 4:

Offences

12. Any person who—

(a) intentionally obstructs a person in the execution of a warrant issued under this Schedule; or

(b) fails without reasonable excuse to give any person executing such a warrant such assistance as he may reasonably require for the execution of the warrant,

shall be guilty of an offence.

(D) Procedural Law

THE POLICE AND CRIMINAL EVIDENCE ACT 1984

PART VII

DOCUMENTARY EVIDENCE IN CRIMINAL PROCEEDINGS

68. Evidence from documentary records

(1) Subject to section 69 below, a statement in a document shall be admissible in any proceedings as evidence of any fact stated therein of which direct oral evidence would be admissible if—
- (a) the document is or forms part of a record compiled by a person acting under a duty from information supplied by a person (whether acting under a duty or not) who had, or may reasonably be supposed to have had, personal knowledge of the matters dealt with in that information; and
- (b) any condition relating to the person who supplied the information which is specified in subsection (2) below is satisfied.

(2) The conditions mentioned in subjection (1)(b) above are—
- (a) that the person who supplied the information—
    - (i) is dead or by reason of his bodily or mental condition unfit to attend as a witness;
    - (ii) is outside the United Kingdom and it is not reasonably practicable to secure his attendance; or
    - (iii) cannot reasonably be expected (having regard to the time which has elapsed since he supplied or acquired the information and to all the circumstances) to have any recollection of the matters dealt with in that information;
- (b) that all reasonable steps have been taken to identify the person who supplied the information but that he cannot be identified; and
- (c) that, the identity of the person who supplied the information being known, all reasonable steps have been taken to find him, but that he cannot be found.

(3) Nothing in this section shall prejudice the admissibility of any evidence that would be admissible apart from this section.

69. Evidence from computer records

(1) In any proceedings, a statement in a document produced by a computer shall not be admissible as evidence of any fact stated therein unless it is shown—
- (a) that there are no reasonable grounds for believing that the statement is inaccurate because of improper use of the computer;
- (b) that at all material times the computer was operating properly, or if not, that any respect in which it was not operating properly or was out of operation was not such as to affect the production of the document or the accuracy of its contents; and
- (c) that any relevant conditions specified in rules of court under subsection (2) below are satisfied.

(2) Provision may be made by rules of court requiring that in any proceedings where it is desired to give a statement in evidence by virtue of this section such information concerning the statement as may be required by the rules shall be provided in such form and at such time as may be so required.

70. Provisions supplementary to sections 68 and 69

(1) Part I of Schedule 3 to this Act shall have effect for the purpose of supplementing section 68 above.

(2) Part II of that Schedule shall have effect for the purpose of supplementing section 69 above.

(3) Part III of that Schedule shall have effect for the purpose of supplementing both sections.

71. Microfilm copies

In any proceedings the contents of a document may (whether or not the document is still in existence) be proved by the production of an enlargement of a microfilm copy of that document or of the material art of it, authenticated in such manner as the court may approve.

72. Part VII–supplementary

(1) In this Part of this Act—

"copy" and "statement" have the same meanings as in Part I of the Civil Evidence Act 1968; and

"proceedings" means criminal proceedings, including—

(a) proceedings in the United Kingdom or elsewhere before a court-martial constituted under the Army Act 1955 or the Air Force Act 1955;

(b) proceedings in the United Kingdom or elsewhere before the Courts-Martial Appeal Court—

(i) on an appeal from a court-martial so constituted or from a court-martial constituted under the Naval Discipline Act 1957; or

(ii) on a reference under section 34 of the Courts-Martial (Appeals) Act 1968; and

(c) proceedings before a Standing Civilian Court.

(2) Nothing in this Part of this Act shall prejudice any power of a court to exclude evidence (whether by preventing questions from being put or otherwise) at its discretion.

SCHEDULE 3

Provisions Supplementary to Sections 68 and 69

Part II

Provisions Supplementary to Section 69

8. In any proceedings where it is desired to give a statement in evidence in accordance with section 69 above, a certificate—

(a) identifying the document containing the statement and describing the manner in which it was produced;

(b) giving such particulars of any device involved in the production of that document as may be appropriate for the purpose of showing that the document was produced by a computer:

(c) dealing with any of the matters mentioned in subsection (1) of section 69 above; and

(d) purporting to be signed by a person occupying a responsible position in relation to the operation of the computer,

shall be evidence of anything stated in it; and for the purposes of this paragraph it shall be sufficient for a matter to be stated to the best of the knowledge and belief of the person stating it.

9. Notwithstanding paragraph 8 above, a court may require oral evidence to be given of anything of which evidence could be given by a certificate under that paragraph.

10. Any person who in a certificate tendered under paragraph 8 above in a magistrates' court, the Crown Court or the Court of Appeal makes a statement which he knows to be false or does not believe to be true shall be guilty of an offence and liable—

(a) on conviction on indictment to imprisonment for a term not exceeding two years or to a fine or to both;

(b) on summary conviction to imprisonment for a term not exceeding six months or to a fine not exceeding the statutory maximum (as defined in section 74 of the Criminal Justice Act 1982) or to both.

11. In estimating the weight, if any, to be attached to a statement regard shall be had to all the circumstances from which any inference can reasonably be drawn as to the accuracy or otherwise of the statement and, in particular—

    (a)   to the question whether or not the information which the information contained in the statement reproduces or is derived from was supplied to the relevant computer, or recorded for the purpose of being supplied to it, contemporaneously with the occurrence or existence of the facts dealt with in that information; and

    (b)   to the question whether or not any person concerned with the supply of information to that computer, or with the operation of that computer or any equipment by means of which the document containing the statement was produced by it, had any incentive to conceal or misrepresent the facts.

12. For the purposes of paragraph 11 above information shall be taken to be supplied to a computer whether it is supplied directly or (with or without human intervention) by means of any appropriate equipment.

UNITED STATES OF AMERICA

(A) Computer-Related Economic Crimes

THE FEDERAL CREDIT CARD FRAUD ACT 1984

Credit Card Fraud Act of 1984 18 USC 1001 note.

Chapter XVI—Credit Card Fraud
  Sec. 1601. This chapter may be cited as the "Credit Card Fraud Act of 1984".
  Sec. 1602. (a) Chapter 47 of title 18 of the United States Code is amended by adding at the end thereof the following:

Penalties.
18 USC 1029.

  "*§ 1029. Fraud and related activity in connection with access devices*

  "(a) Whoever—
    "(1) knowingly and with intent to defraud produces, uses, or traffics in one or more counterfeit access devices;
    "(2) knowingly and with intent to defraud traffics in or uses one or more unauthorized access devices during any one-year period, and by such conduct obtains anything of value aggregating $1,000 or more during that period;
    "(3) knowingly and with intent to defraud possesses fifteen or more devices which are counterfeit or unauthorized access devices; or
    "(4) knowingly, and with intent to defraud, produces, traffics in, has control or custody of, or possesses device-making equipment;
shall, if the offense affects interstate or foreign commerce, be punished as provided in subsection (c) of this section.
  "(b)(1) Whoever attempts to commit an offense under subsection (a) of this section shall be punished as provided in subsection (c) of this section.
  "(2) Whoever is a party to a conspiracy of two or more persons to commit an offense under subsection (a) of this section, if any of the parties engages in any conduct in furtherance of such offense, shall be fined an amount not greater than the amount provided as the maximum fine for such offense under subsection (c) of this section or imprisoned not longer than one-half the period provided as the maximum imprisonment for such offense under subsection (c) of this section, or both.
  "(c) The punishment for an offense under subsection (a) or (b)(1) of this section is:
    "(1) a fine of not more than the greater of $10,000 or twice the value obtained by the offense or imprisonment for not more than ten years, or both, in the case of an offense under subsection (a)(2) or (a)(3) of this section which does not occur after a conviction for another offense under either such subsection, or an attempt to commit an offense punishable under this paragraph;
    "(2) a fine of not more than the greater of $50,000 or twice the value obtained by the offense or imprisonment for not more than fifteen years, or both, in the case of an offense under subsection (a)(1) or (a)(4) of this section which does not occur after a conviction for another offense under either such subsection, or an attempt to commit an offense punishable under this paragraph; and
    "(3) a fine of not more than the greater of $100,000 or twice

the value obtained by the offense or imprisonment for not more than twenty years, or both, in the case of an offense under subsection (a) of this section which occurs after a conviction for another offense under such subsection, or an attempt to commit an offense punishable under this paragraph.

U.S. Secret Service, investigations. "(d) The United States Secret Service shall, in addition to any other agency having such authority, have the authority to investigate offenses under this section. Such authority of the United States Secret Service shall be exercised in accordance with an agreement which shall be entered into by the Secretary of the Treasury and the Attorney General.

"(e) As used in this section—

"(1) the term 'access device' means any card, plate, code, account number, or other means of account access that can be used, alone or in conjunction with another access device, to obtain money, goods, services, or any other thing of value, or that can be used to initiate a transfer of funds (other than a transfer originated solely by paper instrument);

"(2) the term 'counterfeit access device' means any access device that is counterfeit, fictitious, altered, or forged, or an identifiable component of an access device or a counterfeit access device;

"(3) the term 'unauthorized access device' means any access device that is lost, stolen, expired, revoked, canceled, or obtained with intent to defraud;

"(4) the term 'produce' includes design, alter, authenticate, duplicate, or assemble;

"(5) the term 'traffic' means transfer, or otherwise dispose of, to another, or obtain control of with intent to transfer or dispose of; and

"(6) the term 'device-making equipment' means any equipment, mechanism, or impression designed or primarily used for making an access device or a counterfeit access device.

"(f) This section does not prohibit any lawfully authorized investigative, protective, or intelligence activity of a law enforcement agency of the United States, a State, or a political subdivision of a State, or of an intelligence agency of the United States, or any activity authorized under title V of the Organized Crime Control Act of 1970 (18 U.S.C. note prec. 3481.)".

(b) The table of sections at the beginning of chapter 47 of title 18 of the United States Code is amended by adding at the end the following new item:

"1029. Fraud and related activity in connection with access devices".

SEC. 1603. The Attorney General shall report to the Congress annually, during the first three years following the date of the enactment of this joint resolution, concerning prosecutions under the section of title 18 of the United States Code added by this chapter.

THE FEDERAL COUNTERFEIT ACCESS DEVICE AND COMPUTER FRAUD AND ABUSE ACT 1984

Chapter XXI—Access Devices and Computers
SEC. 2101. This chapter may be cited as the "Counterfeit Access Device and Computer Fraud and Abuse Act of 1984".

SEC. 2102. (a) Chapter 47 of title 18 of the United States Code as amended by chapter XVI of this joint resolution is further amended by adding at the end thereof the following:

"§ *1030. Fraud and related activity in connection with computers*

'(a) Whoever—

"(1) knowingly accesses a computer without authorization, or having accessed a computer with authorization, uses the opportunity such access provides for purposes to which such authorization does not extend, and by means of such conduct obtains information that has been determined by the United States Government pursuant to an Executive order or statute to require protection against unauthorized disclosure for reasons of national defense or foreign relations, or any restricted data, as defined in paragraph r. of section 11 of the Atomic Energy Act of 1954, with the intent or reason to believe that such information so obtained is to be used to the injury of the United States, or to the advantage of any foreign nation;

"(2) knowingly accesses a computer without authorization, or having accessed a computer with authorization, uses the opportunity such access provides for purposes to which such authorization does not extend, and thereby obtains information contained in a financial record of a financial institution, as such terms are defined in the Right to Financial Privacy Act of 1978 (12 U.S.C. 3401 et seq.), or contained in a file of a consumer reporting agency on a consumer, as such terms are defined in the Fair Credit Reporting Act (15 U.S.C. 1681 et seq.); or

"(3) knowingly accesses a computer without authorization, or having accessed a computer with authorization, uses the opportunity such access provides for purposes to which such authorization does not extend, and by means of such conduct knowingly uses, modifies, destroys, or discloses information in, or prevents authorized use of, such computer, if such computer is operated for or on behalf of the Government of the United States and such conduct affects such operation;

shall be punished as provided in subsection (c) of this section. It is not an offence under paragraph (2) or (3) of this subsection in the case of a person having accessed a computer with authorization and using the opportunity such access provides for purposes to which such access does not extend, if the using of such opportuinty consists only of the use of the computer.

"(b)(1) Whoever attempts to commit an offense under subsection (a) of this section shall be punished as provided in subsection (c) of this section.

'(2) Whoever is a party to a conspiracy of two or more persons to commit an offense under subsection (a) of this section, if any of the parties engages in any conduct in furtherance of such offense, shall be fined an amount not greater than the amount provided as the maximum fine for such offense under subsection (c) of this section or imprisoned not longer than one-half the period provided as the maximum imprisonment for such offense under subsection (c) of this section, or both.

"(c) The punishment for an offense under subsection (a) or (b)(1) of this section is—

'(1)(A) a fine of not more than the greater of $10,000 or twice the value obtained by the offense or imprisonment for not more than ten years, or both, in the case of an offense under subsection (a)(1) of this section which does not occur after a conviction for another offense under such subsection, or an attempt to commit an offense punishable under this subparagraph; and

'(B) a fine of not more than the greater of $100,000 or twice the value obtained by the offense or imprisonment for not more than twenty years, or both, in the case of an offense under subsection (a)(1) of this section which occurs after a conviction for another offense under such subsection, or an attempt to commit an offense punishable under this subparagraph; and

'(2)(A) a fine of not more than the greater of $5,000 or twice the value obtained or loss created by the offense or imprisonment for not more than one year, or both, in the case of an offense under subsection (a)(2) or (a)(3) of this section which does not occur after a conviction for another offense under such subsection, or an attempt to commit an offense punishable under this subparagraph; and

'(B) a fine of not more than the greater of $10,000 or twice the value obtained or loss created by the offense or imprisonment for not more than ten years, or both, in the case of an offense under subsection (a)(2) or (a)(3) of this section which occurs after a conviction for another offense under such subsection, or an attempt to commit an offense punishable under this subparagraph.

"(d) The United States Secret Service shall, in addition to any other agency having such authority, have the authority to investigate offenses under this section. Such authority of the United States Secret Service shall be exercised in accordance with an agreement which shall be entered into by the Secretary of the Treasury and the Attorney General.

"(e) As used in this section, the term 'computer' means an electronic, magnetic, optical, electrochemical, or other high speed data processing device performing logical, arithmetic, or storage functions, and includes any data storage facility or communications facility directly related to or operating in conjunction with such device, but such term does not include an automated typewriter or typesetter, a portable hand held calculator, or other similar device."

(b) The table of sections at the beginning of chapter 47 of title 18 of the United States Code is amended by adding at the end the following new items:

'1030. Fraud and related activity in connection with computers."

SEC. 2103. The Attorney General shall report to the Congress annually, during the first three years following the date of the enactment of this joint resolution, concerning prosecutions under the sections of title 18 of the United States Code added by this chapter.

THE DEPARTMENT OF JUSTICE'S BILL OF THE 'FEDERAL COMPUTER SYSTEMS PROTECTION ACT 1984'

A Bill

To amend Title 18, United States Code, to make a crime the use, for fraudulent or other illegal purposes, of any computer owned or operated by the United States, certain financial institutions, and entities affecting interstate commerce.

Be it enacted by the Senate and House of Representatives of the United States of America in Congress assembled, That this Act may be cited as the "Federal Computer Systems Protection Act of 1984."

SEC. 2. (a) Chapter 47 of Title 18, United States Code, is amended by adding at the end thereof the following new section: "§ 1028. Computer fraud and abuse.

"(a) Whoever having devised or intending to devise any scheme or artifice to defraud, or for obtaining money or property by false or fraudulent pretenses, representations, or promises, or to embezzle, steal, or convert to his use or the use of another, property not his own, for the purpose of executing such scheme or artifice or embezzlement, theft or conversion or attempting to do so, knowingly accesses or attempts to access a computer, shall, if the computer—

"(1) is owned by, under contract to, or operated for or on behalf of—

"(A) the United States Government; or

"(B) a financial institution, or

(2) operates in, or uses a facility of, interstate commerce,

be fined not more than two times the amount of the gain directly or indirectly derived from the offense or $50,000, whichever is higher, or imprisoned not more than five years, or both.

"(b) Whoever knowingly and willfully without authorization damages, destroys or attempts to damage or destroy a computer described in subsection (a) (1) and (2) or knowingly and willfully without authorization damages or attempts to damage any computer program, or data contained in such computer shall be fined not more than $50,000 or imprisoned not more than five years, or both.

"(c) Whoever intentionally and without authorization accesses a computer as defined in (a) (1), or a computer system or computer network including such computer, shall be guilty of a misdemeanor and shall be fined not more than $25,000 or imprisoned for not more than one year, or both.

"(d) Whoever violates any provision of paragarph (a), (b) or (c) shall forfeit to the United States any interest acquired or maintained in any computer and computer software, which has been used to commit the violation. Upon conviction under this section, the court shall authorize the Attorney General to seize all property or other interest declared forfeited under this section upon such terms and conditions as the court shall deem proper. If a property right or other interest is not exercisable or transferable for value by the United States, it shall expire, and shall not revert to the convicted violator. The United States shall dispose of all such property as soon as commercially feasible, making due provision for the rights of innocent persons.

"(e) DEFINITIONS—For the purpose of this section the term—

"(1) 'computer' means an electronic, magnetic, electrochemical, or other high speed data processing device performing logical, arithmetic, or storage functions, and includes any data storage facility or communications facility directly related to or operating in conjunction with such device;

"(2) 'computer system' means a set of related connected or unconnected computers, computer equipment, devices and software;

"(3) 'computer network' means two or more interconnected computers, computer terminals or computer systems.

"(4) 'financial institution' means—

"(A) a bank with deposits insured by the Federal Deposit Insurance Corporation;

"(B) the Federal Reserve or a member of the Federal Reserve including any Federal Reserve bank;

"(C) an institution with accounts insured by the Federal Savings and Loan Corporation;

"(D) a credit union with accounts insured by the National Credit Union Administration;

"(E) a member of the Federal Home Loan Bank system and any home loan bank;

"(F) a member or business insured by the Securities Investor Protection Corporation; and

"(G) a broker-dealer registered with the Securities and Exchange Commission pursuant to Section 15 of the Securities and Exchange Act of 1934;

"(5) 'property' includes, but is not limited to, financial instruments, information, including electronically processed or produced data, and computer program and computer software in either machine or human readable form, computer services and any other tangible or intangible item of value;

"(6) 'financial instrument' means any check, draft money order, certificate of deposit, letter of credit, bill of exchange, credit card, debit card or marketable security, or any electronic data processing representation thereof;

"(7) 'computer program' means an instruction or statement or a series of instructions or statements, in a form acceptable to a computer, which permits the functioning of a computer system in a manner designed to provide appropriate products from such computer system;

"(8) 'computer software' means a set of computer programs, procedures and associated documentation concerned with the operation of a computer system;

"(9) 'computer services' includes but is not limited to computer time, data processing, and storage functions;

"(10) 'United States Government' includes a branch or agency thereof;

"(11) 'access' means to instruct, communicate with, store data in, retrieve data from, or otherwise make use of any resources of a computer, computer system, or computer network; and

SEC. 3. The table of sections of Chapter 47 of Title 18, United States Code, is

amended by adding at the end thereof the following:
"1028. Computer fraud and abuse."

CALIFORNIAN COMPUTER CRIME ACT 1985
(As the 45 computer-crime State laws cannot be reproduced here, the Californian legislation is taken as an exmple. For the other States' laws see Chapter IV)

Section 502
Definitions; computer system or network; intentional access to defraud or extort, or to obtain money, property or services with false or fraudulent intent, representation or promises, malicious access, alteration, deletion or damage or disruption; violations; penalty, civil action.

(a) For purposes of this section:

(1) "Access" means to instruct, communicate with, store data in, or retrieve data from a computer system or computer network.

(2) "Computer system" means a device or collection of devices, excluding pocket calculators which are not programmable and capable of being used in conjunction with external files, one or more of which contain computer programs and data, that performs functions, including, but not limited to, logic, arithmetic, data stroage and retrieval, communication, and control.

(3) "Computer network" means an interconnection of two or more computer systems.

(4) "Computer program" means an ordered set of instructions or statements and related data that, when automatically executed in actual or modified form in a computer system, causes it to perform specified functions.

(5) "Data" means a representation of information, knowledge, facts, concepts, or instructions, which are being prepared or have been prepared, in a formalized manner, and are intended for use in a computer system or computer network.

(6) "Financial instrument" includes, but is not limited to, any check, draft warrant, money order, note, certificate of deposit, letter of credit, bill of exchange, credit or debit card, transaction authorization mechanism, marketable security, or any computer system representation thereof.

(7) "Property" includes, but is not limited to, financial instruments, data, computer programs, documents associated with computer systems and computer programs, or copies thereof, whether tangible or intangible, including both human and computer system readable data, and data while in transit.

(8) "Services" includes, but is not limited to, the use of the computer system, computer network, computer programs, or data prepared for computer use, or data contained within a computer system, or data contained within a computer network.

(b) Any person who intentionally accesses or causes to be accessed any computer system or computer network for the purpose of (1) devising or executing any scheme or artifice to defraud or extort or (2) obtaining money, property, or services with false or fraudulent intent, representations, or promises, is guilty of a public offense.

(c) Any person who maliciously accesses, alters, deletes, damages, destroys or disrupts the operation of any computer system, computer network, computer program, or data is guilty of a public offense.

(d) Any person who intentionally and without authorization accesses any computer system, computer network, computer program, or data, with knowledge that the access was not authorized, shall be guilty of a public offense. This subdivision shall not apply to any person who accesses his or her employer's computer system, computer network, computer program, or data when acting within the scope of his or her employment.

(e) Any person who violates any provisions of subdivision (b) or (c), unless specified otherwise, is punishable by a fine not exceeding ten thousand dollars ($10,000), or by imprisonment in the state prison for 16 months, or two or three years, or by both such fine and imprisonment, or by a fine not exceeding five thousand dollars ($5,000), or by imprisonment in the county jail not exceeding one year, or by both such fine and imprisonment.

(f)(1) A first violation of subdivision (d) which does not result in injury is an infraction punishable by a fine not exceeding two hundred and fifty dollars ($250).

(2) A violation of subdivision (d) which results in an injury, or a second or subsequent violation of subdivision (d) with no injury is a misdemeanor punishable by a fine not exceeding five thousand dollars ($5,000), or by imprisonment in the county jail not exceeding one year, or by both such fine and imprisonment.

(3) As used in this subdivision "injury" means any alteration, deletion, damage, or destruction of a computer system, computer network, computer program, or data caused by the access or any expenditure reasonably and necessarily incurred by the owner or lessee to verify that a computer system, computer network, computer program, or data was not altered, deleted, damaged, or destroyed by the access.

(g) In addition to any other civil remedy available, the owner or lessee of the computer system, computer network, computer program, or data may bring a civil action against any person convicted under this section for compensatory damages, including any expenditure reasonably and necessarily incurred by the owner or lessee to verify that a computer system, computer network, computer program, or data was not altered, damaged, or deleted by the access. For the purposes of actions authorized by this subdivision, the conduct of an unemancipated minor shall be imputed to the parent or legal guardian having control or custody of the minor, pursuant to the provisions of Section 1714.1 of the Civil Code.

In any action brought pursuant to this subdivision, the court may award attorney's fees to a prevailing plaintiff.

(h) This section shall not be construed to preclude the applicability of any other provision of the criminal law of this state which applies or may apply to any transaction.

(B) Piracy and Counterfeiting

THE FEDERAL PIRACY AND COUNTERFEITING AMENDMENTS ACT OF 24 MAY 1982

Piracy and Counterfeiting Amendments Act of 1982. 18 USC 2311 note.

An Act to amend titles 18 and 17 of the United States Code to strengthen the laws against record, tape, and film piracy and counterfeiting, and for other purposes.

Be it enacted by the Senate and House of Representatives of the United States of America in Congress assembled, That this Act may be cited as the "Piracy and Counterfeiting Amendments Act of 1982".

SEC.2. Section 2318 of title 18, United States Code, is amended to read as follows:

"§2318. Trafficking in counterfeit labels for phonorecords, and copies of motion pictures or other audiovisual works

"(a) Whoever, in any of the circumstances described in subsection (c) of this section, knowingly traffics in a counterfeit label affixed or designed to be affixed to a phonorecord, or a copy of a motion picture or other audiovisual work, shall be fined not more than $250,000 or imprisoned for not more than five years, or both.

Definitions.

"(b) As used in this section—

'(1) the term 'counterfeit label' means an identifying label or container that appears to be genuine, but is not;

"(2) the term 'traffic' means to transport, transfer or otherwise dispose of, to another, as consideration for anything of value or to make or obtain control of with intent to so transport, transfer or dispose of; and

"(3) the terms 'copy', 'phonorecord', 'motion picture', and 'audiovisual work' have, respectively, the meanings given those terms in section 101 (relating to definitions) of title 17.

"(c) The circumstances referred to in subsection (a) of this section are—

"(1) the offense is committed within the special maritime and territorial jurisdiction of the United States; or within the special aircraft jurisdiction of the United States (as defined in section 101 of the Federal Aviation Act of 1958);

49 USC 1301.

"(2) the mail or a facility of interstate or foreign commerce is used or intended to be used in the commission of the offense; or

"(3) the counterfeit label is affixed to or enclose, or is designed to be affixed to or encloses, a copyrighted motion picture or other audiovisual work, or a phonorecord of a copyrighted sound recording.

"(d) When any person is convicted of any violation of subsection (a), the court in its judgment of conviction shall in addition to the penalty therein prescribed, order the forfeiture and destruction or other disposition of all counterfeit labels and all articles to which counterfeit labels have been affixed or which were intended to have had such labels affixed.

"(e) Except to the extent they are inconsistent with the provisions of this title, all provisions of section 509, title 17, United States Code, are applicable to violations of subsection (a).'.

SEC. 3. Title 18, United States Code, is amended by inserting after section 2318 the following new section:

18 USC 2319.

"§2319. Criminal Infringement of a copyright

"(a) Whoever violates section 506(a) (relating to criminal offenses) of title 17 shall be punished as provided in subsection (b) of this section and such penalties shall be in addition to any other provisions of title 17 or any other law.

"(b) Any person who commits an offense under subsection (a) of this section—

"(1) shall be fined not more than $250,000 or imprisoned for not more than five years, or both, if the offense—

"(A) involves the reproduction or distribution, during any one-hundred-and-eighty-day period, of at least one thousand phonorecords or copies infringing the copyright in one or more sound recordings;

"(B) involves the reproduction or distribution, during any one-hundred-and-eighty-day period, of at least sixty-five copies infringing the copyright in one or more motion pictures or other audiovisual works; or

"(C) is a second or subsequent offense under either of subsection (b)(1) or (b)(2) of this section, where a prior offense involved a sound recording, or a motion picture or other audiovisual work;

"(2) shall be fined not more than ($250,000 or imprisoned for not more than two years, or both, if the offense—

"(A) involves the reproduction or distribution, during any one-hundred-and-eighty-day period, of more than one hundred but less than one thousand phonorecords or copies infringing the copyright in one or more sound recordings; or

"(B) involves the reproduction or distribution, during any one-hundred-and-eighty-day period, of more than seven but less than sixty-five copies infringing the copyright in one or more motion pictures or other audiovisual works; and

"(3) shall be fined not more than $25,000 or imprisoned for not more than one year, or both, in any other case.

Definitions.

"(c) As used in this section—

"(1) the terms 'sound recording', 'motion picture', 'audiovisual work', 'phonorecord', and 'copies' have, respectively, the meanings set forth in section 101 (relating to definitions) of title 17; and

"(2) the terms "reproduction" and "distribution" refer to the exclusive rights of a copyright owner under clauses (1) and (3) respectively of section 106 (relating to exclusive rights in copyrighted works), as limited by section 107 through 118, of title 17.".

SEC. 4. The table of sections for chapter 113 of title 18 of the United States Code is amended by striking out the item relating to section 2318 and inserting in lieu thereof the following:

"2318. Trafficking in counterfeit labels for phonorecords and copies of motion pictures or other audiovisual works.

"2319. Criminal infringement of a copyright."

SEC. 5. Section 506(a) of title 17, United States Code, is amended to read as follows:

Ante, p.92.

"(a) CRIMINAL INFRINGEMENT—Any person who infringes a copyright willfully and for purposes of commercial advantage or private financial gain shall be punished as provided in section 2319 of title 18."

(C) Infringements of Semiconductor Chip Products

ENFORCEMENT OF EXCLUSIVE RIGHTS AND CIVIL ACTIONS ACCORDING TO THE FEDERAL SEMICONDUCTOR CHIP PROTECTION ACT OF 1984 (17 USC 910, 911) (CIVIL LAW ONLY)

17 USC 910.

"§ 910. Enforcement of exclusive rights

"(a) Except as otherwise provided in this chapter, any person who violates any of the exclusive rights of the owner of a mask work under this chapter, by conduct in or affecting commerce, shall be liable as an infringer of such rights.

"(b)(1) The owner of a mask work protected under this chapter, or the exclusive licensee of all rights under this chapter with respect to the mask work, shall, after a certificate of registration of a claim of protection in that mask work has been issued under section 908, be entitled to institute a civil action for any infringement with respect to the mask work which is committed after the commencement of protection of the mask work under section 904(a).

"(2) In any case in which an application for registration of a claim of protection in a mask work and the required deposit of identifying material and fee have been received in the Copyright Office in proper form and registration of the mask work has been refused, the applicant is entitled to institute a civil action for infringement under this chapter with respect to the mask work if notice of the action, together with a copy of the complaint, is served on the Register of Copyrights, in accordance with the Federal Rules of Civil Procedure. The Register may, at his or her option, become a party to the action with respect to the issue of whether the claim of protection is eligible for registration by entering an appearance within sixty days after such service, but the failure of the Register to become a party to the action shall not deprive the court of jurisdiction to determine that issue.

Regulations.

"(c)(1) The Secretary of the Treasury and the United States Postal Service shall separately or jointly issue regulations for the enforcement of the rights set forth in section 905 with respect to importation. These regulations may require, as a condition for the exclusion of articles from the United States, that the person seeking exclusion take any one or more of the following actions:

"(A) Obtain a court order enjoining, or an order of the International Trade Commission under section 337 of the Tariff Act of 1930 excluding, importation of the articles.

19 USC 1337.

"(B) Furnish proof that the mask work involved is protected under this chapter and that the importation of the articles would infringe the rights in the mask work under this chapter.

"(C) Post a surety bond for any injury that may result if the detention or exclusion of the articles proves to be unjustified.

Seizure and forfeiture.

"(2) Articles imported in violation of the rights set forth in section 905 are subject to seizure and forfeiture in the same manner as property imported in violation of the customs laws. Any such forfeited articles shall be destroyed as directed by the Secretary of the Treasury or the court, as the case may be, except that the articles may be returned to the country of export whenever it is shown to the satisfaction of the Secretary of the Treasury that the importer had no reasonable grounds for believing that his or her acts constituted a violation of the law.

17 USC 911.

"§911.Civil actions

"(a) Any court having jurisdiction of a civil action arising under this chapter may grant temporary restraining orders, preliminary injunctions, and permanent injunctions on such terms as the court may deem reasonable to prevent or restrain infringement of the exclusive rights in a mask work under this chapter.

"(b) Upon finding an infringer liable, to a person entitled under section 910(b)(1) to institute a civil action, for an infringement of any exclusive right under this chapter, the court shall award such person actual damages suffered by the person as a result of the infringement. The court shall also award such person the infringer's profits that are attributable to the infringement and are not taken into account in computing the award of actual damages. In establishing the infringer's profits, such person is required to present proof only of the infringer's gross revenue, and the infringer is required to prove his or her deductible expenses and the elements of profit attributable to factors other than the mask work.

"(c) At any time before final judgment is rendered, a person entitled to institute a civil action for infringement may elect, instead of actual damages and profits as provided by subsection (b), an award of statutory damages for all infringements involved in the action, with respect to any one mask work for which any one infringer is liable individually, or for which any two or more infringers are liable jointly and severally, in an amount not more than $250,000 as the court considers just.

"(d) An action for infringement under this chapter shall be barred unless the action is commenced within three years after the claim accrues.

"(e)(1) At any time while an action for infringement of the exclusive rights in a mask work under this chapter is pending, the court may order the impounding, on such terms as it may deem reasonable, of all semiconductor chip products, and any drawings, tapes, masks, or other products by means of which such products may be reproduced, that are claimed to have been made, imported, or used in violation of those exclusive rights. Insofar as practicable, applications for orders under this paragraph shall be heard and determined in the same manner as an application for a temporary restraining order or preliminary injunction.

"(2) As part of a final judgment or decree, the court may order the destruction or other disposition of any infringing semiconductor chip products, and any masks, tapes, or other articles by means of which such products may be reproduced.

"(f) In any civil action arising under this chapter, the court in its discretion may allow the recovery of full costs, including reasonable attorneys' fees, to the prevailing party.

(D) Infringements of Privacy

PENAL PROVISION OF SECTION 552 A (RECORDS MAINTAINED ON INDIVIDUALS) OF THE FEDERAL PRIVACY ACT 1974 (5 USC §552 A)

"(i)(1) CRIMINAL PENALTIES.—Any officer or employee of an agency, who by virtue of his employment or official position, has possession of, or access to, agency records which contain individually identifiable information the disclosure of which is prohibited by this section or by rules or regulations established thereunder, and who knowing that disclosure of the specific material is so prohibited, willfully discloses the material in any manner to any person or agency not entitled to receive it, shall be guilty of a misdemeanor and fined not more than $5,000.

"(2) Any officer or employee of any agency who willfully maintains a system of records without meeting the notice requirements of subsection (e) (4) of this section shall be guilty of a misdemeanor and fined not more than $5,000.

"(3) Any person who knowingly and willfully requests or obtains any record concerning an individual from an agency under false pretenses shall be guilty of a misdemeanor and fined not more than $5,000.

CODE OF VIRGINIA (CHAPTER 5 TITLE 18.2 ARTICLE 7.1 'COMPUTER CRIME')

Section 18.2—152.5. Computer invasion of privacy
A. A person is guilty of the crime of computer invasion of privacy when he uses a computer without authority and examines without authority any employment, salary, credit or any other financial or personal information relating to any other person with the intent to injure such person. "Examination" under this section requires the offender to review the information relating to any other person after the time at which the offender knows or should know that he is without authority to view the information displayed.
B. The crime of computer invasion of privacy shall be punishable as a Class 3 misdemeanor.

(E) Procedural Law

CALIFORNIAN EVIDENCE CODE

Section 1500. The best evidence rule
Except as otherwise provided by statute, no evidence other than the original of a writing is admissible to prove the content of a writing. This section shall be known and may be cited as the best evidence rule.

Section 1500.5. Admissibility of printed representation of computer information or computer program
Notwithstanding the provisions of Section 1500, a printed representation of computer

information or a computer program which is being used by or stored on a computer or computer readable storage media shall be admissible to prove the existence and content of the computer information or computer program.

Computer recorded information or computer programs, or copies of computer recorded information or computer programs, shall not be rendered inadmissible by the best evidence rule. Printed representations of computer information and computer programs will be presumed to be accurate representations of the computer information or computer programs that they purport to represent. This presumption, however, will be a presumption affecting the burden of producing evidence only. If any party to a judicial proceeding introduces evidence that such a printed representation is inaccurate or unreliable, the party introducing it into evidence will have the burden of proving, by a preponderance of evidence, that the printed representation is the best available evidence of the existence and content of the computer information or computer programs that it purports to represent.

IOWA CODE

Section 716 A. Printouts Admissible as Evidence

In a prosecution under this chapter, computer printouts shall be admitted as evidence of any computer software, program, or data contained in or taken from a computer notwithstanding an applicable rule of evidence to the contrary.

Index

Access, unauthorized
  legal aspects, 86, 93
  phenomena, 19
Access control system, 122, 127, 128
Access to Information Act (Canada), 97, 205
Accounting practices, 91
Act Concerning the Circuit Layout of a
    Semiconductor Integrated Circuit
    (Japan), 76, 227
Address theft, 12, 132, 140
Aims of security measures, 117
Air conditioning, 15, 126
American Bar Association (ABA), 30
Anton Piller Order, 136
Architectural design of computer centres,
    126–127
Assets identification, 119
Asynchronous attacks, 123
Auditing, 124, 133–134, 139
Australia
  computer crime studies, 31, 34, 184
  law reform, 45–47, 65, 66, 70, 72, 97, 99,
    100–107, 111, 112, 198–199
  traditional law, 41, 54, 58, 65, 66, 70, 75,
    78, 82, 97, 111, 112
Automatic working of computer fraud, 11

Backup system, 15, 127, 129
Balance sheets manipulation, 8, 20, 90–92,
    139
Bank fraud, 4, 6–8, 10, 24
Belgium
  computer crime studies, 32, 184–185
  law reform, 64, 68, 69, 100–107
  traditional law, 38–41, 53, 57, 61, 64, 65,
    78, 81, 82, 86, 87
Berne Convention for the Protection of
    Literary and Artistic Works, 69
Between-the-lines-entry, 124
Bitnapping, 18
Bombing attacks, 15, 18, 127
Brazil, law reform, 73
Breach of trust, 40–41, 61
Building materials, 127
Bundeskriminalamt (Federal State)
    Investigation Agency of Germany), 31,
    33
Business crime
  legal comprehension, 37–93
  phenomena, 3–20
Business records exception, 111

Cable Communications Policy Act (USA),
    98
Californian Computer Crime Act, 43, 87, 89,
    261–262
Camera-supervision, 125, 135
Canada
  computer crime studies, 33, 185–186
  investigation agencies, 143
  law reform, 47, 59, 65, 66, 80, 83, 85–86,
    88, 97, 99, 100–107, 112, 113, 203–208
  traditional law, 39, 40, 55–56, 58, 61, 65,
    66, 78, 82, 83, 86, 97, 111, 113
Cancel-sign-off-technique, 124
Cancer routines, 16
Cash dispenser manipulations
  legal comprehension, 38–41
  phenomena, 5, 9–11
Central Police Bureau (Japan), 33, 34, 143
Centre for the Development of Data
    Technology (Finland), 32
China (Republic of), law reform, 72, 235–236
Chip cards, 11, 128–129
Chips
  illegal copying, 12, 74
  legal protection, 74–77, 93, 214–215,
    265–267
  technical aspects and value, 74
Circumvention of security measures, 7–8, 10,
    13, 35–36, 121–126
Classification of computer crime, 3
CLODO (Committee for the Liquidation
    and Subversion of Computers), 18
COCOM (Co-ordinating Committee for
    Multilateral Export Control), 61
Codes of ethics, 126
Collusion, 12
Commercial secrets, *see* Trade secrets
Commissioner for Data Protection, 102, 110
Competition law, 56–60, 75, 93
Computer(s)
  dependency on, 1
  development, 1, 35–36
  illegal use, 18–19, 81–86
Computer Abuse Research Bureau at the
    Caulfield Institute for Technology
    (Australia), 31, 34
Computer centres
  architectural design, 126–127
  building materials and equipment, 127
Computer Chaos Club (Federal Republic of
    Germany), 19

269